Lecture Notes in Computer Science 6818

Commenced Publication in 1973
Founding and Former Series Editors:
Gerhard Goos, Juris Hartmanis, and Jan van Leeuwen

Yingjiu Li (Ed.)

Data and Applications Security and Privacy XXV

25th Annual IFIP WG 11.3 Conference, DBSec 2011
Richmond, VA, USA, July 11-13, 2011
Proceedings

Volume Editor

Yingjiu Li
Singapore Management University (SMU)
School of Information Systems (SIS)
Room 80 04 049, 80 Stamford Road
Singapore 178902, Singapore
E-mail: yjli@smu.edu.sg

ISSN 0302-9743 e-ISSN 1611-3349
ISBN 978-3-642-22347-1 e-ISBN 978-3-642-22348-8
DOI 10.1007/978-3-642-22348-8
Springer Heidelberg Dordrecht London New York

Library of Congress Control Number: 2011930822

CR Subject Classification (1998): C.2, D.4.6, K.6.5, E.3, H.4, H.3

LNCS Sublibrary: SL 3 – Information Systems and Application, incl. Internet/Web and HCI

Typesetting: Camera-ready by author, data conversion by Scientific Publishing Services, Chennai, India

Printed on acid-free paper

Springer is part of Springer Science+Business Media (www.springer.com)

Preface

This volume contains the papers presented at the 25th Annual WG 11.3 Conference on Data and Applications Security and Privacy held in Richmond, Virginia, USA, July 11-13, 2011. This year's conference celebrated its 25th anniversary and presented the IFIP WG11.3 Outstanding Service Award and IFIP WG11.3 Outstanding Research Contribution Award for significant service contributions and outstanding research contributions, respectively, to the field of data and applications security and privacy.

The program of this year's conference consisted of 14 full papers and 9 short papers, which were selected from 37 submissions after rigorous review and intensive discussion by the Program Committee members and external reviewers. Each submission was reviewed by at least 3, and on average 3.9, Program Committee members or external reviewers. The topics of these papers include access control, privacy-preserving data applications, query and data privacy, authentication and secret sharing. The program also includes four invited papers.

The success of this conference was a result of the efforts of many people. I would like to thank the Organizing Committee members, including Peng Liu (General Chair), Meng Yu (General Co-chair), Adam J. Lee (Publicity Chair), Qijun Gu (Web Chair), Wanyu Zang (Local Arrangements Chair), and Vijay Atluri (IFIP WG 11.3 Chair), for their great effort in organizing this conference. I would also thank the Program Committee members and external reviewers for their hard work in reviewing and discussing papers.

Last but not least, my thanks go to the authors who submitted their papers to this conference and to all of the attendees of this conference. I hope you enjoy reading the proceedings.

July 2011 Yingjiu Li

Organization

Executive Committee

General Chair	Peng Liu, The Pennsylvania State University, USA
General Co-chair	Meng Yu, Virginia Commonwealth University, USA
Program Chair	Yingjiu Li, Singapore Management University, Singapore
Publicity Chair	Adam J. Lee, University of Pittsburgh, USA
Web Chair	Qijun Gu, Texas State University - San Marcos, USA
Local Arrangements Chair	Wanyu Zang, Virginia Commonwealth University, USA
IFIP WG 11.3 Chair	Vijay Atluri, Rutgers University, USA

Program Committee

Claudio Agostino Ardagna	Università degli Studi di Milano, Italy
Vijay Atluri	Rutgers University, USA
Kun Bai	IBM Research T.J. Watson, USA
Steve Barker	King's College, London University, UK
Joachim Biskup	Technische Universität Dortmund, Germany
Marina Blanton	University of Notre Dame, USA
David Chadwick	University of Kent, UK
Frédéric Cuppens	TELECOM Bretagne, France
Nora Cuppens-Boulahia	TELECOM Bretagne, France
Sabrina De Capitani di Vimercati	Università degli Studi di Milano, Italy
Josep Domingo-Ferrer	Universitat Rovira i Virgili, Spain
Eduardo B. Fernandez	Florida Atlantic University, USA
Simone Fischer-Hübner	Karlstad University, Sweden
Simon Foley	University College Cork, Ireland
Sara Foresti	Università degli Studi di Milano, Italy
Qijun Gu	Texas State University - San Marcos, USA
Ehud Gudes	Ben-Gurion University, Israel
Ragib Hasan	Johns Hopkins University, USA
Sokratis Katsikas	University of Piraeus, Greece

Adam J. Lee	University of Pittsburgh, USA
Tieyan Li	Institute for Infocomm Research, Singapore
Yingjiu Li	Singapore Management University, Singapore
Peng Liu	The Pennsylvania State University, USA
Javier Lopez	University of Malaga, Spain
Emil Lupu	Imperial College, UK
Martin Olivier	University of Pretoria, South Africa
Stefano Paraboschi	Università di Bergamo, Italy
Wolter Pieters	University of Twente, The Netherlands
Indrajit Ray	Colorado State University, USA
Indrakshi Ray	Colorado State University, USA
Kui Ren	Illinois Institute of Technology, USA
Mark Ryan	University of Birmingham, UK
Kouchi Sakurai	Kyushu University, Japan
Pierangela Samarati	Università degli Studi di Milano, Italy
Anoop Singhal	NIST, USA
Traian Marius Truta	Northern Kentucky University, USA
Jaideep Vaidya	Rutgers University, USA
Hui Wang	Stevens Institute of Technology, USA
Lingyu Wang	Concordia University, Canada
Xiaokui Xiao	Nanyang Technological University, Singapore
Meng Yu	Virginia Commonwealth University, USA
Xinwen Zhang	Huawei Research Center, Santa Clara, California, USA
Jianying Zhou	Institute for Infocomm Research, Singapore
Zutao Zhu	Google Inc., USA

Additional Reviewers

Chan, Aldar
Chang, Katharine
Cheng, Pengsu
Erola, Arnau
Hori, Yoshiaki
Iliadis, John
Konstantinou, Elisavet
Kourai, Kenichi
Liu, Wen Ming
Livraga, Giovanni
Ma, Jiefei
Mohammed, Noman
Nishide, Takashi
Perez Martinez, Pablo Alejandro
Pulls, Tobias
Scalavino, Enrico
Soria Comas, Jordi
Su, Chunhua
Van Cleeff, André
Xiong, Huijun
Xu, Wenjuan
Zhang, Ge
Zhang, Yulong
Zhao, Bin

Table of Contents

Invited Papers

Access Control I

Privacy-Preserving Data Applications I

Access Control II

Data Confidentiality and Query Verification

Query and Data Privacy

Privacy-Preserving Data Applications II

Authentication and Secret Sharing

Short Papers

Information Flow Containment: A Practical Basis for Malware Defense*

R. Sekar

Stony Brook University

Security threats have escalated rapidly in the past decade. "Zero-day attacks," delivered via web pages, pictures or documents, have become significant threats. Malware is rampant, being installed using phishing, software vulnerability exploits, and software downloads. With the emergence of a lucrative black market in cyber crime, even ordinary users are becoming targets of sophisticated malware attacks.

Existing malware defenses rely mainly on *reactive* approaches such as signature-based scanning, behavior monitoring, and file integrity monitoring. Malware writers are increasingly deploying code obfuscation to fool signature-based detection. They can also modify malware behavior to fool behavior-based techniques. Moreover, to further complicate the development of signatures or profiles, malware is increasingly incorporating anti-analysis and anti-virtualization measures. Finally, sophisticated malware uses rootkit-like techniques to hide its presence from virus scanners and file integrity checkers.

The most commonly deployed *proactive* defense against untrusted (and hence potentially malicious) software is behavior confinement, i.e., restricting access permissions of software using restrictive, fine-grained access control policies. Policies may be enforced on code downloaded from untrusted sources, as well as processes such as web browsers that are at high risk of being compromised. Untrusted processes may be restricted by these policies in terms of their access to system resources (e.g., files) and inter-process or inter-host communication. Unfortunately, an adversary that knows the policy can easily modify their malware so that it can achieve its goals without violating the policy. For instance, if a policy prevents an untrusted process from writing files in system directories, it may simply deposit a shortcut on the desktop with the name of a commonly used application. When the user subsequently double-clicks on this shortcut, malware can do its work without being confined by a policy. Alternatively, malware may deposit files that contain exploits for popular applications such as those used for creation or viewing of documents and pictures, with the actual damage inflicted when a curious user opens them. Indeed, there are numerous ways to mount such multi-step attacks, and it is very difficult, given the complexity of today's applications and operating systems, to eliminate every one of them. Of course, it is possible to impose very restrictive policies, such as preventing any file writes, but this will come at the expense of usability and will likely be rejected by users.

* This work was supported in part by ONR grants N000140110967 and N000140710928, NSF grants CNS-0208877 and CNS-0831298, and AFOSR grant FA9550-09-1-0539.

Y. Li (Ed.): Data and Applications Security and Privacy XXV, LNCS 6818, pp. 1–3, 2011.

A key feature of many malware infections, including the multi-step attacks described above, is the subversion of legitimate (also called *benign*) processes that aren't confined by strict policies. Thus, *rather than focusing on untrusted process confinement,* our research focus has been on *isolating benign processes* from untrusted data and code. In addition to restricting the execution of untrusted code by benign processes, our approach also restricts benign processes from consuming any data that resulted (in part or whole) from an untrusted process. As a result, there can be no causal relationship between the actions of a benign process and those of untrusted malware.

One approach we have developed is based on the concept of *one-way isolation,* where information can flow freely from benign applications (or data) to untrusted applications, but the reverse flow is blocked. In particular, all data created or modified as the result of executing an untrusted application are contained within our *safe-execution environment (SEE),* and is inaccessible to benign applications. SEEs are not only suitable for trying out untrusted software, but have several other interesting applications, including testing of software patches and upgrades, penetration testing, and testing out new software configurations. Our SEE enables these tasks to be performed safely, and without disrupting the operation of benign servers and desktop applications that are running outside the SEE. Moreover, if the result of an SEE execution is determined to be safe by an user, he or she may *commit* the results so that they become visible to the rest of the system. We have developed simple and effective criteria to ensure system consistency after a commit.

Although our SEE is effective in restricting information flows without affecting the usability of untrusted applications, there is one problem it cannot solve by itself: users need to decide whether the results of untrusted execution are "safe" to be committed to the host system. We have explored ways to automate this step. In its most basic form, this automation is achieved by encoding the safety criteria in the form of a program, and by permitting this (trusted) program to examine the state inside the SEE. If the SEE state is determined to be safe, then its contents are committed, as mentioned before. We point out that a policy enforcement mechanism that combines isolated execution with post-execution state examination is more powerful and flexible than a traditional behavior confinement mechanism. In particular, behavior confinement policies need to be written so that every permitted operation leaves the system in a safe state. In contrast, our hybrid approach allows the system to go through intermediate states that are unsafe. For instance, we can permit an execution that deletes a critical file and recreates it, provided the recreated content is equal to the original content (or contains some permitted modifications). In contrast, a traditional behavior confinement system would require aborting the execution at the point the application attempts deletion of the critical file.

We then considered the special but important case of verifying the safety of software installations. Since software installations normally require high privileges, they are a favorite target for malware writers. If malware can trick a user into permitting it to be installed, then, by utilizing the administrative privileges that are available during the installation phase, malware can embed itself deeply into the system. We have developed an approach that can automatically identify the correctness criteria for an untrusted software installation, and verify it after performing the installation within an SEE. Our technique has been implemented for contemporary software installers, specifically, RedHat and Debian package managers.

Most recently, we have been investigating an approach that performs comprehensive information-flow tracking across benign and untrusted applications. The advantage of such an approach is that it can altogether avoid the question of what is "safe." Instead, data that is produced (or influenced) by untrusted applications are marked, and any process (benign or untrusted) that consumes such data is confined by a policy. Moreover, outputs of such processes are also marked as untrusted. Although the concept of information-flow based integrity is very old, its practical application to contemporary operating systems has not had much success. Guided by our experience with SEEs, we have developed an effective and efficient implementation of this approach for contemporary operating systems, specifically, recent versions of Ubuntu Linux. This talk will conclude with a description of our approach, and our experience in using it.

Re-designing the Web's Access Control System*
(Extended Abstract)

Wenliang Du, Xi Tan, Tongbo Luo, Karthick Jayaraman, and Zutao Zhu

Department of Electrical Engineering and Computer Science,
Syracuse University, Syracuse, New York, 13244, USA
Tel.: +1 315 443-9180
wedu@syr.edu

Abstract. The Web is playing a very important role in our lives, and is becoming an essential element of the computing infrastructure. With such a glory come the attacks–the Web has become criminals' preferred targets. Web-based vulnerabilities now outnumber traditional computer security concerns. Although various security solutions have been proposed to address the problems on the Web, few have addressed the root causes of why web applications are so vulnerable to these many attacks. We believe that the Web's current access control models are fundamentally inadequate to satisfy the protection needs of today's web, and they need to be redesigned. In this extended abstract, we explain our position, and summarize our efforts in redesigning the Web's access control systems.

Keywords: web security; access control model.

1 Introduction

The Web is playing a very important role in our lives, and is becoming an essential element of the computing infrastructure. Because of its ubiquity, the Web has become attackers' preferred targets. Web-based vulnerabilities now outnumber traditional computer security concerns [2, 4]. SQL injection, cross-site scripting (XSS), and cross-site request forgery are among the most common attacks on web applications. A recent report shows that over 80 percent of websites *have had* at least one serious vulnerability, and the average number of serious vulnerabilities per website is 16.7 [26].

Attacks on the Web are quite unique, compared to the attacks on the traditional computer systems and networks. From the top 10 list of web attacks recently release by OWASP [19], we can tell that these attacks, to a large degree, are attributed to the unique architecture of web applications. In general, the most common structure for web applications is three-tiered [20]: presentation, application, and storage. The web browser belongs to the first tier, presentation. The web server, using technologies like PHP, ASP, ASP.NET, etc., is the middle tier, which controls the application logic. The database is in the storage tier. Therefore, a typical web application consists of three major components: contents (static and dynamic, such as Javascript code) for the presentation tier, code for the application tier, and interactions with the database.

* This work was supported by Award No. 1017771 from the US National Science Foundation.

Y. Li (Ed.): Data and Applications Security and Privacy XXV, LNCS 6818, pp. 4–11, 2011.

Various security solutions have been proposed to address the problems on the Web [10, 15, 14, 1, 5, 17, 20, 6, 11, 21]; although some of them are quite effective in defending against certain specific type of attacks, few have answered the questions "why is the Web so vulnerable to these many attacks" and "what are the root causes of these problems". If we do not address the root causes, we may be able to address some known problems today, but more and more problems may arise in the future, as the Web is still evolving and new features are being introduced from time to time. We need to study the fundamental problems of why web applications are so vulnerable, and develop solutions to address these fundamental problems, instead of developing point solutions to fix each specific attack.

Most of the vulnerabilities appear to be caused by the mistakes in the programs, but, when we look deeper and think about why the developers make such mistakes, we realize that the real problem is the underlying access control architecture: because of the inadequacy of the access control support from the underlying architecture, developers are forced to implement additional access control in their programs. History has told us that asking average developers to implement access control is dangerous, and that being able to build software systems does not necessarily mean being able to build the security part correctly.

Let us look retrospectively at how the access control in operating systems has been evolved to counter the ever-increasing threats. We can see a clear trend: access control has evolved from the simple access control list, to capability-based access control in Linux [8] and Solaris [23], and to the support of more complicated Mandatory Access Control (MAC) models in SELinux [18] and Windows Vista [3]. These sophisticated access control mechanisms free application developers from building all the access control in their own applications; they can rely on the operating system to do most of the access control work.

Unfortunately, web application developers do not have such a good luck, because the access control mechanisms in the web architecture are quite rudimentary. Although the Web has been evolved quite significantly, with new features being added and new types of data incorporated, the underlying protection model is basically the same as that in the early days, and it has become much insufficient for the Web today. To make up for the insufficiency of the underlying protection model, application developers have to include a lot of access control logics in their programs. This is the exact task that the operating systems strive to free developers from. While much work has been done to secure web applications without changing the fundamental access control model, we take a bold and significantly different position in our research:

> **Our position:** We believe that the current access control models of the web architecture are fundamentally inadequate for the Web; they need to be re-designed to address the protection needs of the current Web. A well-designed access control model can simplify application developers' tasks by enforcing much of the access control within the model, freeing developers from such a complicated and error-prone task.

To understand our position, we need to understand the access control architecture underlying web applications. Conceptually, the access control in web applications can be divided into two parts: browser-side and server-side access control. We will discuss them in the next section.

2 Current Access Control in the Web

2.1 Browser-Side Access Control

Web applications have evolved to become highly interactive applications that execute on both the server and client. As a result, web pages in modern applications are no longer simple documents–they now comprise highly dynamic contents that interact with each other. In some sense, a web page has now become a "system": the dynamic contents are programs running in the system, and they interact with users, access other contents both on the web page and in the hosting browser, invoke the browser APIs, and interact with the programs on the server side. To provide security, web browsers adopt an access control model called *Same Origin Policy (SOP)*. SOP prevents the active contents belonging to one origin from accessing the contents belonging to another origin, but it gives all the active contents from the same origin the same privileges.

Unfortunately, today's web pages no longer draw contents from a single source; contents are now derived from several sources with varying levels of trustworthiness. Contents may be included by the application itself, derived from user-supplied text, or from partially trusted third parties. Web applications merge these contents into web pages, which are then sent to users' browsers at their requests. During parsing, rendering, and execution inside the browser, entities (dynamic and static) in web pages can both act on other entities or be acted upon—in classic security parlance, they can be instantiated as both principals and objects. These principals and objects are only as trustworthy as the sources from which they originate.

With the SOP model, all these contents have the same privileges, because once embedded into a web page, from the browser's perspective, they are indeed from the same origin, and will be treated the same. This is a limitation of the SOP model. Since SOP cannot enforce access control based on contents' actual originating sources, web applications have to implement the control at the server side, even though the access actually takes place at the browser side. The goal of this access control approach is to conduct checking and filtering at the server side before merging the contents into web pages, thereby preventing specific, known attacks from even initiating an action within the generated web pages. For example, to defeat the cross-site scripting attack, one can filter out the code from the contents that are from untrusted sources.

Conducting browser-side access control at the server side has a number of limitations. First, doing the filtering and validation has proven to be difficult; many vulnerabilities are caused by the errors in such a process [7, 9, 12]. For example, despite the fact that `Myspace` had implemented many filtering rules, the Samy worms still found the ways to inject unauthorized Javascript code into users' profiles [13]. Second, if web applications need to run some third-party code (e.g. advertisement and client-side extensions) on a web page, but want to put a limitation on the code (e.g. disallow the access to cookies), it will be difficult, if possible at all, for input validation and filtering to achieve this goal on the server side. In a recent event (September 2009), an unknown person or group, posing as an advertiser, sneaked a rogue advertisement onto New York Times' pages, and successfully compromised the integrity of the publisher's web application using a malicious Javascript program [25]. Third, since the accesses actually take place at the browser side, the server side is fundamentally the wrong place to control these accesses. Access control should be conducted at the run time, when the access is already initiated; this way, we will have all the contexts for access control, including principals, objects, and the condition of the environment.

Therefore, we strongly believe that the browser-side access control should be put back to its proper location, namely, in browsers. This cannot be achieved with the current SOP access control model; a new access control model needs to be developed for web browsers.

2.2 Server-Side Access Control

On the server side, access control is primarily based on sessions. When a user logs into a web application, the server creates a dedicated session for this user, separating him/her from the other users. Sessions are implemented using session cookies; as long as a request carries a session cookie, it will be given all the privileges associated with that session. *Namely, within each session, all requests are given the same privileges, regardless of whether they are initiated by first-party or third-party contents, from client-side or server-side extensions, or from another origin.* We refer to this access control as the "same-session" policy.

Such a single level of granularity, being sufficient for the earlier day's Web, becomes inadequate to address the protection needs of today's Web. The Web, initially designed for primarily serving static contents, has now evolved into a quite dynamic system, consisting of contents and requests from multiple sources, some more trustworthy than others. For example, nowadays, many web applications include *client-side extensions*, i.e., they include links to third-party code or directly include third-party code in their web pages. Examples of client-side extensions include advertisements, Facebook applications, iGoogle's gadgets, etc. Their contents, containing JavaScript code, can be very dangerous if they are vulnerable or malicious,

Unfortunately, the current session-based access control at the web server cannot treat these third-party contents differently. In the current access control systems, it is very difficult to allow the requests from the same web page to access the same session, while preventing some of them from invoking certain server-side services. To achieve such a distinction, applications have to implement their own ad hoc protection logic, such as asking users to confirm their actions, embedding tokens in hidden fields, etc.

The fundamental cause of the above problem is the granularity of a session: it is too coarse. The Web has become more and more complicated, and its client-side contents are no longer uniformly trusted, so requests initiated by these contents are not uniformly trusted either. Therefore, giving all the requests within the same session the same privileges cannot satisfy the protection needs of today's Web anymore. In order not to ask application developers to bear the complete responsibility of implementing those protection needs, we need a better server-side access control system.

3 Our Approaches

Our approach is inspired by the access control in operating systems. Operating systems consider the implementation of access control as their own responsibility, instead of the responsibility of their applications. This is for security reasons, because OS needs to guarantee that all the accesses are mediated; relying on applications to enforce access control simply cannot achieve this goal. Unfortunately, in web applications, because of the lack of appropriate access control models, web applications have to implement their own access control mechanisms, which tend to be error prone: if they miss some places, loopholes may be created.

To satisfy the needs of access control, most operating systems have built in some basic access control models, such as the ACL model in most OSes, an integrity-focused MAC model since Windows Vista [3], and a fine grained MAC model in SELinux [18]. With these models, user applications do not need to worry about implementing some of the access controls if they can be covered by the models. For example, if an application system's protection needs can be satisfied by the underlying ACL model, it only needs to properly *configure* all the objects in the system, and then relies on the operating system to enforce the access control. If an application system needs to enforce a specific MAC policy in SELinux, it only needs to *configure* its system, and then lets SELinux to enforce the access control; the configuration in this case includes setting up the security policies and labeling the subjects and objects.

The benefit of replacing implementation with configuration can be summarized briefly in the following: First, from the implementation perspective, configuring a system is easier than implementing a system, and is thus less error-prone (although errors are still possible). Second, from the verification perspective, because configuration is usually defined based on logics that are much simpler than programming logics, verifying configuration is also much easier than verifying programs. Third, from the error-resistance perspective, configuration is safer: any missing configuration can fall back to a safe default; however, there is no "safe default" if an access control checking is missing. When a web application has over 1000 security checks, missing a few checks is not uncommon [27]. Fourth, configuration allows web applications to put the access control in the place where the access actually takes place.

Motivated by the successful practice in operating systems and the benefit of configuration, *we set out to investigate whether we can develop a better access control system for the Web, such that we can take some of the access control enforcement logic out of web applications, and replace them with configuration, a much easier task.* The enforcement will be done by the access control system that we develop for browsers, servers, and databases. We summarize our ongoing efforts in the following.

Browser-side access control: We have developed two access control models for web browsers: Escudo [11] and Contego [16]. Escudo proposes a ring access control model for web browsers. This model allows web applications to put webpage contents in different rings, based on their trustworthiness: Elements accessible only to more trustworthy principals or from more trusted sources are placed in higher privileged rings. Ring assignments are carried out at the server side, because only the server-side code knows how trustworthy the contents are. Assigning ring labels to contents is called "configuration", and once a web page is "configured", the browser can enforce access control based on the configuration and Escudo's security policies: contents in the lower-privileged rings cannot access the contents in the higher-privileged rings. We implemented Escudo in a browser called Lobo [22].

To provide an even finer granularity, we have developed Contego, a capability-based access control for web browsers. Contego divides the action privileges (e.g. accessing cookies, sending AJAX requests, etc) into small "tokens" (called capabilities). A principal needs to possess the corresponding tokens if it wants to perform certain actions. For example, a Javascript code within a web page will not be able to send AJAX requests if it is not assigned the AJAX-request token. Using these fine-grained capabilities, web applications can assign the least amount of privileges to principals. We implemented Contego in the Google Chrome browser.

Server-side access control: We have developed a fine-grained server-side access control system, which can assign different privileges to the requests in the same session, based on their trustworthiness. The new access control system is called Scuta [24], which is a backward-compatible access control system for web application servers. Extending Escudo's ring model to the server, Scuta labels server-side data (e.g. tables in database) and programs (functions, classes, methods, or files) with rings, based on their protection needs. Programs in a lower-privileged ring cannot access data or code in a higher-privileged ring.

Scuta divides a session into multiple *subsessions*, each mapped to a different ring. Requests from a more trustworthy region in a web page belong to a more privileged subsession. Requests belonging to subsession k are only allowed to access the server-side programs and data in ring k and above (numerically). With the subsession and ring mechanisms, server-side programs can treat the requests in the same session differently, based on the trustworthiness of their initiators, and thus provide access control at a finer granularity. Subsessions in Scuta correspond to the rings in Escudo, i.e., requests initiated from Escudo ring k in a web page is considered as belonging to subsession k, and can thus access the corresponding server-side resources.

To demonstrate the effectiveness of Scuta, we have implemented Scuta in PHP, a widely adopted platform for web applications. We have conducted comprehensive case studies to demonstrate how Scuta can be used to satisfy the diversified protection needs in web applications.

4 Summary

We strongly believe that the access control systems in the current Web infrastructure is fundamentally inadequate to satisfy the protection needs of today's Web, and they have, directly and indirectly, contributed to the dire situation in web applications. It is time to think about whether we can design a better and backward-compatible access control system, instead of developing fixes to patch the existing one in order to defeat certain specific attacks. The web technology is still evolving, so a good design should not only be able to satisfy today's needs, it should also be extensible to satisfy the unknown protection needs that will inevitably come up during the technology evolution. In this extended abstract, we have summarized our pursuit in building a better access control system for the Web.

Acknowledgment

Several other people have also participated in this research, including Amit Bose, Steve Chapin, Tzvetan Devnaliev, Hao Hao, Apoorva Iyer, Balamurugan Rajagopalan, Karthick Soundararaj, Shaonan Wang, and Yifei Wang. We would like to acknowledge their contributions.

References

1. Caja, `http://code.google.com/p/google-caja/`
2. Christey, S., Martin, R.A.: Vulnerability type distributions in cve (version 1.1). MITRE Corporation (2007), `http://cwe.mitre.org/documents/vuln-trends/index.html`
3. Conover, M.: Analysis of the windows vista security model. Symantec Corporation (2007), `http://www.symantec.com/avcenter/reference/Windows_Vista_Security_Model_Analysis.pdf`
4. Symantec Corp. Symantec internet security threat report: Trends for july-december 2007 (executive summary). Page 1–2 (2008)
5. Douglas Crockford. ADSafe, `http://www.adsafe.org`
6. Dalton, M., Kozyrakis, C., Zeldovich, N.: Nemesis: Preventing authentication & access control vulnerabilities in web applications. In: Proceedings of the Eighteenth Usenix Security Symposium (Usenix Security), Montreal, Canada (2009)
7. Grossman, J.: Cross-site scripting worms and viruses. The impending threat and the best defense, `http://www.whitehatsec.com/downloads/WHXSSThreats.pdf`
8. Hallyn, S.E., Morgan, A.G.: Linux capabilities: making them work (2008), `http://ols.fedoraproject.org/OLS/Reprints-2008/hallyn-reprint.pdf`
9. Hansen, R.: XSS cheat sheet, `http://ha.ckers.org/xss.html`
10. Jackson, C., Bortz, A., Boneh, D., Mitchell, J.C.: Protecting browser state from web privacy attacks. In: WWW 2006 (2006)
11. Jayaraman, K., Du, W., Rajagopalan, B., Chapin, S.J.: Escudo: A fine-grained protection model for web browsers. In: Proceedings of the 30th International Conference on Distributed Computing Systems (ICDCS), Genoa, Italy, June 21-25 (2010)
12. Kamkar, S.: The samy worm story (2005), `http://namb.la/popular/`
13. Kamkar, S.: Technical explanation of the myspace worm (2005), `http://namb.la/popular/tech.html`
14. Karlof, C., Shankar, U., Tygar, J.D., Wagner, D.: Dynamic pharming attacks and locked same-origin policies for web browsers. In: CCS 2007 (2007)
15. Livshits, B., Erlingsson, Ú.: Using web application construction frameworks to protect against code injection attacks. In: PLAS 2007 (2007)
16. Luo, T., Du, W.: Contego: Capability-based access control for web browsers. In: Proceedings of the 4th International Conference on Trust and Trustworthy Computing, Pittsburgh, PA (2011)

17. Meyerovich, L.A., Livshits, V.B.: Conscript: Specifying and enforcing fine-grained security policies for javascript in the browser. In: IEEE Symposium on Security and Privacy, pp. 481–496 (2010)
18. National Security Agency. Security-Enhanced Liunx, http://www.nsa.gov/selinux/
19. OWASP. The ten most critical web application security risks (2010), http://www.owasp.org/index.php/File:OWASP_T10_-_2010_rc1.pdf
20. Parno, B., McCune, J.M., Wendlandt, D., Andersen, D.G., Perrig, A.: CLAMP: Practical prevention of large-scale data leaks. In: Proc. IEEE Symposium on Security and Privacy, Oakland, CA (May 2009)
21. Patil, K., Dong, X., Li, X., Liang, Z., Jiang, X.: Towards fine-grained access control in javascript contexts. In: Proceedings of the 31st International Conference on Distributed Computing Systems (ICDCS), Minneapolis, Minnesota, USA, June 20-24 (2011)
22. Solorzano, J.: The Lobo Project, http://lobobrowser.org/
23. SUN Microsystems, Inc. White paper: Trusted Solaris 8 operating environment, http://www.sun.com/software/whitepapers/wp-ts8/ts8-wp.pdf
24. Tan, X., Du, W., Luo, T., Soundararaj, K.: SCUTA: A server-side access control system for web applications. Syracuse University Technical Report (2011)
25. Vance, A.: Times web ads show security breach, http://www.nytimes.com/2009/09/15/technology/internet/15adco.html
26. WhiteHat Security. Whitehat website security statistic report, 10th edn. (2010)
27. Yip, A., Wang, X., Zeldovich, N., Kaashoek, M.F.: Improving application security with data flow assertions. In: Proceedings of the 22nd ACM Symposium on Operating Systems Principles, Big Sky, MT, October 11-14 (2009)

Integrated Management of Security Policies

Stefano Paraboschi

Universitá degli Studi di Bergamo, Italy
parabosc@unibg.it

Abstract. The design of an integrated approach for security management represents a difficult challenge, but the requirements of modern information systems make extremely urgent to dedicate research efforts in this direction. Three perspectives for integration can be identified.

1 Challenges to Security Policy Management

The management of security policies is well known to be a hard problem. Significant attention has been paid in the past to the design of flexible and powerful solutions for the high-level representation of a security policy and its translation to a concrete configuration, but the impact on real systems has been limited. Indeed, most information systems today present an extremely partial support of security policies. Network security is typically the portion of the security domain that exhibits the greater support by tools, with the possibility to define high-level requirements and to get support on mapping them to concrete configuration. The other components of the system are instead managed with labor intensive processes. When automation is used, it relies on configuration scripts and ad hoc solutions. In general, the security policy is documented at the lowest level, as a concrete set of configurations of devices and system modules.

The analysis of long-term trends in the evolution of the ICT scenario makes very clear that the importance and complexity of security policy management is going to increase. Information systems are becoming more extensive, integrate resources of different owners, and offer access to a larger variety of users. Service oriented architectures are an instance of these trends, supporting the realization of large systems that implement functions with the integration of a variety of services executing under the responsibility of potentially independent providers. In addition, modern systems have often to demonstrate compliance with regulations to other parties. For instance, HIPAA, PCI-DSS, and Sarbanes-Oxley Act are leading in their specific domain to an urgent need for better security management solutions.

2 Conceptual, Vertical, and Horizontal Integration

A crucial aspect to consider for the evolution of security management is the need to offer a better integration in the management of security policies. The configuration of the concrete security policy of a specific system in isolation is

Y. Li (Ed.): Data and Applications Security and Privacy XXV, LNCS 6818, pp. 12–13, 2011.

not trivial, but it is not the main obstacle, since it can benefit from sophisticated access control models that have been developed for a variety of systems, from relational database management systems to application servers. The significant obstacles emerge when the need arises to integrate and harmonize the security policies specified in different systems at different levels. Three clear integration perspectives can be identified:

- *Conceptual integration*: security policies have to be described at different levels of abstraction, from the business level to the concrete configuration of modules and devices. Separate models are required for the different levels, as testified by software engineering practice in many areas. Also, some support for translating the policy at a high level to a more concrete policy has to be provided. Describing the correspondence between the policies at different levels, compliance of the concrete policy with the high-level security requirements can be verified in a more effective and efficient way. In addition, a structure with different abstraction levels greatly facilitates the maintenance of the security policy.
- *Vertical integration*: the structure of a modern information system presents several components that can be represented in a vertical stack: physical hardware, virtual hardware, operating system, network, DBMS, application server, application. Security policies can be supported at each of these layers. The security policies at the different layers are typically defined independently, but a clear opportunity exists for their integration. The advantage of a careful integration is both a greater level of security and a greater level of flexibility.
- *Horizontal integration*: Compared to the classical scenarios considered in access control, where a policy is assumed to be enforced by a specific reference monitor, modern information systems present a variety of computational devices cooperating in the execution of a specific user request. The computational infrastructure can be owned by independent parties. In these scenarios, the management of security policies requires to carefully define models and mechanisms able to map a security requirement to a coordinated policy enforced by the different parties. This aspect is particularly difficult when few hypotheses can be made about the specific security management functionality supported by the service providers.

The PoSecCo project [1] plans to investigate these three aspects. Conceptual integration will rely on the design of metamodels structured at three levels: Business, IT, and Landscape. Vertical integration will specifically consider the harmonization between access control and network configuration. Horizontal integration will be considered in a Future Internet scenario, where applications are realized integrating the services of a variety of providers. A shared motif will be the detection and resolution of conflicts in the policies.

Reference

1. PoSecCo, Integrated Project funded by the European Commission, FP7 Call 5 (October 2010-September 2013), `http://www.posecco.eu`

Cooperative Data Access in Multi-cloud Environments*

Meixing Le, Krishna Kant, and Sushil Jajodia

Center for Secure Information Systems,
George Mason University, Fairfax, VA 22030
{mlep,kkant,jajodia}@gmu.edu

Abstract. In this paper, we discuss the problem of enabling cooperative query execution in a multi-cloud environment where the data is owned and managed by multiple enterprises. We assume that each enterprise defines a set of *allow rules* to facilitate access to its data, which is assumed to be stored as relational tables. We propose an efficient algorithm using join properties to decide whether a given query will be allowed. We also allow enterprises to explicitly forbid access to certain data via *deny rules* and propose an efficient algorithm to check for conflicts between allow and deny rules.

Keywords: Cloud, Rule Composition, Join Path.

1 Introduction

With increasing popularity of virtualization, enterprises are deploying clouds to flexibly support the IT needs of their internal business units or departments while providing a degree of isolation between them. Enterprises may need to collaborate with one another in order to run their businesses. For example, an insurance company needs information from a hospital, and vice versa. Clouds remove the physical boundaries of enterprise data so that several enterprises can share the same underlying physical infrastructure. Physical location of the data is important when planning an optimal query plan with data cooperation among enterprises. However, in this work, it suffices to assume that each enterprise has access to a logically separate cloud. We assume that all data is stored in relational databases and accessed via relational queries. The enterprises disclose some information to others based on their collaboration requirements, but would like to avoid leakage of other information.

Similar data sharing scenarios arise in other contexts as well, including those between independently owned data centers and between the enterprise clouds and the underlying physical infrastructure. Figure 1 shows the latter situation

* This material is based upon work supported by the National Science Foundation under grants CCF-1037987 and CT-20013A. Any opinions, findings, and conclusions or recommendations expressed in this material are those of the authors and do not necessarily reflect the views of the sponsoring organizations.

Y. Li (Ed.): Data and Applications Security and Privacy XXV, LNCS 6818, pp. 14–28, 2011.

more clearly where the enterprise clouds A and B run on top of the physical infrastructure I. Similarly, enterprise cloud C runs on top of a different physical infrastructure II. In this case, the enterprise clouds need to know suitable configuration information from the infrastructure providers and the providers may need to know the characteristics of the software deployed by the enterprise clouds. Given the standard CIM [10] (common information model) based storage of configuration data, it may even be necessary to consider access to information that is obtained by combining the stored data in some way (much like joins in normal databases). Thus, the collaboration requirements among these entities can be similar to those in the context of multiple enterprises sharing data.

If in Figure 1, enterprise A needs data from enterprise B to satisfy its business needs, A and B need to negotiate and establish policies regarding the accessibility of each other's data. This results in authorization rules for A and B to follow. With these authorization rules, A is able to answer some queries that require information from B but not others. If A also has authorization rules for cloud C, then A may be able to answer a query that requires some data from both B and C. In the first part of our work, we want to decide whether a given query against enterprise A is allowed according to all the authorization rules given to A.

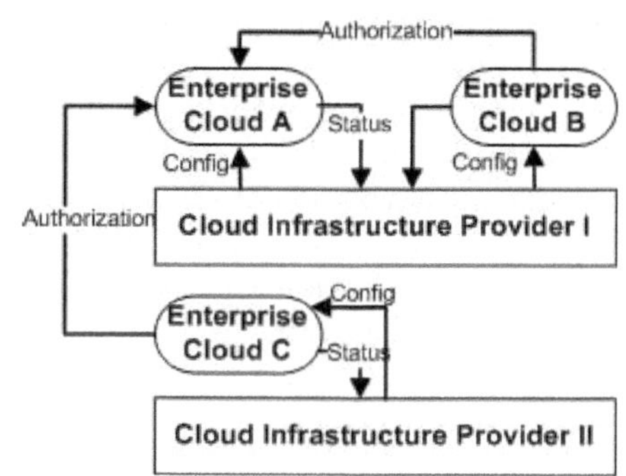

Fig. 1. Cooperative data access in cloud environment

In general, there are two ways of specifying the authorizations: explicit (as in reference [1]), and implicit. The explicit method is easier in that any queries that do not match any explicit authorization rule will not be answered. However, the number of rules could become large and cumbersome to manage. In the implicit approach, the enterprises are only given some basic rules, and are free to compose them and thereby access more information than the rules imply directly. The implicit method can be more concise, and is the focus of this paper. The main problem with implicit method is that there is no way to exclude certain compositions. We fill this gap by introducing deny policies as well.

Deny policies are needed for two reasons. The first reason is simply to avoid certain combinations and thereby achieve the same level of expressiveness as the explicit authorizations. The second reason is that an enterprise may be able to do compositions locally after having obtained the desired data from other enterprises, but such compositions may not be intended.

In this paper, we also present an algorithm to verify whether a deny rule will be violated by the authorization rules. In other words, we check the conflict between allow rules and deny rules. In some cases, the deny rules may still be difficult to enforce with existing parties. In such case, the conflicts found by our algorithm can be used to alert the data owners to change their authorizations or policies in order to remove the conflicts. On the other hand, if it is possible to implement deny rules using a third-party, then they should be given higher priority over the allow rules. Of course, if a deny rule does not conflict with the allow rules, it has no effect and can be ignored. Thus our consistency checking algorithm can be used to reduce the number of deny rules.

The main purpose of this paper is to come up with efficient algorithms for query permission and conflict checking. This paper does not address the next step of actually formulating a query plan as well as the problem of implementing and enforcing all the rules, which will be explored in a subsequent paper.

The outline of the rest of the paper is as follows. Section 2 discusses the related work. Section 3 presents the concepts related to join group and composable rules, and the intuition behind our approach. For checking whether a query originating from a cloud can be authorized, we propose a new two-step algorithm which first selects all the related given rules, and then tries to compose these rules to determine authorization of the query. This is discussed in Section 4. In section 5, we present an algorithm for checking whether the deny rules are consistent with the given authorization rules. Finally, in section 6 we conclude the discussion and outline future work.

2 Related Work

De Capitani di Vimercati, Foresti and Jajodia [1] studied the problem of authorization enforcement for data release among collaborating data owners in a distributed computation so as to make sure the query processing discloses only data that has been explicitly authorized. They proposed an efficient and expressive form of authorization rules which define on the join path of relations and they also devise an algorithm to check if a query with given query plan tree can be authorized using the explicit authorization rules. In our work, we follow the format of authorization rules they proposed. However, it is possible that these explicit authorization rules given to the same enterprise can be composed together to implicitly allow more information to be released through queries.

In another work [2], the same authors evaluate whether the information release the query entails is allowed by all the authorization rules given to a particular user, which is similar to the problem of query permission checking in our work. Their solution uses the graph model to find all the possible compositions of the given rules, and checks the query against all the given allow rules. In our work, the rules are given to different clouds instead of users, and we propose a more efficient algorithm to filter more unrelated rules first. Moreover, we deal with deny policies also.

Processing distributed queries under protection requirements has been studied in [9,12,14]. In these works, each relation/view is constrained by an access pattern, and their goals are to identify the classes of queries that a given set of access patterns can support. These works with access patterns only considers two subjects, the owner of the data and a single user accessing it, whereas the authorization model considered in this work involves independent parties who may cooperate in the execution of a query. There are also classical works on the query processing in centralized and distributed systems [8,13,5], but they do not deal with constraints from the data owners. Superficially, the problem of checking queries against allow and deny rules is similar to checking packets against firewall allow and deny rules [6]. However, firewall rules are usually explicit, and one rule can contain another rule but not compose with another rule.

There are several services such as Sovereign joins [11] to enforce the authorization rule model we used, such a service gets encrypted relations from the participating data providers, and sends the encrypted results to the recipients. Also, there are some research works [3,4,7] about how to secure the data for out-sourced database services. These methods are also useful for enforcing the authorization rules in our work, and their primary purpose is to provide mechanisms for information sharing among untrusted parties.

3 Composing Rules for Query Checking

In order to check if a query is admissible according to the authorization rules, one naive idea is to generate all the possible compositions of the given basic rules, so as to convert each implicit rule into explicit one, and then check the query permission. The problem is that the compositions may generate too many rules, which make the approach very expensive.

Instead of generating all possible compositions, we organize the rules based on join attributes, and then use a two-step algorithm to check whether a given query can be authorized. In the first step, we filter as many rules as possible according to the given query. In the second step, we compose these rules based on their join attributes.

In this section we build up the machinery to enable this checking. In order to illustrate the various concept and models, we start with an e-commerce example that we will use throughout the paper. The example has the following schema:

1. Order (order_id, customer_id, item, quantity) as O
2. Customer (customer_id, name, creditcard_no, address) as C
3. Inventory (item, retail_price, date) as I
4. Warehouse (location, item, supplier_id, stock) as W
5. Supplier (supplier_id, supplier_name, cost_price) as S
6. Shipping (location, customer_id, days, ship_cost) as Sp

The underlined attributes indicate the primary keys of the relations. We assume that relations *Order* and *Customer* are stored at Cloud A, and other relations are on the other clouds. The authorization rules for Cloud A are given below. The first two rules define access to local relations, and the following rules define remote access cooperated with other clouds. Each authorization rule has an attribute set, and is defined on one relation or a join path; the rule is also applied to a specified cloud.

1. (order_id,customer_id,item,quantity),(Order) → Cloud A
2. (customer_id,name,creditcard_no,address),(Customer) → Cloud A
3. (item,supplier_id,supplier_name), (Warehouse, Supplier) → Cloud A
4. (item,order_id,retail_price), (Order, Inventory) → Cloud A
5. (location,supplier_id,retail_price,stock), (Warehouse, Inventory) → Cloud A
6. (location,item,customer_id,ship_cost), (Shipping, Warehouse) → Cloud A
7. (ship_cost,stock, cost_price), (Shipping, Warehouse, Supplier) → Cloud A

For simplicity, we assume identical attributes in different relations have the same name, and queries are in simple *Select-From-Where* form. In addition, relations satisfy the Boyce-Codd Normal Form (BCNF), and possible joins among the relations are all lossless joins. Also, we assume there is no collusion between clouds to bypass access limitations.

To illustrate query authorization, we shall consider two specific queries:

1. ***Select*** name, address, ship_cost, retail_price
   From Customer ***as*** C, Shipping ***as*** Sp, Warehouse ***as*** W, Inventory ***as*** I
   Where C.customer_id = Sp.customer_id ***and*** Sp.location = W.location ***and*** W.item = I.item

2. ***Select*** supplier_name, stock
   From Supplier ***as*** S, Warehouse ***as*** W, Inventory ***as*** I
   Where S.supplier_id = W.supplier_id ***and*** W.item = I.item
   and cost_price>'100'

3.1 Basic Concepts

In order to perform efficient authorization checking, we group relations according to their join capability. For this we define a ***Join Group*** as a set of relations that share the same set of attributes and any subset of them can be joined based on that attribute set. A relation can appear in several Join Groups. A Join Group is identified by the set of attributes that its relations can join over, and we call this as ***Joinable Attribute Set (JAS)*** for the group. In our example, relations $Shipping, Warehouse$ are in the same Join Group, and attribute set $\{location\}$ is the JAS of this group. Other JASes among these relations are: *customer_id*, *supplier_id*, *item*. In order to address information release by joining two or more relations, we define the notation of Join Path.

Definition 1. ***(Join Path)*** *Given a set of relations* $T_1, T_2...T_n$*, a Join Path* $< T_1, T_2...T_n >$ *is an ordered chain of these relations, where each pair of relations* $< T_i, T_{i+1} >$ *are joined with each other on the JAS.*

Each query itself has an associated Join Path called ***Query Join Path***. In contrast, join path associated with a rule is called ***Rule Join Path***. For instance, the Query Join Path of Query 1 is $< C, Sp, W, I >$, and Rule 7 is defined on the join path $< Sp, W, S >$. For each rule, the Join Path defines a view, and the attribute set further refines the view. Therefore, a rule for a cloud defines a view that this cloud can access. Similar to relations, views (rules) can also be joined together. By joining two views, the resulting view is defined over a longer join path. Next, we define the concept of Sub-Path relationships between two join paths, which is useful for determining the relevant rules for checking the authorization.

Definition 2. ***(Sub-Path Relationship)*** *A Join Path A is a Sub-Path of another Join Path B if: 1) The set of relations in Join Path A is a subset of the relation set of Join Path B. 2) For each join pair* $< T_i, T_{i+1} >$ *joins on a* JAS *henceforth denoted as* JAS_i*, and* $< T_i, T_{i+1} >$ *also appears in Join Path B and joined on* JAS_i.

Given two join paths A and B, whether A is a Sub-Path of B cannot be determined by a simple linear matching of Join Paths. It is because the order of the relations may be interchanged in a join path, and JASes in the join path also need to be compared.

3.2 Graph Model to Determine Sub-path Relationship

Here, we use a graph model to determine the Sub-Path relationships. We present Join Path via a labeled graph. $G =< V, E >$, where each node $v \in V$ represents a relation in the Join Path, and each labeled edge $e \in E$ connects two nodes if the two relations form a join pair in the Join Path, and the label indicates the JAS. The graph model applies to both queries and the authorization rules. To determine whether an authorization rule is defined on a Sub-Path of a query is equivalent to checking whether graph $G(r)$ of a rule r is a sub graph of query graph $G(q)$.

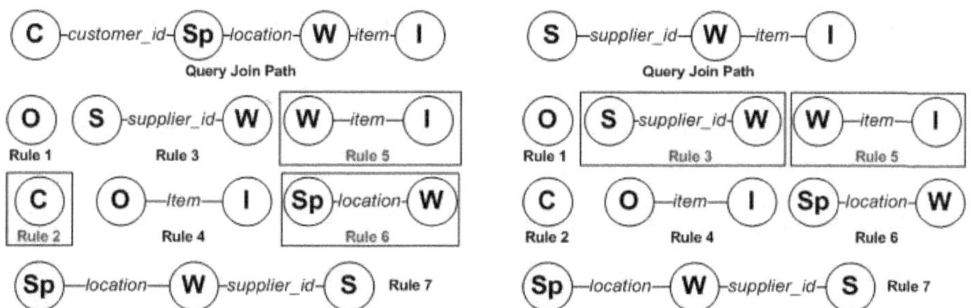

Fig. 2. Rules defined on the Sub-Paths of Query Join Path of Query 1 in example

Fig. 3. Rules defined on the Sub-Paths of Query Join Path of Query 2 in example

Figure 2 shows the query 1 in our example, and the rules in the boxes are the ones defined on the Sub-Path of the Query Join Path. Figure 3 does the same for query 2. For query 1, rules 2, 5, 6 are defined on the Sub-Paths of the Query Join Path. For query 2, the rules are 3 and 5.

Determining Sub-Path relationship is an important step to figure out the composable rules as we shall show later in Theorem 1. However, a rule defined on a Sub-Path of the Query Join Path is not necessarily a composable rule of the query. Hence, we also look at the attributes that can be used to compose rules in the given query. We call the JAS in a Query Join Path as ***Query JAS***. Each Query JAS is also associated with the relation pair that join over it. For example, in query 2, the Query JASes are: $supplier\_id(S, W), item(W, I)$. As rules can be composed using join operations, we define the concept of *Composable rule* below.

Definition 3. ***(Composable rule)*** *An authorization rule is a composable rule, if the attribute set of the rule contains at least one JAS.*

According to the definition, only Rule 7 in our example is not a composable rule because its attribute set does not contain any of the four JASes. Similarly, with a given query, we define ***Query Composable rule*** as an authorization rule whose Join Path is defined on a Sub-Path of the Query Join Path and attribute set contains one Query JAS. For illustration, Rules 2, 5, 6 are the Query composable rules for query 1 since Rule 2 contains *customer_id* and Rule 5 and 6 contain *location*. As join operations can occur in rules, the concept of Join Groups can also be applied to rules instead of basic relations. Within each Join Group of rules, there are the rules whose attribute sets contain a common JAS.

Definition 4. ***(Join Group List)*** *Each entry in a Join Group List is a Join Group of composable rules. There is a unique JAS to identify each entry and within the entry there are composable rules whose attribute sets contain this JAS.*

It is clear that one rule may appear in multiple entries. The Join Group List can be generated with the given rules, and an example of Join Group List can be found in section 5.3. ***Query Join Group List*** is a Join Group List based on the given query. For each entry in such list, it is identified by a Query JAS, and within each entry are the Query composable rules whose attribute set contains this Query JAS. Only rules in the Query Join Group List are the relevant rules that will be considered in the composition step. In section 4.2 we show the Query Join Group Lists of queries in our example.

3.3 Rule Composition Rationale

Our mechanism first checks if a single rule can authorize the query. If not, we compose the relevant rules to see whether the given query can be authorized. All the rules within the same entry of the Query Join Group List can be composed together since they are all composable on that Query JAS. Therefore, rules within one entry can be composed into one single composed rule with longer join path and larger attribute set. If one rule appears in two or more entries of the list, it indicates that this rule can be used to connect these Join Groups so that the composed rules from these entries can be further composed.

Such a composition is also transitive. If a rule r_a appears in entries of JAS_1 and JAS_2 and a rule r_b appears in entries of JAS_2 and JAS_3, then all the rules within these 3 entries can be composed into one rule. It is because r_a and r_b share JAS_2, these two rules can be composed by joining on JAS_2, and their connected entries can be further composed. Therefore, we group the entries in the Query Join Group List based on their connectivity. All the rules within a connected entry group can be composed into one rule. This procedure produces one or more maximally composed rules such that no further composition is possible. If there is more than one such composed rule, at most one of them can be defined on the Query Join Path. This follows from the fact that if two composed rules are defined on the same join path, then they can be further composed together. In addition, since the Query composable rules are all defined on the Sub-Path of the Query Join Path, composition of the rules will not have a join path longer than Query Join Path. Therefore, we only need to check the composed rule which includes the greatest number of relations (longest join path). If this rule is defined on the same join path as the query join path, then we check whether the attribute set of the composed rule is a superset of the attribute set in the query. The query can be authorized if and only if this is the case.

3.4 Theorems and Proofs

In this section, we prove a number of assertions regarding the rule composition and query checking which are useful in formulating the checking algorithm and proving their correctness.

Theorem 1. *All authorization rules that are not defined on a Sub-Path of query Join Path are not useful in the rule composition.*

Proof. Assume a query q has a Join Path of $< T_1, T_2 ... T_n >$. A rule r not defined on a Sub-Path of the Query Join Path will have two possibilities by definition. 1) The Join Path of r includes at least one relation T_m which is not in the set of $\{T_1, T_2 ... T_n\}$. 2) The Join Path of r is defined on the set of relations which is a subset of $\{T_1, T_2 ... T_n\}$, but join over different JASes. The composed rule that can authorize the query must have the same Join Path as Query Join Path. Otherwise, the query results will have incorrect tuples because the underlining views are joined differently, and such a case also means the query is not authorized. Thus, if an authorization rule r has T_m in its Join Path, then any composed rule using this rule will also have T_m in its Join Path which is different from Query Join Path. For the second case, such a rule generates a different view, and any composed rule containing this rule also have a Join Path different from Query Join Path. Therefore, both types of rules need not be included to compose a rule that will authorize the query.

Theorem 2. *Only Query Composable rules are useful in the rule composition.*

Proof. A rule that is not a Query composable rule can have two possibilities: 1) it is not defined on a Sub-Path of Query Join Path. Theorem 1 indicates these rules are not useful. 2) the rule is defined on a Sub-Path of query Join Path, but the attribute set of the rule does not contain any Query JAS. To compose a rule with others to authorize the query, it must join with other rules on Query JAS. Otherwise, either it cannot compose with any other rule, or the composed rule has a join path different from Query Join Path. Therefore, only the Query composable rules should be included for rule composition step.

Theorem 3. *The composition step can cover all the possible ways to authorize the query.*

Proof. From Theorem 2, we know that any composition including non-Query Composable rules will not authorize the query. Then the composition step looks for only possible compositions among Query Composable rules. According to the connectivity among the entries, if two rules are in two disconnected entries, then they cannot be composed into one rule. On the other hand, for rules within the connected entries, we compose them into a maximally composed authorization rule. Such a rule maybe more than enough to authorize the query, but the Join Path of the rule can be at most the same as the Query Join Path. From above two observations, all the possible compositions that may authorize the query are included in these composed rules from separate connected entry groups. Finally, only one composed rule that has the same join path as the Query Join Path can authorize the rule, and there is at most one such composed rule.

4 Verifying Query Admissibility

Our two-step algorithm first builds up the Query Join Group list, and then uses composition step to construct rules that can possibly authorize the query.

4.1 Algorithm for Checking Query Permission

In the first step, the algorithm examines all the given rules and builds the Query Join Group List as discussed above. Each Query composable rule is put into the entries based on its Query JAS. If one rule appears in multiple entries, these entries are connected. Also, each entry is augmented with the relations which are accessible from the rules in this entry. At the end of this step, the algorithm maintains the connected entry group with the greatest number of relations.

In the second step, the algorithm can compose rules efficiently with Query Join Group List. The algorithm only examines all the entries within the connected group that holds the largest number of relations (can be multiple), and entries with only one rule are also ignored. The rules within each connected entry group are composed into one rule as discussed above. As the algorithm examines the groups with most relations, if these composed rules cannot authorize the query, then the query is not authorized.

We assume the complexity of the basic operation that checks whether a given rule r can authorize the query q is C, and there are N given rules, and the query q is defined on a Join Path of m relations. In the algorithm, step one has the worst case complexity of $O(N * C * m)$. It is because the complexity of Sub-Path determination is lower than that of checking the query authorization; both of them need to compare the Join Paths and attribute set. If all the rules pass the Sub-Path checks, then the algorithm compares each rule with the $m - 1$ Query JASes to decide which entries to put in. None of the rest operations is more expensive than C. Similarly, in step two, at most m entries and N rules are checked, and composing the rules is not expensive than C also, thus, the complexity of step two is $O(N * C)$. Therefore, the overall complexity of the algorithm is $O(N * C * m)$. Considering the fact that most join paths in practice involves less than 4 or 5 relations, the number of m is expected to be very small in most cases. Therefore, in average cases, we can expect the complexity of the algorithm close to $O(N * C)$.

Algorithm 1. Query Permission Checking Algorithm

```
Require: Set of authorization rules, the query q
Ensure: Query can be authorized or not
  STEP ONE:
for each authorization rule r do
    if r authorizes q then
        q is authorized
        return true
    else if Sub-Path(r, q) then
        for each Query JAS in q do
            if r is composable on this JAS then
                Add r into the entry of this JAS in Query Join Group List
                Connect this entry with previous entry that r also appears
                Update the relation set associated with this entry
for each unvisited entry in Query Join Group List do
    Follow the link to the connected entries
    Update the relation set associated with each entries in the same group
Keep the largest connected entry groups with most relations
  STEP TWO:
Construct an empty rule r_c
for each largest connected groups do
    Begin from one entry in the group
    Follow the link to the connected entries
    Compose the rules in entry with the existing composed rule r_c
    Generate a composed rule r_c
    if r_c authorizes q then
        q is authorized
        return true
q is denied
return false
```

4.2 Illustration with the Running Example

We begin with query 1. In the first step, the algorithm examines all the rules. As no single rule is defined on the Query Join Path, none of the given rule can authorize this query. Based on the definitions, rules 1, 3, 4, 7 are not defined on the Sub-Path of the Query Join Path, so that they are not useful to authorize the query. The Query Join Group List is:

1. customer_id (C, Sp) → {Rule 2, Rule 6}.
2. location (Sp, W) → {Rule 5, Rule 6}.
3. item (W, I) → {Rule 6}.

Since Rule 6 appears in all three entries, these three entries form the only connected entry group in this list. Then in second step of the algorithm, the entry *item* is ignored since there is only one rule in the group, and Rule 6 is composed with Rule 2 by joining on Query JAS *customer_id* which further composes with Rule 5 by joining on Query JAS *location*. Thus, the composed rule is "(*customer_id*, *name*, *creditcard_no*, *item*, *address*, *retail_price*, *stock*, *ship_cost*, *location*), (*Customer*, *Shipping*, *Warehouse*, *Inventory*) → Cloud *A*". This composed rule is defined on the Query Join Path of query 1, and the attribute set contains all the attributes required in query 1. Therefore, the query is authorized.

Query 2 has Query Join Path $< S, W, I >$, attribute set {*supplier_name*, *stock*, *cost_price*}, and Query JASes are {*supplier_id* (*S*,*W*), *item* (*W*,*I*)}. Here, attribute *cost_price* appears in ***Where*** clause is put into the attribute set, since the query needs the authorization on that attribute to do the select operation. As no single rule can authorize the query, the algorithm builds the Query Join Group List during the first step. Rules 1, 2, 4, 6, 7 are filtered as their Join Paths are not Sub-Paths of Query Join Path. The Query Join Group List is:

1. supplier_id (S, W)→ {Rule 3, Rule 5}.
2. item (W, I) → {Rule 3}.

Then the algorithm ignores entry *item*, and composes the Rule 3, 5 by joining on Query JAS *supplier_id*. The resulting composed rule is "(*item*, *supplier_name*, *supplier_id*, *retail_price*, *stock*), (*Supplier*, *Warehouse*, *Inventory*) → Cloud *A*". Since attribute *cost_price* is not in the attribute set of the composed rule, this query cannot be authorized.

5 Checking Consistency with Deny Policies

In addition to the authorization rules to allow access, cloud owners usually have deny rules to make sure that certain combinations of attributes are not accessible so that the information contained in such a relationship will not be released. We want to check using all the given authorization rules whether there exists any possible authorized query that violates the deny rules. For example, we can have a deny rule as below:

1. (Inventory.item, Inventory.retail_price, Supplier.cost_price) → Cloud *A*

This rule means the Cloud A does not allow to get these three attributes from two tables at the same time (in one tuple), however the appearance of two of the attributes at the same time is allowed. Unlike the authorization rule, deny rules are not defined on join paths because such a rule is more restrictive than the one defined on a join path from the perspective of deny. Without join path, a deny rule prohibits any composition result that make the attribute set appear together no matter which join path is used. Since they are not defined on join paths so that they cannot be composed, and we always check them one at a time. To make sure a deny rule is not violated, all the possible join paths and rule compositions that will allow the attribute set need to be checked. To do so, one naive idea is to generate all the possible authorization rules and check if any one of them violates the given deny rules. Again, this is highly inefficient and we need a better algorithm.

5.1 Join Group List Approach

If the attributes within one deny rule are not explicitly allowed by an authorization rule, then the only possible way to violate it is the composition of the given authorization rules. We use the Join Group List to check the possible rule compositions that may violate the deny rules. Unlike query authorization considered earlier, the rule composition here is not constrained by the Query Join Path, and any composition of the rules that may violate the deny rule should be considered. Similar to the above algorithm, rules in a connected entry group of the Join Group List can be composed into one rule. Beginning with one basic rule and following all the connected entries, we can get a maximally composed rule including that basic rule.

To test whether a given deny rule is violated, we begin with the deny rule by randomly pick an attribute from the rule. We can randomly pick the first attribute because that for the attributes in a deny rule to appear together in one tuple, there must exist a composed or given rule to include all these attributes. After picking the first attribute, we choose all the basic rules that include this attribute. It is because any composed rule that violates the deny rule must be composed with at least one of such rules. We then compose the rules much like that for the query authorization one. In addition, there is no need to generate the real composed rule, as we are only concerned with the attribute set of the composed rule. This can be achieved by taking the union of the attribute set from all the connected Join Group List entries.

5.2 Deny Rule Verification Algorithm

The deny rule verification algorithm first generates the Join Group List with given rule, and then composes rules to check violation. The first step of the algorithm can be treated as a pre-computation step since once the authorization rules are given, the list can be generated. According to the definition, by examining the authorization rules with each JAS, putting the rules in the corresponding entries, and creating the connections among the entries, the list is generated. In the second step, the algorithm goes through all the rules containing the randomly picked attribute and tries to compose maximum possible rules to violate the rule. If and only if one of such rule is found, the deny rule is violated. Algorithm 2 is the detail description of Deny Rule Verification procedure.

Algorithm 2. Deny Rule Verification Algorithm

Require: Set of authorization rules, the deny rule d, the JAS set
Ensure: Deny rule can be violated or not

```
STEP ONE(Join Group List Generation):
for each authorization rule r do
  for each JAS do
    if JAS ⊆ Attribute set of r then
      Add r into the entry of this JAS in Join Group List
      Connect this entry with previous entry that r also appears
STEP TWO(Verification):
Pick one attribute A from deny rule d
Create an empty attribute set UA
for each rule r includes attribute A do
  if r is in Join Group List and not visited then
    Get the attribute set from the rules in the entry that includes r
    Follow the links among the entries to get all connected entries
    Union all the attributes from the rules in these entries, get set UA
    if The attribute set of deny rule d ⊆ UA then
      Deny Rule can be violated
      return true
  else
    if The attribute set of deny rule d ⊆ The attribute set of r then
      Deny Rule can be violated
      return true
Deny Rule cannot be violated
return false
```

In order to examine its complexity, suppose that there are N given rules, and there are m possible JASes among them, and the cost of checking whether an attribute is included in a set is C. Then the complexity of step one is $O(N*C*m)$. If the largest number of rules in each entry in the list is t, and basic operation cost for getting the attribute set from a rule is C, the worst complexity of step two is $O(N*C*t)$. It is because in step two, at most N rules are examined, and for each entry, at most t rules are checked. Therefore, the overall complexity depends on the number of given rules and the relationships among them. On the other hand, since such verification can be done offline with all given authorization rules and deny rules, complexity is not a big concern here.

5.3 Illustration of Deny Rule Checking

Based on the definition in section 3, the Join Group List of our running example including all the relations is:

1. (customer_id) → (Rule 1, Rule 2, Rule 6)
2. (supplier_id) → (Rule 3, Rule 5)
3. (item) → (Rule 1, Rule 3, Rule 4, Rule 6)
4. (location) → (Rule 5, Rule 6)

For the verification, the algorithm randomly picks one attribute, let us say *retail_price*. Since *retail_price* appears in Rule 4 and Rule 5, the algorithm only needs to begin with these two rules. Starting with Rule 4, the algorithm first gets the attribute set of the rules within entry *item*, and then examines the connected entry group including entry *item*. Since entries *location* and *customer_id* connect to *item* with Rule 6, and entry *supplier_id* connects entry *location* with Rule 5, all the entries in this list are connected. Therefore, Rule 5 does not need to be checked again. Figure 4 depicts how the rules 1 to 6 are composed together with JASes to obtain the attribute set. The resulting composed rule will have the attribute set which is the union of the attribute sets from rule 1 to 6. Because this set is not a superset of $\{item, retail\_price, cost\_price\}$, the deny rule cannot be violated.

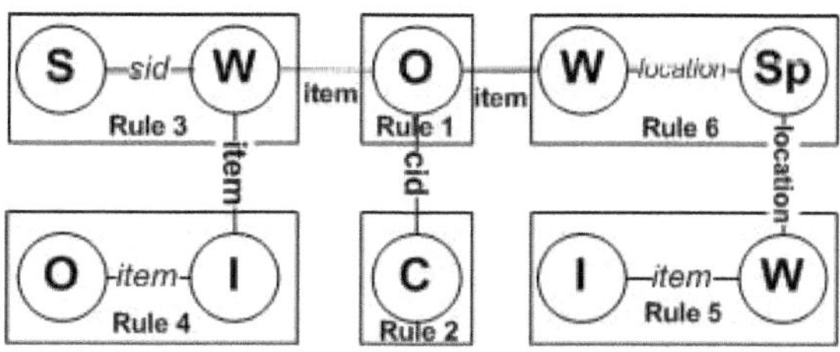

Fig. 4. Composition of the rules 1 to 6

6 Conclusions and Future Work

In this paper, we examined the problem of cooperative data access in multi-cloud environments. Given the authorization rules for allow policies, using the join properties among the given rules, we presented an efficient algorithm to decide whether a given query can be authorized. In addition, we proposed an algorithm to check whether the given authorization rules are consistent with the deny rules that the enterprises may have specified to ensure that sensitive data is not released.

As stated earlier, we do not consider the generation of actual query plans in this paper. Generating a query plan may require the help of a trusted third-party in order to do the required join operations without violating the authorizations and deny rules. The query plan generation also involves performance considerations, which, in a multi-cloud environment would require consideration of location of data. The implementation of authorization checks may need to be done at all the parties that contribute data to the query before the query execution can begin. The query execution itself must decide what operations are done where in order to avoid any unauthorized leakage of information.

It may be possible to formulate the query authorization problem formally with first-order logic so as to use traditional SAT based techniques; however, the feasibility and complexity of this approach remain to be investigated.

References

1. De Capitani di Vimercati, S., Foresti, S., Jajodia, S., Paraboschi, S., Samarati, P.: Controlled Information Sharing in Collaborative Distributed Query Processing. In: Proc. of ICDCS 2008, Beijing, China (June 2008)
2. De Capitani di Vimercati, S., Foresti, S., Jajodia, S., Paraboschi, S., Samarati, P.: Assessing query privileges via safe and efficient permission composition. In: Proc. of ACM Conference on Computer and Communications Security 2008, Alexandria, VA, U.S.A. (October 2008)
3. Aggarwal, G., Bawa, M., Ganesan, P., Garcia-Molina, H., Kenthapadi, K., Motwani, R., Srivastava, U., Thomas, D., Xu, Y.: Two can keep a secret: A distributed architecture for secure database services. In: Proc. of CIDR 2005, Asilomar, CA, USA (January 2005)
4. Ciriani, V., De Capitani di Vimercati, S., Foresti, S., Jajodia, S., Paraboschi, S., Samarati, P.: Keep a few: Outsourcing data while maintaining confidentiality. In: Backes, M., Ning, P. (eds.) ESORICS 2009. LNCS, vol. 5789, pp. 440–455. Springer, Heidelberg (2009)
5. Kossmann, D.: The state of the art in distributed query processing. ACM CSUR 32(4), 422–469 (2000)
6. Gouda, M., Liu, A.: Firewall Design: Consistency, Completeness, and Compactness. In: Proc. of ICDCS 2004, Tokyo, Japan (2004)
7. Sion, R.: Query execution assurance for outsourced databases. In: Proc. of VLDB 2005, Trondheim, Norway (2005)
8. Bernstein, P., Goodman, N., Wong, E., Reeve, C., Rothnie, J.J.B.: Query processing in a system for distributed databases (SDD-1). ACM TODS 6(4), 602–625 (1981)
9. Cali, A., Martinenghi, D.: Querying data under access limitations. In: Proc. of ICDE 2008, Cancun (April 2008)
10. Common Information Model, `http://dmtf.org/standards/cim`
11. Agrawal, R., Asonov, D., Kantarcioglu, M., Li, Y.: Sovereign joins. In: Proc. of ICDE 2006, Atlanta (April 2006)
12. Florescu, D., Levy, A.Y., Manolescu, I., Suciu, D.: Query optimization in the presence of limited access patterns. In: Proc. of SIGMOD 1999, Philadelphia, PA (June 1999)
13. Aho, A.V., Beeri, C., Ullman, J.D.: The theory of joins in relational databases. ACM TODS 4(3), 297–314 (1979)
14. Li, C.: Computing complete answers to queries in the presence of limited access patterns. VLDB Journal 12(3) (2003)

Multiparty Authorization Framework for Data Sharing in Online Social Networks*

Hongxin Hu and Gail-Joon Ahn

Arizona State University, Tempe, AZ 85287, USA
{hxhu,gahn}@asu.edu

Abstract. Online social networks (OSNs) have experienced tremendous growth in recent years and become a *de facto* portal for hundreds of millions of Internet users. These OSNs offer attractive means for digital social interactions and information sharing, but also raise a number of security and privacy issues. While OSNs allow users to restrict access to shared data, they currently do not provide effective mechanisms to enforce privacy concerns over data associated with multiple users. In this paper, we propose a multiparty authorization framework that enables collaborative management of shared data in OSNs. An access control model is formulated to capture the essence of multiparty authorization requirements. We also demonstrate the applicability of our approach by implementing a proof-of-concept prototype hosted in Facebook.

Keywords: Social network, Multiparty, Access control, Privacy, Data sharing.

1 Introduction

In recent years, we have seen unprecedented growth in the application of OSNs. For example, Facebook, one of representative social network sites, claims that it has over 500 million active users and over 30 billion pieces of shared contents each month [2], including web links, news stories, blog posts, notes and photo albums. To protect user data, access control has become a central feature of OSNs [1,3].

A typical OSN provides each user with a virtual space containing profile information, a list of the user's friends, and web pages, such as *wall* in Facebook, where users and friends can post contents and leave messages. A user profile usually includes information with respect to the user's birthday, gender, interests, education and work history, and contact information. In addition, users can not only upload a content into their own or others' spaces but also *tag* other users who appear in the content. Each tag is an explicit reference that links to a user's space. For the protection of user data, current OSNs indirectly require users to be system and policy administrators for regulating their data, where users can restrict data sharing to a specific set of trusted users. OSNs often use *user relationship* and *group membership* to distinguish between trusted and untrusted users. For example, in Facebook, users can allow *friends*, *friends of friends*, *specific groups* or *everyone* to access their data, relying on their personal authorization and privacy requirements.

* This work was partially supported by the grants from National Science Foundation (NSF-IIS-0900970 and NSF-CNS-0831360) and Department of Energy (DE-SC0004308).

Y. Li (Ed.): Data and Applications Security and Privacy XXV, LNCS 6818, pp. 29–43, 2011.

Although OSNs currently provide simple access control mechanisms allowing users to govern access to information contained in their own spaces, users, unfortunately, have no control over data residing outside their spaces. For instance, if a user posts a comment in a friend's space, s/he cannot specify which users can view the comment. In another case, when a user uploads a photo and tags friends who appear in the photo, the tagged friends cannot restrict who can see this photo, even though the tagged friends may have different privacy concerns about the photo. To address such an issue, preliminary protection mechanisms have been offered by existing OSNs. For example, Facebook allows tagged users to remove the tags linked to their profiles. However, removing a tag from a photo can only prevent other members from seeing a user's profile by means of the association link, but the user's image is still contained in the photo. Since original access control policies cannot be changed, the user's image continues to be accessed by all authorized users. Hence, it is essential to develop an effective and flexible access control mechanism for OSNs, accommodating the special authorization requirements coming from multiple associated users for collaboratively managing the shared data.

In this paper, we propose a multiparty authorization framework (MAF) to model and realize multiparty access control in OSNs. We begin by examining how the lack of multiparty access control for data sharing in OSNs can undermine the protection of user data. A multiparty authorization model is then formulated to capture the core features of multiparty authorization requirements which have not been accommodated so far by existing access control systems and models for OSNs (e.g., [6,7,13,14,19]). Meanwhile, as conflicts are inevitable in multiparty authorization specification and enforcement, systematic conflict resolution mechanism is also addressed to cope with authorization and privacy conflicts in our framework.

The rest of the paper is organized as follows. Section 2 gives a brief overview of related work. In Section 3, we present multiparty authorization requirements and articulate our proposed multiparty authorization model, including multiparty authorization specification and multiparty policy evaluation. Implementation details and experimental results are described in Section 4. Section 5 concludes this paper.

2 Related Work

Access control for OSNs is still a relatively new research area. Several access control models for OSNs have been introduced (e.g., [6,7,13,14,19]). Early access control solutions for OSNs introduced trust-based access control inspired by the developments of trust and reputation computation in OSNs. The D-FOAF system [19] is primarily a Friend of a Friend (FOAF) ontology-based distributed identity management system for OSNs, where relationships are associated with a trust level, which indicates the level of friendship between the users participating in a given relationship. Carminati et al. [6] introduced a conceptually-similar but more comprehensive trust-based access control model. This model allows the specification of access rules for online resources, where authorized users are denoted in terms of the relationship type, depth, and trust level between users in OSNs. They further presented a semi-decentralized discretionary access control model and a related enforcement mechanism for controlled sharing of information in OSNs [7]. Fong et al. [14] proposed an access control model that formalizes and generalizes the access control mechanism implemented in Facebook, admitting arbitrary policy vocabularies that are based on theoretical graph properties. Gates [8] described relationship-based access control as one of new security paradigms that addresses unique requirements of Web 2.0. Then, Fong [13] recently formulated this paradigm called a Relationship-Based Access Control (ReBAC) model that bases authorization decisions on the relationships between the resource owner and the resource accessor in an OSN. However, none of these existing work could model and analyze access control requirements with respect to collaborative authorization management of shared data in OSNs.

Recently, semantic web technologies have been used to model and express fine-grained access control policies for OSNs (e.g., [5,10,21]). Especially, Carminati et al. [5] proposed a semantic web based access control framework for social networks. Three types of policies are defined in their framework, including authorization policy, filtering policy and admin policy, which are modeled with the Web Ontology Language (OWL) and the Semantic Web Rule Language (SWRL). Access control policies regulate how resources can be accessed by the participants; filtering policies specify how resources have to be filtered out when a user fetches an OSN page; and admin policies can determine who is authorized to specify policies. Although they claimed that flexible admin policies are needed to bring a system to a scenario where several access control policies specified by distinct users can be applied to the same resource, the lack of formal descriptions and concrete implementation of the proposed approach leaves behind the ambiguities of their solution.

The need of joint management for data sharing, especially photo sharing, in OSNs has been recognized by the recent work [4,24,26]. The closest work to this paper is probably the solution provided by Squicciarini et al. [24] for collective privacy management in OSNs. Their work considered access control policies of a content that is co-owned by multiple users in an OSN, such that each co-owner may separately specify her/his own privacy preference for the shared content. The Clarke-Tax mechanism was adopted to enable the collective enforcement of policies for shared contents. Game theory was applied to evaluate the scheme. However, a general drawback of their solution is the usability issue, as it could be very hard for ordinary OSN users to comprehend the Clarke-Tax mechanism and specify appropriate bid values for auctions. In addition, the auction process adopted in their approach indicates that only the winning bids could determine who can access the data, instead of accommodating all stakeholders' privacy preferences. In contrast, our work proposes a formal model to address the multiparty access control issue in OSNs, along with a general policy specification scheme and a simple but flexible conflict resolution mechanism for collaborative management of shared data in OSNs.

Other related work include general conflict resolution mechanisms for access control [12,15,16,17,18,20] and learn-based generation of privacy policies for OSNs [11,22,23]. All of those related work are orthogonal to our work.

3 Multiparty Authorization for OSNs

In this section, we analyze the requirements of multiparty authorization (Section 3.1) and address the modeling approach we utilize to represent OSNs (Section 3.2). We also

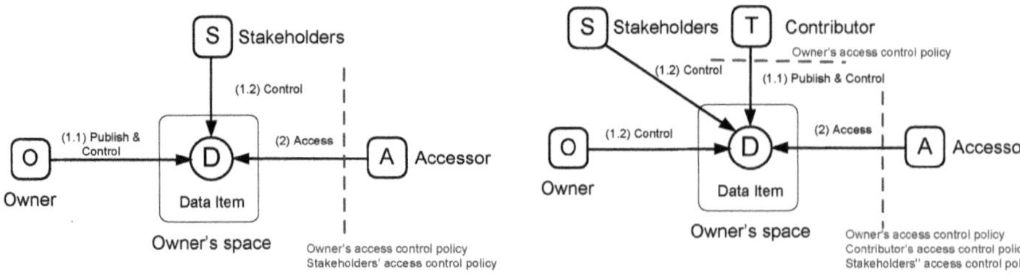

(a) A shared data item has multiple stakeholders

(b) A shared data item is published by a contributor

Fig. 1. Scenarios of Multiparty Authorization in OSNs

introduce a policy scheme (Section 3.3) and an authorization evaluation mechanism (Section 3.4) for the specification and enforcement of multiparty access control policies in OSNs.

3.1 Requirements

OSNs provide built-in mechanisms enabling users to communicate and share data with other members. OSN users can post statuses and notes, upload photos and videos in their own spaces, and tag others to their contents and share the contents with their friends. On the other hand, users can also post contents in their friends' spaces. The shared contents may be connected with multiple users. Consider an example where a photograph contains three users, Alice, Bob and Carol. If Alice uploads it to her own space and tags both Bob and Carol in the photo, we call Alice an *owner* of the photo, and Bob and Carol *stakeholders* of the photo. All of these users may specify access control policies over this photo. Figure 1(a) depicts a data sharing scenario where the owner of a data item shares the data item with other OSN members, and the data item has multiple stakeholders who may also want to involve in the control of data sharing. In another case, when Alice posts a note stating *"I will attend a party on Friday night with @Carol"* to Bob's space, we call Alice a *contributor* of the note and she may want to make the control over her notes. In addition, since Carol is explicitly identified by *@-mention* (at-mention) in this note, she is considered as a *stakeholder* of the note and may also want to control the exposure of this note. Figure 1(b) shows another data sharing scenario where a contributor publishes a data item to someone else's space and the data item may also have multiple stakeholders (e.g., tagged users). All associated users should be allowed to define access control policies for the shared data item.

OSNs also enable users to share others' data. For example, when Alice views a photo in Bob's space and selects to share this photo with her friends, the photo will be in turn posted to her space and she can specify access control policies to authorize her friends to see this photo. In this case, Alice is a *disseminator* of the photo. Since Alice may adopt a weaker control saying the photo is visible to everyone, the initial access control requirements of this photo should be complied with, preventing from the possible leakage of sensitive information via the procedure of data dissemination. For a more complicated case, the disseminated data may be further *re-disseminated* by disseminator's friends, where effective access control mechanisms should be applied in each procedure to regulate *sharing* behaviors. Especially, regardless of how many steps the data item has been re-disseminated, the original access control policies should be always enforced to protect the data dissemination.

3.2 Modeling Social Networks

An OSN can be represented by a relationship network, a set of user groups and a collection of user data. The relationship network of an OSN is a directed labeled graph, where each node denotes a user, and each edge represents a relationship between users. The label associated with each edge indicates the type of the relationship. Edge direction denotes that the initial node of an edge establishes the relationship and the terminal node of the edge accepts the relationship. The number and type of supported relationships rely on the specific OSNs and its purposes. Besides, OSNs include an important feature that allows users to be organized in groups [28,27], where each group has a unique name. This feature enables users of an OSN to easily find other users with whom they might share specific interests (e.g., same hobbies), demographic groups (e.g., studying at the same schools), political orientation, and so on. Users can join in groups without any approval from other group members. Furthermore, OSNs provide each member with a web space where users can store and manage their personal data including profile information, friend list and user content.

We now formally model and define an online social network as follows:

Definition 1 ***(Online Social Network)***. *An online social network is modeled as a 9-tuple* $OSN =< U, G, PC, RT, RC, TT, CC, UU, UG >$, *where*

- U *is a set of users of the OSN. Each user has a unique identifier;*
- G *is a set of groups to which the users can belong. Each group also has a unique identifier;*
- PC *is a collection of user profile sets,* $\{p_1, \ldots, p_n\}$, *where* $p_i = \{pi_1, \ldots, pi_m\}$ *is the profile set of a user* $i \in U$. *Each profile entry is a* <attribute: profile value> *pair,* $pi_j =< attr_j : pvalue_j >$;
- RT *is a set of relationship types supported by the OSN. Each user in an OSN may be connected with others by relationships of different types;*
- RC *is a collection of user relationship sets,* $\{r_1, \ldots, r_n\}$, *where* $r_i = \{ri_1, \ldots, ri_m\}$ *is the relationship set of a user* $i \in U$. *Each relationship entry is a* <user: relationship type> *pair,* $ri_j =< u_j : rt_j >$, *where* $u_j \in U$ *and* $rt_j \in RT$;
- TT *is a set of content types supported by the OSN. Supported content types are photo, video, note, event, status, message, link, and so on;*
- CC *is a collection of user content sets,* $\{c_1, \ldots, c_n\}$, *where* $c_i = \{ci_1, \ldots, ci_m\}$ *is a set of contents of a user* $i \in U$. *Each content entry is a* <content: content type> *pair,* $ci_j =< cont_j : tt_j >$, *where* $cont_j$ *is a content identifier and* $tt_j \in TT$;
- UU *is a collection of uni-directional binary user-to-user relations,* $\{UU_{rt_1}, \ldots, UU_{rt_n}\}$, *where* $UU_{rt_i} \subseteq U \times U$ *specifies the pairs of users in a relationship type* $rt_i \in RT$; *and*
- $UG \subseteq U \times G$ *is a binary user-to-group membership relation;*

Figure 2 shows an example of social network representation. It describes relationships of five individuals, Alice (*A*), Bob (*B*), Carol (*C*), Dave (*D*) and Edward (*E*), along with their groups of interest and their own spaces of data. Note that two users may be directly connected by more than one edge labeled with different relationship types in the relationship network. For example, in Figure 2, Alice (*A*) has a direct relationship

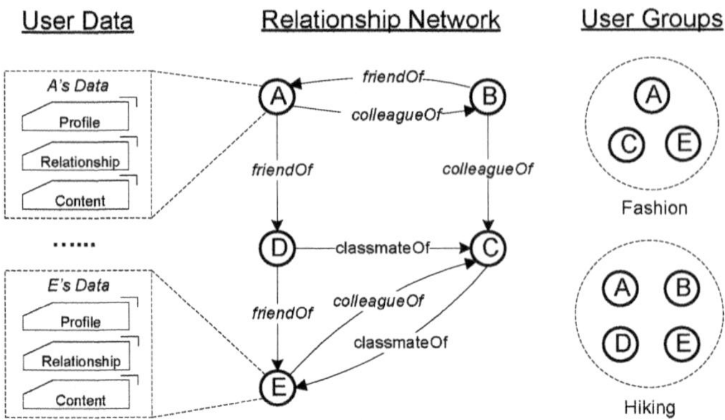

Fig. 2. An Example of Social Network Representation

of type *colleagueOf* with Bob (*B*), whereas Bob (*B*) has a relationship of *friendOf* with Alice (*A*). Moreover, in this example, we can notice there are two groups that users can participate in: the "*Fashion*" group and the "*Hiking*" group, and some users, such as Alice (*A*) and Edward (*E*), may join in multiple groups.

3.3 Multiparty Authorization Specification

To enable a collaborative authorization management of data sharing in OSNs, it is essential for multiparty access control policies to be in place to regulate access over shared data, representing authorization requirements from multiple associated users. Our policy specification scheme is built upon the above-mentioned OSN model (Section 3.2).

Recently, several access control schemes (e.g., [6,13,14]) have been proposed to support fine-grained authorization specifications for OSNs. Unfortunately, these schemes can only allow a single controller (*the resource owner*) to specify access control policies. Indeed, a flexible access control mechanism in a multi-user environment like OSNs is necessary to allow multiple controllers associated with the shared data item to specify access control policies. As we discussed in Section 3.1, in addition to the *owner* of data, other controllers, including the *contributor*, *stakeholder* and *disseminator* of data, also desire to regulate access to the shared data. We formally define these controllers as follows:

Definition 2 ***(Owner)***. *Let d be a shared data item in the space of a user $i \in U$ in the social network. The user i is called the owner of d, denoted as OW_d^i.*

Definition 3 ***(Contributor)***. *Let d be a shared data item published by a user $i \in U$ in someone else's space in the social network. The user i is called the contributor of d, denoted as CB_d^i.*

Definition 4 ***(Stakeholder)***. *Let d be a shared data item published in the space of a user in the social network. Let T be the set of tagged users associated with d. A user $i \in U$ is called a stakeholder of d, denoted as SH_d^i, if $i \in T$.*

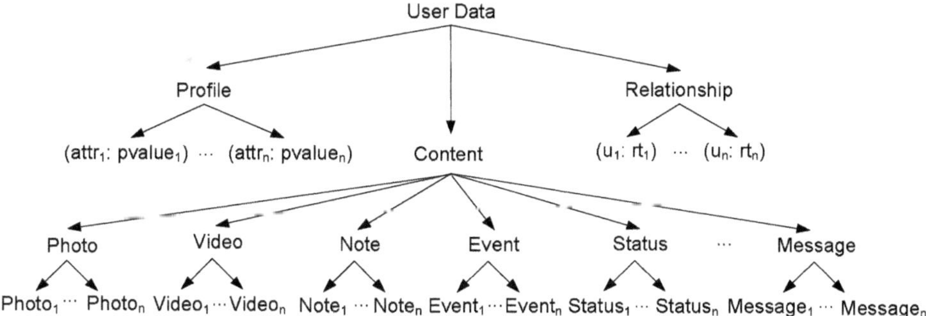

Fig. 3. Hierarchical User Data in OSNs

Definition 5 ***(Disseminator)***. *Let d be a shared data item disseminated by a user $i \in U$ from someone else's space to her/his space in the social network. The user i is called a disseminator of d, denoted as DS_d^i.*

In the context of an OSN, user data is composed of three types of information: *User profile* describes who the user is in the OSN, including identity and personal information, such as name, birthday, interests and contact information. *User relationship* shows who the user knows in the OSN, including a list of friends to represent the connections with family members, coworkers, colleagues, and so on. *User content* indicates what the user has in the OSN, including photos, videos, statuses, and all other data objects created through various activities in the OSN. Formally, we define user data as follows:

Definition 6 ***(User Data)***. *The user data is a collection of data sets, $\{d_1, \ldots, d_n\}$, where $d_i = p_i \cup r_i \cup c_i$ is a set of data of a user $i \in U$ representing the user's profile p_i, the user's relationship list r_i, and the user's content set c_i, respectively.*

User data in OSNs can be organized as a hierarchical structure, whose leaves represent the instances of data, and whose intermediate nodes represent classifications of data. Figure 3 depicts a hierarchical structure of user data where the root node, *user data*, is classified into three types, *profile*, *relationship* and *content*. The content is further divided into multiple categories, such as *photo*, *video*, *note*, *event*, *status*, etc. In this way, access control policies can be specified over both data classifications and instances. Especially, access control policies specified on classifications can be automatically propagated down in the hierarchy. For instance, if access for the parent node *photo* is allowed, access for all children nodes of *photo* is also allowed. As a consequence, such a hierarchical structure of user data can be used to improve the expressiveness of access control policies and simplify the authorization management.

To summarize the aforementioned features and elements, we introduce a formal definition of multiparty access control policies as follows:

Definition 7 ***(Multiparty Access Control Policy)***. *A multiparty access control policy is a 7-tuple $P =< controller, ctype, accessor, atype, data, action, effect >$, where*

- $controller \in U$ *is a user who can regulate access to data;*
- $ctype \in \{OW, CB, SH, DS\}$ *is the type of the controller (*owner, contributor, stakeholder, *and* disseminator, *respectively);*
- *accessor is a set of users to whom the authorization is granted, representing with a set of user names, a set of relationship types or a set of group names. Note that patterns are allowed to specify* any set *by using the the wildcard (*) instead of a specific name;*
- $atype \in \{UN, RN, GN\}$ *is the type of the accessor specification (*user name, relationship type, *and* group name, *respectively);*
- $data \in d_i \cup TT \cup DT$ *is a data item* $di_j \in d_i$*, a content type* $tt \in TT$*, or a data type* $dt \in DT = \{profile, relationship, content\}$*, where* $i \in U$*;*
- $action = view$ *is an action being authorized or forbidden;*[1] *and*
- $effect \in \{permit, deny\}$ *is the authorization effect of the policy.*

Note that different representations of *accessor* in our policy specification scheme have different semantics. If the *accessor* is represented with a set of user names $\{u_1, \ldots, u_n\}$, the semantics of this user name set can be explained as $u_1 \vee \ldots \vee u_n$, which means that any user contained in the user name set is treated as an authorized accessor. On the other hand, if the *accessor* is expressed as a set of relationship types $\{rt_1, \ldots, rt_n\}$ or a set of group names $\{g_1, \ldots, g_n\}$, the semantics of the relationship type set or group name set are interpreted as $rt_1 \wedge \ldots \wedge rt_n$ or $g_1 \wedge \ldots \wedge g_n$. Examples of multiparty access control policies are as follows:

1. $p_1 = (Alice, OW, \{friendOf\}, RN, < statusId, status >, view, permit)$: $Alice$ authorizes her friends to view her status identified by $statusId$. In this policy, $Alice$ is an owner of the status.
2. $p_2 = (Bob, CB, \{colleageOf\}, RN, photo, view, permit)$: Bob authorizes his colleagues to view *all* photos he publishes to others' spaces. In this policy, Bob is a contributor of the photos.
3. $p_3 = (Carol, ST, \{friendOf, colleageOf\}, RN, < photoId, photo >, view, permit)$: $Carol$ authorizes users who are both her friends and her colleagues to view one photo $photoId$ she is tagged in. In this policy, $Carol$ is a stakeholder of the photo.
4. $p_4 = (Dave, OW, \{Bob, Carol\}, UN, < eventId, event >, view, deny)$: $Dave$ disallows Bob and $Carol$ to view his event $eventId$.
5. $p_5 = (Edward, DS, \{fashion, hiking\}, GN, < videoId, video >, view, permit)$: $Edward$ authorizes users who are in both groups, $fashion$ and $hiking$, to view a video $videoId$ that he disseminates. In this policy, $Edward$ is a disseminator of the video.

3.4 Multiparty Policy Evaluation

In our proposed multiparty authorization model, each controller can specify a set of policies, which may contains both positive and negative policies, to regulate access of

[1] We limit our consideration to $view$ action. The support of more actions such as $post$, $comment$, tag, and $update$ does not significantly complicate our approach proposed in this paper.

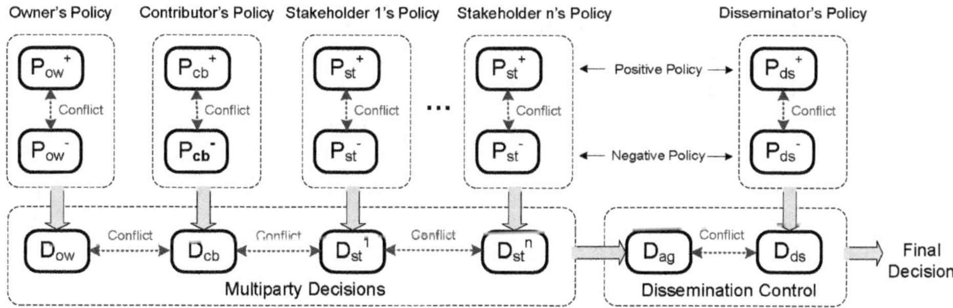

Fig. 4. Conflict Identification for Multiparty Policy Evaluation

the shared data item. Two steps should be performed to evaluate an access request over multiparty access control policies. The first step checks the access request against policies of each controller and yields a decision for the controller. Bringing in both positive and negative policies in the policy set of a controller raises potential policy conflicts. In the second step, decisions from all controllers responding to the access request are aggregated to make a final decision for the access request. Since those controllers may generate different decisions (`permit` and `deny`) for the access request, conflicts may occurs again. Figure 4 illustrates potential conflicts identified during the evaluation of multiparty access control policies. In order to make an unambiguous final decision for each access request, it is crucial to adopt a systematic conflict resolution mechanism to resolve those identified conflicts during multiparty policy evaluation.

Policy Conflict Resolution in One Party. In the first step of multiparty policy evaluation, policies belonging to each controller are evaluated in sequence, and the *accessor* element in a policy decides whether the policy is applicable to a request. If the user who sends the request belongs to the user set derived from the *accessor* of a policy, the policy is applicable and the evaluation process returns a response with the decision (either `permit` or `deny`) indicated by the *effect* element in the policy. Otherwise, the response yields `NotApplicable`. In the context of OSNs, controllers generally utilize a positive policy to define a set of trusted users to whom the shared data item is visible, and a negative policy to exclude some specific untrusted users from whom the shared data item should be hidden. Some general conflict resolution strategies for access control have been introduced [12,15,16]. For example, *deny-overrides* (this strategy indicates that "deny" policy take precedence over "allow" policy), *allow-overrides* (this strategy states that "allow" policy take precedence over "deny" policy), *specificity-overrides* (this strategy states a more specific policy overrides more general policies), and *recency-overrides* (this strategy indicates that policies take precedence over policies specified earlier). We can adopt these strategies to resolve policy conflicts in our conflict resolution mechanism when evaluating a controller's policies. Since some strategies, such as *specificity-overrides* and *recency-overrides* are nondeterministic, and *deny-overrides* strategy is too restricted in general for conflict resolution, it is desirable to combine these strategies together to achieve a more effective conflict resolution. Thus, a strategy chain can be constructed to address this issue, which has been discussed in our previous work [17,18].

Resolving Multiparty Privacy Conflicts. When two users disagree on whom the shared data item should be exposed to, we say a *privacy conflict* occurs. The essential reason leading to the privacy conflicts is that multiple controllers of the shared data item often have different privacy concerns over the data item. For example, assume that Alice and Bob are two controllers of a photo. Each of them defines an access control policy stating only her/his friends can view this photo. Since it is almost impossible that Alice and Bob have the same set of friends, privacy conflicts may always exist considering multiparty control over the shared data item.

A *naive* solution for resolving multiparty privacy conflicts is to only allow the common users of accessor sets defined by the multiple controllers to access the data. Unfortunately, this strategy is too restrictive in many cases and may not produce desirable results for resolving multiparty privacy conflicts. Let's consider an example that four users, Alice, Bob, Carol and Dave, are the controllers of a photo, and each of them allows her/his friends to see the photo. Suppose that Alice, Bob and Carol are close friends and have many common friends, but Dave has no common friends with them and also has a pretty weak privacy concern on the photo. In this case, adopting the *naive* solution for conflict resolution may turn out that no one can access this photo. Nevertheless, it is reasonable to give the view permission to the common friends of Alice, Bob and Carol.

A strong conflict resolution strategy may provide a better privacy protection. In the meanwhile, it reduces the social value of data sharing in OSNs. Therefore, it is important to consider the tradeoff between *privacy* and *utility* when resolving privacy conflicts. To address this issue, we introduce a flexible mechanism for resolving multiparty privacy conflicts in OSNs based on a voting scheme. Several simple and intuitive strategies can be derived from the voting scheme as well.

Our voting scheme contains two voting mechanisms, *decision voting* and *sensitivity voting*. In the decision voting, an aggregated decision value from multiple controllers with respect to the results of policy evaluation is computed. In addition, each controller assigns a sensitivity level to the shared data item to reflect her/his privacy concern. Then, a sensitivity score for the data item can be calculated as well through aggregating each controller's sensitivity level value. Based on the aggregated decision value and the sensitivity score, our decision making approach provides two conflict resolution solutions: *automatic* conflict resolution and *strategy-based* conflict resolution. A basic idea of our approach for automatic conflict resolution is that the sensitivity score can be utilized as a *threshold* for decision making. Intuitively, if the sensitivity score is higher, the final decision is likely to *deny* access, taking into account the privacy protection of high sensitive data. Otherwise, the final decision is very likely to *allow* access. Hence, the utility of OSN services cannot be affected. In the second solution, the sensitivity score of a data item is considered as a guideline for the owner of shared data item in selecting an appropriate strategy for conflict resolution. Several specific strategies can be used for resolving multiparty privacy conflicts in OSNs. For example, *owner-overrides* (the owner's decision has the highest priority), *full-consensus-permit* (if any controller denies the access, the final decision is `deny`), *majority-permit* (this strategy permits a request if over 1/2 controllers permit it), *strong-majority-permit* (this strategy permits a request if over 2/3 controllers permit it), and *super-majority-permit* (this strategy permits a request if over 3/4 controllers permit it).

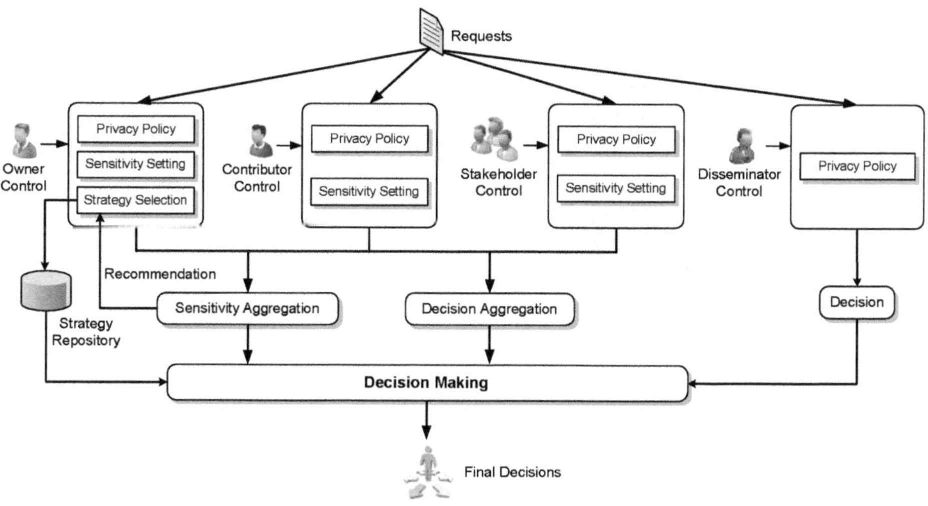

Fig. 5. System Architecture of Decision Making in MController

Conflict Resolution for Disseminated Data. A user can *share* others' contents with her/his friends in OSNs. In this case, the user is a disseminator of the content, and the content will be posted in the disseminator's space and visible to her/his friends or the public. Since a disseminator may adopt a weaker control over the disseminated content but the content may be much sensitive from the perspective of original controllers of the content, the privacy concerns from the original controllers of the content should be always complied with, preventing inadvertent disclosure of sensitive contents. In other words, the original access control policies should be always enforced to restrict access to the disseminated content. Thus, the final decision for an access request to the disseminated content is a composition of the decisions aggregated from original controllers and the decision from the current disseminator. In order to eliminate the risk of possible leakage of sensitive information from the procedure of data dissemination, we leverage the restrictive conflict resolution strategy, `Deny-overrides`, to resolve conflicts between original controllers' decision and the disseminator's decision. In such a context, if either of those decisions is to `deny` the access request, the final decision is `deny`. Otherwise, if both of them are `permit`, the final decision is `permit`.

4 Prototype Implementation and Evaluation

To demonstrate the feasibility of our authorization model and mechanism, we implemented a Facebook-based application called *MController* for supporting collaborative management of shared data. Our prototype application enables multiple associated users to specify their authorization policies and privacy preferences to co-control a shared data item. We currently restrict our prototype to deal with photo sharing in OSNs. Obversely, our approach can be generalized to handle other kinds of data, such as videos and comments, in OSNs as long as the stakeholders of shared data can be identified with effective methods like tagging or searching.

Fig. 6. MController for Owner Control on Facebook

MController is deployed as a third-party application of Facebook, which is hosted in an Apache Tomcat application server supporting PHP and MySQL database. *MController* application is based on the iFrame external application approach, adopting the Facebook REST-based APIs and supporting Facebook Markup Language (FBML), where Facebook server acts as an intermediary between users and the application server. Facebook server accepts inputs from users, then forwards them to the application server. The application server is responsible for the input processing and collaborative management of shared data. Information related to user data such as user identifiers, friend lists, user groups, and user contents are stored in the MySQL database.

Once a user installs *MController* in her/his Facebook space, *MController* can access user's basic information and contents. In particular, *MController* can retrieve and list all photos, which are owned or uploaded by the user, or where the user was tagged. Then, the user can select any photo to define the privacy preference. If the user is not the owner of selected photo, s/he can only edit the privacy setting and sensitivity setting of the photo. Otherwise, if the user is an owner of the photo, s/he can further configure the conflict resolution mechanism for the shared photo.

A core component of *MController* is the decision making module, which processes access requests and returns responses (either `permit` or `deny`) for the requests. Figure 5 depicts a system architecture of the decision making module in *MController*. To evaluate an access request, the policies of each controller of the targeted content are enforced first to generate a decision for the controller. Then, the decisions of all controllers are aggregated to yield a final decision as the response of the request. During the procedure of decision making, policy conflicts are resolved when evaluating controllers'

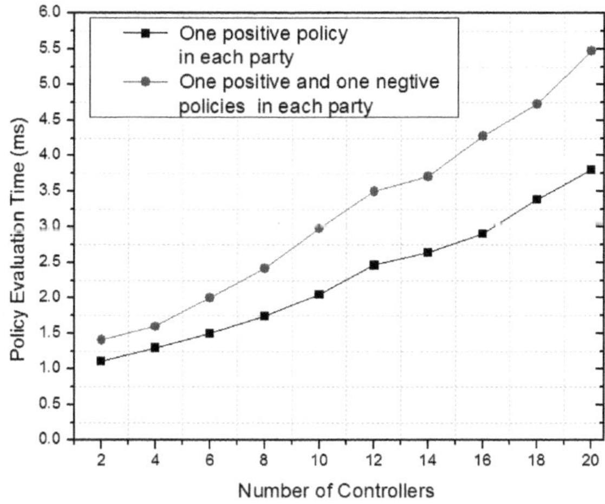

Fig. 7. Performance of Policy Evaluation Mechanism

policies by adopting a strategy chain pre-defined by the controllers. In addition, multiparty privacy conflicts are resolved based on the configured conflict resolution mechanism when aggregating the decisions of controllers. If the owner of the content chooses automatic conflict resolution, the aggregated sensitivity value is utilized as a threshold for making a decision. Otherwise, multiparty privacy conflicts are resolved by applying the strategy selected by the owner, and the aggregated sensitivity score is considered as a recommendation for the strategy selection. Regarding access requests to the disseminated contents, the final decision is made by combining the disseminator's decision and original controllers' decision through a *deny-overrides* combination strategy.

A snapshot of *MController* for owner control is shown in Figure 6, where an owner of a photo can assign weight values to different types of controllers of the shared photo, and select either *automatic* or *manual* mechanism for conflict resolution. If the owner chooses *manual* conflict resolution, s/he can further select an appropriate conflict resolution strategy referring to the recommendation derived from the sensitivity score of the photo. Note that *MController* currently requires all controllers of a shared photo should define their privacy preferences before applying our authorization mechanism to evaluate the requests. Otherwise, the photo is only visible to the controllers. Since a user may be involved in the control of hundreds of photos, manual input of the privacy preferences is a time-consuming and tedious task. As part of our future work, we would study inference-based techniques [11] for automatically configuring controllers' privacy preferences.

To evaluate the performance of the policy evaluation mechanism in *MController*, we changed the number of the controllers of a shared photo from 1 to 20. Also, we considered two cases for our evaluation. In the first case, each controller has only one positive policy. The second case examines two policies (one positive policy and one negative policy) of each controller. Figure 7 shows the policy evaluation cost while changing the number of the controllers. For both cases, the experimental results show that the policy evaluation cost increased slightly with the increase of the number of the controllers. Also, we can observe that *MController* performs fast enough to handle even a large number of controllers for collaboratively managing the shared data.

5 Conclusion and Future Work

In this paper, we have proposed a novel authorization framework that facilitates collaborative management of the shared data in OSNs. We have given an analysis of multiparty authorization requirements in OSNs, and formulated a multiparty access control model. Our access control model is accompanied with a multiparty policy specification scheme and corresponding policy evaluation mechanism. Moreover, we have described a proof-of-concept implementation of our approach called *MController*, which is a Facebook application, along with performance analysis.

As our future work, we will incorporate a logic-based reasoning feature into our approach to provide a variety of analysis services for collaborative management of the shared data. Also, we are planning to conduct extensive user studies to evaluate the usability of our proof-of-concept implementation, *MController*. In addition, as effective automated algorithms (e.g., facial recognition [9,25]) are being developed to recognize people accurately in contents such as photos and then generate tags automatically, access and privacy controls will become even more problematic in the future. Consequently, we would extend our work to explore more sophisticated and effective solutions to address emerging security and privacy challenges for sharing various data in OSNs.

References

1. Facebook Privacy Policy, `http://www.facebook.com/policy.php/`
2. Facebook Statistics, `http://www.facebook.com/press/info.php?statistics`
3. Myspace Privacy Policy, `http://www.myspace.com/index.cfm?fuseaction=misc.privacy/`
4. Besmer, A., Lipford, H.R.: Moving beyond untagging: Photo privacy in a tagged world. In: Proceedings of the 28th International Conference on Human Factors in Computing Systems, pp. 1563–1572. ACM, New York (2010)
5. Brands, S.A.: Rethinking public key infrastructures and digital certificates: building in privacy. The MIT Press, Cambridge (2000)
6. Carminati, B., Ferrari, E., Perego, A.: Rule-based access control for social networks. In: Meersman, R., Tari, Z., Herrero, P. (eds.) OTM 2006 Workshops. LNCS, vol. 4278, pp. 1734–1744. Springer, Heidelberg (2006)
7. Carminati, B., Ferrari, E., Perego, A.: Enforcing access control in web-based social networks. ACM Transactions on Information and System Security (TISSEC) 13(1), 1–38 (2009)
8. Carrie, E.: Access Control Requirements for Web 2.0 Security and Privacy. In: Proc. of Workshop on Web 2.0 Security & Privacy (W2SP), Citeseer (2007)
9. Choi, J., De Neve, W., Plataniotis, K., Ro, Y., Lee, S., Sohn, H., Yoo, H., Neve, W., Kim, C., Ro, Y., et al.: Collaborative Face Recognition for Improved Face Annotation in Personal Photo Collections Shared on Online Social Networks. IEEE Transactions on Multimedia, 1–14 (2010)
10. Elahi, N., Chowdhury, M., Noll, J.: Semantic Access Control in Web Based Communities. In: Proceedings of the Third International Multi-Conference on Computing in the Global Information Technology, pp. 131–136. IEEE, Los Alamitos (2008)

11. Fang, L., LeFevre, K.: Privacy wizards for social networking sites. In: Proceedings of the 19th International Conference on World Wide Web, pp. 351–360. ACM, New York (2010)
12. Fisler, K., Krishnamurthi, S., Meyerovich, L.A., Tschantz, M.C.: Verification and change-impact analysis of access-control policies. In: ICSE 2005: Proceedings of the 27th International Conference on Software Engineering, pp. 196–205. ACM, New York (2005)
13. Fong, P.: Relationship-Based Access Control: Protection Model and Policy Language. In: Proceedings of the First ACM Conference on Data and Application Security and Privacy. ACM, New York (2011)
14. Fong, P., Anwar, M., Zhao, Z.: A privacy preservation model for facebook-style social network systems. In: Backes, M., Ning, P. (eds.) ESORICS 2009. LNCS, vol. 5789, pp. 303–320. Springer, Heidelberg (2009)
15. Fundulaki, I., Marx, M.: Specifying access control policies for XML documents with XPath. In: Proceedings of the Ninth ACM Symposium on Access Control Models and Technologies, pp. 61–69. ACM, New York (2004)
16. Jajodia, S., Samarati, P., Subrahmanian, V.S.: A logical language for expressing authorizations. In: IEEE Symposium on Security and Privacy, Oakland, CA, pp. 31–42 (May 1997)
17. Jin, J., Ahn, G., Hu, H., Covington, M., Zhang, X.: Patient-centric authorization framework for sharing electronic health records. In: Proceedings of the 14th ACM Symposium on Access Control Models and Technologies, pp. 125–134. ACM, New York (2009)
18. Jin, J., Ahn, G.J., Hu, H., Covington, M.J., Zhang, X.: Patient-centric authorization framework for electronic healthcare services. Computers & Security 30(2-3), 116–127 (2011)
19. Kruk, S., Grzonkowski, S., Gzella, A., Woroniecki, T., Choi, H.: D-FOAF: Distributed identity management with access rights delegation. In: Mizoguchi, R., Shi, Z.-Z., Giunchiglia, F. (eds.) ASWC 2006. LNCS, vol. 4185, pp. 140–154. Springer, Heidelberg (2006)
20. Li, N., Wang, Q., Qardaji, W., Bertino, E., Rao, P., Lobo, J., Lin, D.: Access control policy combining: theory meets practice. In: Proceedings of the 14th ACM Symposium on Access Control Models and Technologies, pp. 135–144. ACM, New York (2009)
21. Masoumzadeh, A., Joshi, J.: Osnac: An ontology-based access control model for social networking systems. In: IEEE International Conference on Privacy, Security, Risk and Trust, pp. 751–759 (2010)
22. Shehab, M., Cheek, G., Touati, H., Squicciarini, A., Cheng, P.: User Centric Policy Management in Online Social Networks. In: 2010 IEEE International Symposium on Policies for Distributed Systems and Networks, pp. 9–13. IEEE, Los Alamitos (2010)
23. Squicciarini, A., Paci, F., Sundareswaran, S.: PriMa: an effective privacy protection mechanism for social networks. In: Proceedings of the 5th ACM Symposium on Information, Computer and Communications Security, pp. 320–323. ACM, New York (2010)
24. Squicciarini, A., Shehab, M., Paci, F.: Collective privacy management in social networks. In: Proceedings of the 18th International Conference on World Wide Web, pp. 521–530. ACM, New York (2009)
25. Stone, Z., Zickler, T., Darrell, T.: Autotagging Facebook: Social network context improves photo annotation. In: IEEE Computer Society Conference on Computer Vision and Pattern Recognition Workshops, CVPRW 2008, pp. 1–8. IEEE, Los Alamitos (2008)
26. Wishart, R., Corapi, D., Marinovic, S., Sloman, M.: Collaborative Privacy Policy Authoring in a Social Networking Context. In: 2010 IEEE International Symposium on Policies for Distributed Systems and Networks, pp. 1–8. IEEE, Los Alamitos (2010)
27. Wondracek, G., Holz, T., Kirda, E., Kruegel, C.: A practical attack to de-anonymize social network users. In: 2010 IEEE Symposium on Security and Privacy, pp. 223–238. IEEE, Los Alamitos (2010)
28. Zheleva, E., Getoor, L.: To join or not to join: the illusion of privacy in social networks with mixed public and private user profiles. In: Proceedings of the 18th International Conference on World Wide Web, pp. 531–540. ACM, New York (2009)

Enforcing Confidentiality and Data Visibility Constraints: An OBDD Approach

Valentina Ciriani, Sabrina De Capitani di Vimercati,
Sara Foresti, Giovanni Livraga, and Pierangela Samarati

DTI - Università degli Studi di Milano, 26013 Crema, Italia
firstname.lastname@unimi.it

Abstract. The problem of enabling privacy-preserving data releases has become more and more important in the last years thanks to the increasing needs of sharing and disseminating information. In this paper we address the problem of computing data releases in the form of *fragments* (vertical views) over a relational table, which satisfy both confidentiality and visibility constraints, expressing needs for information protection and release, respectively. We propose a modeling of constraints and of the data fragmentation problem based on Boolean formulas and Ordered Binary Decision Diagrams (OBDDs). Exploiting OBDDs, we efficiently manipulate Boolean formulas, thus easily computing data fragments that satisfy the constraints.

Keywords: Privacy, fragmentation, confidentiality and visibility constraints, OBDDs.

1 Introduction

Information sharing and dissemination are typically selective processes. While on one side, there is a need - or demand - for making certain information available to others, there is on the other side an equally strong need to ensure proper protection of sensitive information. It is therefore important to provide data holders with means to express and enforce possible constraints over their data, modeling the need for information of the data recipients (visibility constraints) and the need for protecting confidential information from an improper disclosure (confidentiality constraints).

Recent proposals considering confidentiality and visibility constraints have put forward the idea of computing vertical fragments over the original data structure (typically a relation) in such a way that constraints are satisfied [1,7,8,10]. While such proposals have been introduced as a way of departing from data encryption when relying on external storage services, data fragmentation can result appealing also in data publication scenarios. In fact, data fragments can be seen as different (vertical) views that a data holder can release to external parties to satisfy their demand for information while at the same time guaranteeing that confidential information is not disclosed. The problem of computing data views in a way that explicitly takes into consideration both privacy needs

Y. Li (Ed.): Data and Applications Security and Privacy XXV, LNCS 6818, pp. 44–59, 2011.

and visibility requirements makes however the data fragmentation problem far from trivial. In particular, ensuring some meaningful form of minimality of the computed fragments (to the aim of avoiding unnecessary fragmentation), makes the problem NP-hard [10].

In this paper we propose a new modeling of the fragmentation problem that exploits the representation of confidentiality and visibility constraints as Boolean formulas, and of fragments as truth assignments over Boolean variables corresponding to attributes in the original relation. In this way, the computation of a fragmentation that satisfies the given constraints greatly relies on the efficiency with which Boolean formulas are manipulated and represented. Since the classical methods for operating on Boolean formulas are impractical for large-scale problems, we exploit reduced Ordered Binary Decision Diagrams (OBDDs). OBDDs are a canonical form for Boolean formulas that can be manipulated efficiently, thus being suitable for compactly representing large Boolean formulas [18]. The size of an OBDD does not directly depend on the size of the corresponding formula and therefore the complexity of the Boolean operators depends on the OBBD size only. Although the size of an OBDD could be, in the worst case, exponential in the number of variables appearing in the formula, the majority of Boolean formulas can be represented by very compact OBDDs. Our approach then consists in transforming all the inputs of the fragmentation problem into Boolean formulas, and in exploiting their representation through OBDDs to process different constraints simultaneously, and to easily check whether a fragmentation reflects the given confidentiality and visibility constraints.

The remainder of this paper is organized as follows. Section 2 introduces confidentiality and visibility constraints, and describes the fragmentation problem. Section 3 presents our modeling of the problem, defining OBDDs corresponding to constraints and truth assignments satisfying them, and illustrating how truth assignments can be composed for computing a solution to the problem. Section 4 illustrates an algorithm exploiting the OBDD-based modeling for determining a fragmentation. Section 5 discusses related work. Finally, Section 6 reports our conclusions.

2 Preliminary Concepts

We consider a scenario where, consistently with other proposals (e.g., [1,8,10,19]), the data undergoing possible external release are represented with a single relation r over a relation schema $R(a_1, \ldots, a_n)$. We use standard notations of relational database theory and, when clear from the context, we will use R to denote either the relation schema R or the set $\{a_1, \ldots, a_n\}$ of attributes in R. We consider two kinds of constraints on data: *confidentiality constraints* that impose restrictions on the (joint) visibility of values of attributes in R, and *visibility constraints* expressing requirements on data views [8,10].

Definition 1 (Confidentiality constraint). *Given a relation schema* $R(a_1, \ldots, a_n)$*, a* confidentiality constraint c *over* R *is a subset of* $\{a_1, \ldots, a_n\}$.

CensusData

SSN	Name	Birth	ZIP	Job	Employer
123-45-6789	Alice	56/12/07	94101	spy	special units
234-56-7654	Bob	79/03/01	94123	agent	FBI
345-67-8123	Carol	51/11/11	95173	sniper	army
456-78-9876	David	67/05/09	96234	undercover agent	FBI
567-89-0534	Emma	80/11/12	94143	scientist	army

(a)

$\mathcal{C}$

$c_1 = \{$SSN$\}$
$c_2 = \{$Name, Job$\}$
$c_3 = \{$Name, Employer$\}$
$c_4 = \{$Birth, ZIP, Job$\}$
$c_5 = \{$Birth, ZIP, Employer$\}$

(b)

$\mathcal{V}$

$v_1 =$ ZIP $\vee$ Employer
$v_2 =$ SSN $\vee$ (Birth $\wedge$ ZIP)
$v_3 =$ Job $\wedge$ Employer

(c)

Fig. 1. An example of relation (a), confidentiality (b) and visibility constraints (c)

Confidentiality constraints state that the values assumed by an attribute (*singleton constraint*) or the associations among the values of a given set of attributes (*association constraint*) are sensitive and should not be visible. More precisely, a singleton constraint $\{a\}$ states that the values of attribute a should not be visible. An association constraint $\{a_{i_1}, \ldots, a_{i_m}\}$ states that the values of attributes $a_{i_1}, \ldots, a_{i_m}$ should not be visible in association. For instance, Figure 1(b) illustrates one singleton (c_1) and four association ($c_2, \ldots, c_5$) constraints for relation CensusData in Figure 1(a).

Visibility constraints are defined as follows.

Definition 2 (Visibility constraint). *Given a relation schema $R(a_1, \ldots, a_n)$, a* visibility constraint *v over R is a monotonic Boolean formula over attributes in R.*

Intuitively, a visibility constraint imposes the release of an attribute or the joint release of a set of attributes. Visibility constraint $v{=}a$ states that the values assumed by attribute a must be visible. Visibility constraint $v{=}v_i{\wedge}v_j$ states that v_i and v_j must be jointly visible (e.g., constraint v_3 in Figure 1(c) requires the joint release of attributes `Job` and `Employer` since the associations between their values must be visible). Visibility constraint $v{=}v_i{\vee}v_j$ states that at least one between v_i and v_j must be visible (e.g., constraint v_1 in Figure 1(c) requires that the values of attribute `ZIP` or the values of attribute `Employer` are released). Note that negations are not used in the definition of visibility constraints since they model requirements of non-visibility, which are already captured by confidentiality constraints.

Confidentiality and visibility constraints can be enforced by splitting (fragmenting) attributes in R in different sets (*fragments*). A fragmentation of relation R is a set of fragments, as formally defined in the following.

Definition 3 (Fragmentation). *Given a relation schema $R(a_1, \ldots, a_n)$, a* fragmentation *$\mathcal{F}$ of R is a set $\{F_1, \ldots, F_l\}$ of fragments, where each fragment F_i, $i = 1, \ldots, l$, is a subset of $\{a_1, \ldots, a_n\}$.*

Given a relation R, a set $\mathcal{C}$ of confidentiality constraints, and a set $\mathcal{V}$ of visibility constraints, a fragmentation $\mathcal{F}$ of R is *correct* if it satisfies all the confidentiality constraints in $\mathcal{C}$ and all the visibility constraints in $\mathcal{V}$. Formally, a correct fragmentation is defined as follows.

Definition 4 (Correctness). *Given a relation schema $R(a_1, \ldots, a_n)$, a set $\mathcal{C}$ of confidentiality constraints over R, and a set $\mathcal{V}$ of visibility constraints over R, a fragmentation $\mathcal{F}$ of R is* correct *with respect to $\mathcal{C}$ and $\mathcal{V}$ iff:*

F_1

Birth	ZIP
56/12/07	94101
79/03/01	94123
51/11/11	95173
67/05/09	96234
80/11/12	94143

F_2

Job	Employer
spy	special units
agent	FBI
sniper	army
undercover agent	FBI
scientist	army

Fig. 2. An example of correct fragmentation of relation CensusData in Figure 1(a)

1. $\forall c \in \mathcal{C}$, $\forall F \in \mathcal{F}$: $c \not\subseteq F$ (*confidentiality*);
2. $\forall v \in \mathcal{V}$, $\exists F \in \mathcal{F}$: F *satisfies* v (*visibility*);
3. $\forall F_i, F_j \in \mathcal{F}$, $i \neq j$: $F_i \cap F_j = \emptyset$ (*un-linkability*).

Condition 1 ensures that neither sensitive attributes nor sensitive associations are visible in a fragment. Condition 2 ensures that visibility constraints are satisfied. Condition 3 ensures that fragments do not have common attributes and therefore that association constraints cannot be violated by possibly joining fragments. We note that singleton constraints can be satisfied only by not releasing the corresponding sensitive attributes. Association constraints can be satisfied either by not releasing at least one of the attributes in the constraints, or by distributing the attributes among different (un-linkable) fragments. Visibility constraints are satisfied by ensuring that each constraint is satisfied by at least one fragment.

Given a set of confidentiality and visibility constraints, we are interested in a fragmentation that does not split attributes among fragments when it is not necessary for constraint satisfaction. The rationale is that maintaining a set of attributes in the same fragment releases their values and also their associations, thus maximizing the visibility over the data. Our goal is then to compute a *minimal* fragmentation, that is, a fragmentation that does not include fragments that can be merged without violating confidentiality constraints. The problem of computing a minimal fragmentation can be defined as follows.

Problem 1 (Min-Frag). Given a relation schema $R(a_1, \ldots, a_n)$, a set $\mathcal{C}$ of confidentiality constraints over R, and a set $\mathcal{V}$ of visibility constraints over R, determine (if it exists) a correct fragmentation $\mathcal{F}$ of R with respect to $\mathcal{C}$ and $\mathcal{V}$ such that there does not exist another correct fragmentation $\mathcal{F}'$ obtained by merging fragments in $\mathcal{F}$.

For instance, the fragmentation in Figure 2 is a minimal fragmentation since merging F_1 with F_2 would violate confidentiality constraints c_4 and c_5.

3 OBDD-Based Modeling of the Fragmentation Problem

We model the fragmentation problem as the problem of managing a set of Boolean formulas that are conveniently represented through *reduced and ordered binary decision diagrams* (OBDDs) [3]. OBDDs allow us to efficiently manipulate confidentiality and visibility constraints, and to easily compute a minimal fragmentation (see Section 4).

$\mathcal{B}$	$\mathcal{C}$	$\mathcal{V}$
SSN	c_1 = SSN	v_1 = ZIP∨Employer
Name	c_2 = Name∧Job	v_2 = SSN∨(Birth∧ZIP)
Birth	c_3 = Name∧Employer	v_3 = Job∧Employer
ZIP	c_4 = Birth∧ZIP∧Job	
Job	c_5 = Birth∧ZIP∧Employer	
Employer		

Fig. 3. Boolean interpretation of the inputs of the MIN-FRAG problem in Figure 1

3.1 OBDD Representation of Constraints

In our modeling, attributes in R are interpreted as Boolean variables. Visibility constraints have already been defined as Boolean formulas (Definition 2). Each confidentiality constraint in $\mathcal{C}$ can be represented as the conjunction of the variables corresponding to the attributes in the constraint. For instance, Figure 3 represents the Boolean interpretation of the inputs of the MIN-FRAG problem in Figure 1, where $\mathcal{B}$ denotes the set of Boolean variables.

We use OBDDs as an effective and efficient solution to represent and manipulate Boolean formulas. An OBDD represents a Boolean formula as a rooted directed acyclic graph with two leaf nodes labeled 1 (true) and 0 (false), respectively, corresponding to the truth values of the formula. Each internal node in the graph represents a Boolean variable in the formula and has two outgoing edges, labeled 1 and 0, representing the assignment of values 1 and 0, respectively, to the variable. The variables occur in the same order on all the paths of the graph. Also, to guarantee a compact representation of the Boolean formula, the subgraphs rooted at the two direct descendants of each internal node in the graph are disjoint, and any possible pair of subgraphs rooted at two different nodes are not isomorphic. Figure 4 and Figure 5 illustrate the OBDDs of the Boolean formulas in Figure 3 that model the confidentiality and visibility constraints, respectively, in Figure 1. Here and in the following, edges labeled 1 are represented by solid lines, and edges labeled 0 are represented by dashed lines. A truth assignment to the Boolean variables in a formula corresponds to a path from the root to one of the leaf nodes of the OBDD of the formula. The outgoing edge of a node in the path is the value assigned to the variable represented by the node. For instance, with respect to the OBDD of v_1 in Figure 5, path ⟨ZIP, Employer, 1⟩ represents truth assignment [ZIP=0, Employer=1] since the edge in the path outgoing from node ZIP is labeled 0, and the edge in the path outgoing from node Employer is labeled 1. We call *one-paths* (*zero-paths*, respectively) all the paths of an OBDD that reach leaf node 1 (0, respectively), which correspond to the assignments that satisfy (do not satisfy, respectively) the formula. For instance, with respect to the OBDD of v_1 in Figure 5, path ⟨ZIP, Employer, 1⟩ is a one-path of the OBDD. Variables in the formula that do not occur in a path from the root to a leaf node are called *don't care* variables, that is, variables whose values do not influence the truth value of the formula. For instance, with respect to the one-path ⟨ZIP, 1⟩ of the OBDD of v_1 in Figure 5, Employer is a don't care variable. If there is at least a don't care variable along a path, the corresponding truth assignment is *partial* (in contrast to *complete*), since only a

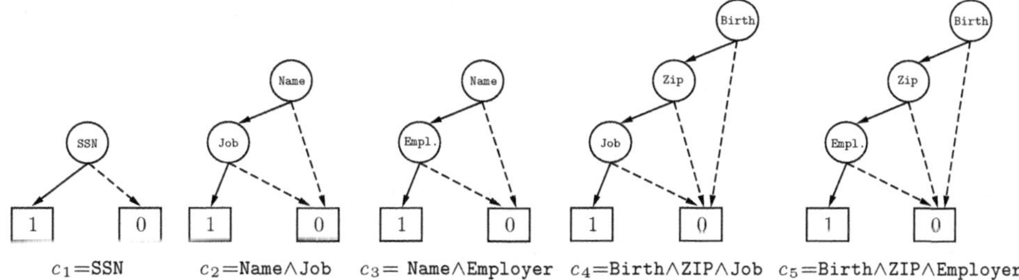

Fig. 4. OBDDs representing the confidentiality constraints in Figure 3

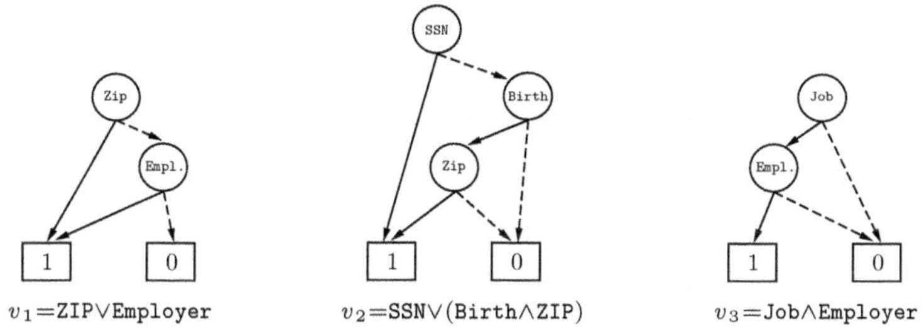

Fig. 5. OBDDs representing the visibility constraints in Figure 3

subset of the variables in the formula is assigned a value. We note that a partial truth assignment with k don't care variables is a compact representation of a set of 2^k complete truth assignments, obtained by assigning to the don't care variables value 1 or 0. For instance, the OBDD of v_1 in Figure 5 has two one-paths, corresponding to truth assignments [ZIP=1] and [ZIP=0, Employer=1]. Partial truth assignment [ZIP=1] is a shorthand for [ZIP=1, Employer=1] and [ZIP=1, Employer=0], where don't care variable Employer has value 1 and 0, respectively.

3.2 Truth Assignments

In the Boolean modeling of the fragmentation problem, a fragment $F \in \mathcal{F}$ can be interpreted as a complete truth assignment, denoted I_F, over the set $\mathcal{B}$ of Boolean variables. Function I_F assigns value 1 to each variable corresponding to an attribute in F, and value 0 to all the other variables. A fragmentation is then represented by a set of complete truth assignments, which is formally defined as follows.

Definition 5 (Set of truth assignments). *Given a set $\mathcal{B}$ of Boolean variables, a* set $\mathcal{I}$ of truth assignments *is a set $\{I_1, \ldots, I_l\}$ of functions, such that each I_i in $\mathcal{I}$, $i = 1, \ldots, l$, is defined as $I_i : \mathcal{B} \rightarrow \{0,1\}$.*

With a slight abuse of notation, we use I to denote also the list of truth values assigned by I to variables in $\mathcal{B}$. For instance, fragmentation $\mathcal{F}$ in Figure 2 corresponds to the set $\mathcal{I}=\{I_{F_1},I_{F_2}\}$ of truth assignments, where I_{F_1} = [SSN=0, Name=0, Birth=1, ZIP=1, Job=0, Employer=0] and I_{F_2} = [SSN=0, Name=0, Birth=0, ZIP=0, Job=1, Employer=1]. Given a Boolean formula f, defined over Boolean variables $\mathcal{B}$, and a truth assignment I, $I(f)$ denotes the result of the evaluation of f with respect to truth assignment I. A set $\mathcal{I}$ of truth assignments corresponds to a correct fragmentation if it satisfies all confidentiality and visibility constraints and each Boolean variable is set to true by at most one truth assignment, as formally defined in the following.

Definition 6 (Correct set of truth assignments). *Given a set $\mathcal{B}$ of Boolean variables, a set $\mathcal{C}$ of confidentiality constraints over $\mathcal{B}$, and a set $\mathcal{V}$ of visibility constraints over $\mathcal{B}$, a set $\mathcal{I}$ of truth assignments is* correct *with respect to $\mathcal{C}$ and $\mathcal{V}$ iff:*

1. $\forall c \in \mathcal{C}$, $\forall I \in \mathcal{I}$: $I(c) = 0$ *(confidentiality);*
2. $\forall v \in \mathcal{V}$, $\exists I \in \mathcal{I}$: $I(v) = 1$ *(visibility);*
3. $\forall I_i, I_j \in \mathcal{I}, i \neq j$, $\forall a \in \mathcal{B}$ *s.t.* $I_i(a) = 1$: $I_j(a) = 0$ *(un-linkability).*

Condition 1 ensures that the evaluation of any confidentiality constraint with respect to any truth assignment (fragment) is false (i.e., no confidentiality constraint is violated). Condition 2 ensures that, for each visibility constraint, there is at least one truth assignment (fragment) that makes the visibility constraint true (i.e., all visibility constraints are satisfied). Condition 3 ensures that there is at most one truth assignment (fragment) that sets a variable to true (i.e., different fragments do not have common attributes). It is immediate to see that a set of truth assignments is correct with respect to $\mathcal{C}$ and $\mathcal{V}$ iff the corresponding fragmentation is correct with respect to $\mathcal{C}$ and $\mathcal{V}$ (i.e., Definition 6 is equivalent to Definition 4). The correctness of a set $\mathcal{I}$ of truth assignments can be efficiently verified by using the OBDDs representing the confidentiality and visibility constraints: *i)* each assignment I must correspond to a zero-path in all the OBDDs of the confidentiality constraints; and *ii)* for each visibility constraint, at least one assignment I must correspond to a one-path in the OBDD of the constraint. For instance, consider the OBDDs of confidentiality and visibility constraints in Figure 4 and Figure 5 and the set $\mathcal{I} = \{I_{F_1}, I_{F_2}\}$ of truth assignments representing the fragmentation in Figure 2. $\mathcal{I}$ is correct, since: *1)* I_{F_1} and I_{F_2} correspond to zero-paths of the OBDDs of the confidentiality constraints (confidentiality); *2)* I_{F_2} corresponds to a one-path of the OBDDs of v_1 and v_3, and I_{F_1} corresponds to a one-path of the OBDD of v_2 (visibility); and *3)* each variable in $\mathcal{B}$ is set to 1 by at most one between I_{F_1} and I_{F_2} (un-linkability).

Note that given two fragments F_i and F_j and the corresponding truth assignments I_{F_i} and I_{F_j}, the truth assignment representing merged fragment $F_{ij}=F_i \cup F_j$ is $I_{F_{ij}}=I_{F_i} \vee I_{F_j}$. The Min-Frag problem can now be reformulated as follows.

*Problem 2 (*Min-Truth*).* Given a set $\mathcal{B}$ of Boolean variables, a set $\mathcal{C}$ of confidentiality constraints over $\mathcal{B}$, and a set $\mathcal{V}$ of visibility constraints over $\mathcal{B}$, determine (if it exists) a correct set $\mathcal{I}$ of truth assignments such that there does not exist

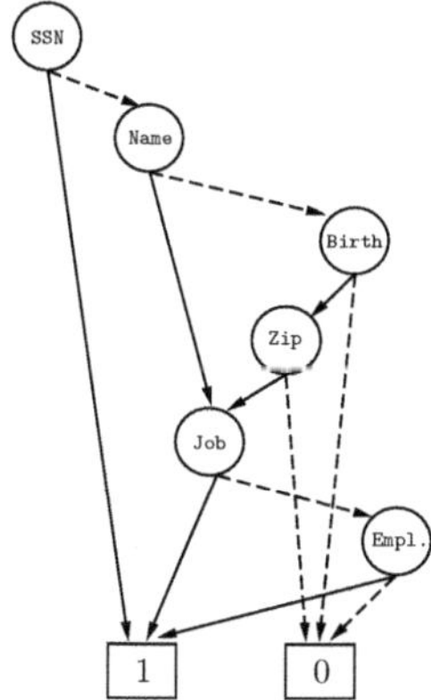

Fig. 6. OBDD representing the disjunction $(c_1 \vee c_2 \vee c_3 \vee c_4 \vee c_5)$

another correct set $\mathcal{I}'$ of truth assignments obtained by combining two truth assignments in $\mathcal{I}$ through the OR operator.

Our approach to solve the MIN-TRUTH problem exploits properties of the OBDDs to efficiently check if a set of truth assignments is correct. In principle, a set of truth assignments should be checked for correctness against each confidentiality and each visibility constraint. We can cut down on such controls by noting that if a truth assignment I does not make true any confidentiality constraint, Boolean formula $c_1 \vee \ldots \vee c_m$ evaluates to false with respect to I. Also, if truth assignment I makes true at least one of the confidentiality constraints in $\mathcal{C}$, Boolean formula $c_1 \vee \ldots \vee c_m$ evaluates to true with respect to I. In other words, we can check all the confidentiality constraints together in a single step. Formally, this observation is expressed as follows.

Observation 1. *Given a set $\mathcal{B} = \{a_1, \ldots, a_n\}$ of Boolean variables, a set $\mathcal{C} = \{c_1, \ldots, c_m\}$ of confidentiality constraints over $\mathcal{B}$, and a truth assignment I:*

$$\forall c \in \mathcal{C},\ I(c) = 0 \iff I(c_1 \vee \ldots \vee c_m) = 0.$$

To verify whether a truth assignment I satisfies the confidentiality constraints, we can then simply check if I characterizes a zero-path of the OBDD representing the disjunction of confidentiality constraints. For instance, consider the confidentiality constraints in Figure 3, the OBDD representing their disjunction in Figure 6, and truth assignment I_{F_2} = [`SSN`=0, `Name`=0, `Birth`=0, `ZIP`=0, `Job`=1, `Employer`=1], representing fragment F_2 in Figure 2. I_{F_2} corresponds to a zero-path in the OBDD in Figure 6, implying that I_{F_2} does not violate the confidentiality constraints.

For each visibility constraint v, a correct set of truth assignments must include at least a truth assignment I satisfying v, while not violating confidentiality constraints (i.e., $I(v)$=1 and $I(c_1 \vee \ldots \vee c_m)$=0). This is equivalent to say that the evaluation of Boolean formula $v \wedge \neg(c_1 \vee \ldots \vee c_m)$ with respect to truth assignment I is true, as formally observed in the following.

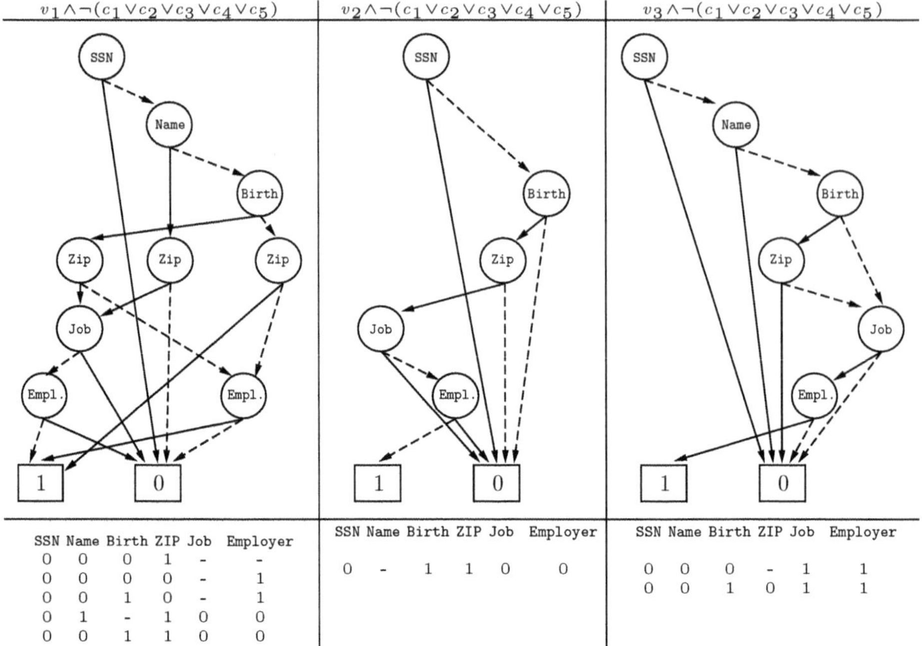

SSN	Name	Birth	ZIP	Job	Employer
0	0	0	1	-	-
0	0	0	0	-	1
0	0	1	0	-	1
0	1	-	1	0	0
0	0	1	1	0	0

SSN	Name	Birth	ZIP	Job	Employer
0	-	1	1	0	0

SSN	Name	Birth	ZIP	Job	Employer
0	0	0	-	1	1
0	0	1	0	1	1

Fig. 7. OBDDs representing the composition of each visibility constraint in Figure 5 with the negated disjunction of the confidentiality constraints in Figure 4, and their one-paths

Observation 2. *Given a set $\mathcal{B} = \{a_1, \ldots, a_n\}$ of Boolean variables, a set $\mathcal{C} = \{c_1, \ldots, c_m\}$ of confidentiality constraints over $\mathcal{B}$, a visibility constraint v over $\mathcal{B}$, and a truth assignment I:*

$$I(v) = 1 \text{ and } I(c_1 \vee \ldots \vee c_m) = 0 \iff I(v \wedge \neg(c_1 \vee \ldots \vee c_m)) = 1.$$

In other words, the one-paths of the OBDD, denoted O_i, of Boolean formula $v_i \wedge \neg(c_1 \vee \ldots \vee c_m)$, represent in a compact way all and only the truth assignments that satisfy v_i and that do not violate any confidentiality constraint. Note that all variables in $\mathcal{B}$ not appearing in the formula are considered as don't care variables. For instance, consider the confidentiality and visibility constraints in Figure 4 and in Figure 5. Figure 7 illustrates the OBDDs of formulas $v_i \wedge \neg(c_1 \vee \ldots \vee c_5)$, $i = 1, \ldots, 3$, along with their one-paths. In the figure and in the remainder of the paper, we use '-' as value for the don't care variables. For instance, attribute `Name` does not appear in the OBDD representing $v_2 \wedge \neg(c_1 \vee \ldots \vee c_5)$ and therefore it appears as a don't care variable in the one-path of O_2 (i.e., [`SSN`=0, `Name`=-, `Birth`=1, `ZIP`=1, `Job`=0, `Employer`=0]). To satisfy Condition 1 (confidentiality) and Condition 2 (visibility) in Definition 6, a set $\mathcal{I}$ of truth assignments must include, for each $v_i \in \mathcal{V}$, one truth assignment in the set of one-paths of O_i. However, not all the sets of truth assignments that include one of the one-paths of O_i for each $v_i \in \mathcal{V}$ are correct, since they may violate Condition 3 in Definition 6 (un-linkability). In the following, we discuss how to combine truth assignments representing one-paths of $O_1, \ldots, O_k$ to incrementally compute a correct set $\mathcal{I}$ of truth assignments. We note that one-paths of O_i may represent partial truth assignments, while a correct set of truth assignments is composed of complete assignments only (Definition 5). As a consequence, don't care variables must be set either to 0 or 1 before inserting one-paths of $O_1, \ldots, O_k$ into $\mathcal{I}$.

3.3 Comparison of Assignments

Goal of our approach is to incrementally create a correct set of truth assignments that solves the MIN-TRUTH problem and that corresponds to a correct and minimal fragmentation. To this purpose, we first introduce the concepts of *linkable* and *mergeable* truth assignments.

Definition 7 (Linkable truth assignments). *Given two assignments I_i and I_j over Boolean variables $\mathcal{B}$, we say that I_i and I_j are* linkable *iff $\exists a \in \mathcal{B}$: $I_i(a) = I_j(a) = 1$.*

According to Definition 7, two assignments are linkable iff there is a Boolean variable in $\mathcal{B}$ such that the truth value of the variable is 1 with respect to the given assignments. Intuitively, this implies that the fragments corresponding to them have an attribute in common. For instance, the two assignments [SSN=0, Name=0, Birth=0, ZIP=-, Job=1, Employer=1] and [SSN=0, Name=0, Birth=0, ZIP=-, Job=1, Employer=-] are linkable since they both assign 1 to variable Job.

Definition 8 (Mergeable truth assignments). *Given two assignments I_i and I_j over Boolean variables $\mathcal{B}$, we say that I_i and I_j are* mergeable *iff $\forall a \in \mathcal{B}$ s.t. $I_i(a)$=1, $I_j(a)$=1 or $I_j(a)$=- and vice versa.*

According to Definition 8, two truth assignments are mergeable iff for each variable a in $\mathcal{B}$ the truth values of the variable in the two assignments are not in contrast, where being in contrast for variable a means that a is assigned 1 by one assignment while being assigned 0 by the other one. Intuitively, two mergeable assignments define the truth value of variables in a way that they can be represented through a single assignment. As an example, consider the two assignments [SSN=0, Name=-, Birth=0, ZIP=-, Job=-, Employer=1] and [SSN=0, Name=0, Birth=-, ZIP=1, Job=-, Employer=-]. For each variable set to 1 in one of these assignments, the correspondent truth value in the other assignment is either 1 or -, and therefore the two assignments are mergeable. Assignments [SSN=0, Name=0, Birth=1, ZIP=0, Job=-, Employer=1] and [SSN=0, Name=0, Birth=1, ZIP=1, Job=0, Employer=-] are linkable (Birth is set to 1 by both assignments) but not mergeable since there is a conflict on variable ZIP. Note that the presence of don't care variables does not influence the linkability or mergeability of two truth assignments.

Mergeable assignments can be composed according to the composition operator $\odot$ in Figure 8. The composition of two mergeable truth assignments I_i

$\odot$	0	1	-
0	0	n.a.	0
1	n.a.	1	1
-	0	1	-

Fig. 8. Assignment composition operator

and I_j results in a new truth assignment, where the truth value of a variable coincides with its truth value in the assignment in which it does not appear as a don't care variable. If a variable appears as a don't care variable in both I_i and I_j, then its value in the new assignment remains don't care. For instance, assignments [`SSN`=0, `Name`=-, `Birth`=0, `ZIP`=-, `Job`=-, `Employer`=1] and [`SSN`=0, `Name`=0, `Birth`=-, `ZIP`=1, `Job`=-, `Employer`=-] are mergeable and the result of their composition is assignment [`SSN`=0, `Name`=0, `Birth`=0, `ZIP`=1, `Job`=-, `Employer`=1].

4 Computing a Minimal Set of Truth Assignments

Figure 9 illustrates our heuristic algorithm for computing a solution to the Min-Truth problem (Problem 2). The algorithm takes as input a set $\mathcal{B}$ of Boolean variables, a set $\mathcal{C} = \{c_1, \ldots, c_m\}$ of confidentiality constraints, and a set $\mathcal{V} = \{v_1, \ldots, v_k\}$ of visibility constraints. It incrementally builds a correct set of truth assignments by inserting, for each v in $\mathcal{V}$, a truth assignment satisfying v while not violating confidentiality constraints. A truth assignment can be inserted in an existing set either as a new truth assignment (if it is not linkable with any assignment in the set) or by composing it with an existing assignment (if it is linkable and mergeable with an assignment in the set). It returns a correct and minimal set $\mathcal{I}_{sol}$ of truth assignments, if such a set exists; it returns NULL, otherwise.

The algorithm first defines, for each $v_i \in \mathcal{V}$, the OBDD representing Boolean formula $v_i \wedge \neg(c_1 \vee \ldots \vee c_m)$, extracts the set $\mathcal{I}_{v_i}$ of one-paths, and orders them by decreasing number of don't care variables (lines 1-4). The reason for this ordering is that truth assignments with a high number of don't care variables impose less constraints on subsequent choices, and therefore are less likely to be in contrast with them. Also, $\mathcal{I}_{v_1}, \ldots, \mathcal{I}_{v_k}$ are ordered by increasing number of truth assignments (line 5). The reason for such ordering is to consider first sets for which fewer truth assignments are possible.

The algorithm calls function **DefineAssignments** (line 6), which receives as input a set $\mathcal{I}_{sol}$ of truth assignments and an integer number i, $1 \leq i \leq k$, indicating that $\mathcal{I}_{sol}$ has been obtained by combining one truth assignment from each $\mathcal{I}_j$, $j = 1, \ldots, (i-1)$. Function **DefineAssignments** tries to insert into $\mathcal{I}_{sol}$ a truth assignment that belongs to $\mathcal{I}_i$, possibly composing it, through the $\odot$ operator, with a truth assignment in $\mathcal{I}_{sol}$ if they are linkable and mergeable. For the j-th truth assignment $\mathcal{I}_i[j]$ in $\mathcal{I}_i$ ($j = 1, \ldots, |\mathcal{I}_i|$), the function first identifies the set *LinkableAssignments* of truth assignments in $\mathcal{I}_{sol}$ linkable with $\mathcal{I}_i[j]$

INPUT
$\mathcal{B} = \{a_1,\ldots,a_n\}$ /* Boolean variables */
$\mathcal{C} = \{c_1,\ldots,c_m\}$ /* Boolean interpretation of confidentiality constraints */
$\mathcal{V} = \{v_1,\ldots,v_k\}$ /* visibility constraints */
OUTPUT
$\mathcal{I}_{sol} = \{I_1,\ldots,I_l\}$ /* correct and minimal set of truth assignments */
MAIN
1: **for each** $v_i \in \mathcal{V}$ **do** /* define the OBDDs representing the constraints */
2: let O_i be the OBDD representing $v_i \wedge \neg(c_1 \vee \ldots \vee c_m)$
3: let $\mathcal{I}_{v_i}$ be the set of one-paths of O_i
4: order $\mathcal{I}_{v_i}$ by decreasing number of -
5: let $[\mathcal{I}_1,\ldots,\mathcal{I}_k]$ be the list obtained ordering $\{\mathcal{I}_{v_1},\ldots,\mathcal{I}_{v_k}\}$ by increasing number of one-paths
6: $\mathcal{I}_{sol}$:= **DefineAssignments**($\emptyset$,1) /* compute a correct set of truth assignments */
7: **if** $\mathcal{I}_{sol} \neq$NULL **then** /* a correct set of truth assignments exists */
8: **for** i:=1,...,($|\mathcal{I}_{sol}|-1$) **do** /* compose truth assignments to make $\mathcal{I}_{sol}$ minimal */
9: **for** j:=($i+1$),...,$|\mathcal{I}_{sol}|$ **do**
10: **if** MERGEABLE($\mathcal{I}_{sol}[i]$,$\mathcal{I}_{sol}[j]$) **then**
11: $\mathcal{I}_{sol}[i] := \mathcal{I}_{sol}[i] \odot \mathcal{I}_{sol}[j]$
12: remove $\mathcal{I}_{sol}[j]$ from $\mathcal{I}_{sol}$
13: **for each** $I \in \mathcal{I}_{sol}$ **do** assign 0 to don't care variables in I
14: **return**($\mathcal{I}_{sol}$)

DEFINEASSIGNMENTS($\mathcal{I}_{sol}$,i)
15: **for** j:=1,...,$|\mathcal{I}_i|$ **do**
16: *satisfied* := TRUE /* true if $\mathcal{I}'_{sol}$ includes a truth assignment from $\mathcal{I}_i$ */
17: *LinkableAssignments* := $\{I \in \mathcal{I}_{sol}$:LINKABLE($\mathcal{I}_i[j]$,$I$)$\}$ /* assignments linkable with $\mathcal{I}_i[j]$ */
18: $\mathcal{I}'_{sol}$:=$\mathcal{I}_{sol} \setminus$*LinkableAssignments* /* remove assignments linkable with $\mathcal{I}_i[j]$ */
19: I_{new}:=$\mathcal{I}_i[j]$
20: **while**(*satisfied* AND *LinkableAssignments* $\neq \emptyset$) **do**
21: I:= **ExtractAssignment**(*LinkableAssignments*)
22: **if** MERGEABLE(I_{new},I) **then** $I_{new} := I_{new} \odot I$ /* compose truth assignments */
23: **else** *satisfied* := FALSE /* I is linkable but not mergeable with I_{new} */
24: **if** *satisfied* **then**
25: $\mathcal{I}'_{sol}$:=$\mathcal{I}_{sol} \cup \{I_{new}\}$
26: **if** i=k **then return**($\mathcal{I}'_{sol}$) /* $\mathcal{I}'_{sol}$ is correct */
27: $\mathcal{I}'_{sol}$:= **DefineAssignments**($\mathcal{I}'_{sol}$,$i+1$) /* recursive call */
28: **if** $\mathcal{I}'_{sol} \neq$NULL **then return**($\mathcal{I}'_{sol}$) /* $\mathcal{I}'_{sol}$ is correct */
29: **return**(NULL)

Fig. 9. Algorithm that computes a correct and minimal set of truth assignments

(line 17) and iteratively composes them with $\mathcal{I}_i[j]$, obtaining truth assignment I_{new} (lines 19-23). We note that mergeable assignments that are not linkable are kept separate, even if they could be composed without violating any confidentiality constraint. In fact, by composing a pair of not linkable truth assignments, the algorithm would discard, without evaluation, all the correct solutions where the two truth assignments are kept separate. If $\mathcal{I}_i[j]$ and *LinkableAssignments* are not mergeable, $\mathcal{I}_i[j]$ can be inserted into $\mathcal{I}_{sol}$ neither as an un-linkable assignment nor by composing it with existing assignments (variable *satisfied*=FALSE). Otherwise, $\mathcal{I}'_{sol}$ is obtained removing *LinkableAssignments* and including I_{new} into $\mathcal{I}_{sol}$ (line 25). If i=k, $\mathcal{I}'_{sol}$ represents a correct fragmentation and is returned (line 26); **DefineAssignments** is recursively called over $\mathcal{I}'_{sol}$ and $i+1$, otherwise (line 27). If the set $\mathcal{I}'_{sol}$ resulting from the recursive call is not NULL, it is correct and is returned (line 28). If no assignment in $\mathcal{I}_i$ can be inserted into $\mathcal{I}_{sol}$, the function returns NULL (line 29).

The set $\mathcal{I}_{sol}$ computed by function **DefineAssignments** may not be minimal, since it may include mergeable truth assignments that are not linkable. The algorithm therefore possibly composes each truth assignment $\mathcal{I}_{sol}[i]$ with each

$\mathcal{I}_{sol}[j]$, $j > i$ (lines 7-12). We note that it is not necessary to check the truth assignment resulting from the composition with assignments $\mathcal{I}_{sol}[l]$, $l < i$, since if $\mathcal{I}_{sol}[l]$ and $\mathcal{I}_{sol}[i]$ are not mergeable, then also $\mathcal{I}_{sol}[l]$ and $\mathcal{I}_{sol}[i] \odot \mathcal{I}_{sol}[j]$ are not mergeable. The algorithm finally assigns 0 to don't care variables in $\mathcal{I}_{sol}$ and returns $\mathcal{I}_{sol}$ (lines 13-14).

Example 1. Consider relation CENSUSDATA and the confidentiality and visibility constraints over it in Figure 1. First, the algorithm builds O_1, O_2, and O_3 in Figure 7, representing the conjunction of each visibility constraint (v_1, v_2, and v_3) with the disjunction ($c_1 \vee \ldots \vee c_5$) of confidentiality constraints. It then extracts their one-paths, orders the one-paths of each $\mathcal{I}_v$ by decreasing number of -, and orders the set of $\mathcal{I}_v$ by increasing number of one-paths. The ordered list [$\mathcal{I}_1$,$\mathcal{I}_2$,$\mathcal{I}_3$] of sets of truth assignments is illustrated in Figure 10, where $\mathcal{I}_1 = \mathcal{I}_{v_2}$, $\mathcal{I}_2 = \mathcal{I}_{v_3}$, and $\mathcal{I}_3 = \mathcal{I}_{v_1}$. Figure 10 presents the recursive calls to function **DefineAssignments** illustrating for each execution: the value of input parameters $\mathcal{I}_{sol}$ and i; the candidate truth assignment $\mathcal{I}_i[j]$ in $\mathcal{I}_i$; the set *LinkableAssignments* of assignments in $\mathcal{I}_{sol}$ that are linkable with $\mathcal{I}_i[j]$; the iterative composition of $\mathcal{I}_i[j]$ with the assignments in *LinkableAssignments* and the resulting truth assignment $\mathcal{I}_{new}$; and the computed set $\mathcal{I}'_{sol}$. In the figure, for simplicity, we do not report attribute names in truth assignments and we assume that truth values are assigned, in the order, to `SSN`, `Name`, `Birth`, `ZIP`, `Job`, `Employer`. The fragmentation corresponding to the set of truth assignments returned by the algorithm is illustrated in Figure 2.

The correctness and complexity of the algorithm in Figure 9 are stated by the following theorems. The proofs of the theorems are omitted for space constraints.

Theorem 1 (Correctness). *Given a set $\mathcal{B}$ of Boolean variables, a set $\mathcal{C}$ of confidentiality constraints over $\mathcal{B}$, and a set $\mathcal{V}$ of visibility constraints over $\mathcal{B}$, the algorithm in Figure 9 terminates and computes, if it exists, a correct and minimal set of truth assignments with respect to $\mathcal{C}$ and $\mathcal{V}$.*

Theorem 2 (Complexity). *Given a set $\mathcal{B}$ of Boolean variables, a set $\mathcal{C}$ of confidentiality constraints over $\mathcal{B}$, and a set $\mathcal{V}$ of visibility constraints over $\mathcal{B}$, the complexity of the algorithm in Figure 9 is $O(\prod_{v \in \mathcal{V}} |\mathcal{I}_v| \cdot |\mathcal{B}| + (|\mathcal{V}| + |\mathcal{C}|)2^{|\mathcal{B}|})$ in time, where $\mathcal{I}_v$ is the set of one-paths of the OBDD representing $v \wedge \neg(c_1 \vee \ldots \vee c_m)$.*

The computational cost of the algorithm is obtained as the sum of the cost of building the OBDDs, which is $O((|\mathcal{V}| + |\mathcal{C}|)2^{|\mathcal{B}|})$, and the cost of determining $\mathcal{I}_{sol}$ through recursive function **DefineAssignments**, which is $O(\prod_{v \in \mathcal{V}} |\mathcal{I}_v| \cdot |\mathcal{B}|)$. We note that the computational cost of the construction of the OBDDs is exponential in the worst case, but in the majority of real-world applications OBBD-based approaches are computationally efficient [3,16].

$\mathcal{I}_1$:=([0,-,1,1,0,0])
$\mathcal{I}_2$:=([0,0,0,-,1,1],[0,0,1,0,1,1])
$\mathcal{I}_3$:=([0,0,0,1,-,-],[0,0,0,0,-,1],[0,0,1,0,-,1],[0,1,-,1,0,0],[0,0,1,1,0,0])
DefineAssignments(∅,1)
$\mathcal{I}_1$[1]=[0,-,1,1,0,0]
LinkableAssignments:=∅
I_{new}:=[0,-,1,1,0,0]
$\mathcal{I}'_{sol}$:={[0,-,1,1,0,0]}
DefineAssignments({[0,-,1,1,0,0]},2)
$\mathcal{I}_2$[1]=[0,0,0,-,1,1]
LinkableAssignments:=∅
I_{new}:=[0,0,0,-,1,1]
$\mathcal{I}'_{sol}$:{[0,-,1,1,0,0],[0,0,0,-,1,1]}
DefineAssignments({[0,-,1,1,0,0],[0,0,0,-,1,1]},3)
$\mathcal{I}_3$[1]=[0,0,0,1,-,-]
LinkableAssignments:={[0,-,1,1,0,0]}
I_{new}:=[0,0,0,1,-,-]
MERGEABLE([0,0,0,1,-,-],[0,-,1,1,0,0])=FALSE
$\mathcal{I}_3$[2]=[0,0,0,0,-,1]
LinkableAssignments:={[0,0,0,-,1,1]}
I_{new}:=[0,0,0,0,-,1]
MERGEABLE([0,0,0,0,-,1],[0,0,0,-,1,1])=TRUE
I_{new}:=[0,0,0,0,-,1] ⊙ [0,0,0,-,1,1]:=[0,0,0,0,1,1]
return({[0,-,1,1,0,0],[0,0,0,0,1,1]})

Fig. 10. Example of the execution of the algorithm in Figure 9 with the inputs in Figure 3

5 Related Work

Data fragmentation has been studied as a solution to enforce confidentiality constraints while ensuring an efficient query execution in outsourcing scenarios, where data are stored and managed at external honest-but-curious servers [9,14,20]. In particular, the proposals based on fragmentation can be classified as solutions that: *1)* combine fragmentation and encryption and split data between two fragments stored on two non-communicating servers [1], or among multiple fragments [8], possibly stored on a single server, in such a way to minimize query execution costs [6]; *2)* depart from encryption [7,21] and satisfy confidentiality constraints by splitting the data over two fragments, one of which is stored at the data owner. Although our approach shares with these proposals the use of fragmentation for properly protecting sensitive data and/or associations, we take into consideration a different scenario and address a different problem. In fact, our proposal considers a data publishing scenario, in contrast to data outsourcing, and aims at satisfying also visibility constraints, which have been introduced in [10] where the authors exploit SAT solvers to compute a correct fragmentation.

The work presented in this paper has some affinity with the proposals that introduce a policy based classification of the data to protect their confidentiality (e.g., [2]). Such solutions however do not use fragmentation and are concerned with returning to users query results that do not contain combinations of values that are sensitive or that can be exploited for inferring sensitive information.

Other related work is represented by proposals that introduce OBDD-based approaches for solving constraint satisfaction problems (or CSPs, e.g. [13,15,17]). These approaches aim at computing a truth assignment for a set of variables that satisfies a set of constraints among the variable values. The solution described in this paper differs from the techniques proposed for general constraint satisfaction problems, since our approach takes advantage of the monotonicity of confidentiality and visibility constrains and therefore fully exploits the implicit representation of sets of truth assignments provided by OBDDs. These peculiarities of the minimal fragmentation problem permit to limit the computational effort required to compute an optimal solution.

6 Conclusions

We presented a novel OBDD-based approach for computing a fragmentation that fulfills both the need of properly protecting sensitive data and the need of guaranteeing visibility requirements when a dataset is publicly released. Our modeling of the fragmentation problem relies on the interpretation of both confidentiality and visibility constraints as Boolean formulas and of fragments as truth assignments to variables. OBDDs allow us to compactly represent multiple constraints and to simply check whether a fragmentation satisfies them.

Acknowledgments

This work was supported in part by the EU within the 7FP project "PrimeLife" under grant agreement 216483, by the Italian Ministry of Research within the PRIN 2008 project "PEPPER" (2008SY2PH4), and by the Università degli Studi di Milano within the "UNIMI per il Futuro - 5 per Mille" project "PREVIOUS".

References

1. Aggarwal, G., Bawa, M., Ganesan, P., Garcia-Molina, H., Kenthapadi, K., Motwani, R., Srivastava, U., Thomas, D., Xu, Y.: Two can keep a secret: A distributed architecture for secure database services. In: Proc. of CIDR 2005, Asilomar, CA, USA (January 2005)
2. Biskup, J., Wiese, L.: Combining consistency and confidentiality requirements in first-order databases. In: Samarati, P., Yung, M., Martinelli, F., Ardagna, C.A. (eds.) ISC 2009. LNCS, vol. 5735, pp. 121–134. Springer, Heidelberg (2009)
3. Bryant, R.: Graph-based algorithms for Boolean function manipulation. IEEE TC 35(8), 677–691 (1986)

4. Cao, N., Wang, C., Li, M., Ren, K., Lou, W.: Privacy-preserving multi-keyword ranked search over encrypted cloud data. In: Proc. of INFOCOM 2011, Shanghai, China (April 2011)
5. Cimato, S., Gamassi, M., Piuri, V., Sassi, R., Scotti, F.: Privacy-aware biometrics: Design and implementation of a multimodal verification system. In: Proc. of ACSAC 2008, Anaheim, CA, USA (December 2008)
6. Ciriani, V., De Capitani di Vimercati, S., Foresti, S., Jajodia, S., Paraboschi, S., Samarati, P.: Fragmentation design for efficient query execution over sensitive distributed databases. In: Proc. of ICDCS 2009, Montreal, Canada (June 2009)
7. Ciriani, V., De Capitani di Vimercati, S., Foresti, S., Jajodia, S., Paraboschi, S., Samarati, P.: Keep a few: Outsourcing data while maintaining confidentiality. In: Backes, M., Ning, P. (eds.) ESORICS 2009. LNCS, vol. 5789, pp. 440–455. Springer, Heidelberg (2009)
8. Ciriani, V., De Capitani di Vimercati, S., Foresti, S., Jajodia, S., Paraboschi, S., Samarati, P.: Combining fragmentation and encryption to protect privacy in data storage. ACM TISSEC 13(3), 22:1–22:33 (2010)
9. Damiani, E., De Capitani di Vimercati, S., Jajodia, S., Paraboschi, S., Samarati, P.: Balancing confidentiality and efficiency in untrusted relational DBMSs. In: Proc. of CCS 2003, Washington, DC, USA (October 2003)
10. De Capitani di Vimercati, S., Foresti, S., Jajodia, S., Paraboschi, S., Samarati, P.: Fragments and loose associations: Respecting privacy in data publishing. Proc. of the VLDB Endowment 3(1), 1370–1381 (2010)
11. Gamassi, M., Lazzaroni, M., Misino, M., Piuri, V., Sana, D., Scotti, F.: Accuracy and performance of biometric systems. In: Proc. of IMTC 2004, Como, Italy (May 2004)
12. Gamassi, M., Piuri, V., Sana, D., Scotti, F.: Robust fingerprint detection for access control. In: Proc. of RoboCare Workshop 2005, Rome, Italy (May 2005)
13. Gange, G., Stuckey, P.J., Lagoon, V.: Fast set bounds propagation using a bdd-sat hybrid. J. Artif. Int. Res. 38, 307–338 (2010)
14. Hacigümüs, H., Iyer, B., Mehrotra, S.: Providing database as a service. In: Proc. of ICDE 2002, San Jose, CA, USA (February 2002)
15. Hadzic, T., Hansen, E.R., O'Sullivan, B.: On automata, MDDs and BDDs in constraint satisfaction. In: Proc. of ECAI 2008, Patras, Greece (July 2008)
16. Knuth, D.E.: The Art of Computer Programming. Fascicle 1: Bitwise Tricks & Techniques; Binary Decision Diagrams, vol. 4. Addison-Wesley Professional, Reading (2009)
17. Kurihara, M., Kondo, H.: Efficient BDD encodings for partial order constraints with application to expert systems in software verification. In: Orchard, B., Yang, C., Ali, M. (eds.) Innovations in Applied Artificial Intelligence. Springer, Heidelberg (2004)
18. Meinel, C., Theobald, T.: Algorithms and Data Structures in VLSI Design. Springer, Heidelberg (1998)
19. Samarati, P.: Protecting respondents' identities in microdata release. IEEE TKDE 13(6), 1010–1027 (2001)
20. Samarati, P., De Capitani di Vimercati, S.: Data protection in outsourcing scenarios: Issues and directions. In: Proc. of ASIACCS 2010, Beijing, China (April 2010)
21. Wiese, L.: Horizontal fragmentation for data outsourcing with formula-based confidentiality constraints. In: Echizen, I., Kunihiro, N., Sasaki, R. (eds.) IWSEC 2010. LNCS, vol. 6434, pp. 101–116. Springer, Heidelberg (2010)

Public-Key Encrypted Bloom Filters with Applications to Supply Chain Integrity

Florian Kerschbaum

SAP Research
Karlsruhe, Germany
florian.kerschbaum@sap.com

Abstract. Bloom filters provide a space- and time-efficient mean to check the inclusion of an element in a set. In some applications it is beneficial, if the set represented by the Bloom filter is only revealed to authorized parties. Particularly, operations data in supply chain management can be very sensitive and Bloom filters can be applied to supply chain integrity validation. Despite the protection of the represented set, Bloom filter operations, such as the verification of set inclusion, need to be still feasible. In this paper we present privacy-preserving, publicly verifiable Bloom filters which offer both: privacy for the represented set and public Bloom filter operations. We give security proofs in the standard model.

1 Introduction

Bloom filters provide a space- and time-efficient mean to check the inclusion of an element in a set in constant time. We apply them to supply chain integrity (see Section 2). Yet, they have many more applications in computer science, e.g. in databases [1,15] or networks [5].

We consider situations where the confidentiality of the set represented by the Bloom filter is important. Given an unprotected Bloom filter anyone can check for the inclusion of an element and maybe even enumerate all included elements. In many scenarios this is an undesired property, e.g. when the Bloom filter is stored or used by untrusted service provider [1,15]. The content (i.e. its bit mask representing the contained set) of the Bloom filter should remain private. This is particularly true in supply chain integrity where there are risks of industrial espionage [9,28].

Our idea starts by encrypting the Bloom filter content. Regular encryption renders the Bloom filter content useless. We therefore use a special, carefully crafted form of encryption: public-key and (partially) homomorphic. Now, only the private-key holder can access the Bloom filter content, but in order for the encrypted Bloom filter to be useful we need to still enable regular operations on it despite the encryption.

First, we enable the public-key holder to add elements to the Bloom filter by encrypting them – without interaction. Second, we enable the public-key holder to verify the inclusion or exclusion of an element – also without interaction.

Y. Li (Ed.): Data and Applications Security and Privacy XXV, LNCS 6818, pp. 60–75, 2011.

For these purposes we exploit the homomorphism of the encryption scheme to evaluate the Bloom filter operations and then employ zero-knowledge proofs (ZKP) [16] for validating the result. Our ZKPs guarantee that the private-key holder cannot make false claims about the Bloom filter content, yet the public-key holder will learn nothing beyond the validity of the claims. We emphasize that our secured Bloom filter operations can still be computed and verified in constant time.

We propose to apply these Bloom filters to supply chain integrity. Several important supply chain integrity checks can be reduced to set in- or exclusion. Any participant in the supply chain – whether supplier or customer – can verify using our privacy-preserving Bloom filters set inclusion and thereby e.g. product authenticity. Most importantly, no such check will violate any supplier's desire for privacy.

In summary, our contributions are

- the adaptation of a *public-key encryption* scheme for Bloom filters
- *non-interactive operations* for element addition, element inclusion or exclusion verification and filter content comparison
- *security proofs* in the standard model

The remainder of the paper is structured as follows. In the next section we present our example application of supply chain integrity and its security requirements. In Section 3 we present our building blocks of Bloom filters, public key encryption schemes and ZKPs. We describe our main result – a public-key encrypted Bloom filter – in Section 4. In Section 5 we review related work before we conclude the paper in Section 6.

2 Problem: Supply Chain Integrity

Supply chain integrity refers to the integrity of the flow of goods through a supply chain. This integrity can, e.g., be compromised by the introduction of counterfeit products or by the distribution of genuine products on gray markets. The sale of counterfeit products alone costs the United States an estimated 200 billion dollars annually [32].

Clearly, tracking of items and increased visibility of items throughout the supply chain help protecting supply chain integrity [30]. Nevertheless, this tracking also implies a number of novel security and privacy risks [28]. Given detailed information about one's supply chain operation one can infer strategic relationships, business volumes or planned promotions. Companies are therefore very reluctant to disclose this information despite its benefits [9].

In this paper we present secure methods for checking supply chain integrity that disclose nothing but the validity of the integrity check. We assume a generic model for item-level tracking in supply chains [30]. Each item is equipped with an unique identifier. Let $I = \{i_0, \ldots, i_n\}$ be the set of item identifiers. Also each supplier has an unique identifier. Let $S = \{s_0, \ldots, s_m\}$ be the set of supplier identifiers.

As an item i progresses through the supply chain it is handled by a number of different suppliers s. We can perform a number of simple, yet efficient checks on this process.

As a first application we can collect the set S_i of suppliers that have handled an item i. We create a Bloom filter d that represents the set of suppliers and transport it along with the item. This transport can be electronic in an accompanying network message (advanced shipping notification) or even on the item, e.g. an RFID tag [11]. Before a supplier ships the item to another supplier it adds the new supplier to the Bloom filter.

Given this Bloom filter d we can perform two distinct checks. First, we can compare the set S_i against a black list S_{bl} of known violators. These violators can be e.g. companies dealing on grey markets.

$$\forall s \in S_{bl}.s \notin S_i$$

Second, we can check the set S_i against a white list S_{wl} of mandatory suppliers. These suppliers can be e.g. the authentic manufacturers of the item.

$$\forall s \in S_{wl}.s \in S_i$$

For the technical implementation we need to be able to check whether an element s is in a set S_i. As already mentioned, Bloom filters offer a space- and time-efficient mean for this operation. We just need to protect the confidentiality of the represented set.

As a second application we can collect the set I_s of items that a supplier s has handled. We again create a Bloom filter d, but maintain it at one supplier. Each time this supplier handles an item i it adds it to the Bloom filter.

This time we can perform another check. Given two Bloom filters d_1 and d_2 at two suppliers s_1 and s_2, respectively, we can compare whether they encode the same set I. If they do, we are assured that there is no intermediate diversion of the flow of goods between the two suppliers.

$$I_{s_1} = I_{s_2}$$

For the technical implementation we need to be able to compare Bloom filter contents. This may seem simple, but we encrypt the Bloom filter contents using IND-CPA secure encryption [20], such that an equality comparison of the ciphertexts will fail.

Figure 1 exemplarily depicts these checks in a supply chain and how they capture illegitimate items. There are five suppliers s_1 to s_5 and three items i_1 to i_3. Each item takes a different path through the supply chain. Supplier s_1 is on the white list, while supplier s_4 is on the black list. The final customer (or any participant of the supply chain) can perform the following exemplar checks: First, for authentic item i_1 it can check whether it has been handled by supplier s_1: $s_1 \in S_1$. Second, for authentic item i_2 it check whether it has not been handled by supplier s_4: $s_4 \notin S_2$. Third, it can compare the set I_1 of supplier s_1 to the set I_5 of supplier s_5. While this check succeeds in our example, it would fail if supplier s_4 would have sold the item on the grey market (and thereby avoid the second check).

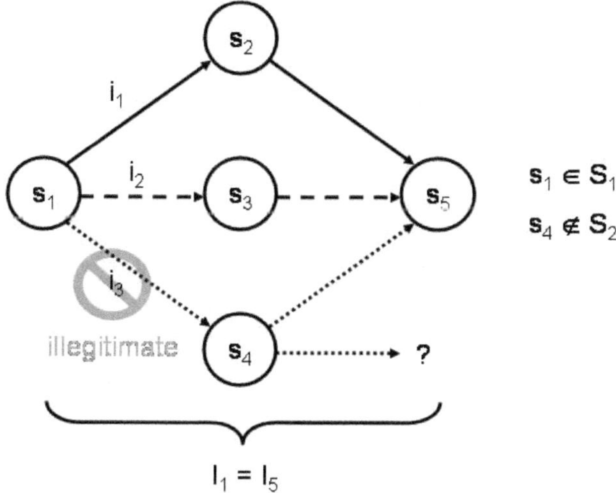

Fig. 1. Example Supply Chain with Illegitimate Item

2.1 Security Desiderata

Given a Bloom filter d we require a number of security properties. We distinguish only two parties: an authority and a supplier. The authority controls the Bloom filter. Its help is needed to perform the operations described above. The authority can be the manufacturer of an item or even an independent organization, such as an industry association. The supplier can add elements to the set and verify the checks described above, i.e. the supplier participates in the supply chain by handling goods and verifying the integrity of the supply chain. Loosely speaking, the goal of our algorithms is to protect against malicious suppliers. Most importantly, we do not distinguish between malicious and honest suppliers. This commonly made distinction is difficult to perform in practice, since the reliability of a supplier can vary over time and is difficult to assess. We assume that all suppliers may be malicious and may perform all operations on the Bloom filter.

Furthermore we assume that an attacker has full control over the network. We model the supply chain as a directed graph with vertices representing suppliers and edges representing transportation links. Items pass through the supply chain and along with each item i a Bloom filter for its set of suppliers S_i. Furthermore, each supplier s maintains a Bloom filter I_s of all of its items. An attacker may read and write any Bloom filter at any point in the graph. Given this powerful type of attacker some attacks cannot be prevented: disruption and cloning. We limit our protection goals to privacy and unlinkability.

Disruption. An attacker may simply destroy the Bloom filter and disrupt the communication. This cannot be prevented. Nevertheless, we can assume a default decision. Items without proper security checks can be considered illegitimate.

Then an attacker disrupting the supply chain cannot insert counterfeit items, but he can cause false positives resulting in a disruption of goods supply. Alternatively, items without proper security checks could be considered legitimate. This current practice prevents disruptions due to false positives, but the problem of counterfeits is prevalent.

Cloning. An attacker may simply copy the information of one Bloom filter to another. This attack is called cloning and is a common problem for anti-counterfeiting. There are no item-level (on-tag) countermeasures, but given a global data view, prevention is feasible [21,23,26,33]. We propose to augment both solutions, since our mechanism can protect against more supply chain integrity threats than just cloning.

Privacy. The content of a Bloom filter (i.e. the represented set) should remain private. Given any Bloom filter d an attacker should not be able to tell whether an element e is in the set or not (except with negligible probability). Even given several successful checks of inclusion or exclusion for elements e_i, an attacker should not be able to tell whether an element e' ($\forall i.e' \neq e_i$) is in the set or not (except with a small probability of false positives). Furthermore, given several successful checks of equality or inequality of sets, an attacker should still not be able to tell.

Unlinkability. An attacker should not be able to link a Bloom filter before and after the addition of an element. Given a pair of Bloom filters d_0 and d_1, an element e and a randomly chosen Bloom filter $d_b \in \{d_0 \cup \{e\}, d_1 \cup \{e\}\}$ with the element e added, an attacker should not be able to tell the random choice b (except with negligible advantage). This prevents an attacker from tracing items through the supply chain. It augments our privacy requirement in preventing supply chain espionage.

3 Background

3.1 Bloom Filter

Bloom filters [3] provide a space- and time-efficient mean to check the inclusion of an element in a set. An empty Bloom filter b consists of m bits, all set to 0, and k hash functions f_i ($0 \leq i < k$). We write b_j ($0 \leq j < m$) for the j-th bit of Bloom filter b. Bloom filters support the operations $add(x)$ for addition of element x to the set and $test(x)$ to test for inclusion of element x.
$Create(m)$: m bits ($0 \leq j < m$) are set to 0

$$\forall j.b_j = 0$$

and k hash functions f_i ($0 \leq i < k$) are published

$$\forall i.f_i : \{0,1\}^* \mapsto \{0, \ldots, m-1\}$$

Add(x): The element x is hashed with all k hash functions f_i and the k bits at the resulting indices l_i are set to 1.

$$\forall i. l_i = f_i(x) \wedge b_{l_i} = 1$$

$Test(x)$: Again, the element x is hashed with all k hash functions f_i and if all k bits at the resulting indices l_i are set, then the test function returns true.

$$\bigwedge_{i=0}^{k-1} b_{f_i(x)}$$

Using Bloom filters false positive are possible, but false negatives are not. The more elements are added to the set, the more likely false positives are. Given the number n of elements to be added and a desired maximum false positive rate p, one can compute the necessary size m of the Bloom filter as [3]

$$m = -\frac{n \ln p}{\ln 2}$$

3.2 Goldwasser Micali Encryption

Goldwasser-Micali (GM) encryption [17] is a public-key, semantically-secure (IND-CPA), homomorphic encryption scheme. Its plaintext length is only 1 bit. GM encryption uses quadratic residuosity modulo a composite of two large primes p and q. A quadratic residue r is a number, such that there exists a number s: $s^2 = r \bmod n$. GM encodes a 1 as a quadratic non-residue and a 0 as a quadratic residue. Particularly, the quadratic non-residues are pseudo quadratic residues, i.e. their Jacobi symbols are all 1. Note that differentiating pseudo quadratic residues and quadratic residues implies factoring.

Let $n = pq$ be the composite of two large primes and v be pseudo quadratic residue. The public key is n, v and the private key is p and q. To encrypt a 0 one chooses a random number r and computes $r^2 \bmod n$ (a quadratic residue). To encrypt a 1 one also chooses a random number r and computes $vr^2 \bmod n$ (a quadratic non-residue). To decrypt one computes whether it is a quadratic residue.

We can summarize the operations as follows

KeyGen(κ): Let κ be a security parameter. Given κ generate the private key $sk = \{p, q\}$ and the public key $pk = \{n = pq, v\}$.

Encrypt(x, pk): Given plaintext x and public key pk produces ciphertext c.

Decrypt(c, sk): Given ciphertext c and private key sk produces plaintext x.

Let $E(x)$ denote encryption of x under GM public key pk. Multiplying two ciphertexts, e.g. $E(x) \cdot E(y)$, results in an encryption of the exclusive-or (XOR) denoted by $\oplus$.

$$E(x) \cdot E(y) = E(x \oplus y)$$

GM encryption is semantically-secure (IND-CPA) [20], i.e. one cannot infer from a ciphertext and the public key whether the ciphertext has a specific plaintext, e.g. by encrypting the plaintext and then comparing it.

3.3 Sander Young Yung Technique

Sander, Young and Yung operate on GM encryptions and allow the computation of one logical AND operation [29]. Recall that we can perform any number of logical XOR operations on the ciphertexts. A ciphertext $E(x)$ is expanded as follows.

Expand(c, pk): Given ciphertext $c = E(x)$ and public key pk compute σ_i. We repeat this operation u times $(0 \leq i < u)$.

1. Flip a fresh random coin $r_i \in \{0, 1\}$ $(i = 1, \ldots, u)$.
2. Choose plaintext e_i according to the random coin and set

$$\sigma_i \leftarrow E(e_i) = \begin{cases} E(x) \cdot E(1) = E(x \oplus 1) & \text{if } r_i = 0 \\ E(0) & \text{if } r_i = 1 \end{cases}$$

The result is a u-length vector $\boldsymbol{\sigma} = (\sigma_1, \ldots, \sigma_k)$ which we call expanded ciphertext. If $x = 1$, then $x \oplus 1 = 0$ and $e_i = 0$. Then also $\sigma_i = E(0)$ for $i = 1, \ldots, u$. Otherwise, if $x = 0$, e_i is randomly distributed in $\{0, 1\}$ and σ_i is a GM ciphertext of a random bit.

We can now compute a logical AND of two expanded ciphertexts $\boldsymbol{\sigma}$ (for $E(x)$) and $\boldsymbol{\rho}$ (for $E(y)$). We denote $\sigma_i = E(e_i)$ and $\rho_i = E(d_i)$. Logical AND is performed by pair-wise multiplication of the elements of the expanded ciphertext vectors: $\tau_i = \sigma_i \cdot \rho_i$. If $x \wedge y = 1$, then $\tau_i = E(c_i) = E(e_i) \cdot E(d_i) = E(e_i \oplus d_i) = E(0 \oplus 0) = E(0)$ for $i = 1, \ldots, u$, but if $x \wedge y = 0$, then c_i remains randomly distributed in $\{0, 1\}$, since at least one of e_i or d_i is randomly distributed in $\{0, 1\}$. Therefore $\boldsymbol{\tau}$ is the expanded ciphertext of $x \wedge y$. In order to decrypt an expanded ciphertext $\boldsymbol{\sigma}$ one decrypts each element $D(\sigma_i) = e_i$. If $e_i = 0$ for $i = 1, \ldots, u$, then the final plaintext $x = 1$; otherwise $x = 0$. There is a 2^{-u} probability that it is falsely decrypted as 1, since for an expanded ciphertext $\boldsymbol{\sigma}$ of $x = 0$ the plaintexts e_i are randomly distributed in $\{0, 1\}^u$.

3.4 Quadratic Residuosity Zero-Knowledge Proofs

A simple proof that a ciphertext has plaintext 0 is to present a root s $(s^2 = r)$. It can be verified by squaring s and is zero-knowledge, since it does not reveal the secret key p and q. Furthermore, if r is a quadratic non-residue, no such s exists.

Proof-QR(r):
Common input: r, $n = pq$
Prover's secret input: p, q

1. The prover outputs s.
2. The verifier accepts, if $s^2 = r$.

Nevertheless, this proof cannot be used to prove that a ciphertext has plaintext 1. If the prover claims that there is no root s, there is no way for the verifier to check it. In [10] Fiat and Shamir present a zero-knowledge proof (ZKP) that

r is a quadratic residue. The proof is analogous to the general ZKP for graph isomorphism by Goldreich, Micali and Widgerson in [16]. Furthermore in [16] they present a ZKP for graph non-isomorphism. We adapt this proof to quadratic residues and present a ZKP that r is a quadratic non-residue. We present its interactive form.

Proof-QNR(r):
  Common input: r, $n - pq$
  Prover's secret input: p, q

1. The verifier uniformly chooses a random number s and a bit $b \in \{0, 1\}$. If $b = 0$, then the verifier sends s^2 to the prover. If $b = 1$, then the verifier sends rs^2 to the prover.
2. The prover outputs a guess b' of b. The prover also sends a guess s' of s.
3. The verifier accepts if $b' = b$ and $s' = s$.

For a ZKP one has to prove three properties: (honest-verifier) zero-knowledge, completeness and soundness. Zero-knowledge means that the verifier learns nothing about the secret input of the prover. We can do so by showing a simulator of the verifier's view from its input (including random coin tosses) and output (of a successful proof). In this case, the simulator is particularly simple, since it simply mirrors the verifier's random choices b and s.

Completeness means that if r is indeed a quadratic non-residue an honest verifier will always accept. Clearly, if r is a quadratic non-residue then rs^2 is a quadratic non-residue, but s^2 is always a quadratic residue. Therefore the prover can distinguish the choice b by computing quadratic residuosity.

Soundness means that if r is not a quadratic non-residue, i.e. $t^2 = r$ an honest verifier will reject with high probability. If $b = 1$ and $t^2 = r$, then there exist a $s' = st$, such that $s'^2 = rs^2$. The message from the verifier is therefore indistinguishable to the prover for both cases of b. The probability of a right guess b' is then at most $\frac{1}{2}$.

In order to increase the probability for rejecting the ZKP in case of a quadratic residue we can repeat the above ZKP n times in parallel. The probability of a false accept is then 2^{-n}.

Furthermore, we can apply the technique by Blum, Feldman and Micali to make the ZKP non-interactive [4]. Given access to a common random string we can simulate the messages from the verifier. In our case it is critical to not simulate the random choices b, but just the messages themselves, i.e. the verifier sends a sequence of numbers u. We can non-interactively verify the correct guess of b by b' using s'. If the verifier sends a quadratic non-residue u (which he does with probability $\frac{1}{2}$) and r is a quadratic residue ($t^2 = r$), then there exists no s', since ur^{-1} is quadratic non-residue.

3.5 Shuffle Zero-Knowledge Proof

In addition to the quadratic residuosity ZKPs we need a further ZKP. Let $\boldsymbol{\sigma}$ be a u-length vector of GM ciphertexts $E(e_i)$. Let π be a random permutation for

$1, \ldots, u$ and $\boldsymbol{\rho}$ be a u-length vector of GM ciphertexts with plaintext 0. We can compute a shuffle $\boldsymbol{\tau} = \pi(\boldsymbol{\sigma}) \cdot \boldsymbol{\rho}$, such that given $\boldsymbol{\sigma}$ and $\boldsymbol{\tau}$ (but not the secret key) nothing is revealed about π.

A shuffle ZKP proves that $\boldsymbol{\tau}$ is indeed a permutation of $\boldsymbol{\sigma}$, i.e. there exist π and $\boldsymbol{\rho}$.

Proof-Shuffle($\boldsymbol{\sigma}$, $\boldsymbol{\tau}$):

Common input: $\boldsymbol{\sigma}$, $\boldsymbol{\tau}$

Prover's secret input: π, $\boldsymbol{\rho} = (E(0), \ldots)$, such that $\boldsymbol{\tau} = \pi(\boldsymbol{\sigma}) \cdot \boldsymbol{\rho}$.

Groth and Ishai present a shuffle ZKP that has sub-linear communication complexity [18]. Sub-linear communication complexity means that less than u elements are transmitted.

4 Public-Key Encrypted Bloom Filter

In this section we present our main result: privacy-preserving, publicly verifiable Bloom filter. Due to our use of public-key encryption we call them public-key encrypted Bloom filter (PEBF). The basic idea of a PEBF is to encrypt each bit b_j of the Bloom filter using GM encryption. We present its operations $PEBF-Create(m, \kappa)$, $PEBF-Add(x)$, $PEBF-Test(x)$ and $PEBF-Compare(E(\boldsymbol{b}'))$.

PEBF-Create(m, κ):

1. Create a public-, private-key pair in the GM encryption scheme using $KeyGen(\kappa)$.
$$pk, sk \leftarrow KeyGen(\kappa)$$
2. Create a Bloom filter
$$b_j, f_i \leftarrow Create(m)$$
3. Encrypt each bit of the Bloom filter
$$E(b_j) \leftarrow Encrypt(b_j, pk)$$

Let $E(\boldsymbol{b})$ denote the element-wise encryption of $\boldsymbol{b} = (\ldots, b_j, \ldots)$ with the public key pk. The public part of the PEBF is $E(\boldsymbol{b}), f_i, pk$ and the private part is sk.

We give our first theorem that the public part of the PEBF does not leak any information about the content of the Bloom filter.

Theorem 1. *Let the adversary $\mathcal{A}$ choose two Bloom filter contents $\boldsymbol{b}_0 = (\ldots, b_{0,j}, \ldots)$ and $\boldsymbol{b}_1 = (\ldots, b_{1,j}, \ldots)$. Given a random choice β and the public part of a PEBF $E(\boldsymbol{b}_\beta), f_i, pk$, the probability that any adversary $\mathcal{A}$ outputs β is at most*
$$Pr\left[\mathcal{A}\left(\boldsymbol{b}_0, \boldsymbol{b}_1, E\left(\boldsymbol{b}_\beta\right), f_i, pk\right) = \beta\right] \leq \frac{1}{2} + \frac{1}{poly(\kappa)}$$
where $poly(\kappa)$ is an arbitrary polynomial in κ.

Proof. The proof is simple. Such an adversary $\mathcal{A}$ would contradict the IND-CPA security of GM encryption. We can simulate a successful adversary against GM encryption by embedding the challenge into the challenge of the adversary $\mathcal{A}$.

PEBF-Add(x):

1. Compute indices of Bloom filter for addition

$$l_i \leftarrow f_i(x)$$

2. Recompute each bit of the Bloom filter by replacing it with a plaintext 1 if it is set by the *Add*(x) operation and re-randomizing if it is not set

$$E(b_j) = \begin{cases} E(1) & \text{if } \exists i.j = l_i \\ E(b_j) \cdot E(0) = E(b_j \oplus 0) & \text{otherwise} \end{cases}$$

We can rest assured that the public part of the PEBF before and after an addition does not leak any information about the added item. In fact, this is a corollary of Theorem 1.

Corollary 2. *Given two public parts $E(\boldsymbol{b}), f_i, pk$ for the same PEBF, but for Bloom filter contents $\boldsymbol{b}_0 = (\ldots, b_{0,j}, \ldots)$ and $\boldsymbol{b}_1 = (\ldots, b_{1,j}, \ldots)$, such that there exist an index h where $b_{0,h} \neq b_{1,h}$, the probability that any adversary $\mathcal{A}$ outputs h is at most*

$$Pr\left[\mathcal{A}\left(E\left(\boldsymbol{b}_0\right), E\left(\boldsymbol{b}_1\right), f_i, pk\right) = h\right] \leq \frac{1}{m} + \frac{1}{poly(\kappa)}$$

Proof. Construct an adversary $\mathcal{A}^\star$ for Theorem 1 by handing both ciphertexts $\boldsymbol{b}_0$ and $\boldsymbol{b}_1$ to adversary $\mathcal{A}$. If $\mathcal{A}$ guesses correctly, then $\mathcal{A}^\star$ guesses correctly.

PEBF-Test(x): Checking whether a PEBF contains an element x requires the private key sk. We construct a ZKP $PEBF-Test_{true}$ that x is contained within the public PEBF part $E(\boldsymbol{b})$, f_i, pk.

Common input: x, $E(\boldsymbol{b})$, f_i, pk
Prover's secret input: sk

1. Compute the set Bloom filter indices for x

$$l_i \leftarrow f_i(x)$$

2. Expand the ciphertext for each set Bloom filter bit

$$\boldsymbol{\sigma}_{l_i} \leftarrow Expand(E(b_{l_i}), pk)$$

3. Compute the logical AND of all set Bloom filter bits using the homomorphism

$$\boldsymbol{\sigma} \leftarrow \boldsymbol{\sigma}_{l_1} \cdot \ldots \cdot \boldsymbol{\sigma}_{l_k}$$

4. Proof in zero-knowledge that σ_j $(0 \leq j < u)$ is a quadratic residue

$$Proof - QR(\sigma_j)$$

Figure 2 depicts the process of ciphertext expansion on a PEBF.

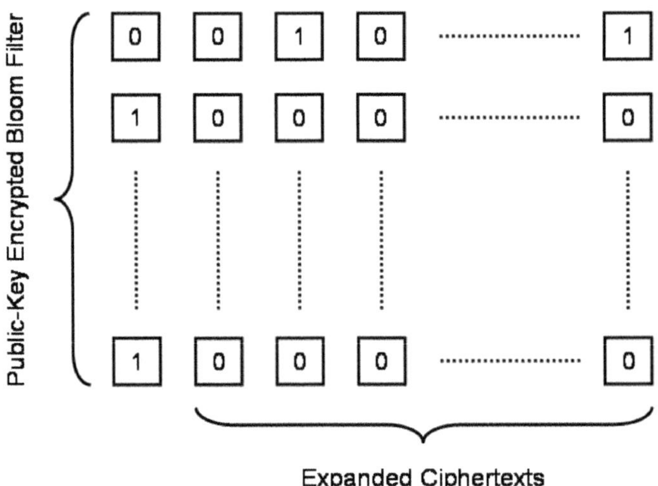

Fig. 2. Public-Key Encrypted Bloom Filter and Ciphertext Expansion

Theorem 3. *The zero-knowledge proof* $PEBF{-}Test_{true}$ *is honest-verifier zero-knowledge, complete and sound.*

Proof. For honest-verifier zero-knowledge we need to show a simulator for the view of the verifier. The simulator computes steps 1 to 3. It then invokes u times the simulator for *Proof-QR*(s^2).

We emphasize that the proof reveals that σ_i is a quadratic residue and (w.h.p.) that $E(b_{l_i})$ is a quadratic non-residue, but this is implied by the output of the ZKP.

For completeness we need to show that if $test(x) = true$, then $PEBF - Test_{true}$ is accepted by an honest verifier. If $test(x) = true$, then $E(b_{l_i})$ is a quadratic non-residue, $\sigma_{l_i,j}$ is a quadratic residue and consequently all σ_j are quadratic residues.

For soundness we need to show that if $test(x) = false$, then $PEBF{-}Test_{true}$ will be reject by an honest verifier with high probability. If $test(x) = false$, then there exist an index h ($0 \leq h < k$), such that $l_h = f_h(x)$ and $b_{l_h} = 0$. Then $\sigma_{l_h,j}$ is (uniformly) randomly distributed in $\{E(0), E(1)\}$ and so is σ_j. Then at least one ZKP for quadratic residuosity will fail with probability $1 - 2^{-u}$.

In order to prove that an element x is not contained in a PEBF we need to prove that at least one index of $\boldsymbol{\sigma}$ has a quadratic non-residue. Unfortunately, knowing that σ_j is a quadratic non-residue may imply (w.h.p.) that (one specific) $b_j = 0$. Simply assume that the random choices in the *Expand*() operation, are such that the ciphertext of only one $E(b_j)$ is used and the others are fixed to $E(0)$.

We therefore need to construct a more complicated ZKP $PEBF - Test_{false}$.

1. Perform steps 1 to 3 as in $PEBF - Test_{true}$.
2. Choose a random permutation π of $(1, ldots, u)$ and a u-length vector of ciphertexts $\boldsymbol{\rho} = (E(0), \ldots)$. Compute

$$\boldsymbol{\tau} \leftarrow \pi(\boldsymbol{\sigma}) \cdot \boldsymbol{\rho}$$

3. Proof in zero-knowledge that $\boldsymbol{\tau}$ is a shuffle of $\boldsymbol{\sigma}$.

$$Proof - Shuffle(\boldsymbol{\sigma}, \boldsymbol{\tau})$$

4. Reveal an index h, such that τ_h is a quadratic non-residue and prove it in zero-knowledge

$$Proof - QNR(\tau_h)$$

Theorem 4. *The zero-knowledge proof* $PEBF - Test_{false}$ *is honest-verifier zero-knowledge, complete and sound.*

Proof. The proof for the properties of completeness and soundness are analogous to the proof for $PEBF - Test_{true}$.

For honest-verifier zero-knowledge we give the following simulator. Uniformly choose a random h. For $\boldsymbol{\tau}$ choose a random permutation of the ciphertexts $\boldsymbol{\sigma}$ except for τ_h choose one with plaintext 1 (a quadratic non-residue). Note that we might replace a quadratic residue at index h. Invoke the simulator for $Proof - Shuffle(\boldsymbol{\sigma}, \boldsymbol{\tau})$. If the simulator fails, because we did replace a quadratic residue, then rewind and choose a new h. The choice of h will fall on a quadratic non-residue with probability $\frac{1}{2}$. Therefore we succeed with high probability. Then invoke the simulator for $Proof - QNR(\tau_h)$.

PEBF-Compare($E(\boldsymbol{b}')$): Let $E(\boldsymbol{b}')$ be the encrypted Bloom filter content for the same hash functions f_i. Using the secret key *sk* we construct a ZKP $PEBF - Compare$ that $\boldsymbol{b}$ of the public part of a PEBF is equal.

Common input: $E(\boldsymbol{b}')$, $E(\boldsymbol{b})$, *pk*

Prover's secret input: *sk*

1. Compute the negated, logical XOR of the two encrypted Bloom filter contents using the homomorphism of the encryption scheme

$$E(\boldsymbol{b}'') \leftarrow E(\boldsymbol{b}) \cdot E(\boldsymbol{b}') \cdot E(1^m) = E(\boldsymbol{b} \oplus \boldsymbol{b}' \oplus 1^m)$$

2. Expand the ciphertext for each Bloom filter bit $(0 \leq i < m)$

$$\boldsymbol{\sigma}_i \leftarrow Expand(E(b_i''), pk)$$

3. Compute the logical AND of Bloom filter bits using the homomorphism

$$\boldsymbol{\sigma} \leftarrow \boldsymbol{\sigma}_0 \cdot \ldots \cdot \boldsymbol{\sigma}_{m-1}$$

4. Proof in zero-knowledge that σ_j $(0 \leq j < u)$ is a quadratic residue

$$Proof - QR(\sigma_j)$$

Theorem 5. *The zero-knowledge proof $PEBF - Compare$ is honest-verifier zero-knowledge, complete and sound.*

Proof. The proof for honest-verifier zero-knowledge is equal to the proof for honest-verifier zero-knowledge for $PEBF - Test_{true}$. We can use the same simulator.

For completeness we need to show that if $\boldsymbol{b} = \boldsymbol{b}'$, then $PEBF - Compare$ is accepted by an honest verifier. If $\boldsymbol{b} = \boldsymbol{b}'$, then $\boldsymbol{b}'' = 1^m$ and $\boldsymbol{\sigma}$ are all quadratic residues.

For soundness we need to show that if $\boldsymbol{b} \neq \boldsymbol{b}'$, then $PEBF - Compare$ will be reject by an honest verifier with high probability. If $\boldsymbol{b} \neq \boldsymbol{b}'$, then $\boldsymbol{b}''$ contains a 0 and $\boldsymbol{\sigma}$ contains a quadratic non-residue with probability $1 - 2^{-u}$. Consequently, at least one ZKP $Proof - QR(\sigma_j)$ will be rejected with high probability.

The construction of a ZKP that $\boldsymbol{b} \neq \boldsymbol{b}'$ follows the same ideas as ZKP $PEBF - Test_{false}$. We omit it for brevity.

5 Related Work

Our work is related to cryptographically secure Bloom filters [1,15,25], private set intersection [6,7,8,12,19,22] and anti-counterfeiting [2,21,23,24,26,27,31,33].

Cryptographically protected Bloom filters have been proposed before [1,15,25]. Nevertheless, the type of protection differs significantly from our approach.

In [1,15] Bloom filters are used for securely searching documents. It enables checking whether a document contains certain keywords without disclosing all of them. Their protection mechanism is to compute the hash function as a cryptographic pseudo-random function. This prevents reversing the Bloom filter, but it also prevents non-interactively adding an element which we enable.

In [25] an interactive protocol for securely checking set inclusion via Bloom filters without disclosing the Bloom filter content or the checked element. They also do not enable non-interactive (or even privacy-preserving) element addition. They use blind signatures in order to protect the Bloom filter content.

A related problem is private set intersection. Given two parties, each input a set of elements, privately compute the intersection of these two sets without disclosing either set. The first protocol secure in the semi-honest model has been presented in [22]. Efficiency improvements have been made in [12]. The malicious model has been first considered in [19] and further efficiency improvements have been made in [7,8]. An authority to certify the sets has been proposed in [6]. Note that – as opposed to all work on private set intersection – our operations work non-interactively. This also makes the distinction between semi-honest and malicious adversaries less applicable. Our security definitions are closer to public-key encryption.

The benefits of item tracking for anti-counterfeiting have been first recognized in [31]. They already outline the two basic approaches beyond item identification itself: on-tag and in-network.

In-network protection collects information about all items and correlates it. It can prevent cloning attacks. A statistical method based on detection of low probability events is presented in [23]. This method requires sharing of information. A similar method that protects this information using secure multi-party computation has been presented in [33]. A deterministic method for detecting integrity violations has been presented in [26]. It also requires sharing of information. A secure variant using cryptographic hashing has been presented in [21].

On-tag protection only stores information on the RFID tag. Methods using more powerful RFID tags that support cryptographic hashing have been proposed first [24,27]. Recently, a method using only storage on the RFID tag has been described [2]. Our public-key encrypted Bloom filters (augmented with standard signatures) implement not only their full functionality, but surpass it in several aspects. First, we enable more checks than just path verification, such as our compare operation. Second, we provide security against the verifier of integrity considering an attacker that is part of the supply chain.

6 Conclusions

In this paper we have presented public-key encrypted Bloom filters. The content of the Bloom filter is encrypted using public-key, homomorphic encryption. Only the private-key holder can access the Bloom filter content. We enable the public-key holder to non-interactively add elements by encrypting them. Furthermore, we present zero-knowledge proofs for non-interactively verifying the inclusion or exclusion of an element and the equality of two Bloom filter contents.

Given such protected Bloom filters one can perform several privacy-preserving supply chain integrity checks. One can check the path of item through a supply chain against black lists, white lists or for equality. The public-key encryption protects the confidentiality of the Bloom filter content during all these operations.

There are a few possible improvements for future work. First, the set inclusion or exclusion zero-knowledge proofs reveal the element checked. This could be prevented by also encrypting it, but the homomorphism of existing (efficient) public-key encryption schemes is insufficient. When fully homomorphic encryption [14] becomes practical, it may provide a further avenue.

Second, the set inclusion or exclusion zero-knowledge proofs also require the knowledge of the ciphertext. Ideally the private-key holder could issue a security token without knowing the ciphertext in question. This could be done using searchable encryption, but the existing searchable encryption schemes do not support homomorphisms. Given improved, searchable encryption schemes, a new construction might become feasible.

Third, the bit-wise encryption of Goldwasser-Micali encryption is quite storage-intensive. While RFID tags with sufficient storage capacity – up to 64 KByte – exist [13], a reduction of the storage requirements would enable using cheaper RFID tags. Of course, this is no restriction for the collection of all handled items at one supplier.

References

1. Bellovin, S., Cheswick, W.: Privacy-Enhanced Searches Using Encrypted Bloom Filters. Cryptology ePrint Archive Report 2004/022 (2004)
2. Blass, E., Elkhiyaoui, K., Molva, R.: Tracker: Security and Privacy for RFID-based Supply Chains. In: Proceedinsg of the 18th Network and Distributed System Security Symposium, pp. 455–472 (2011)
3. Bloom, B.: Space/Time Trade-offs in Hash Coding with Allowable Errors. Communication of the ACM 13(7), 422–426 (1970)
4. Blum, M., Feldman, P., Micali, S.: Non-Interactive Zero-Knowledge and Its Applications. In: Proceedings of the 20th ACM Symposium on Theory of Computing, pp. 103–112 (1988)
5. Broder, A., Mitzenmacher, M.: Network Applications of Bloom Filters: A Survey. Internet Mathematics 1(4), 485–509 (2003)
6. Camenisch, J., Zaverucha, G.: Private Intersection of Certified Sets. In: Dingledine, R., Golle, P. (eds.) FC 2009. LNCS, vol. 5628, pp. 108–127. Springer, Heidelberg (2009)
7. Dachman-Soled, D., Malkin, T., Raykova, M., Yung, M.: Efficient Robust Private Set Intersection. In: Abdalla, M., Pointcheval, D., Fouque, P.-A., Vergnaud, D. (eds.) ACNS 2009. LNCS, vol. 5536, pp. 125–142. Springer, Heidelberg (2009)
8. De Cristofaro, E., Kim, J., Tsudik, G.: Linear-Complexity Private Set Intersection Protocols Secure in Malicious Model. In: Abe, M. (ed.) ASIACRYPT 2010. LNCS, vol. 6477, pp. 213–231. Springer, Heidelberg (2010)
9. Eurich, M., Oertel, N., Boutellier, R.: The Impact of Perceived Privacy Risks on Organizations' Willingness to Share Item-Level Event Data Across the Supply Chain. Electronic Commerce Research 10(3-4), 423–440 (2010)
10. Fiat, A., Shamir, A.: How to Prove Yourself: Practical Solutions to Identification and Signature Problems. In: Odlyzko, A.M. (ed.) CRYPTO 1986. LNCS, vol. 263, pp. 186–194. Springer, Heidelberg (1987)
11. Finkenzeller, K.: RFID Handbook: Fundamentals and Applications in Contactless Smart Cards and Identification. John Wiley & Sons, Inc., Chichester (2003)
12. Freedman, M., Nissim, K., Pinkas, B.: Efficient Private Matching and Set Intersection. In: Cachin, C., Camenisch, J.L. (eds.) EUROCRYPT 2004. LNCS, vol. 3027, pp. 1–19. Springer, Heidelberg (2004)
13. Fujitsu. Fujitsu Develops World's First 64KByte High-Capacity FRAM RFID Tag for Aviation Applications. Press Release (2008), `http://www.fujitsu.com/global/news/pr/archives/month/2008/20080109-01.html`
14. Gentry, C.: Fully Homomorphic Encryption using Ideal Lattices. In: Proceedings of the 41st ACM Symposium on Theory of Computing, pp. 169–178 (2009)
15. Goh, E.: Secure Indexes. Cryptology ePrint Archive Report 2003/216 (2003)
16. Goldreich, O., Micali, S., Wigderson, A.: Proofs that Yield Nothing but Their Validity or All Languages in NP have Zero-Knowledge Proof Systems. Journal of the ACM 38(3), 690–728 (1991)
17. Goldwasser, S., Micali, S.: Probabilistic Encryption. Journal of Computer and Systems Science 28(2), 270–299 (1984)
18. Groth, J., Ishai, Y.: Sub-Linear Zero-Knowledge Argument for Correctness of a Shuffle. In: Smart, N.P. (ed.) EUROCRYPT 2008. LNCS, vol. 4965, pp. 379–396. Springer, Heidelberg (2008)
19. Hazay, C., Lindell, Y.: Efficient Protocols for Set Intersection and Pattern Matching with Security Against Malicious and Covert Adversaries. In: Canetti, R. (ed.) TCC 2008. LNCS, vol. 4948, pp. 155–175. Springer, Heidelberg (2008)

20. Katz, J., Lindell, Y.: Introduction to Modern Cryptography: Principles and Protocols. Chapman & Hall/CRC (2007)
21. Kerschbaum, F., Oertel, N.: Privacy-Preserving Pattern Matching for Anomaly Detection in RFID Anti-Counterfeiting. In: Ors Yalcin, S.B. (ed.) RFIDSec 2010. LNCS, vol. 6370, pp. 124–137. Springer, Heidelberg (2010)
22. Kissner, L., Song, D.: Privacy-Preserving Set Operations. In: Shoup, V. (ed.) CRYPTO 2005. LNCS, vol. 3621, pp. 241–257. Springer, Heidelberg (2005)
23. Lehtonen, M., Michahelles, F., Fleisch, E.: How to Detect Cloned Tags in a Reliable Way from Incomplete RFID Traces. In: Proceedings of the IEEE RFID Conference, pp. 257–264 (2009)
24. Li, Y., Ding, X.: Protecting RFID Communications in Supply Chains. In: Proceedings of the ACM Symposium on Information, Computer and Communications Security, pp. 234–241 (2007)
25. Nojima, R., Kadobayashi, Y.: Cryptographically Secure Bloom-Filters. Transactions on Data Privacy 2, 131–139 (2009)
26. Oertel, N.: Tracking based product authentication: Catching intruders in the supply chain. In: Proceedings of the 17th European Conference on Information Systems (2008)
27. Ouafi, K., Vaudenay, S.: Pathchecker: an RFID Application for Tracing Products in Suply-Chains. In: Proceedings of the 5th Workshop on RFID Security (2009)
28. Santos, B., Smith, L.: RFID in the supply chain: panacea or pandora's box? Communications of the ACM 51(10), 127–131 (2008)
29. Sander, T., Young, A., Yung, M.: Non-Interactive CryptoComputing For NC1. In: Proceedings of the 40th Symposium on Foundations of Computer Science, pp. 554–567 (1999)
30. Sarma, S., Brock, D., Engels, D.: Radio frequency identification and the electronic product code. IEEE Micro 21(6), 50–54 (2001)
31. Staake, T., Thiesse, F., Fleisch, E.: Extending the EPC Network – The Potential of RFID in Anti-Counterfeiting. In: Proceedings of the 20th ACM Symposium on Applied Computing, pp. 1607–1612 (2005)
32. Waldbaum, M., Nguyen, X.: Using Creativity to Fight a $60 Billion Consumer Problem – Counterfeit Goods. Loyola Chicago Consumer Law Review 10(1), 88 (1998)
33. Zanetti, D., Fellmann, L., Capkun, S.: Privacy-preserving Clone Detection for RFID-enabled Supply Chains. In: Proceedings of the IEEE International Conference on RFID, pp. 37–44 (2010)

An Optimization Model for the Extended Role Mining Problem

Emre Uzun, Vijayalakshmi Atluri, Haibing Lu, and Jaideep Vaidya

MSIS Department and CIMIC, Rutgers University, USA
{emreu,atluri,haibing,jsvaidya}@cimic.rutgers.edu

Abstract. The primary purpose of Role Mining is to effectively determine the roles in an enterprise using the permissions that have already been assigned to the users. If this permission assignment is viewed as a 0-1 matrix, then Role Mining aims to decompose this matrix into two matrices which represent user-role and role-permission assignments. This decomposition is known as Boolean Matrix Decomposition (BMD). In this paper, we use an Extended BMD (EBMD) to consider separation of duty constraints (SOD) and exceptions, that are common to any security system, in the role mining process. Essentially, in EBMD, we introduce negative assignments. An additional benefit of allowing negative assignments in roles is that, a less number of roles can be used to reconstruct the same given user-permission assignments. We introduce Extended Role Mining Problem and its variants and present their optimization models. We also propose a heuristic algorithm that is capable of utilizing these models to find good decompositions.

1 Introduction

The recent developments in the usage of information technology in many different enterprises facilitate access to data. This situation brings out security issues that must be seriously considered in order to maintain confidentiality. In order to cope with this issue, many enterprises enforce strict access control policies on various data resources that they administer. A typical implementation is to have a 0-1 (Boolean) User-Permission Assignment (UPA) Matrix which indicates whether a particular user has access to a particular resource in the system. An example of this matrix is given in Figure 1.

	Resource 1	Resource 2	Resource 3
User 1	1	1	0
User 2	0	1	1
User 3	1	1	1

Fig. 1. A 0-1 User-Permission Access Control Matrix

Basically, this method can be used in small enterprises with relatively small number of resources. However, administration of this method gets complicated in large enterprises with many resources. Hence, companies seek for a more efficient way of managing permission assignments. As a result, Role Based Access Control (RBAC)

Y. Li (Ed.): Data and Applications Security and Privacy XXV, LNCS 6818, pp. 76–89, 2011.

methodologies are developed. The purpose of RBAC is to define roles which can be considered as a set of permissions and assign roles to users in order to grant permissions. This process makes the security administration easier, since the number of roles are significantly smaller than the number of users.

According to Edward Coyne, ‘Definition of the roles with their assigned permissions must be accomplished before all the benefits of RBAC can be realized. The goal is to define a set of roles that is complete, correct and efficient’ [2]. There are mainly two different approaches in determining roles: Top-down and bottom-up. Top-down approach is to determine the roles by carefully examining the business processes and identifying the potential roles which is in practice, defining job functions from scratch and associating the necessary permissions to the role. However, this method ignores the existing permission assignments and it is costly and labor intensive in large enterprises with large number of business processes and permissions [1],[2]. There are some implementations of top-down approach available in the literature such as [6]. The bottom-up approach, on the other hand utilizes the existing user-permission assignments and tries to aggregate them to obtain potential roles. However, the existing business processes are ignored and as a result of this, the roles that are obtained may not fully represent the existing job functions in the enterprise [8]. Basically, the bottom-up approach is called Role Mining (RM).

There are many different algorithms proposed in RM area. The very first algorithms aim to find a decomposition to a given UPA matrix. CompleteMiner, FastMiner [9] and ORCA [7] are some of these algorithms. After the formalization of the role mining problem (RMP) and its variants by Vaidya et al. [8], many different new algorithms that are capable of handling the new objectives are proposed. Many of these new algorithms are basically an adaptation of the solution procedures of an existing problem. Some examples are: Utilizing Minimum Database Tiling Problem, Discrete Basis Problem, Minimum Biclique Cover Problem and Graph Optimization [11], [1], [8]. Moreover, [4] provides computational tests and comparisons of most of these algorithms.

It is clear that the purpose of RM is to generate a user-to-role (UA) and a role-to-permission (PA) matrix from a given UPA matrix. This is in fact analogous to have a Boolean Matrix Decomposition (BMD) where the UPA matrix is decomposed into two Boolean matrices UA and PA [3]. This decomposition literally means that UPA matrix can exactly be represented by UA and PA matrices using the Boolean Matrix Multiplication operator described by Vaidya et al.[8]. Now, consider that one of the decomposed matrices is allowed to contain -1 in addition to 0 and 1. The purpose of having -1, or namely, negative assignments, is to introduce exception and separation of duty constraints. For instance, suppose that there are three roles in an enterprise: Manager, Auditor and Employee, where Managers have access to all of the permissions that Auditors and Employees have. Now suppose that a new manager, say John, is not allowed to access Auditor’s permissions. Such exceptions are quite common to real world policies. This is supported through a negative assignment as it does not make sense to create a new role specifically to John alone. Negative user-role assignments mean that if a role is assigned to a user negatively, the user cannot have access to any permission of that role. The negative user-role assignment is superior to the positive (or regular) user-role assignment. If the user is already assigned to a permission positively

	p_1	p_2	p_3	p_4
u_1	1	0	1	1
u_2	1	0	1	1
u_3	1	1	0	1
u_4	0	1	0	1

Fig. 2. UPA Matrix

	r_1	r_2	r_3
u_1	1	0	1
u_2	1	0	1
u_3	1	1	0
u_4	0	1	0

$\otimes$

	p_1	p_2	p_3	p_4
r_1	1	0	0	1
r_2	0	1	0	1
r_3	0	0	1	0

Fig. 3. BMD Decomposition of the sample UPA Matrix in Figure 2

	r_1	r_2
u_1	1	0
u_2	1	0
u_3	1	1
u_4	0	1

$\odot$

	p_1	p_2	p_3	p_4
r_1	1	0	1	1
r_2	0	1	-1	1

Fig. 4. EBMD Decomposition of the sample UPA Matrix in Figure 2

through another role, this assignment is automatically revoked. If the user is assigned to a permission positively in the future, it still does not become effective.

We observe that in addition to increasing administration flexibility, negative assignments can help discover alternative representations of UPA matrices. Consider the example of existing user-permission assignments UPA as shown in Figure 2, where $\{u_1, u_2, u_3, u_4\}$ denote users and $\{p_1, p_2, p_3, p_4\}$ denote permissions.

In Figure 3 the classical BMD decomposition and in Figure 4, a decomposition with negative role assignments are shown. Clearly, the UPA matrix can be represented by fewer number of roles using negative role assignments.

The matrix decomposition with negative assignments is proposed by Lu et al.[5] and called Extended Boolean Matrix Decomposition (EBMD). We use their notion and definitions to utilize Extended Boolean Matrices in Role Mining area and develop Extended Role Mining (ERM), where we allow the UA matrix to contain negative assignments in addition to positive assignments.

RM only aims to decompose the UPA matrix without any objective, which implies any decomposition is indeed a RM task. Vaidya et al. [8] formulate RMP as an optimization problem seeking to minimize the number of roles. Furthermore, they also propose certain variants to RMP with different objectives like minimizing roles given a noise threshold or minimizing noise. In this paper, we propose Extended Role Mining Problem (ERMP) and its variants, in which we optimize the decomposition allowing one of the matrices contain negative assignments.

Since RMP and ERMP and their variants are optimization problems, they can be formulated using Mixed Integer Programming (MIP) techniques. Lu et al. [3] propose a MIP formulation for RMP and its variants. In this paper, we develop MIP formulations for ERMP and its variants. The main advantage of using MIP formulations is that, we can directly adopt many different tools developed for specifically for MIP to obtain a solution, which is guaranteed to be optimal.

Our contributions in this paper are: We define the Extended Role Mining Problem (ERMP) and its variants using EBMD. We propose MIP formulations for these problems. Moreover, we develop a heuristic procedure that seeks to find a good decomposition to a given UPA matrix using the proposed MIP formulations.

The rest of the paper is organized as follows. In the Section 2, a more formal problem definition and some preliminary background information is given. In Section 3, we introduce our Mixed Integer Programming formulations for ERMP and its variants. We present our heuristic algorithm for the ERMP and its variants in Section 4. Finally, conclusions and remarks are noted at Section 6.

2 Problem Definition and Preliminaries

In this section necessary notations and definitions are given.

2.1 Notations and Preliminary Definitions

RBAC

- Let M, K, OPS, and OBJ be the set of users, roles, operations and objects, respectively.
- Let $UA \subseteq M \times K$, be a many-to-many mapping user-to-role assignment relation.
- N(the set of permissions) $\subseteq \{(op, obj)|op \in OPS$ and $obj \in OBJ\}$
- Let $PA \subseteq K \times N$ be a many-to-many mapping of role-to-permission assignments.
- Let $UPA \subseteq M \times N$ be a many-to-many mapping of user-to-role assignments.
- Let $assigned\_users(k) = \{m \in M|(m, k) \in UA\}$ be the mapping of role k onto a set of users.
- Let $assigned\_permissions(k) = \{n \in N|(n, k) \in PA\}$ be the mapping of role k onto the set of permissions.

Boolean Matrix Multiplication. A Boolean matrix multiplication between Boolean Matrices $A \in \{0,1\}^{m \times k}$ and $B \in \{0,1\}^{k \times n}$ is $A \otimes B = C$ where C is in space $\{0,1\}^{m \times n}$ and

$$c_{ij} = \bigvee_{l=1}^{k}(a_{il} \wedge b_{lj}).$$

Boolean Matrix Decomposition. If $A = B \otimes C$, where A, B, C are Boolean matrices, $B \otimes C$ is called the decomposition of A.

Extended Boolean Matrix Multiplication. Given a matrix $C_{k\times n} \in \{0,1\}^{k\times n}$ and a matrix $B_{m\times k} \in \{-1,0,1\}^{m\times k}$, the matrix $A_{m\times n}$ obtained from the operation $B \odot C$ has the following properties:

- If $\exists t_1 : (c_{it_1} = 1 \wedge b_{t_1 j} = 1) \wedge \neg\exists t_2 : (c_{it_2} = 1 \wedge b_{t_2 j} = -1),\ then\ a_{ij} = 1$
- If $\neg\exists t_1 : (c_{it_1} = 1 \wedge b_{t_1 j} = 1) \vee \exists t_2 : (c_{it_2} = 1 \wedge b_{t_2 j} = -1),\ then\ a_{ij} = 0$

where $i \in \{1,..,m\}$ and $j \in \{1,..,n\}$

Extended Boolean Matrix Decomposition. Given matrices $A_{m\times n} \in \{0,1\}^{m\times n}$ and $C_{k\times n} \in \{0,1\}^{k\times n}$ and a matrix $B_{m\times k} \in \{-1,0,1\}^{m\times k}$, $A = B \odot C$ is called the EBMD of A, if $A_j = \cup_{b_{ij}=1} C_i \setminus \cup_{b_{ij}=-1} C_i$ where A_j denotes the item subset corresponding to elements of 1 in the jth column of A and C_i denotes similarly.

δ-Consistency. A given user-to-role assignment UA, role-to-permission assignment PA and user-to-permission assignment UPA are δ-consistent if and only if

$$||M(UA) \otimes M(PA) - M(UPA)||_1 \leq \delta$$

where $M(UA), M(PA)$ and $M(UPA)$ denote the matrix representation of UA, PA and UPA, respectively.

If negative assignments are allowed in UA, then the condition to be satisfied changes to

$$||M(UA) \odot M(PA) - M(UPA)||_1 \leq \delta$$

where $M(UA), M(PA)$ and $M(UPA)$ denote the matrix representation of UA, PA and UPA, respectively.

L_1 Norm The L_1 Norm of a d-dimensional vector $v \in X^d$, for some set X is,

$$||v||_1 = \sum_{i=1}^{d} |v_i|$$

This definition can be expanded to a distance metric between two vectors v and w as

$$||v - w||_1 = \sum_{i=1}^{d} |v_i - w_i|$$

Furthermore, the definition can be applied to $n \times m$ matrices A and B as

$$||A - B||_1 = \sum_{i=1}^{n} ||a_i - b_i||_1 = \sum_{i=1}^{n} \sum_{i=1}^{m} |a_{ij} - b_{ij}|$$

2.2 Problem Definitions

Vaidya et al. [8] describe the Role Mining Problem (RMP) as follows:

Role Mining Problem (RMP): Given a set of users M, a set of permissions N and a user-permission assignment UPA, find a set of roles $ROLES$, a user-to-role assignment UA and a role-to-permission assignment PA that is 0-consistent with UPA and minimizing the number of roles, k.

The purpose of RMP is to decompose the UPA into PA and UA in such a way that the decomposition exactly describes the UPA and the number of roles are minimized. In theory, enterprises would like to implement RMP to obtain a set of roles. However, obtaining an exact decomposition is not always practical in large UPA matrices. If one allows some amount of "noise" in the decomposition, then the UA and PA matrices obtained from the decomposition do not fully represent the original UPA matrix ($UA \otimes PA = UPA' \neq UPA$), meaning that some of the entries in UPA' matrix are different than the original UPA matrix. Vaidya et al. [8] discuss the situation of having an noised decomposition and define the Minimum Noise RMP.

Minimum Noise RMP: Given a set of users M, a set of permissions N, a user-permission assignment UPA, and the number of roles k, find a set of k roles K, a-user-to-role assignment UA and a role-to-permission assignment PA minimizing

$$||M(UA) \otimes M(PA) - M(UPA)||_1$$

where $M(UA), M(PA)$ and $M(UPA)$ denote the matrix representation of UA, PA and UPA, respectively.

One other variation of RMP is the Edge RMP problem. The difference of Edge RMP is that rather than minimizing the number of roles, minimize the number of user-role and role-permission assignments [3].

Edge RMP: Given a set of users M, a set of permissions N and a user-permission assignment UPA, find a set of roles K, a user-to-role assignment UA and a role-to-permission assignment PA that is 0-consistent with UPA and minimizing $|UA|+|PA|$.

RMP, Minimum Noise RMP and Edge RMP are all NP-Complete problems [8]. These problems are all optimization problems and they only deal with Boolean matrices. Using the Extended Boolean Matrix Decomposition, we now can define the Extended Role Mining Problem and its variants:

Extended Role Mining Problem (ERMP): Given a set of users M, a set of permissions N and a user-permission assignment UPA, find a set of roles K, a user-to-role assignment UA where negative assignments are allowed and a role-to-permission assignment PA that is 0-consistent with UPA and minimizing the number of roles, k.

Extended Minimum Noise Role Mining Problem (Minnoise ERMP): Given a set of users M, a set of permissions N, a user-permission assignment UPA, and the number of roles k, find a set of k roles K, a-user-to-role assignment UA where negative assignments are allowed and a role-to-permission assignment PA minimizing

$$||M(UA) \odot M(PA) - M(UPA)||_1$$

where $M(UA), M(PA)$ and $M(UPA)$ denote the matrix representation of UA, PA and UPA, respectively.

Note that, unlike BMD in which we use the symbol $\otimes$, in EBMD we use the symbol $\odot$ as the matrices contains 0, 1 and -1.

Extended Edge Role Mining Problem (Edge ERMP): Given a set of users M, a set of permissions N and a user-permission assignment UPA, find a set of roles K, a user-to-role assignment UA where negative assignments are allowed and a role-to-permission assignment PA that is 0-consistent with UPA and minimizing $|UA|+|PA|$.

3 Mathematical Models for ERMP and Its Variants

In this section, we present the MIP formulations for the ERMP and its variants. Each of these models utilize an initial decomposition of UPA matrix, which can be obtained using an algorithm proposed in the literature such as FastMiner [9]. The main purpose of using an initial decomposition is due to the fact that the optimization models become non-linear unless one of the matrices UA or PA is known. This is the same approach used by Lu et al. [3] to formulate mathematical models for RMP. Given Boolean matrices UPA and PA, our models try to establish a decomposition consisting of an Extended Boolean UA matrix and a Boolean PA matrix while improving the decomposition in terms of the objective metric. In our analysis, we assume Extended Boolean UA and Boolean PA matrices, and perform our experiments based on this assumption. The opposite case is symmetric and not covered in this paper.

The following models are used to obtain a (0,1,-1) UA matrix given PA and UPA matrices. The decision variables and the parameters used in these models are as follows:

Decision Variables

- Let $x^+_{ik} = \begin{cases} 1, \; if\; the\; user\; i\; is\; positively\; assigned\; to\; role\; k, \; k \in K, \; i \in M \\ 0, \; otherwise \end{cases}$
- Let $x^-_{kj} = \begin{cases} 1, \; if\; the\; user\; i\; is\; negatively\; assigned\; to\; role\; k, \; k \in K, \; i \in M \\ 0, \; otherwise \end{cases}$
- Let $y_k = \begin{cases} 1, \; if\; role\; k\; is\; used \\ 0, \; otherwise \end{cases}$
- Let $t_{ij} \in \{0,1\}$ be an indicator variable, $i \in M, \; j \in N$
- Let u^+_{ij} denote the amount of noise caused by positively realized x^+_{ik} variables, $i \in M, \; j \in N \; k \in K$
- Let u^-_{ij} denote the amount of noise caused by positively realized x^-_{ik} variables, $i \in M, \; j \in N \; k \in K$

Parameters

- Let a_{ij} denote the entry (i,j) of matrix UPA.
- Let c_{kj} denote the entry (k,j) of matrix PA.

The objective of the ERMP problem is to minimize the total number of roles that are used. On the other hand, Minnoise ERMP seeks to minimize the number of noise in the decomposition given a fixed number of roles and Edge ERMP seeks to find the decomposition that has the least number of role assignments. The primary purpose of using Extended Boolean Matrix Decomposition instead of classic Boolean Matrix Decomposition is to further decrease the size of the resulting matrices (as discussed in Section 1), hence in our case, decreasing the number of roles. Although Minnoise ERMP and Edge ERMP does not have an objective of minimizing the number of roles, to capture the effect of using Extended Boolean Matrices, we slightly alter the objectives of Minnoise ERMP and Edge ERMP to reflect this property. Hence the objective functions of these problems are composed of two components, one being the sum of the roles.

Other than the objective functions, the feasible region declarations of all of these three models are very similar. Thus, here we give a common explanation to the constraints of each of these models. Constraints 2 and 3, 12 and 13, and 24 and 25 ensure the $\odot$ property of the entries valued 1 in the UPA matrix in ERMP, Minnoise ERMP and Edge ERMP Models, respectively. For each of these entries, both constraints must be satisfied. Constraints 2 and 24 force that there exists at least one positive matching entry in the UA and PA matrices that will satisfy the $\odot$ property. Similarly, Constraints 3 and 25 force that there does not exist any negative matching entries in the UA and PA matrices. The logic in the Constraints 12 and 13 is the same but the main difference is that the $\odot$ property does not have to be satisfied (which implies a noise in the decomposition). Constraints 2 and 3, 12 and 13, and 24 and 25 ensure the $\odot$ property of the entries valued 0 in the UPA matrix in ERMP, Minnoise ERMP and Edge ERMP Models, respectively. The structure of these constraints are similar to the first set of constraints. However the major difference is that for each 0 entry in the UPA matrix, either one of these constraint tuples or both must be satisfied. This is handled using the decision variable t_{ij} which sets at least one of these constraints to be enforced. The constant M in these constraints is a value sufficiently big to make any of these constraints redundant depending on the value of t_{ij}. In constraints 12, 13, 14 and 15, the amount of noise is determined by u_{ij}^{+} and u_{ij}^{-} variables. Constraints 6, 16 and 28 ensure that only one of the variables x_{ik}^{+} and x_{ik}^{-} can take positive value at the same time (i.e: a cell in the UA matrix cannot take 1 and -1 values at the same time) in ERMP, Minnoise ERMP and Edge ERMP Models, respectively. However, they can both be 0 at the same time which indicates a 0 in the corresponding cell. Constraints 7 and 8, 17 and 18, and 29 and 30 ensure that a role is active whenever there is at least one user assigned either positively or negatively to that role.

3.1 MIP Formulation for ERMP

$$min \sum_{k \in K} y_k \tag{1}$$

$$s.t$$

$$\sum_{k \in K s.t. a_{ij}=1} x_{ik}^{+} c_{kj} \geq 1, \; \forall i \in M, \; j \in N \tag{2}$$

$$\sum_{k \in K s.t. a_{ij}=1} x_{ik}^{-} c_{kj} = 0, \; \forall i \in M, \; j \in N \tag{3}$$

$$\sum_{k \in K s.t. a_{ij}=0} x_{ik}^{+} c_{kj} \leq t_{ij} M, \; \forall i \in M, \; j \in N \tag{4}$$

$$\sum_{k \in K s.t. a_{ij}=0} x_{ik}^{-} c_{kj} \geq 1 - (1 - t_{ij}) M, \; \forall i \in M, \; j \in N \tag{5}$$

$$x_{ik}^{+} + x_{ik}^{-} \leq 1, \; \forall k, j \tag{6}$$

$$y_k \geq x_{ik}^{+}, \; \forall k \in K, \; i \in M \tag{7}$$

$$y_k \geq x_{ik}^{-}, \; \forall k \in K, \; i \in M \tag{8}$$

$$t_{ij} \in \{0, 1\}, \; \forall i \in M, j \in N \tag{9}$$

$$x_{ik}^{+}, x_{ik}^{-} \in \{0, 1\}, \; \forall k \in K, i \in M \tag{10}$$

3.2 MIP Formulation for Minnoise ERMP

$$min \sum_{i\in M}\sum_{j\in N} u_{ij} + \sum_{k\in K} y_k \tag{11}$$

$$s.t.$$

$$\sum_{k\in K s.t. a_{ij}=1} x^+_{ik} c_{kj} + u^+_{ij} \geq 1,\ \forall i \in M,\ j \in N \tag{12}$$

$$\sum_{k\in K s.t. a_{ij}=1} x^-_{ik} c_{kj} - u^-_{ij} = 0,\ \forall i \in M,\ j \in N \tag{13}$$

$$\sum_{k\in K s.t. a_{ij}=0} x^+_{ik} c_{kj} - u^+_{ij} \leq t_{ij} M,\ \forall i \in M,\ j \in N \tag{14}$$

$$\sum_{k\in K s.t. a_{ij}=0} x^-_{ik} c_{kj} + u^-_{ij} \geq 1 - (1 - t_{ij})M,\ \forall i \in M,\ j \in N \tag{15}$$

$$x^+_{ik} + x^-_{ik} \leq 1,\ \forall k, j \tag{16}$$

$$y_k \geq x^+_{ik},\ \forall k \in K,\ i \in M \tag{17}$$

$$y_k \geq x^-_{ik},\ \forall k \in K,\ i \in M \tag{18}$$

$$t_{ij} \in \{0, 1\},\ \forall i \in M, j \in N \tag{19}$$

$$x^+_{ik}, x^-_{ik} \in \{0, 1\},\ \forall k \in K, i \in M \tag{20}$$

$$u^+_{ij}, u^-_{ij} \geq 0, \forall i \in M, j \in N \tag{21}$$

(22)

3.3 MIP Formulation for Edge ERMP

$$min \sum_{i\in M}\sum_{k\in K} x^+_{ik} + x^-_{ik} + \sum_{k\in K} y_k \tag{23}$$

$$s.t.$$

$$\sum_{k\in K s.t. a_{ij}=1} x^+_{ik} c_{kj} \geq 1,\ \forall i \in M,\ j \in N \tag{24}$$

$$\sum_{k\in K s.t. a_{ij}=1} x^-_{ik} c_{kj} = 0,\ \forall i \in M,\ j \in N \tag{25}$$

$$\sum_{k\in K s.t. a_{ij}=0} x^+_{ik} c_{kj} \leq t_{ij} M,\ \forall i \in M,\ j \in N \tag{26}$$

$$\sum_{k\in K s.t. a_{ij}=0} x^-_{ik} c_{kj} \geq 1 - (1 - t_{ij})M,\ \forall i \in M,\ j \in N \tag{27}$$

$$x^+_{ik} + x^-_{ik} \leq 1,\ \forall k, j \tag{28}$$

$$y_k \geq x^+_{ik},\ \forall k \in K,\ i \in M \tag{29}$$

$$y_k \geq x^-_{ik},\ \forall k \in K,\ i \in M \tag{30}$$

$$t_{ij} \in \{0, 1\},\ \forall i \in M, j \in N \tag{31}$$

$$x^+_{ik}, x^-_{ik} \in \{0, 1\},\ \forall k \in K, i \in M \tag{32}$$

4 Heuristic Procedure

In this section, we introduce the heuristic algorithm we propose to find good decompositions to ERMP, Minnoise ERMP and Edge ERMP utilizing the Mixed Integer Programming formulations. Our algorithm is an iterative algorithm which takes a Boolean UPA matrix and a corresponding Boolean PA matrix as an input and tries to improve the decomposition by finding better Extended Boolean UA and Boolean PA matrices at each iteration. The algorithm mainly has two stages: Preprocessing Stage and Iterative Stage. We now explain each stage in detail.

We need a Preprocessing Stage since the MIP formulations that we propose require an initial PA matrix. This PA matrix can be obtained using one of the heuristic Boolean matrix decomposition procedures available in the literature. We use the algorithm described in Vaidya et al. [10] for this purpose. When we implement this algorithm, we get Boolean UA and PA matrices for the corresponding Boolean UPA matrix. Although this PA matrix can be used as the initial PA matrix of our heuristic algorithm, we use RMP formulation described by Lu et al. [3] to further improve it. This RMP formulation takes the UPA and UA matrices as input and constructs the the corresponding optimal PA' matrix, while minimizing the number of roles. This PA' matrix is expected to have smaller (or equal) number of roles when compared to the PA matrix and it is used as the initial matrix of the Iterative Stage of our heuristic procedure. This initial decomposition is not the optimal Boolean Matrix Decomposition of the UPA matrix, rather we obtain a heuristic decomposition and try to improve it as much as we can to get a good starting matrix. Note that none of the matrices used in this stage contains -1 entries.

At each iteration of the Iterative Stage, we either obtain the corresponding optimal Extended Boolean UA matrix given the Boolean PA matrix of the previous iteration, or we obtain the corresponding Boolean PA matrix given the Extended Boolean UA matrix of the previous iteration. The purpose of doing this round-robin operation lies under the fact that in each iteration when we obtain a corresponding optimal UA (PA) matrix using a PA (UA) matrix, the PA (UA) matrix may not be the optimal given the new UA (PA) matrix. Hence we need to do this round-robin operation until we do not observe any improvement in the decomposition. We define the improvement metric and termination criteria later in this section. At an iteration, if a UA matrix is to be obtained given a PA matrix, then one of the ERMP, Minnoise ERMP or Edge ERMP model is used (This selection is fixed throughout the algorithm). On the other hand, if a PA matrix is to be obtained given a UA matrix, then we need an additional model. Notice that our proposed MIP formulations require a Boolean PA matrix to construct an Extended Boolean UA matrix. However, we cannot use these formulations to obtain a Boolean PA matrix, given an Extended Boolean UA matrix. For this purpose, we develop a Reverse ERMP model as a MIP formulation seeking to minimize number of roles. We do not present the model here since it is very similar to our proposed formulations. See Appendix A for the model formulation. In summary, in the Iterative Stage, we bounce back and forth in a round-robin fashion constructing UA given PA and PA given UA using the selected ERMP formulation and Reverse ERMP formulation, respectively, until we observe N_I consecutive iterations without any improvement or we observe a decomposition which is exactly the same as the minimum solution observed so far (this implies that we are in an infinite loop). Note that, in the Minnoise ERMP

Algorithm 1. Algorithm for ERMP Problem and its Variants

```
Initialize
Do preprocessing
while n_i < N_I do
    Obtain the corresponding optimal UA matrix
    if There is an improvement then
        Update statistics
    else if Same decomposition observed again then
        break
    else
        Increment n_i
    end if
    Obtain the corresponding optimal PA matrix
    if There is an improvement then
        Update statistics
    else if Same decomposition observed again then
        break
    else
        Increment n_i
    end if
end while
```

case, the solution we obtain may contain some noise, which implies that the resulting UA and PA matrices do not fully represent the UPA matrix. In this case, we cannot use this result to bounce back using the Reverse ERMP Model, because it requires an exact decomposition. So, during the iterative step, if we observe noise in decomposition, we terminate the algorithm at that point. Also note that, although we use MIP formulations and obtain optimal corresponding matrices at each iteration, the overall algorithm is heuristic and may not terminate at a global optimum since we start with a heuristic decomposition and improve only one matrix at a time.

In order to define the improvement metric in our algorithm, we first need to define certain algorithm parameters:

Let $|UA|$ and $|PA|$ denote the number of nonnegative entries in matrices UA and PA, respectively. Let $cur(|UA|)$ and $cur(|PA|)$ be the current values and $min(|UA|)$ and $min(|PA|)$ be the minimum observed values of $|UA|$ and $|PA|$, respectively and let $cur(k)$ be the current and $min(k)$ be the minimum observed value of the number of roles, k. Then, an improvement occurs iff

$$[cur(|UA|) + cur(|PA|) \leq min(|UA|) + min(|PA|)] \vee cur(k) < min(k)$$

Another parameter is n_i which denotes the current number of iterations in which no improvement occurs. Then, the algorithm terminates iff

$$n_i = N_I \vee [cur(|UA|) = min(|UA|) \wedge cur(|PA|) = min(|PA|) \wedge cur(k) = min(k)]$$

This expression denotes that we terminate the algorithm if we do not observe any improvement in N_I consecutive iterations or we observe the minimum solution again which implies that the algorithm enters an infinite loop.

Now, we give our algorithm to ERMP and its variants:

5 Computational Experiments and Results

In this section, we present the results of our computational experiments. We code basic structure of our algorithm using C programming language which communicates with CPLEX 12 Optimization Package via CPLEX Callable Library to perform the optimization. We perform our experiments on a Intel Core2Duo 2.00 GHz machine with 2.00 GB memory running 32-bit Windows 7. We have 2 real and 9 randomly generated synthetic data sets with various different sizes. The synthetic data sets can be separated into three groups according to their sizes (There are 3 synthetic data sets with 100 users and 50 permissions; 3 data sets for 200 users and 100 permissions and 3 data sets for 300 users and 150 permissions).

The results are summarized in Table 1. In this table, Size column denotes the number of users (M) and permissions (N). The Initial Decomposition column denotes the statistics of the initial solution, and the other columns state the results of ERMP, Minnoise ERMP and Edge ERMP, respectively. The % column denotes the percentage improvement in the number of roles in each case. In the results, we take the average of 3 synthetic data sets with equal sizes.

According to the results we see that in the Synthetic data sets our algorithm performs better when the problem size increases. Especially, the improvement of the starting solution in terms of the number of roles in the Data Set 3 is significant as we have an improvement of 8%. Furthermore, Edge ERMP performs better when compared to the ERMP and Minnoise ERMP since there is always a decrease in the number of assignments, which is in fact reasonable when we migrate from BMD to EBMD. We believe that the reason for getting small improvements is due to the pure random nature of the Synthetic Data Sets. However, since the Real Data Sets are not purely random (i.e, it is reasonable to assume that there can be a pattern in the distribution of the user-permission assignments), the improvement is more significant in terms of the number of roles. For instance, the improvement in Real Data Set 1 for ERMP is 31%.

The limitations of our algorithm is that, since it utilizes MIP formulations, the problem cannot easily be solved for large data sets. CPLEX and other MIP optimizers use Branch and Cut techniques which tend to grow exponentially as the problem size increases. Moreover, although we use MIP formulations and obtain optimal corresponding matrices at each iteration, the overall algorithm is heuristic and may not terminate at a global optimum since we start with a heuristic decomposition and improve only one matrix at a time.

Table 1. Computational Results

Data Set	Size	Initial Decompst.			ERMP				Minnoise ERMP				Edge ERMP			
	$(M-N)$	$\lvert UA\rvert$	$\lvert PA\rvert$	K	$\lvert UA\rvert$	$\lvert PA\rvert$	K	%	$\lvert UA\rvert$	$\lvert PA\rvert$	K	%	$\lvert UA\rvert$	$\lvert PA\rvert$	K	%
Syn.D.1	100 - 50	400.6	59	20	400.6	59	20	0	400.6	59	20	0	315.6	59	20	0
Syn.D.2	200 - 100	767.6	271.6	50.6	751.6	257.3	49.3	2.6	751.6	257	49.3	2.6	611	265	50.6	0
Syn.D.3	300 - 150	1618	903.6	111	1506.6	729	102	8.1	1594.3	864	108.6	2.1	886	911	106.6	3.9
Real D.1	231 - 79	726	152	22	682	233	15	31	625	145	20	10	581	145	20	10
Real D.2	46 - 46	438	381	17	228	317	14	17	354	317	14	17	53	317	14	17

6 Conclusions

The advancements in Role Mining aids in finding better role distributions that will increase effectiveness and efficiency of RBAC systems. Since a basic RBAC scheme is composed of Boolean matrices which represent the user-role assignments, usage of negative assignments in extended Boolean matrices can take into account exceptions and separation of duty constraints while performing role mining. In this paper, we propose the Extended Role Mining Problem and its variants, which allow negative assignments. We present the MIP formulations for each of these problems. We also develop a heuristic procedure which utilizes these formulations to obtain a better decomposition. Our experimental results indicate that EBMD can result in significantly less number of roles when compared to BMD.

Some of the future work can be a better evaluation of the heuristic algorithm with more test runs and using synthetic data where the optimal decomposition is known. Furthermore, the Reverse ERMP model can be improved to cover Minnoise ERMP and Edge ERMP objectives of minimizing noise and assignments rather than only minimizing number of roles in the decomposition.

References

1. Ene, A., Horne, W., Milosavljevic, N., Rao, P., Schreiber, R., Tarjan, R.E.: Fast exact and heuristic methods for role minimization problems. In: Proceedings of Symposium on Access Control Models and Technologies (SACMAT), pp. 1–10 (2008)
2. Kuhlmann, M., Shohat, D., Schimpf, G.: Role mining - revealing business roles for security administration using data mining technology. In: Symposium on Access Control Models and Technologies, SACMAT (2003)
3. Lu, H., Vaidya, J., Atluri, V.: Optimal boolean matrix decomposition: Application to role engineering. In: Proceedings of International Conference on Data Engineering (ICDE), pp. 297–306 (2008)
4. Molloy, I., Li, N., Li, T., Mao, Z., Wang, Q., Lobo, J.: Evaluating Role Mining Algorithms. In: Proceedings of ACM Symposium on Access Control Models and Technologies, SACMAT (2009)
5. Lu, H., Vaidya, J., Atluri, V., Hong, Y.: Extended boolean matrix decomposition. In: Ninth IEEE International Conference on Data Mining (ICDM), pp. 317–326 (2009)
6. Schaad, A., Moffett, J., Jacob, J.: The role-based access control system of a european bank: A case study and discussion. In: Proceedings of ACM Symposisum on Access Control Models and Technologies, pp. 3–9 (2001)
7. Schlegelmilch, J., Steffens, U.: Role mining with ORCA. In: Symposium on Access Control Models and Technologies, SACMAT (2005)
8. Vaidya, J., Atluri, V., Guo, Q.: The role mining problem: Finding a minimal descriptive set of roles. In: Proceedings of Symposium on Access Control Models and Technologies (SACMAT), pp. 175–184 (2007)
9. Vaidya, J., Atluri, V., Warner, J.: Roleminer: mining roles using subset enumeration. In: Proceedings of the ACM Conference on Computer and Communications Security, pp. 144–153 (2006)
10. Vaidya, J., Atluri, V., Guo, Q.: The role mining problem: A formal perspective. ACM Trans. Inf. Syst. Secur. 13(3), 1–31 (2010)
11. Zhang, D., Ramamohanrao, K., Ebringer, T.: Role engineering using graph optimisation. In: Symposium on Access Control Models and Technologies (SACMAT), pp. 139–144 (2007)

A Reverse ERMP Model

The following model is used to obtain a Boolean PA matrix given an Extended Boolean UA matrix. The formulation is similar to the ERMP formulation given in the previous section. However, the only difference is that the objective is to minimize the number of roles only.

Decision Variables

– Let $y_k = \begin{cases} 1, \; if \; role \; k \; is \; used \\ 0, \; otherwise \end{cases}$
– Let $x_{kj} = \begin{cases} 1, \; if \; permission \; j \; is \; assigned \; to \; role \; k \\ 0, \; otherwise \end{cases}$
– Let $t_{ij} \in \{0, 1\}$ be an indicator variable, $i \in M, \; j \in N$

Parameters

– Let a_{ij} denote the entry (i, j) of matrix UPA.
– Let b^+_{ik} is 1 if the entry (i, k) of matrix UA is 1, 0 otherwise.
– Let b^-_{ik} is 1 if the entry (i, k) of matrix UA is -1, 0 otherwise.

Then the model is as follows:

$$min \sum_{k \in K} y_k \tag{33}$$

$$s.t.$$

$$\sum_{k \in K s.t. a_{ij}=1} b^+_{ik} x_{kj} \geq 1, \; \forall i \in M, \; j \in N \tag{34}$$

$$\sum_{k \in K s.t. a_{ij}=1} b^-_{ik} x_{kj} = 0, \; \forall i \in M, \; j \in N \tag{35}$$

$$\sum_{k \in K s.t. a_{ij}=0} b^+_{ik} x_{kj} \leq t_{ij} M, \; \forall i \in M, \; j \in N \tag{36}$$

$$\sum_{k \in K s.t. a_{ij}=0} b^-_{ik} x_{kj} \geq 1 - (1 - t_{ij}) M, \; \forall i \in M, \; j \in N \tag{37}$$

$$y_k \geq x_{kj}, \; \forall k \in K, \; j \in N \tag{38}$$

$$t_{ij} \in \{0, 1\}, \; \forall i \in M, j \in N \tag{39}$$

$$x_{kj} \in \{0, 1\}, \; \forall k \in K, j \in N \tag{40}$$

Dynamics in Delegation and Revocation Schemes: A Logical Approach

Guillaume Aucher[1], Steve Barker[2], Guido Boella[3], Valerio Genovese[3,4], and Leendert van der Torre[4]

[1] University of Rennes 1 - INRIA, France
[2] King's College London, UK
[3] University of Torino, Italy
[4] University of Luxembourg, Luxembourg

Abstract. In this paper we first introduce a logic for describing formally a family of delegation and revocation models that are based on the work in Hagström *et al.*. We then extend our logic to accommodate an epistemic interpretation of trust within the framework that we define. What emerges from this work is a rich framework of formally well-defined delegation and revocation schemes that accommodates an important trust component.

1 Introduction

Delegation and revocation are broad concepts that are fundamentally important in modelling and reasoning about (dynamic) distributed systems. In the context of multi-agent systems (MAS), delegation is important in relation to the coordination of agents and for the coordinating of activities within organizational structures [5]. Trust is, in turn, a fundamental notion in delegation and revocation; ordinarily, a principal i may delegate an access privilege a on an object o to a principal j iff i trusts j sufficiently not to abuse the trust i has in j to perform the action a in relation to o. In the context of revocation, it is when i loses trust in j, in relation to exercising the privilege a on o, that i revokes the a privilege on o from j. Although the importance of the trust dimension has been recognized in delegation-revocation, it is our contention that more work is required on the formal specification and reasoning about trust in the context of delegation and revocation. In this paper, our focus is on formally defining a general, dynamic delegation-revocation framework that accommodates an important aspect of trust. A feature of MAS is that agents are autonomous and therefore they can act with respect to a subjective perception of the environment. For instance, a verifier may decide not to concede access to agents that she does not trust or that have been delegated by other untrusted agents. In relation to this observation, in this paper we contribute to the study of delegation and revocation in the context of distributed systems, and multi-agent systems in particular, by addressing the following key research question: *How to define a formal framework to model and reason about delegation and revocation in the context of multi-agent (and*

Y. Li (Ed.): Data and Applications Security and Privacy XXV, LNCS 6818, pp. 90–105, 2011.

other distributed) systems? This generally stated question breaks down into at least three important sub-questions that we intend to address: *How to update privileges on objects in a dynamic, multi-agent environment? How to specify and reason about different types of delegation and revocation schemes? How to study delegation of access privileges when trust interferes with the fact that an agent has been permitted to access?*

Our main question and each of the subquestions that we consider have been considered in the past, but the novelty of what we describe is to be understood in terms of the new formal approaches that we introduce to address them. The need for formal representations of security concepts is well understood (e.g., formal representations of security concepts are important for constructing assurance proofs). Our work is also motivated by the more specific observations that distributed access control systems can be seen as a type of a multi-agent system for which delegation models in "classical" security need to be extended. We need to also *use* our logical framework to reason about delegation-revocation policies and we require fast and effective tools for that. Delegation is an intrinsically dynamic process, therefore we additionally need to define dynamic operators that formalize a range of delegation-revocation schemes. The explicit representation of trust that we accommodate requires us to face two challenges: first, how to make the verifier autonomous to decide whether to give access in case of there being authorized but untrusted agents. Second, how to generalize the revocation policies of Hagström *et al.* [9] by considering whether an agent who delegated a permission is trusted or not. We address all of these issues in this paper.

The methodology that we employ in addressing these issues can be understood in the following way. First, we show that our framework can embody delegation and revocation schemes as addressed by the distributed access control community. In particular, we model all of the revocation schemes that are semi-formally introduced in [9] by using a dynamic variant of propositional logic. The work in [9] is among the most general models to handle dynamics in delegation chains and is the basis of several applied delegation models in security (Section 5 of [9]). Second, we extend the proposed framework to study relationships between trust and privilege delegation by explicitly modeling beliefs about trust relationships among agents.

Our contributions on these things can be summarized thus: (i) we formalize, in logic, the Hagström *et al.* framework (in [9], a semi-formal account is provided), (ii) we demonstrate the translation of our logic into "programs" (a notion that we will define later) that describe the effects of performing delegation and revocation actions, and (iii) we describe an extended form of our logic that allows for representing and reasoning about the beliefs that agents have of principals in a distributed delegation-revocation framework.

In Section 2, we describe a general authorization system, along the lines of [9], and we give some basic definitions. In Section 3, we introduce the logic that we use in order to represent formally the range of delegation and revocation schemes, of the Hagström *et al.* type, that we consider. In Section 4, we describe the use of our logic for representing delegation policies and, in Section 5, we describe the use of our logic for representing revocation schemes. In Section 6, we make the key move of extending the formalization of policies expressible in the Hagström *et al.* framework to accommodate an epistemic logic of trust. The latter is used to account for reasoning about belief and trust in the delegation-revocation context. In Section 7, we describe related work and, in Section 8, we draw conclusions and make some suggestions for further work.

2 System Description

In this Section, we formalize the general concepts and notation introduced informally in [9]. The notation is intended to represent a generic access control framework using an ownership-based model with grant option for both positive and negative permissions, and where negative permissions dominate positive ones. We draw the reader's to a simplified version of the distributed authoriza-

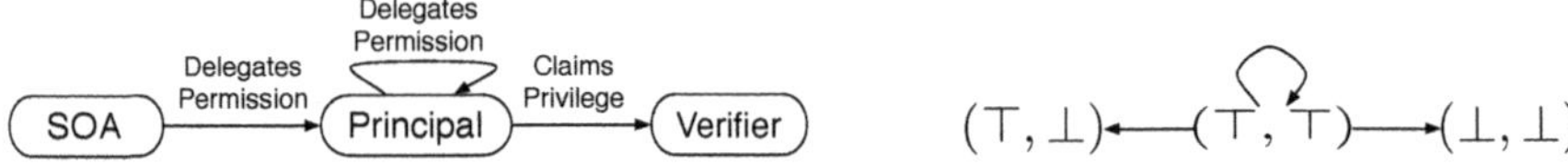

Fig. 1. The Authorization Model

Fig. 2. Dominance Relation $\mathcal{R}$

tion model described in [1,8], and illustrated in Figure 1, where an agent receives a privilege, directly or indirectly, from a *source of authority* (SOA). The SOA is an agent that has full power over a resource and is the ultimate authority w.r.t. accesses to that specific resource. The verifier is a particular agent in charge of checking whether another agent, who received a privilege directly or indirectly from the SOA, that wants to exercise an access permission is authorized so to do.

2.1 Basics

Let $\mathbb{AG}$ be a finite set of *agents* (users) in the authorization system. Let $\mathbb{O}$ be the (finite) set of system *objects* for which authorizations can be stated. Finally, let $\mathbb{A}$ be the (finite) set of *accesses* over objects; by accesses we mean the actions that agents may perform on objects. We assume that all authorizations in the system are stored in an authorization specification $AUTH$, and that every authorization is of the form $(i, j, (a, o), alp, dlp)$ where, i and j are two agents, the *grantor* and the *subject*; (a, o) is an *access type* and specifies an action a on a object o; $alp \in \{\top, \bot\}$ (access level permission) is a flag which specifies if the authorization is an access level permission $alp = \top$ or an access level denial $alp = \bot$; $dlp \in \{\top, \bot\}$ (delegation level permission) is a flag which specifies whether or not the authorization gives to j the authority to further delegate the permission. For instance, the authorization $(i, j, (a, o), \top, \top) \in AUTH$ says that agent i gives agent j the permission to perform action a on object o and the authority to further delegate this permission to other principals. On the contrary $(i, j, (a, o), \top, \bot) \in AUTH$ means that j still gets from i the permission to perform the a action on o but she is not granted by i to further delegate the permission. In case of an authorization being a denial, i.e., $alp = \bot$, we require also dlp to be $\bot$ in order to represent that the agent cannot delegate a permission to access what she does not have herself. Hence, in our model we have three possible permissions (i.e., $(\top, \top)$, $(\top, \bot)$, $(\bot, \bot)$).

Definition 1 (Positive and Negative Permissions). *Given an authorization $(i, j, (a, o), alp, dlp)$, we refer to (alp, dlp) as a* negative permission *if $alp = \bot$; otherwise, we call it a* positive permission.

When a user receives both a positive and a negative permission for the same $(action, object)$ pair, there is a "conflict" between the two assignments. Hence, the set of permissions is divided into one set of *active permissions* and one set of *inactive permissions.* Active permissions can be inactivated when a negative permission is granted (e.g., during a revocation). Inactive permissions, instead, can be activated when a negative permission for the same target is removed.

In Figure 2, we illustrate a dominance relation $\mathcal{R}$ between permissions such that if $(alp, dlp)\mathcal{R}(alp', dlp')$ reads as, if an agent i has permission (alp, dlp) then it can grant an authorization of type $(i, \_, (\_, \_), alp', dlp')$. Intuitively, (alp, dlp) $\mathcal{R}(alp', dlp')$ means that permission (alp, dlp) is stronger than (alp', dlp').

In line with [9], we require an authorization specification to satisfy the following property:

Definition 2 (Connectivity Property). *For all authorizations in $AUTH$, if an agent i is the grantor of a permission (alp, dlp) for permissions target (a, o) to the subject j, then i must have a permission (alp', dlp') such that $(alp', dlp')\mathcal{R}(alp, dlp)$.*

The connectivity property can be considered as a constraint over the authorization specification $AUTH$. Intuitively, it assures that if an agent i delegates a permission (alp, dlp) to j for the access type (a, o) then she has the permission to do so.

Definition 3 (Delegation Chain). *Given an access type (a, o), a* delegation chain *$[x_1, x_2, \ldots, x_n]_{(a,o)}$ is a sequence of authorizations of the form $(x_1, x_2, (a, o), alp_1, dlp_1)$, $\ldots$, $(x_{n-1}, x_n, (a, o), alp_n, dlp_n)$.*

An agent j is granted the access type (a, o) if and only if the verifier can check the existence of a *rooted delegation chain*, which we define next.

Definition 4 (Rooted Delegation Chain). *A delegation chain $[x_1, x_2, \ldots, x_n]_{(a,o)}$ is* rooted *if and only if the following hold: x_1 is a source of authority for object o; all agents $x_2, \ldots, x_{n-1}$ have an active privilege $(\top, \top)$ for access type (a, o); agent x_n has an active privilege $(\top, dlp)$ with $dlp \in \{\top, \bot\}$.*

The notion of rooted delegation chain is pivotal because it corresponds to the notion of permission in standard access control. In this view, the connectivity property assures that if $(i, j, (a, o), alp, dlp) \in AUTH$ then there is a rooted delegation chain that links j to a source of authority for o. In [9], Hagström *et al.* impose the above property to hold in *any* authorization specification. However, in highly distributed scenarios (e.g., GRID systems) it may be extremely difficult to enforce the connectivity property *a priori* for every access type (a, o) (see [8] for an example). In Section 3, we relax this requirement and we give a formal account of the properties reported above in order to check whether a node in the authorization specification is part of a rooted chain.

As reported in [9], the chains of granted authorizations in a system can be represented by directed graphs. The nodes contain information about subject, object and access type, and the arcs are labelled with the granted permission (alp, dlp). There is an arc from node $(i, (a, o))$ to node $(j, (a, o))$ if there is an entry in the authorization specification with $(i, j, (a, o), alp, dlp)$. An arc from node i to node j is labelled with the permission granted by user i to user j.

Active arcs have unbroken lines and inactive arcs have dashed lines to indicate that although they are still in $AUTH$, they are not in effect because they have been overruled by a negative permission.

3 The Logic

We extend the propositional language *Prop* with dynamic operators to specify programs that update an authorization specification by issuing (or revoking) credentials certificates.

Definition 5 (Syntax). *We define inductively the language $\mathcal{L}$ as follows:*

$$\varphi ::= p \mid \varphi \wedge \varphi \mid \neg\varphi \mid [\pi]\varphi \qquad \pi ::= +p \mid -p \mid \varphi? \mid \pi \cup \pi \mid \pi;\pi$$

where p ranges over $\Phi = \{soa_{i,o}, (i,(a,o),j)^D_+, (i,(a,o),j)^D_-, (i,(a,o),j)^P_+, (i,(a,o), j)^P_- \mid a \in \mathbb{A}, o \in \mathbb{O}, i, j \in \mathbb{AG}\}$, with $\mathbb{A}, \mathbb{O}$ and $\mathbb{AG}$ being finite sets.

The propositional atoms in Φ describe the state of the authorization system. $soa_{i,o}$ reads as: "agent i is the source of authority over object o". To describe the steps of delegation chains we use triples such that $(i,(a,o),j)^P_+$ (resp. $(i,(a,o),j)^D_+$) reads as: "there is a certificate supporting that i delegates an access (resp. delegation) level permission to j" while $(i,(a,o),j)^P_-$ (resp. $(i,(a,o),j)^D_-$) reads as: "there is a certificate supporting that i gives a negative access (resp. delegation) level permission".

Given a generic dynamic formula $[\pi]\varphi$ we read it as follows: "after executing program π, the formula φ holds true". A program is therefore intended as a sequence of instructions such that : $[+p]\varphi$ (resp. $[-p]\varphi$) reads as: "after making p true (resp. false), φ holds"; $[\varphi?]\psi$ reads as: "If φ is true, then ψ is the case"; $[\pi \cup \pi']\varphi$ reads as: "after executing π, φ holds *and*, after executing π', φ holds"; $[\pi;\pi']\varphi$ reads as: "After executing π and then π', φ holds". For readability, we adopt the following abbreviations: $(i,(a,o),j)^{P,D}_+ \overset{\text{def}}{=} (i,(a,o),j)^P_+ \wedge$

$(i,(a,o),j)^{D}_{+}$; $\neg(i,(a,o),j)^{P,D}_{-} \stackrel{\text{def}}{=} \neg(i,(a,o),j)^{P}_{-} \wedge \neg(i,(a,o),j)^{D}_{-}$; `if` φ `then` τ_1 `else` $\tau_2 \stackrel{\text{def}}{=} ((\varphi?;\tau_1) \cup (\neg\varphi?;\tau_2))$; `for all` $(x \in \{s_1,\ldots,s_n\})$ `do` $\tau_1(x)$ `end for` $\stackrel{\text{def}}{=} \tau_1(s_1);\ldots;\tau_1(s_n)$.

Definition 6 (Semantics). *A valuation Θ is a function assigning a truth value to each propositional atom: $\Theta : \Phi \to \{\top,\bot\}$. Given a valuation Θ of propositional logic and $p \in \Phi$, the updates Θ^{+p} and Θ^{-p} are defined as follows.*

$$\Theta^{+p}(q) = \begin{cases} \top & \text{if } p = q, \\ \Theta(q) & \text{otherwise.} \end{cases} \quad \Theta^{-p}(q) = \begin{cases} \bot & \text{if } p = q, \\ \Theta(q) & \text{otherwise.} \end{cases}$$

Let Θ be a valuation and $\phi \in \mathcal{L}$. The satisfaction relation $\Theta \models \phi$ is defined inductively as follows (we omit $\neg$ and $\wedge$).

$$\begin{array}{llll} \Theta \models p & \text{iff } \Theta(p) = \top & \Theta \models [\psi?]\phi & \text{iff } \Theta \models \psi \to \phi \\ \Theta \models [+p]\phi & \text{iff } \Theta^{+p} \models \phi & \Theta \models [\pi;\pi']\phi & \text{iff } \Theta \models [\pi][\pi']\phi \\ \Theta \models [-p]\phi & \text{iff } \Theta^{-p} \models \phi & \Theta \models [\pi \cup \pi']\phi & \text{iff } \Theta \models [\pi]\phi \wedge [\pi']\phi \end{array}$$

We exploit our basic dynamic operators to model certificate creation (granting) and deletion (revoking) by defining the following programs: $i \xrightarrow{(a,o)}_D j \stackrel{\text{def}}{=} +(i,(a,o),j)^{D}_{+}$; $i \xleftarrow{(a,o)}_D j \stackrel{\text{def}}{=} -(i,(a,o),j)^{D}_{+}$; $i \xrightarrow{(a,o)}_P j \stackrel{\text{def}}{=} +(i,(a,o),j)^{P}_{+}$; $i \xleftarrow{(a,o)}_P j \stackrel{\text{def}}{=} -(i,(a,o),j)^{P}_{+}$; $i \xrightarrow{-(a,o)} j \stackrel{\text{def}}{=} +(i,(a,o),j)^{P}_{-};+(i,(a,o),j)^{D}_{-}$; $i \xleftarrow{-(a,o)} j \stackrel{\text{def}}{=} -(i,(a,o),j)^{P}_{-};-(i,(a,o),j)^{D}_{-}$. For instance, $i \xrightarrow{(a,o)}_D j$ reads as: "a certificate supporting that i grants j the authority to delegate (a,o) is issued." while $i \xrightarrow{-(a,o)}_P j$ reads as: "a certificate supporting a negative permission granted by i to j for (a,o) is issued".

Next, we define the logic that we use for our delegation-revocation framework.

Definition 7. *The logic* L *is defined by the following axiom schemes and inference rules.*

Taut	$\vdash \phi$ *for all propositional tautologies* ϕ *based on* Φ	
K+	$\vdash [+p](\phi \to \psi) \to ([+p]\phi \to [+p]\psi)$	
K-	$\vdash [-p](\phi \to \psi) \to ([-p]\phi \to [-p]\psi)$	
Det+	$\vdash \neg[+p]\phi \leftrightarrow [+p]\neg\phi$	
Det-	$\vdash \neg[-p]\phi \leftrightarrow [-p]\neg\phi$	
Test	$\vdash [\psi?]\phi \leftrightarrow (\psi \to \phi)$	
Red1	$\vdash [+p]p$	
Red2	$\vdash [+p]q \leftrightarrow q$	*if* $p \neq q$
Red3	$\vdash [-p]\neg p$	
Red4	$\vdash [-p]q \leftrightarrow q$	*if* $p \neq q$
Comp	$\vdash [\pi;\pi']\phi \leftrightarrow [\pi][\pi']\phi$	
Choice	$\vdash [\pi \cup \pi']\phi \leftrightarrow [\pi]\phi \wedge [\pi']\phi$	
Nec	*If* $\vdash \phi$ *then* $\vdash [+p]\phi$ *and* $\vdash [-p]\phi$	
MP	*If* $\vdash \phi$ *and* $\vdash \phi \to \psi$ *then* $\vdash \psi$	

Proposition 1. *For all formula $\phi \in \mathcal{L}_D$, there is $Red(\phi) \in Prop$ such that $\vdash \phi \leftrightarrow Red(\phi)$. The reduction of ϕ to $Red(\phi)$ is polynomial in the size of ϕ*

Proof (sketch). We prove it by successive inductions. We use in great extent the 'reduction' axioms K+, K-, Det+, Det-, Test, Red1 to Red4: they all 'push through' the connectives, except for the basic cases Test and Red1-Red4 where the dynamic modalities [+p] and [-p] disappear.

The above proposition is extremely important because it shows that *every* dynamic formula of the type $[\pi]\varphi$ can be reduced in an *equivalent* static formula in standard propositional logic. As a consequence of Proposition 1 we get the following theorem:

Theorem 1. *The semantics of $\mathcal{L}_D$ is sound and complete w.r.t. the logic* L. *The logic* L *is also decidable and* NP*-complete.*

Definition 8 (Rooted Delegation Chain). *In the system represented by a valuation Θ, there is a rooted delegation chain ending at the node $(j,(a,o))$ iff $\Theta \models \mathcal{CP}_\emptyset(j,(a,o))$, where*

$$\begin{aligned}&\mathcal{CP}_S(j,(a,o)) = \\ &\quad \bigvee_{i\notin S} (((i,(a,o),j)^P_+ \wedge \neg(i,(a,o),j)^P_- \wedge soa_{i,o}) \vee \\ &\quad ((i,(a,o),j)^P_+ \wedge \neg(i,(a,o),j)^P_- \wedge \mathcal{CP}^{P,D}_{S\cup\{i,j\}}(i,(a,o)))\end{aligned}$$

$$\begin{aligned}&\mathcal{CP}^{P,D}_S(j,(a,o)) = \\ &\quad \bigvee_{i\notin S} (((i,(a,o),j)^{P,D}_+ \wedge \neg(i,(a,o),j)^{P,D}_- \wedge soa_{i,o}) \vee \\ &\quad ((i,(a,o),j)^{P,D}_+ \wedge \neg(i,(a,o),j)^{P,D}_- \wedge \mathcal{CP}^{P,D}_{S\cup\{i,j\}}(i,(a,o)))\end{aligned}$$

Intuitively, $\mathcal{CP}_S(j,(a,o))$ reads as: "There is a rooted delegation chain (with no agent in S) such that j is granted an access level permission (i.e., $alp = \top$) for (a,o)". Notice that our definition of $\mathcal{CP}_S(j,(a,o))$ is well-founded because we have a finite number of agents, object and actions.

An authorization that has the connectivity property as reported in Definition 2 can be seen as a particular valuation which complies with the following definition.

Definition 9 (Connectivity Property). *A system represented by a valuation Θ has the connectivity property iff for all access types (a,o), $\Theta \models \mathcal{CP}(a,o)$, where $\mathcal{CP}(a,o) = \bigwedge_{i\in\mathbb{AG}} ((i,(a,o),j)^P_+ \rightarrow \mathcal{CP}_\emptyset(i,(a,o)))$*

We now introduce two notions that are pivotal in formally defining the revocation schemes presented in Section 5.

Definition 10 (Independency). *In a system represented by Θ, given a subject j with a permission (alp, dlp) for access type (a,o), j is said to be* independent *of a subject i iff $\Theta \models \mathcal{CP}_{\{i\}}(j,(a,o))$*

Definition 11 (Reachability). *In a system represented by a valuation Θ we say that j is reachable from i via a delegation chain for access type (a,o) iff $\Theta \models R_\emptyset(j,i,(a,o))$ where $R_S(j,i,(a,o)) = (i,(a,o),j)^P_+ \vee \bigvee_{x\notin S} ((x,(a,o),j)^{P,D}_+ \wedge R_{S\cup\{x\}}(x,i,(a,o)))$*[1]

[1] Notice that we do not check for the arc in the delegation chain to be active.

Automated Theorem Proving. As shown in Proposition 1, the logic defined above is sound and complete w.r.t. propositional logic. In order to show how to use state of the art theorem provers to reason about delegation and revocation schemes, we developed a parser (written in SCHEME) which implements a set of complete reduction axioms and translates dynamic formulas, as reported in Definition 5, into (static) propositional logic. The parser translates a set of formulas written in our logical framework into first-order formulas compatible with SPASS [15] syntax. Due that our language is finite, SPASS automatically instantiates the translated formulas into propositional logic and then uses a SAT solver to check satisfiability[2].

4 Delegation Schemes

As pointed out in [8], in the information security literature, *delegation* normally describes the act of distributing privileges to agents in distributed systems. In general, there are two possible kinds of delegation:

Delegation as creation of new privilege: the delegatee receives its own privilege which is independent of the delegator's privilege in the sense that if the delegator's privilege is revoked, then it does not necessarily mean that the delegatee's privilege is revoked. A special case is the *transfer* of a new privilege, which models the creation of a new privilege and a revocation of an old one;

Delegation by proxy: The delegatee does not receive its own privilege, but can exercise the privilege through the delegator, in the sense that the delegator *speaks for* or *acts on behalf of* the delegator.

On the first type of delegation, an agent i has a direct privilege to act on an object o if she is the SOA for it (i.e., $soa_{i,o}$). To model delegation by proxy instead, we need to keep track of the delegation chains (represented through atoms like $(i,(a,o),j)_{+}^{P,D}$) on which an agent depends for a given privilege.

We can accommodate the different types of delegation by exploiting the dynamic operators defined in the previous section. For instance, we can model delegation as creation of new privileges with the following programs: "Agent i assigns (if she has the power) a new privilege on object o to agent j": ($\texttt{if}\ soa_{i,o}\ \texttt{then}\ {+soa_{j,o}}$); "Agent i transfers her privilege over o to agent j": ($\texttt{if}\ soa_{i,o}\ \texttt{then}\ {-soa_{i,o}}; {+soa_{j,o}}$).

5 Revocation Schemes

In this section, we define the revocation operations that are informally described in [9]. The following schemes are sufficiently general to model a great deal of real-world distributed authorization architectures. The main contribution of this section is that for each revocation scheme S we define a program π_S such that we read $[\pi_S]\varphi$ as: "after the execution of a revocation operation S, φ holds".

[2] The parser is available at `http://www.di.unito.it/~genovese/tools/delegation2spass.zip`

Due to space constraints, we refer to $\pi_S[n-m]$ as the block instructions from line n to m of the program π_S.

As in [9], we divide revocation schemes into *positive* and *negative*, depending on the revocation action of deleting a certificate or of issuing a negative permission.

When i revokes a permission to j, we identify two types of agents: (i) those that are not independent from i and delegated the same permission to j (see Definition 10) and (ii) those that are reachable from j (see Definition 11) in the delegation chain. We classify a revocation operation as *weak/strong* and *local/global*, depending on how it influences agents of type (i) and (ii). A revocation operation is *weak* (resp. *strong*) if, in revoking a permission from i to j, none (resp. all) of the agents of type (i) are forced to revoke their delegation. Instead, we classify a revocation operation as *local* (resp. *strong*) if the algorithm influences none (resp. all) of the agents of type (ii).

An important property of *all* the programs implementing the revocation schemes is as follows

Theorem 2 (Invariance under connectivity). *After the execution of* any *program implementing the revocation schemes, the resulting delegation chain satisfies the connectivity property.*

5.1 Positive Revocation Schemes

Weak Local Delete. The *weak local delete* operation is the simplest form of revocation. After the application of the weak local delete operation on a permission (alp, dlp) for a given access type (a, o) granted by agent i to j, the following three post-conditions must be satisfied [9]: i no longer grants j the permission (alp, dlp); Permissions for (a, o) granted to j by users other than i are intact; Permissions for subjects other than j are intact. However, the grantors of permissions for users directly following j in the graph for (a, o) may have changed in order for the connectivity property to be satisfied;

In Figure 4 we show the resulting delegation chain after the execution of program $WLD_{i,j}$.

Strong Local Delete. The application of the *strong local delete* operation on a permission (alp, dlp) for access type (a, o) granted by agent i to agent j has to satisfy the following post-conditions: i no longer grants j the permission (alp, dlp); Permissions for access type (a, o) granted to j by every agent z other than i are intact if they are independent of i. Otherwise, they are restricted to satisfy the connectivity property for those paths from z that are independent of i; Positive (and negative) permissions for agents other than j are intact. However, the grantors of permissions for agents directly following j in the graph for (a, o) may have changed in order for the connectivity property to be satisfied. In Figure 6, we show the resulting delegation chain after the execution of program $SLD_{i,j}$.

Weak global delete. After the application of a weak global delete operation on a permission (alp, dlp) for an access type (a, o) granted by i to j, the following

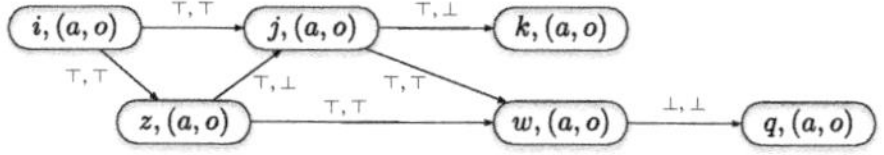

Fig. 3. A Delegation Chain

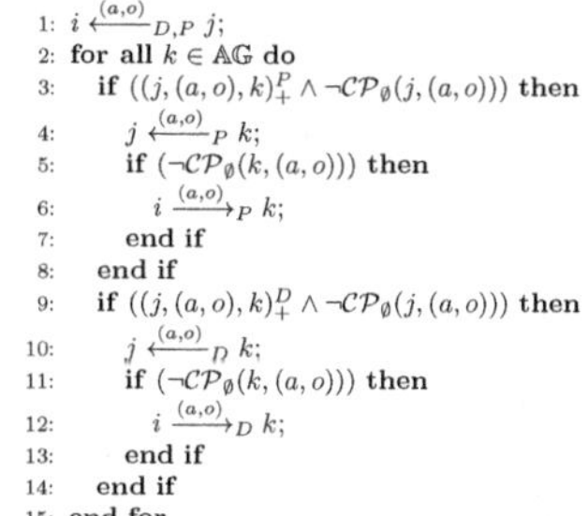

$i \xleftarrow{(a,o)}_{D,P} j$;
for all $k \in \mathbb{AG}$ **do**
  if $((j,(a,o),k)^{P}_{+} \wedge \neg\mathcal{CP}_{\emptyset}(j,(a,o)))$ **then**
    $j \xleftarrow{(a,o)}_{P} k$;
    if $(\neg\mathcal{CP}_{\emptyset}(k,(a,o)))$ **then**
      $i \xrightarrow{(a,o)}_{P} k$;
    end if
  end if
  if $((j,(a,o),k)^{D}_{+} \wedge \neg\mathcal{CP}_{\emptyset}(j,(a,o)))$ **then**
    $j \xleftarrow{(a,o)}_{D} k$;
    if $(\neg\mathcal{CP}_{\emptyset}(k,(a,o)))$ **then**
      $i \xrightarrow{(a,o)}_{D} k$;
    end if
  end if
end for

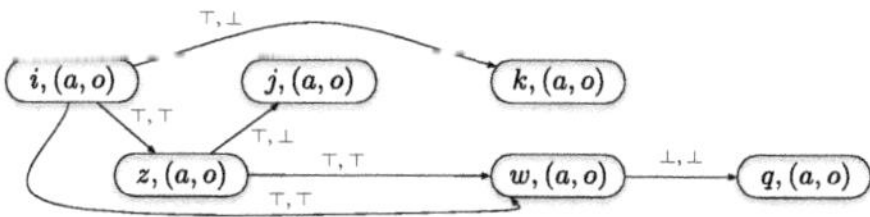

Fig. 4. Weak Local Delete

Fig. 5. $WLD_{i,j}$ Program

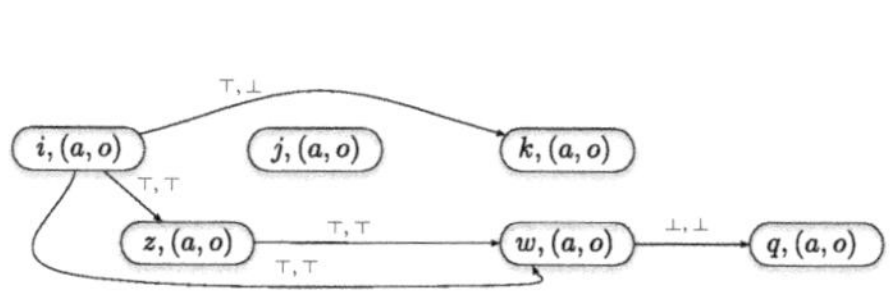

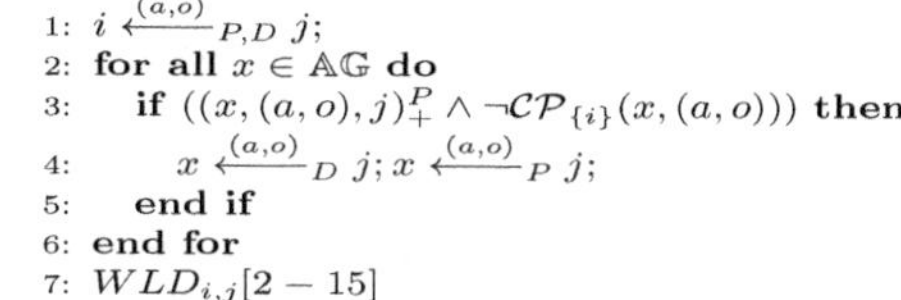

$i \xleftarrow{(a,o)}_{P,D} j$;
for all $x \in \mathbb{AG}$ **do**
  if $((x,(a,o),j)^{P}_{+} \wedge \neg\mathcal{CP}_{\{i\}}(x,(a,o)))$ **then**
    $x \xleftarrow{(a,o)}_{D} j; x \xleftarrow{(a,o)}_{P} j$;
  end if
end for
$WLD_{i,j}[2-15]$

Fig. 6. Strong Local Delete

Fig. 7. $SLD_{i,j}$ Program

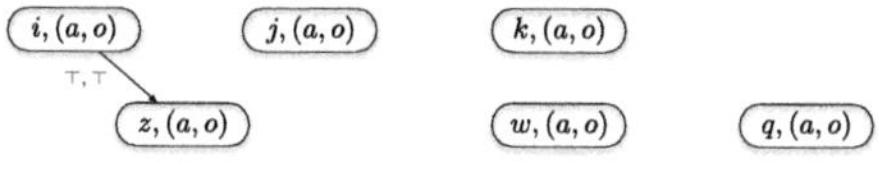

Fig. 8. Strong Global Delete

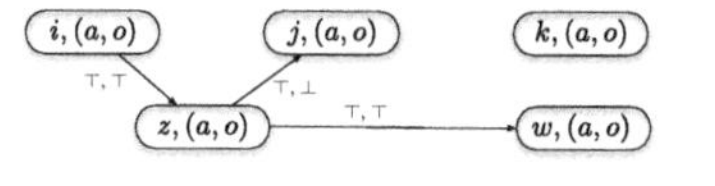

Fig. 9. Weak Global Delete

post-conditions must satisfied: i no longer grants j the permission (alp, dlp) for access type (a, o); Permissions from the same access type (alp, dlp) granted to j by users other than i are intact; The permissions of all subjects that have been granted by j may change depending on whether other principals granted some permission for the same access type. A suitable situation to use the weak global delete operation is when i loses her trust in j but she still trusts that other guarantees to make their own judgements about him. Also, since i no longer trusts j with the permission previously given, in turn she no longer trusts any subject trusted by j, and so on. In Figure 9, we show the resulting delegation chain after the execution of program $WGD_{i,j}$.

Strong global delete. After the application of a strong global delete operation on a permission (alp, dlp) for an access type (a, o) granted by i to j, the following post-conditions must be satisfied: i no longer grants j the permission (alp, dlp); Positive permissions for the same access type (a, o) granted to j or any descendant of j by every user z other than i are intact if they are independent of i. Otherwise, they are adjusted (i.e., restricted) to satisfy the connectivity

1: $i \xleftarrow{(a,o)}_{P,D} j$;
2: **for all** $x \in \mathbb{AG}$ **do**
3: **if** $((x,(a,o),j)^P_+ \wedge \neg\mathcal{CP}_{\{i\}}(x,(a,o)))$ **then**
4: $x \xleftarrow{(a,o)}_P j; x \xleftarrow{(a,o)}_D j$;
5: **end if**
6: **if** $R_\emptyset(x,j,(a,o))$ **then**
7: $WGD_{i,j}[2-10]$
8: **end if**
9: **end for**

Fig. 10. $SGD_{i,j} Program$

1: $i \xleftarrow{(a,o)}_{P,D} j$;
2: **for all** $x \in \mathbb{AG}$ **do**
3: **if** $R_\emptyset(x,j,(a,o))$ **then**
4: **for all** $y \in \mathbb{AG}$ **do**
5: **if** $((y,(a,o),x)^P_+ \wedge \neg\mathcal{CP}_\emptyset(y,(a,o)))$ **then**
6: $y \xleftarrow{(a,o)}_P x; y \xleftarrow{(a,o)}_D x$;
7: **end if**
8: **end for**
9: **end if**
10: **end for**

Fig. 11. $WGD_{i,j}$ Program

property for those paths from z back to a SOA that is independent of i. Negative permissions of the same type are intact; The permissions of all subjects that have been granted either directly or transitively, by j may have been adjusted in order for the connectivity property to be satisfied. In Figure 8 we show the resulting delegation chain after the execution of program $SGD_{i,j}$.

Negative Revocation Schemes. Negative revocation schemes differ from positive ones in that revocation is done not by deleting a positive certificate but by issuing a negative permission. The outcome of such schemes is exactly the same as the positive ones (permission is revoked) but a negative permission make it easier to go back to the previous state when negative permission is in turn revoked. For this reason we refer to [9] for an intuitive description of the schemes.[3]

6 An Epistemic Approach to Trust

The outcomes of executing a delegation or a revocation action, as presented in Sections 4 and 5, depend only on the authorization policy. The decision points of the programs presented so far are checked against the presence of information that is at system (institutional) level, like "is this agent a source of authority?" or "do we have evidence of a particular delegation certificate being held?".

However, one of the features of MAS is that agents are autonomous and therefore they can act w.r.t. a subjective and internal perception of the environment. We next show that this subjective dimension can be naturally accommodated in our logic by explicitly representing *beliefs* of agents with a standard epistemic modal operator.

A crucial subjective dimension in authorization is the one of *trust* among agents. In particular, we are interested in policy requirements like: *"An agent i trusts agent j on (a, o) while j is not considered trustworthy by agent k".*

The possibility of expressing subjective statements about trust enriches the model, which we describe above, in several respects:

[3] For space constraints we refer to a companion technical report [4] for a formalization of negative schemes.

Verification: For a verifier to grant a privilege it is not sufficient that the delegation chain is rooted according to Definition 4, but we require the chain to be such that all the agents are trusted by the verifier.

Delegation: An agent i delegates a permission to agent j not only if i has the privilege to do so but also if i trusts j.

Revocation: The introduction of trust can generalize the revocation schemes presented in Section 5. To see that, suppose that agent i wants to revoke a permission from agent j, then depending on whether i trusts j or not: 1. The agent i may want to remove the same permission from of all the other agents delegated by j that are not trusted by i; 2. The agent i may force all the other agents that gave the same privilege to j to revoke it if i does not trust them.

In what follows, we give a formal account of how to accommodate trust in all of the different respects that we reported above.

Definition 12. *A* trust model *is a tuple $M = (W, R, V, w)$ where: W is a set of possible worlds and $w \in W$; $R : \mathbb{AG} \to 2^{W \times W}$ is a function assigning to each agent an accessibility relation on W; $V : \Phi \to 2^W$ is a function assigning to each propositional letter a set of possible worlds.*

Definition 13. *The language $\mathcal{L}_T$ is defined inductively as follows:*

$$\mathcal{L} : \phi ::= p \mid \neg\phi \mid \phi \wedge \phi \mid B_j\phi$$

where p in $\Phi_T = \{t(i,(a,o)), \mid a \in \mathbb{A}, o \in \mathbb{O}, i, j \in \mathbb{AG}\}$.

The truth conditions of the relation $M, w \models \phi$ are defined inductively as usual (we omit $\neg$ and $\wedge$).

$$\begin{array}{lll} M, w \models p & \textit{iff} & w \in V(p) \\ M, w \models B_j\phi & \textit{iff} & \textit{for all } v \in R_j(w), M, v \models \phi \end{array}$$

Intuitively, $t(j,(a,o))$ reads as: "j is trusted on (a,o)" and $B_i t(j,(a,o))$ reads as: "i trusts j on (a,o)".

In the remainder of this section, we show how we can (independently) merge the trust model as described above, with the delegation model introduced in previous sections.

Definition 14. *A* trust-authorization model *is a pair $\{(M, w), \Theta\}$ of an internal trust-model (M, w) and a valuation Θ on Φ.*

Definition 15. *We define inductively the language $\mathcal{L}$ as follows:*

$$\phi ::= p \mid \psi \mid \phi \wedge \phi \mid \neg\phi \mid [\pi]\phi \qquad \pi ::= +p \mid -p \mid \phi? \mid \pi \cup \pi \mid \pi;\pi$$

where p ranges over Φ and ψ ranges over $\mathcal{L}_T$. Its truth conditions on the set of internal trust delegation models are defined as follows (we omit $\neg$ and $\wedge$):

$$\begin{array}{lll} \{(M, w), \Theta\} \models p & \textit{iff} & \Theta \models p \\ \{(M, w), \Theta\} \models \psi & \textit{iff} & M, w \models \psi \\ \{(M, w), \Theta\} \models [\pi]\phi & \textit{iff} & \{(M, w), \Theta^\pi\} \models \phi \end{array}$$

Theorem 3. *The semantics of the language $\mathcal{L}$ is completely axiomatized by the following axiom schemes and inference rules:*

L_D	*All axiom schemes and inference rules of* L_D
K_B	$\vdash B_j(\phi \rightarrow \phi') \rightarrow (B_j\phi \rightarrow B_j\phi')$
Red5	$\vdash [\pi]\psi \leftrightarrow \psi$
Nec	*If* $\vdash \phi$ *then* $\vdash B_j\phi$

where ψ *ranges over* $\mathcal{L}_T$ *and* j *over* $\mathbb{AG}$.

More generally, as put forward by Abadi in [2], the use of an (epistemic) modal language permits to specify and reason about authorization in distributed environments by associating policies (i.e., formulae) to agents. For space constraints, we only give some examples of how to express such policies: If the computer science department supports that the university is trusted on (a, o), then the department will trust any other agent trusted by the university on the same access type: $(B_{cs\_dep}t(uni, (a, o)) \rightarrow \bigwedge_{j \in \mathbb{AG}} (B_{uni}t(j, (a, o)) \rightarrow B_{cs\_dep}t(j, (a, o))))$; If j does not trust i then he will not trust any other agent k that delegates a permission to j: $(B_j(\neg t(i, (a, o))) \rightarrow \bigwedge_{k \in \mathbb{AG}} ((k, (a, o), j)^P_+ \rightarrow B_j \neg t(k, (a, o))))$; Whatever is supported by the university is supported by the computer science department too: $(B_{uni}\varphi \rightarrow B_{cs\_dep}\varphi)$, for any φ[4].

Verification. When a verifier i has to check whether an agent j is permitted to perform action a on object o, she does not check for a rooted chain in which all the agents involved are trusted by i. Note that this is an inherently internal perspective which is independent from the external point of view of institutional notions, like authorization and permission. Faced with the same request, two verifiers can react differently depending on which agents they trust.

Definition 16. *In a trust-authorization system represented by* $\{(M, w), \Theta\}$ *a verifier* i *supports that* j *has the privilege for* (a, o) *iff* $\{(M, w), \Theta\} \models \mathcal{DT}_\emptyset(i, j, (a, o))$*, where*

$$\begin{aligned}
&\mathcal{DT}_S(i, j, (a, o)) = B_it(j, (a, o)) \wedge \\
&\quad (\bigvee_{w \notin S} (((w, (a, o), j)^P_+ \wedge \neg(w, (a, o), j)^P_- \wedge soa_{w,o} \\
&\quad \wedge B_it(w, (a, o)) \wedge B_it(j, (a, o))) \vee \\
&\quad ((w, (a, o), j)^P_+ \wedge \neg(w, (a, o), j)^P_- \wedge B_it(w, (a, o)) \wedge B_it(j, (a, o)) \\
&\quad \wedge \mathcal{DT}^{P,D}_{S \cup \{w,j\}}(i, w, (a, o)))
\end{aligned}$$

$$\begin{aligned}
&\mathcal{DT}^{P,D}_S(i, j, (a, o)) = B_it(j, (a, o)) \wedge \\
&\quad (\bigvee_{w \notin S} (((w, (a, o), j)^{P,D}_+ \wedge \neg(w, (a, o), j)^{P,D}_- \wedge soa_{w,o} \\
&\quad \wedge B_it(w, (a, o)) \wedge B_it(j, (a, o))) \vee \\
&\quad ((w, (a, o), j)^{P,D}_+ \wedge \neg(w, (a, o), j)^{P,D}_- \wedge B_it(w, (a, o)) \wedge B_it(j, (a, o)) \wedge \\
&\quad \mathcal{DT}^{P,D}_{S \cup \{w,j\}}(i, w, (a, o)))
\end{aligned}$$

---

[4] This formula has to be intended as an axiom schema, the corresponding canonical property is: $\forall x, y(xR_{cs\_dep}y \rightarrow xR_{uni}y)$.

Delegation. Also delegation schemes can be naturally parameterized in terms of a subjective dimension of trust. For instance, w.r.t. *delegation via transfer* we can define the following programs: - (`if` $(soa_{i,o} \wedge B_i(t(j,o)))$ `then` $+soa_{j,o}$) - (`if` $(soa_{i,o} \wedge B_i(t(j,o)))$ `then` $-soa_{i,o}; +soa_{j,o}$)

Revocation. The schemes in Section 5 can be generalized with the revocation program in Figure 12 whose effects depend on the trust relationships between the revokee and the other agents in the delegation chain. The program generalizes the *weak/strong* and *global/local* dimensions of positive[5] revocation algorithms as presented in Section 5. For instance, in [9] $WGD_{i,j}$ is motivated as "…agent i loses trust in agent j but still trusts other agents to make their own judgement on j". The block $TBR[21 - 25]$ generalizes precisely this case, depending on whether i trusts other agents that are not independent from him, the relative permission may be revoked.

1: $i \xleftarrow{(a,o)}_{P,D} j$;
2: **if** $B_i t(j,(a,o))$ **then**
3:   **for all** $x \in \mathbb{AG}$ **do**
4:     **if** $(x,(a,o),j)^P_+ \wedge \neg\mathcal{CP}_{\{i\}}(x,(a,o)) \wedge B_i \neg t(x,(a,o))$ **then**
5:       $x \xleftarrow{(a,o)}_{P,D} j$;
6:     **end if**
7:     **if** $((j,(a,o),x)^P_+ \wedge \neg\mathcal{CP}_\emptyset(j,(a,o)))$ **then**
8:       $j \xleftarrow{(a,o)}_{P} x$;
9:       **if** $(\neg\mathcal{CP}_\emptyset(x,(a,o)) \wedge B_i t(x,(a,o)))$ **then**
10:         $i \xrightarrow{(a,o)}_{P} x$;
11:       **end if**
12:     **end if**
13:     **if** $((j,(a,o),x)^D_+ \wedge \neg\mathcal{CP}_\emptyset(j,(a,o)))$ **then**
14:       $j \xleftarrow{(a,o)}_{D} x$;
15:       **if** $(\neg\mathcal{CP}_\emptyset(x,(a,o)) \wedge B_i t(x,(a,o)))$ **then**
16:         $i \xrightarrow{(a,o)}_{D} x$;
17:       **end if**
18:     **end if**
19:   **end for**
20: **end if**
21: **if** $B_i \neg t(j,(a,o))$ **then**
22:   **for all** $x \in \mathbb{AG}$ **do**
23:     **if** $((x,(a,o),j)^P_+ \wedge \neg\mathcal{CP}_{\{i\}}(x,(a,o)) \wedge B_i t(x,(a,o))$ **then**
24:       $x \xleftarrow{(a,o)}_{P} j; x \xleftarrow{(a,o)}_{D} j$;
25:     **end if**
26:     **if** $R_\emptyset(x,j,(a,o)) \wedge \neg B_i t(x,(a,o))$ **then**
27:       **for all** $y \in \mathbb{AG}$ **do**
28:         **if** $((y,(a,o),x)^P_+ \wedge \neg\mathcal{CP}_i(y,(a,o)))$ **then**
29:           $y \xleftarrow{(a,o)}_{P} x; y \xleftarrow{(a,o)}_{D} x$;
30:         **end if**
31:       **end for**
32:     **end if**
33:   **end for**
34: **end if**

Fig. 12. Trust Based Revocation Program $TBR_{i,j}$

7 Related Work

As we have stressed throughout our discussion, the delegation-revocation framework described by Hagström *et al.* is the basis for much of what we have described. The Hagström *et al.* work gives a semi-formal account of a range of delegation-revocation schemes, which we have formally represented in the logic language that we have introduced. We have also described an extension that allows for representing and reasoning about the beliefs.

We note that ABLP logic [3] and the RT^D model [12] allow for some restricted forms of delegation policies to be represented, but neither approach accommodates the rich range of delegation *and* revocation schemes that our approach admits. SPKI/SDSI [6] allows for delegation of privileges on objects via authorization certificates. However, the delegation policies that may be represented in the SPKI/SDSI approach are limited to a simple 1-step passing on of privileges

[5] The algorithm can be adapted to work over negative permissions.

on objects; revocation is limited to being typically effected via the expiration of short-lived certificates.

Hoek et al. [14] introduce a logic to reason how the abilities of agents and coalitions of agents are altered by transferring control from one agent to another. They adopt a dynamic propositional language in which atomic programs are of the form "agent i transfers the control of variable p to agent j". Herzig et al. [10] generalize the logic introduced in [14] by relaxing the assumption that at most one agent can control a variable. Nevertheless, delegation is still modelled as transfer and it is not possible to keep track of the delegation chain. In [13], the main focus is on reasoning about the dynamics of how responsibility can be acquired, transferred and discharged; delegation is analyzed in relation to obligations. The approach of accounting for delegation in terms of obligation creation has some merit, but the proposal does not naturally accommodate the very rich delegation-revocation framework that we have described. The work by Demolombe [7] is related to ours in the sense that an epistemic logic is described for reasoning about trust. However, Demolombe does not consider trust in the context of the range of delegation-revocation schemes that we have.

8 Conclusions and Further Work

Recall that the principal research question that we have considered is how to define a formal framework to model and reason about management structures for distributing access privileges in multi-agent systems? On that, we have described a very general framework for modelling and reasoning about delegation and revocation schemes in the context of multi-agent authorization. In particular, we introduced a (dynamic) propositional logic (Section 3) for formulating policies, we demonstrated how a range of delegation schemes (Section 4) and revocation schemes (Section 5) can be treated formally within our logic language. Our logic enables the effects of delegation and revocation actions to be expressed in terms of the changes they make to a delegation graph. The effects of performing delegation and revocation actions are expressible in terms of the "programs" that we have defined. Evidence for the applicability of our formalization is apparent in our demonstration that the eight revocation schemes informally presented in [9] and the delegation types presented in [8] can be represented in our formal framework. We also showed (Section 6) how a notion of trust can be incorporated into an extended form of our delegation-revocation framework. To the best of our knowledge, ours is the first logical framework for distributed authorization that is able to represent the range of delegation-revocation schemes that are described in [9] and [8] and that accommodates an epistemic language for explicitly representing trust relations among agents.

In terms of future work, we plan to extend the epistemic model for trust that we have introduced (Section 6). In distributed authorization, it is often quite reasonable to model trust as a simple relation between predicates (see [16]). However, in MAS things can be more complex. For instance, we may need to admit a transitive model of trust [11] and express policies like "If i believes that j trusts z then i believes that z is trustworthy" (e.g., $B_iB_jt(z,(a,o)) \rightarrow B_it(z,(a,o)))$. In such cases, it is useful to have a modal language to nest belief modalities. The development of such a language is a matter for future work. We also intend to investigate the possibility of further developing our delegation-revocation framework to incorporate a notion of time, e.g., for time-constrained delegation of privileges on objects.

Acknowledgements. Valerio Genovese is supported by the National Research Fund, Luxembourg. The authors thank the reviewers for their comments, which proved to be helpful for improving the clarity of the paper.

References

1. FPDAM on Certificate Extensions. Final Proposed Draft Amendment on Certificate Extensions (V6), Collaborative ITU and ISO/IEC USA (April 1999)
2. Abadi, M.: Logic in access control. In: 18th IEEE Symposium on Logic in Computer Science (LICS), p. 228 (2003)
3. Abadi, M., Burrows, M., Lampson, B., Plotkin, G.: A calculus for access control in distributed systems. ACM Trans. Program. Lang. Syst. 15(4), 706–734 (1993)
4. Aucher, G., Barker, S., Boella, G., Genovese, V., van der Torre, L.: Dynamics in delegation and revocation schemes: a logical approach, technical report (2011), `http://www.di.unito.it/~genovese/publications.html`
5. Boella, G., van der Torre, L.W.N.: Delegation of power in normative multiagent systems. In: Goble, L., Meyer, J.-J.C. (eds.) DEON 2006. LNCS (LNAI), vol. 4048, pp. 36–52. Springer, Heidelberg (2006)
6. Clarke, D.E., Elien, J.-E., Ellison, C.M., Fredette, M., Morcos, A., Rivest, R.L.: Certificate chain discovery in SPKI/SDSI. J. Comp. Sec. 9(4), 285–322 (2001)
7. Demolombe, R.: Reasoning about trust: A formal logical framework. In: Jensen, C., Poslad, S., Dimitrakos, T. (eds.) iTrust 2004. LNCS, vol. 2995, pp. 291–303. Springer, Heidelberg (2004)
8. Firozabadi, B.S., Sergot, M.J., Bandmann, O.L.: Using authority certificates to create management structures. In: Christianson, B., Crispo, B., Malcolm, J.A., Roe, M. (eds.) Security Protocols 2001. LNCS, vol. 2467, pp. 134–145. Springer, Heidelberg (2002)
9. Hagström, Å., Jajodia, S., Parisi-Presicce, F., Wijesekera, D.: Revocations-a classification. In: Procs. of CSFW-14, pp. 44–58 (2001)
10. Herzig, A., Troquard, N.: The dynamic logic of propositional control. In: Procs. of LIS@ESSLLI2010, pp. 107–121 (2010)
11. Kuntze, N., Schmidt, A.U.: Transitive trust in mobile scenarios. In: Müller, G. (ed.) ETRICS 2006. LNCS, vol. 3995, pp. 73–85. Springer, Heidelberg (2006)
12. Li, N., Mitchell, J., Winsborough, W.: Design of a role-based trust-management framework. In: IEEE Symp. on Sec. and Privacy, pp. 114–130 (2002)
13. Norman, T.J., Reed, C.: A logic of delegation. Artif. Intell. 174(1), 51–71 (2010)
14. van der Hoek, W., Walther, D., Wooldridge, M.: Reasoning about the transfer of control. J. Artif. Intell. Res. (JAIR) 37, 437–477 (2010)
15. Weidenbach, C., Dimova, D., Fietzke, A., Kumar, R., Suda, M., Wischnewski, P.: SPASS version 3.5. In: Schmidt, R.A. (ed.) CADE-22. LNCS, vol. 5663, pp. 140–145. Springer, Heidelberg (2009)
16. Wen, W., Mizoguchi, F.: An authorization-based trust model for multiagent systems. Applied Artif. Intell. 14(9), 909–925 (2000)

History-Dependent Inference Control of Queries by Dynamic Policy Adaption*

Joachim Biskup

Technische Universität Dortmund, Dortmund, Germany
joachim.biskup@cs.tu-dortmund.de

Abstract. Policy-based inference control of queries submitted to a logic-oriented information system requires us to consider the history of queries and answers to a particular user. In most previous approaches, the control system captures the history by maintaining a fictitious view the user is supposed to generate by exploiting rational reasoning. In this paper, we propose and explore an alternative option to represent the history, namely by suitably adapting the confidentiality policy after returning an answer to a query. Basically, such a policy adaption precomputes all relevant steps of formal proofs that the fictitious view logically implies some policy element. We focus on propositional information systems.

Keywords: a priori knowledge, closed query, confidentiality policy, Controlled Query Evaluation, inference control, information system, interaction history, policy adaption, propositional logic, refusal, view.

1 Introduction

Inference control is a crucial though costly mechanism to protect *information* rather than just the underlying *data*, as achieved by traditional access control or simple encryption [4]. In general, dynamic *inference control* of *queries* submitted to an *information system* necessarily requires us to consider the *history* of queries and answers related to a particular user. In most of the previous work, including those on Controlled Query Evaluation (CQE) [5], the control employs the user's history in two ways: First, the control generates an (assumption about the) *view* that the user (supposingly) infers to represent his knowledge about the instance of the information system. This instance itself, however, remains hidden to the user, except that he has seen the *previous answers* and might have access to some *a priori knowledge*. Second, the control investigates whether that view combined with the correct answer to the next submitted query (or some closely related information) would be harmful w.r.t. a *confidentiality policy* specifically declared for the user.

In this context the intuitive meaning of *harmful* is the following: the user will be able to infer that some sentence contained in the policy actually holds in the

* This work has been performed within the framework of the Collaborative Research Center "Providing Information by Resource-Constrained Data Analysis", supported by the Deutsche Forschungsgemeinschaft under grant SFB 876/A5.

Y. Li (Ed.): Data and Applications Security and Privacy XXV, LNCS 6818, pp. 106–121, 2011.

instance. If this will be the case, the control reacts with a suitable *distortion* of the correct answer to avoid a security violation. In any case, after returning a reaction to the user, the control has to appropriately adjust the view generated for the user. Thus, over the time, the control enforces a suitable *invariant* to ensure that the view will be never harmful.

Notably, the view is *dynamically* updated after each reaction to a query, whereas the policy is kept unchanged once it has been *statically* declared by a security officer. We can rephrase this approach to dealing with the history as follows: at any point in time, the control has to confine the entailment relationship between the increasingly powerful (knowledgeable) view and the static policy.

We will illustrate this *view-based approach* to inference control by the following simple and straightforward example. Suppose that the policy requests to keep the propositional sentence $\varphi_1 \wedge \varphi_2$ secret. Furthermore, the user is assumed to have no a priori knowledge about the instance, for which both φ_1 and φ_2 are supposed to hold, and thus $\varphi_1 \wedge \varphi_2$ as well. Initially, the control generates an empty view. Then, as a first query, the user submits the sentence φ_1 in order to ask whether this sentence holds. The correct answer, φ_1, i.e., that this sentence holds, together with the empty view does not entail the single policy element, and thus the control returns the correct answer to the user in undistorted form and, accordingly, updates the view, which now comprises just the returned answer φ_1. Finally, as a second query, the user submits φ_2. Now, the correct answer, φ_2, together with the content of the updated view, φ_1, obviously entails the policy element, $\varphi_1 \wedge \varphi_2$, and thus the control must suitably distort the answer. Note the dynamic "last-minute behavior" of the control: if the queries were submitted in reverse order, first φ_2 and then φ_1, then φ_2 would have been correctly answered and the answer to φ_1 would have been distorted.

In this work, we will explore an alternative approach to employ the user's history. The alternative approach aims to represent the user's history by *dynamically adapting the policy*, thereby getting rid of the need to generate and maintain a view for the user. Intuitively, over the time, we will increasingly strengthen the policy, making it more and more restrictive as a countermeasure to the knowledge accumulated by previous answers.

To illustrate this alternative *policy-adaption based approach*, we reconsider the example presented above. Initially, the policy contains the sentence $\varphi_1 \wedge \varphi_2$. Since the first query, φ_1, is harmless, the correct answer is returned to the user. Now, once one of the conjuncts occurring in the original policy element is known to the user, he must not learn the other conjunct as well. Accordingly, the control replaces the previous policy element $\varphi_1 \wedge \varphi_2$ by φ_2 to be kept secret in future. If afterwards the second query, φ_2, is submitted, the control will immediately detect that the correct answer would violate the adapted policy and thus will distort the answer, as in the view-based approach.

We can also describe the policy-adaption based approach in terms of *theorem-proving*, as sketched in the following and elaborated in more detail in the remainder of this paper. In the starting step, for each sentence contained in the declared policy and thus explicitly wanted to be kept secret to the user while returning answers to him, the user is supposed to aim at proving (the validity of) that sentence from the answers received. Acccordingly, for simplicity here assuming no a priori knowledge, the user initially considers every sentence contained in the declared policy to be a *current proof obligation*. Having received a new answer Φ_i in step i, the user can analyze all possible formal proofs for any of the current proof obligations whether and how Φ_i will be helpful to prove it. If the user detects such a situation, he can determine the resulting remaining proof obligations and, potentially, try to satisfy them by issuing further queries. Correspondingly, inference control can track the user's abilities, and thus control can dynamically adapt the policy by always setting it to the current set of proof obligations. In the example given above, the sole initial proof obligation is $\varphi_1 \wedge \varphi_2$, which can be replaced by the new proof obligation φ_2, once φ_1 is known.

Dynamic inference control is costly, at least in general, due to the inevitable need to suitably keeping track of the history and performing some kind of theorem-proving. The basic features of policy adaption suggest the possibility of substantial improvements in computational costs *at query time* in comparison with the view-based approach, at least in special situations: (1) the control no longer has to maintain a separate data structure for reflecting the user's view, and (2) analyzing and remembering remaining proof obligations can bee seen as a kind of stored *precomputation* for the task of checking whether subsequent queries are harmful or not. Moreover, we might be able to find appropriate *data structures* to actually benefit from the potentials.

In the following we roughly outline such an improvement for a restricted *propositional* situation, where *queries* are just propositional *atoms* of the form a_i and elements of the *confidentiality policy* are *conjunctions* of such atoms, thus of the form $a_{i_1} \wedge \ldots \wedge a_{i_k}$ with $1 \leq k$. Moreover, we will make policies *redundancy-free* in the sense that no policy element is a subconjunction of another policy element, just by discarding the larger one. As an example, let the policy be $\{a_1 \wedge a_2 \wedge a_3, a_3 \wedge a_4, a_4 \wedge a_5, a_6\}$, and consider the query sequence $\langle a_1, a_2 \rangle$.

The current policy will be represented by a data structure that is composed of two linked parts. The "look-up part" contains all *atoms* still occurring in the policy, and the "reduced part" comprises the *nontrivial conjunctions* (having at least 2 different atoms) still to be checked. Moreover, each atom in the former part is linked to each of the conjunctions in which it occurs in the latter part. Fig. 1 shows the initial state of the data structure for the example.

If an atom a_i is submitted as a query, the control first searches for that atom in the look-up part. If the atom is not found there, the query is censored to be *harmless* and correctly answered. Otherwise, there are two cases: If the atom is not linked to any nontrivial conjunction, then the atom is *harmful* by itself and the answer must be distorted. Otherwise, if there are links, the query is censored to be *harmless* and correctly answered, but the policy must be adapted by manipulating the current state of the data structure appropriately: (1) the query atom a_i is removed from the look-up part; (2) the query atom a_i is deleted from all the conjunctions in which it occurs; (3) if after the deletion a remaining

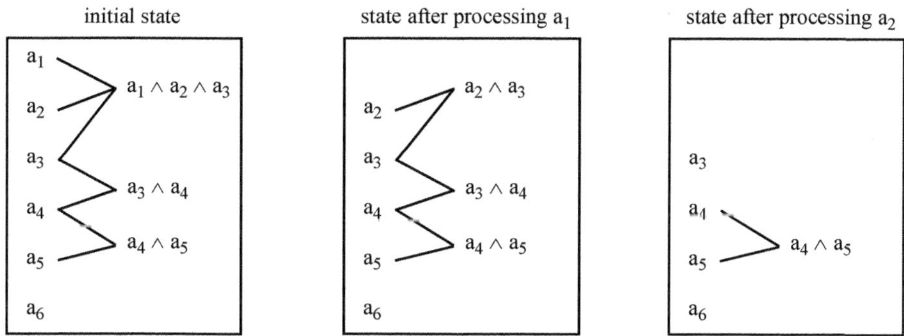

Fig. 1. Initial and subsequent states of a data structure for dynamic policy adaption

conjunction is reduced to a single atom a_j, then the conjunction is dropped at all and the corresponding link from a_j is deleted as well; moreover, all other conjunctions in which a_j occurs are deleted with all their links, too. Finally, if – by these deletions – another atom in the look-up part has lost all its links, then that atom is deleted from the look-up part.

Fig. 1 visualizes how the control operates for the parameters specified above. Querying the atom a_1 is harmless and leads to its removal from the look-up part by (1) and its deletion from the first conjunction, which is thus reduced to $a_2 \wedge a_3$ by (2). Then querying the atom a_2 is harmless again and leads to its removal from the look-up part by (1) and its deletion from the reduced conjunction, which thus becomes the single atom a_3 by (2); but this trivial conjunction is then totally dropped by (3), and the conjunction $a_3 \wedge a_4$ is deleted as well.

Since only some searching and elementary link manipulations are used, the *efficiency* of the procedure should be evident. A full justification of the *correctness* is elaborated in Sect. 3 for a more general situation. Roughly summarizing, in this article we will provide the following main contributions:

- We propose the policy-adaption based approach to keeping track of the history as a promising alternative to the view-based approach (this Sect. 1).
- After introducing our basic notations, briefly reviewing the view-based approach and commenting on complexity issues (Sect. 2), we fully elaborate the new approach for a special but reasonably expressive situation of Controlled Query Evaluation. This situation employs refusal as the sole distortion option and deals with a propositional information system (Sect. 3).
- We relate our approach to previous work, briefly discuss first-order information systems and evaluate the expected potentials and limitations (Sect. 4).

2 Basic Notations and View-Based Approach

Restricting to propositional information systems, we first introduce our basic notations. Then we briefly describe the view-based approach and state some observations on the complexity of deciding the pertinent logical implications.

2.1 Basic Notations

We employ a logic-oriented approach to information systems (see, e.g., [1]), which establishes formal semantics for both query answering and updating (not considered in this paper). For simplicity, we only consider *complete* information systems, and we focus on *propositional logic.* We assume a vocabulary of propositional *atoms*, from which we can construct propositional *sentences* in the standard way, using the propositional connectives of *negation* and *disjunction* and further derived connectives. A *literal* is either an atom or a negated atom.

The *schema* (of the information system) is given by the vocabulary and the *integrity constraints*, which are expressed as a finite set *con* of sentences over this vocabulary. We consider the integrity constraints as part of any user's a priori knowledge, which in each case is given as a set of sentences over the vocabulary.

An *instance db* (of the information system) is a set of literals formed as follows: For each atom α of the vocabulary, either the atom α itself or the negated atom $\neg\alpha$ is an element. Given the vocabulary, it suffices to explicitly specify only those atoms that are contained in an instance (implicitly assuming for the remaining atoms that their negations are elements by default, as a kind of closed world assumption). An instance *db* defines a *truth-value assignment* to propositional atoms by making each atom $\alpha \in db$ *true* and all the remaining atoms *false.* Such a truth-value assignment (interpretation) is inductively extended to arbitrary sentences Φ by giving the connectives the standard meaning; $eval(\Phi)(db)$ denotes the truth value assigned to Φ by *db*. The standard notion of logical *implication*, or *entailment*, between (sets of) sentences is designated by $\models$.

As a (closed, yes/no-) *query*, we allow any sentence Φ of the underlying propositional logic. The *correct answer* to the query Φ under an instance *db* is given by the pertinent truth value $eval(\Phi)(db)$; however, for convenience, we alternatively express the correct answer by $eval^*(\Phi)(db)$ that denotes either Φ or $\neg\Phi$ in a straightforward way. We aim at controlling any sequence of queries $Q := \langle\, \Phi_1, \Phi_2, \ldots, \Phi_i, \ldots, \Phi_k \,\rangle$ where the query Φ_i is submitted by some user at the point in time i; for simplicity of the presentation, we focus on only one user.

While the user is granted a general access right for reading (querying), a security officer declares a *confidentiality policy* as a finite set *psec* of propositional sentences, called *potential secrets*, in order to confine the actual information gain that can be achieved by the user. Here the qualification "potential" indicates that these sentences are not necessarily true in the actual instance. Following the principle of open design, the user is supposed to be *aware* of this declaration, as well as of all other features of the control mechanism. In order to prevent the user from ever inferring that any sentence $\Psi \in psec$ actually holds, we follow the *refusal* approach to inference control [11,6,5], i.e., if an informative answer to a query would be harmful, then the control reacts by returning a special symbol `mum`. In general, the refusal approach has to examine not only whether the correct answer to a query is harmful but also whether its negation would be harmful, in order to prevent so-called meta-inferences.

Besides the policy, in general the control mechanism also has to consider the (postulated) *a priori knowledge* of the user and the *answers* to previously issued queries. To do so, the control might maintain a *user log*. Basically, such a user log then just contains a set *log* of propositional sentences. In principle, both the policy and the user log might be updated while processing queries; the current versions of them taken together form the current *state* $s_i := (psec_i, log_i)$ of the control mechanism. The *initial state* is obtained by setting $psec_0 := psec$ and $log_0 := prior$, where *prior* can be any suitable superset of the constraints *con* not being in conflict with *psec*, i.e., $prior \not\models \Psi$ for all $\Psi \in psec$. In this work, for simplicity, we will not elaborate the treatment of the a priori knowledge *prior* in depth: we just leave it empty in our examples, and we simply process it like a sequence of queries within our initialization subprotocol.

Definition 1 (controlled query evaluation). *Let be given an instance db, a finite set log_{i-1} of sentences (for explicitly reflecting the assumed user's current knowledge about the instance), and a finite set $psec_{i-1}$ of sentences (for representing the current version of the confidentiality policy). Then a function $cqe(db, psec_{i-1}, log_{i-1}, \Phi_i)$ defines a* controlled query evaluation *of a query Φ_i by generating a triple $(ans_i, psec_i, log_i)$, where ans_i is the answer returned to the user, and $psec_i$ and log_i together form the updated state.*

Furthermore, for the initializations specified above, this function is inductively extended to any query sequence $Q := \langle\, \Phi_1, \ldots, \Phi_i, \ldots, \Phi_k \,\rangle$ by applying it stepwise in a straightforward way:

$$\begin{aligned} &cqe(db, psec_0, log_0, Q) := \\ &\big\langle (ans_1, psec_1, log_1), \ldots, (ans_i, psec_i, log_i), \ldots, (ans_k, psec_k, , log_k) \big\rangle \end{aligned} \tag{1}$$

We are now ready to present our formal definition of the confidentiality requirement we want to achieve by a controlled query evaluation. Roughly summarized, given a potential secret Ψ declared in the (original) policy *psec*, this requirement is expressed in terms of the *indistinguishability* – from the point of view of the user – of the actual instance *db* from an alternative instance db^s that does not satisfy the potential secret considered.

Definition 2 (confidentiality). *A controlled query evaluation cqe* preserves confidentiality *iff*
for all instances db,
for all finite sets of sentences psec (original confidentiality policy),
for all finite sets of sentences prior (a priori knowledge)
satisfied by db and such that $prior \not\models \Psi$ for all $\Psi \in psec$,
for all query sequences Q, and
for all potential secrets $\Psi \in psec$
there exists an alternative instance db^s satisfying prior such that:

1. [indistinguishability]*:*

$$cqe(db, psec, prior, Q) = cqe(db^s, psec, prior, Q) \tag{2}$$

2. [possibility of false potential secrets]*:*

$$eval^*(\Psi)(db^s) = \neg\Psi \tag{3}$$

2.2 View-Based Approach

The view-based approach to Controlled Query Evaluation, as surveyed in [5], keeps track of the history by only updating the user log, while leaving the original policy unchanged. For the specific setting described above, i.e., refusal under known potential secrets for a propositional information system dealing with closed (yes/no-)queries, the function cqe^{view} is defined by its outputs as follows:

$$\begin{aligned} ans_i \quad &:= \texttt{if } log_{i-1} \models eval^*(\Phi_i)(db) \texttt{ then } eval^*(\Phi_i)(db) \texttt{ else} \\ &\quad \texttt{if } (\text{exists } \Psi)(\Psi \in psec \text{ and} \\ &\qquad (log_{i-1} \cup \{\Phi_i\} \models \Psi \text{ or } log_{i-1} \cup \{\neg\Phi_i\} \models \Psi)) \\ &\quad \texttt{then mum else } eval^*(\Phi_i)(db) \end{aligned} \tag{4}$$

$$psec_i \quad := psec \tag{5}$$

$$log_i \quad := \texttt{if } ans_i = \texttt{mum then } log_{i-1} \texttt{ else } log_{i-1} \cup \{ans_i\} \tag{6}$$

Proposition 1 ([6]). *The function cqe^{view} preserves confidentiality in the sense of Def. 2.*

Definition (4) of the controlled answer indicates that the task of inference control is closely related to the problem of deciding on logical implications of the form $\chi \models \Psi$, where the finite set of sentences χ – equivalently identified with the corresponding sentence formed as the conjunction over this set – denotes some potential knowledge of the user and Ψ is a policy element. This decision problem is well-known to be of high computational complexity in general, and thus we can expect to control answers efficiently only under some restrictions of the expressiveness of the languages for the sentences χ and Ψ, respectively.

As a starting point, we first observe the following: If both χ and Ψ are already specified in *disjunctive normal form* for a finite vocabulary, i.e., as a disjunction of so-called *minterms* that are built as a conjunction of literals (atoms or negated atoms) ranging over all atoms in the vocabulary, then $\chi \models \Psi$ holds if and only if each minterm of χ is also a minterm of Ψ.

For a slightly relaxed situation where both χ and Ψ are specified as a *disjunctive form*, i.e., a disjunction of conjunctions of literals ranging over different atoms in the vocabulary, the sufficiency part of this observation can be generalized along the following lines of reasoning, often referred to as subsumption. First, if some disjunctive sentences η_1 and η_2 are (syntactically) related such that each disjunct of η_1 is also a disjunct of η_2 – or at least (semantically) implies some disjunct of η_2 –, then the (semantic) implication $\eta_1 \models \eta_2$ holds, since η_2 is an obvious weakening of η_1. Dually, if some conjunctive sentences θ_1 and θ_2 are (syntactically) related such that each conjunct of θ_1 is also a conjunct of θ_2 – or is at least (semantically) implied by some conjunct of θ_2 –, then the (semantic) implication $\theta_2 \models \theta_1$ holds, since θ_2 is an obvious strengthening of θ_1.

Unfortunately, the necessity part of the observation stated above cannot be generalized for arbitrary disjunctive forms. However, the necessity part holds indeed, if the sentence Ψ consists of *all* the *prime implicants* of Ψ, i.e., (1) each disjunct of Ψ is *minimal* in the sense that discarding any of the literals in the conjunction that constitutes this disjunct would result in a non-equivalent sentence, and (2) Ψ contains all minimal disjuncts (conjunctions of literals ranging over different atoms in the vocabulary) that imply Ψ.

Proposition 2. *Let χ be a disjunctive form and Ψ a disjunctive form that consists of all its prime implicants. Then $\chi \models \Psi$ holds if and only if for each disjunct of χ there is a disjunct of Ψ such that each literal occurring as a conjunct of the latter disjunct also appears as a conjunct of the former disjunct.*

3 Policy Adaption for Propositional Information Systems

We now present our new concept of the policy-adaption based approach in detail, exhibit an appropriate data structure for representing the current policy, and then demonstrate the correctness and comment on the efficiency.

3.1 Outline and Examples

To elaborate the policy-adaption based approach, we aim at defining the corresponding function cqe^{pol} for controlled query evaluation such that the following properties (further explained below) hold:

1. The parameter *log* could be dropped.
2. The history is reflected in the current version $psec_i$ of the policy.
3. The generated outputs ans_i are the same as for cqe^{view}.
4. The current version $psec_i$ is converted to be redundancy-free (see below).
5. The current version $psec_i$ is converted to be fully vulnerable (see below).

We first outline the basic techniques to achieve these properties, then exemplify these techniques, and finally present and verify a comprehensive algorithm for cqe^{pol} leading to a controlled query evaluation based on these techniques.

By property 3 and as a corollary to the result for cqe^{view} stated in Prop. 1, the function cqe^{pol} will preserve confidentiality in the sense of Def. 2 as well.

Regarding property 4, demanding the policy to be *redundancy-free*, we can observe the following by inspecting the guarding condition in the second line and the third line of (4): If a policy *psec* contains two different potential secrets Ψ_1 and Ψ_2 such that $\Psi_1 \models \Psi_2$, then we can remove Ψ_1 from the policy without affecting the answer. For, if a user knowledge $log \cup \{\Phi\}$ or $log \cup \{\neg\Phi\}$, respectively, implies Ψ_1, then that knowledge also implies Ψ_2; thus the outcome of the guarding condition remains the same after removing Ψ_1. Accordingly, we will keep the set *psec* redundancy-free in the sense that none of its elements implies another one.

Regarding property 5, demanding the policy to be *fully vulnerable*, we further observe the following: If a policy *psec* contains a potential secret Ψ such that $log \models \neg\Psi$ holds for the current user knowledge *log*, then we can remove Ψ from the policy. For, by monotonicity, this property will always be preserved later on and thus the confidentiality requirement expressed by Ψ will never be hurt.

Regarding the properties 2 and 3, which demand an *appropriate reflection of the history* in $psec_i$ such that the same outputs are generated as in the view-based approach, again by inspecting the guarding condition in the second line and the third line of (4), we have to inductively achieve an equivalence of the following kind (to be made more precise later on), where Δ_i denotes the query Φ_i or its negation $\neg\Phi_i$, respectively:

$$(\text{exists } \Psi)(\Psi \in psec \text{ and } log_{i-1} \cup \{\Delta_i\} \models \Psi) \text{ iff} \quad (7)$$

$$(\text{exists } \Psi)(\Psi \in psec_{i-1} \text{ and } \{\Delta_i\} \models \Psi) \quad (8)$$

To attain such a goal, we first impose all queries Φ_i and all policy elements Ψ to be given as a disjunctive form. Moreover, we additionally extend each policy element such that it contains all its prime implicants in order to profit from the efficiently verifiable characteristic property of $\chi \models \Psi$ given in Prop. 2.

Next, again for easily exploiting that property, in general we aim at representing a policy element of the form $\Psi = \Psi_1 \vee \ldots \vee \Psi_m$ that constitutes a nontrivial disjunction with $2 \leq m$ as the *set* of its disjuncts $\{\Psi_1, \ldots, \Psi_m\}$. To achieve a homogeneous treatment with a policy element of the form $\Psi = \Psi_1$ having only one disjunct, we then have to represent such an element as the singleton set $\{\Psi_1\}$. The set representations introduced will not affect the wanted equivalence, since they are functional equivalent with the original forms. If there are no semantic ambiguities, i.e., from a special context under consideration it is clear whether two disjuncts (implicants) belong to the same policy element or not, as in the examples below, we will omit the set notation for the sake of readibility.

Finally, to deal with disjunctive answers of the form $\Phi = \Phi_1 \vee \ldots \vee \Phi_n$ with $2 \leq n$, we will introduce *policy branches*: for each disjunct Φ_l, a copy of the current policy is generated and then inspected regarding implications that result from Φ_l alone. Subsequently, each of these branches has to be maintained with reference to the pertinent Φ_l until a definite answer that $\neg\Phi_l$ holds is given; then the branch is obviously contradictory and thus must be removed.

Example 1. Consider the following situation:
$db := \{a_1, \neg a_2, \neg a_3, a_4\}$ is the instance,
$Q := \langle\ a_1, a_2, a_3, a_4\ \rangle$ is the query sequence,
$psec := \{\neg a_1 \wedge \neg a_2 \wedge a_3 \wedge \neg a_4, a_1 \wedge \neg a_2 \wedge \neg a_3 \wedge a_4\}$ is the policy, and
$log_0 := \emptyset$ is the void a priori knowledge.

Then $\langle\ a_1, \neg a_2, \neg a_3, a_4\ \rangle$ is the correct answer sequence, and the instance defines the first potential secret to be *false* and the second one to be *true*.

Controlling the first query a_1, we see that neither a_1 nor $\neg a_1$ implies any of the potential secrets, and thus the correct answer a_1 can be returned, and it would be inserted into the user log by the view-based approach such that we would have $log_1 := \{a_1\}$. Since the first potential secret is no longer vulnerable, we can remove it from the policy. Furthermore, once the user knows a_1, we now have to protect the remainder of the second potential secret, i.e., we can drop a_1 from $a_1 \wedge \neg a_2 \wedge \neg a_3 \wedge a_4$. Thus we get
$psec_1 := \{\neg a_2 \wedge \neg a_3 \wedge a_4\}$.

Description and Branch	**Disjuncts (given prime implicants)**	**Disjuncts (additional prime implicants)**
sole element (original)	$a_1 \land \neg a_3 \land \neg a_4$ $a_1 \land \neg a_2 \land a_4$ $a_2 \land a_3 \land a_4$ $\neg a_1 \land a_2 \land \neg a_3$	$a_2 \land \neg a_3 \land \neg a_4$ $a_1 \land \neg a_2 \land \neg a_3$ $a_1 \land a_3 \land a_4$ $\neg a_1 \land a_2 \land a_4$
sole element (after answer a_1)	$\neg a_3 \land \neg a_4$ $\neg a_2 \land a_4$ $a_2 \land a_3 \land a_4$ (complementary)	$a_2 \land \neg a_3 \land \neg a_4$ $\neg a_2 \land \neg a_3$ $a_3 \land a_4$ (complementary)
sole element (after answer a_1 and subsumption)	$\neg a_3 \land \neg a_4$ $\neg a_2 \land a_4$ (subsumed) (complementary)	(subsumed) $\neg a_2 \land \neg a_3$ $a_3 \land a_4$ (complementary)
sole element (after answers a_1, $\neg a_2 \lor a_3$) for branch $\{\neg a_2\}$	$\neg a_3 \land \neg a_4$ a_4 (subsumed) (complementary)	(subsumed) $\neg a_3$ $a_3 \land a_4$ (complementary)
sole element (after answers a_1, $\neg a_2 \lor a_3$) for branch $\{a_3\}$	(complementary) $\neg a_2 \land a_4$ (subsumed) (complementary)	(subsumed) (complementary) a_4 (complementary)
sole element (after answers a_1, $\neg a_2 \lor a_3$ and subsumption) for branch $\{\neg a_2\}$	(subsumed) a_4 (subsumed) (complementary)	(subsumed) $\neg a_3$ (subsumed) (complementary)
sole element (after answers a_1, $\neg a_2 \lor a_3$ and subsumption) for branch $\{a_3\}$	(complementary) (subsumed) (subsumed) (complementary)	(subsumed) (complementary) a_4 (complementary)

Fig. 2. A converted and then stepwise adapted confidentiality policy

Similarly, stepwise controlling the second query a_2 and the third query a_3, we (would) get the following:

$log_2 := \{a_1, \neg a_2\}$, $\quad psec_2 := \{\neg a_3 \land a_4\}$,

$log_3 := \{a_1, \neg a_2, \neg a_3\}$, $\quad psec_3 := \{a_4\}$.

Finally, controlling the fourth query a_4, we immediately see that the correct answer violates the policy, and thus the answer must be refused. Notably, if the correct answer was $\neg a_4$, then that answer would have to be refused as well.

Example 2. Consider the following situation, the processing of which is further illustrated in Fig. 2:

$db := \{a_1, \neg a_2, \neg a_3, a_4\}$ is the instance, the same as before,

$Q := \langle\, a_1, \neg a_2 \lor a_3, a_3, a_4 \,\rangle$ is the query sequence,

$psec := \{\, a_1 \land \neg a_3 \land \neg a_4 \;\lor\; a_1 \land \neg a_2 \land a_4 \;\lor\; a_1 \land a_2 \land a_3 \land a_4$
$\lor\; \neg a_1 \land a_2 \land a_3 \land a_4 \;\lor\; \neg a_1 \land a_2 \land \neg a_3 \,\}$ is the policy, and

$log_0 := \emptyset$ is the void a priori knowledge.

Obviously, then $\langle\, a_1, \neg a_2 \lor a_3, \neg a_3, a_4 \,\rangle$ is the correct answer sequence, and the instance defines the sole potential secret to be *true*.

At initialization time, we observe that the sole policy element can be equivalently simplified by combining the two disjuncts $a_1 \wedge a_2 \wedge a_3 \wedge a_4$ and $\neg a_1 \wedge a_2 \wedge a_3 \wedge a_4$ into the prime implicant $a_2 \wedge a_3 \wedge a_4$. Furthermore, even afterwards the policy element does not contain all its prime implicants; in fact, we have to add four further prime implicants, namely
$a_2 \wedge \neg a_3 \wedge \neg a_4$, $a_1 \wedge \neg a_2 \wedge \neg a_3$, $a_1 \wedge a_3 \wedge a_4$, and $\neg a_1 \wedge a_2 \wedge a_4$.
Subsequently, we replace the sole policy element by the set of its disjuncts (prime implicants) and get the following representation of the policy:

$$psec_0 := \{a_1 \wedge \neg a_3 \wedge \neg a_4,\ \ a_1 \wedge \neg a_2 \wedge a_4,\ \ a_2 \wedge a_3 \wedge a_4,\ \ \neg a_1 \wedge a_2 \wedge \neg a_3,\ \ a_2 \wedge \neg a_3 \wedge \neg a_4,\ \ a_1 \wedge \neg a_2 \wedge \neg a_3,\ \ a_1 \wedge a_3 \wedge a_4,\ \ \neg a_1 \wedge a_2 \wedge a_4\}.$$

Controlling the first query a_1, we see that neither a_1 nor $\neg a_1$ implies any of the potential secrets, and thus the correct answer a_1 can be returned. Since the policy elements containing the complementary literal $\neg a_1$ are no longer vulnerable, we can remove them from the policy. Furthermore, once the user knows a_1, we can drop a_1 from the remaining elements. Additionally, we can remove elements that have become redundant, which is equivalent to being subsumed by a shorter disjunct. Altogether we get

$$psec_1 := \{\neg a_3 \wedge \neg a_4,\ \neg a_2 \wedge a_4,\ \neg a_2 \wedge \neg a_3,\ a_3 \wedge a_4\}.$$

Controlling the second query $\neg a_2 \vee a_3$, we see again that neither the positive answer $\neg a_2 \vee a_3$ nor the negative answer $a_2 \wedge \neg a_3$ implies any of the potential secrets, and thus the correct answer can be returned. However, since the correct answer is a disjunction, we split the policy into branches, one for the case that $\neg a_2$ is actually *true* and another one for the case that a_3 is actually *true*.

In the branch for $\neg a_2$, we can drop the occurrences of $\neg a_2$ from two of the elements, yielding the reduced elements a_4 and $\neg a_3$. As there are no occurrences of the complementary literal a_2, all elements are still vulnerable. Additionally, however, we can remove the then subsumed elements $\neg a_3 \wedge \neg a_4$ and $a_3 \wedge a_4$. Thus we get

$$psec_2[\neg a_2] := \{a_4, \neg a_3\}.$$

In the branch for a_3, we can drop the occurrence of a_3 from one of the elements, yielding the reduced element a_4, and we can remove the elements $\neg a_3 \wedge \neg a_4$ and $\neg a_2 \wedge \neg a_3$, in which the complementary literal $\neg a_3$ occurs. Additionally, the element $\neg a_2 \wedge a_4$ is now subsumed and thus can be removed. Thus we get

$$psec_2[a_3] := \{a_4\}.$$

Controlling the third query a_3, we see that the correct answer $\neg a_3$ makes the policy branch for a_3 contradictory and implies an element in the remaining branch for $\neg a_2$. Accordingly, the answer must be refused and both policy branches remain unchanged. Finally, controlling the fourth query a_4, we see that the correct answer a_4 implies a policy element in both branches, and thus the answer must be refused as well.

3.2 Protocol for Policy Adaption and Correctness

Having introduced the basic techniques, we are now ready to specify the types, inputs and methods of our new approach of policy adaption more formally.

Protocol for Policy Adaption.
types.

$\mathscr{L}$ propositional sentences;
$\mathscr{L}_{\mathrm{df}} \subseteq \mathscr{L}$ propositional sentences in disjunctive form;
$\mathscr{L}_{\mathrm{pi}} \subseteq \mathscr{L}_{\mathrm{df}}$ propositional sentences that consist of all their prime implicants;
$\mathscr{L}_{\mathrm{li}} \subseteq \mathscr{L}_{\mathrm{pi}}$ literals;
$\mathscr{L}_{\mathrm{im}} \subseteq \mathscr{L}_{\mathrm{df}}$ implicants (conjunctions of literals over distinct atoms);
$\mathscr{C} \subseteq_{\mathit{finite}} \wp\mathscr{L}$ declared confidentiality policies;
$\mathscr{M} \subseteq_{\mathit{finite}} \wp\wp\mathscr{L}_{\mathrm{im}}$ converted confidentiality policies as multisets of "identified policy elements";
$\mathscr{B} \subseteq_{\mathit{finite}} \mathscr{M} \times \wp\mathscr{L}_{\mathrm{li}}$ policy branches; //written as $imsets[liset]$;
$\mathscr{Q} \subseteq \mathscr{L}$ queries.

subprotocol: initialization.
input: $psec : \mathscr{C}$;
$prior : \wp\mathscr{L}$;
method:

1. $sec_\emptyset := psec$;
2. modify $sec_\emptyset$ as follows:
   foreach $\Psi \in sec_\emptyset$ **do**
   convert Ψ such that it becomes the disjunction of all its prime implicants;
   foreach $\Psi \in sec_\emptyset$ **do**
   replace Ψ having form $\Psi_1 \vee \ldots \vee \Psi_m$ by the representing set $\{\Psi_1, \ldots, \Psi_m\}_\Psi$;
3. $psecb_0 := \{sec_\emptyset[\emptyset]\}$; // only one policy branch of form $\{\{\ldots\}, \ldots, \{\ldots\}\}[\emptyset]$
4. process $prior$ like a sequence of queries. //not elaborated for lack of space

subprotocol: generation (of answer and policy).
input: $\Phi_i : \mathscr{L}$;
$psecb_{i-1} : \mathscr{B}$;
method:

1. convert Φ_i into disjunctive form $\Phi_{i,1} \vee \ldots \vee \Phi_{i,n}$;
2. $ans_i :=$ **if** Φ_i violates $psecb_{i-1}$ **or** $\neg\Phi_i$ violates $psecb_{i-1}$
   then mum
   else $eval^*(\Phi_i)(db)$;
3. **if** $ans_i = \Phi_i$ (let $\Phi_i = \Phi_{i,1} \vee \ldots \vee \Phi_{i,n}$)
   then $psecb_i := \emptyset$;
   foreach disjunct $\Phi_{i,j}$ of Φ_i **do**
   $lit_j := \{\varphi \mid \varphi \text{ occurs in } \Phi_{i,j}\}$;
   $copy_j := \{sec[D \cup lit_j] \mid sec[D] \in psecb_{i-1}\}$;
   foreach literal φ of $\Phi_{i,j}$ **do** perform policy adaption for φ and $copy_j$;
   $psecb_i := psecb_i \cup copy_j$

   elseif $ans_i = \neg\Phi_i$ (let $\neg\Phi_i = \neg\Phi_{i,1} \wedge \ldots \wedge \neg\Phi_{i,n}$)
   then $psecb_i := psecb_{i-1}$;
   foreach conjunct $\neg\Phi_{i,j}$ of $\neg\Phi_i$ (let $\neg\Phi_{i,j} = \varphi_1 \vee \ldots \vee \varphi_k$) **do**
   $copy := \emptyset$;
   foreach literal φ_l of $\neg\Phi_{i,j}$ **do**
   $copy_l := \{sec[D \cup \{\varphi_l\}] \mid sec[D] \in psecb_i\}$;
   perform policy adaption for φ_l and $copy_l$;
   $copy := copy \cup copy_l$;
   $psecb_i := copy$.

subprotocol: violation (test).
input: $\Phi : \mathscr{L}$;
$psecb : \mathscr{B}$;
method:
convert Φ into disjunctive form;
//nothing to do if $\Phi = \Phi_i$, i.e., violation test is performed for current query
`if` there exists a branch $sec[D]$ of policy $psecb$ and
there exists a disjunct Φ_j of (negated) query Φ
such that $\Phi_j \wedge \bigwedge_{\varphi \in D} \varphi$ is not contradictory
//guaranteed if $\Phi = eval^*(\Phi_i)(db)$
`and`
there exists $\{\ldots\}_{\tilde{\Psi}} \in sec_\emptyset$ such that // $\tilde{\Psi}$ "uniformly identifies" a policy element
for all branches $sec[D]$ of policy $psecb$ and
for all disjuncts Φ_j of (negated) query Φ
such that $\Phi_j \wedge \bigwedge_{\varphi \in D} \varphi$ is not contradictory
there exists a disjunct $\tilde{\Psi}_r \in \{\ldots\}_{\tilde{\Psi}} \in sec$ such that $\Phi_j \models \tilde{\Psi}_r$ (by subsumption)
`then` return *true* (violation)
`else` return *false* (no violation).

subprotocol: adaption (for literal and policy copy).
input: $\varphi : \mathscr{L}_{\mathrm{li}}$;
`var` *copy* : $\mathscr{B}$; // *copy* is used as input-and-output parameter
method: // modify *copy* as follows
`foreach` policy branch $sec_j[D_j] \in copy$ `do`
1. `if` $\neg\varphi \in D_j$
`then` delete branch $sec_j[D_j]$
`else foreach` $\{\chi_1, \ldots, \chi_r\}_\Psi \in sec_j$ `do`
`foreach` $\chi \in \{\chi_1, \ldots, \chi_r\}_\Psi$ `do`
`if` φ occurs in χ `then` drop φ from χ;
`if` $\neg\varphi$ occurs in χ `then` remove χ from $\{\chi_1, \ldots, \chi_r\}_\Psi$;
`foreach` distinct $\chi_1, \chi_2 \in \{\chi_1, \ldots, \chi_r\}_\Psi$ `do`
`if` $\chi_1 \models \chi_2$ (by subsumption) `then` remove χ_1 from $\{\chi_1, \ldots, \chi_r\}_\Psi$;
2. `foreach` $\{\chi_1, \ldots, \chi_r\}_\Psi, \{\bar{\chi}_1, \ldots, \bar{\chi}_{\bar{r}}\}_{\bar{\Psi}} \in sec_j$ with $\Psi \neq \bar{\Psi}$ `do`
`if` $\chi_1 \vee \ldots \vee \chi_r \models \bar{\chi}_1 \vee \ldots \vee \bar{\chi}_{\bar{r}}$
`then` replace $\{\chi_1, \ldots, \chi_r\}_\Psi$ by $\emptyset_\Psi$ // consider $\emptyset_\Psi$ as removed.

As explained in Sect. 3.1, the protocol for policy adaption has been designed to achieve the same effects as the view-based approach. Thus the protocol is claimed to be *correct* with respect to the view-based approach and, accordingly by Prop. 1, to *preserve confidentiality.* The latter claim is stated in the following theorem, the proof of which justifies the former claim.

Theorem 1. *The function cqe^{pol} as defined by the Protocol for Policy Adaption preserves confidentiality in the sense of Def. 2.*

Proof. For lack of space, we only outline the inductive proof, which follows the informal arguments presented in Sect. 3.1. Basically, the induction will deal with the following items and notations:

- $hist_{i-1} := \bigvee_k \bigwedge_l \beta_{k,l}$ equivalently represents the user log log_{i-1} under the view-based approach as a single sentence converted into disjunctive form.
- $\Delta_i := \bigvee_{k''} \chi_{k''}$ in disjunctive form denotes the query Φ_i or its negation $\neg\Phi_i$.
- $tent_i := hist_{i-1} \wedge \Delta_i = \bigvee_{k,k''}(\bigwedge_l \beta_{k,l} \wedge \chi_{k''})$ then represents a left-hand side in a violation test according to (4), but so far ignoring that contradictory disjuncts might occur.
- $tent_i^{red} := \bigvee_{\bar{k},\bar{k}''}(\bigwedge_l \beta_{\bar{k},l} \wedge \chi_{\bar{k}''})$ in disjunctive form results from $tent_i$ by discarding all contradictory disjuncts (containing both an atom α and the negated literal $\neg\alpha$). The special case that $tent_i^{red}$ becomes the empty disjunction only happens if $log_{i-1} \models eval^*(\Phi_i)(db)$ and $\Delta_i = \neg eval^*(\Phi_i)(db)$.
- $\mathscr{D}_{i-1}$ is the set of tags D occurring in the current policy $psecb_{i-1}$.
- $psecb_{i-1} := \{sec_D[D] \mid D \in \mathscr{D}_{i-1}\}$ then describes the elements of that policy.

One can verify that the generation subprotocol establishes a one-to-one correspondance between the set of non-contradictory disjuncts $\bigwedge_l \beta_{k,l}$ of $hist_{i-1}$, ranging over all pertinent k, and $\mathscr{D}_{i-1}$, such that for each k the corresponding tag D satisfies $D = \{\beta \mid \beta = \beta_{k,l}$ for some $l\}$. Note that if the generation subprotocol tentatively forms a branch corresponding to a contradictory disjunct, then this fact is detected by performing the adaption subprotocol, which leads to an immediate deletion of that branch.

Then we assert and comment the equivalence of the following assertions:

1. (exists Ψ)($\Psi \in psec$ and $log_{i-1} \cup \{\Delta_i\} \models \Psi$).
   Such a kind of assertion is checked by the view-based approach according to (4), to be shown to satisfy the equivalence given by "(7) iff (8)".
2. (exists Ψ)($\Psi \in psec$ and $tent_i^{red} \models \Psi$).
   The set on the left-hand side of $\models$ is represented as a single sentence, which is formed as the conjunction over all elements of that set and then converted into disjunctive form (with discarding of contradictory disjuncts).
3. (exists $\tilde{\Psi}_s$)($\tilde{\Psi}_s = \{\tilde{\Psi}_{s,1}, \ldots, \tilde{\Psi}_{s,m}\} \in sec_\emptyset$ and $\bigvee_{\bar{k},\bar{k}''}(\bigwedge_l \beta_{\bar{k},l} \wedge \chi_{\bar{k}''}) \models \bigvee_r \tilde{\Psi}_{s,r}$).
   Here $\{\tilde{\Psi}_{s,1}, \ldots, \tilde{\Psi}_{s,m}\}$ are the initially determined prime implicants of $\tilde{\Psi}_s$.
4. (exists $\tilde{\Psi}_s$)($\tilde{\Psi}_s = \{\tilde{\Psi}_{s,1}, \ldots, \tilde{\Psi}_{s,m}\} \in sec_\emptyset$ and (for all $\bar{k}''$)(for all $\bar{k}$) (exists $\tilde{\Psi}_{s,r}$)($\tilde{\Psi}_{s,r} \in \tilde{\Psi}_s$ and $\bigwedge_l \beta_{\bar{k},l} \wedge \chi_{\bar{k}''} \models \tilde{\Psi}_{s,r}$)).
   We have exploited Prop. 2 for treating the implication problems.
5. (exists $\tilde{\Psi}_s$)($\tilde{\Psi}_s = \{\tilde{\Psi}_{s,1}, \ldots, \tilde{\Psi}_{s,m}\} \in sec_\emptyset$ and (for all $\bar{k}''$)(for all "non-contradictory"$\bar{D} \in \mathscr{D}_{i-1}$) (exists $\tilde{\Psi}_{s,r}$)($\tilde{\Psi}_{s,r} \in \tilde{\Psi}_s$ and $\bigwedge_l \beta_{k(\bar{D}),l} \wedge \chi_{\bar{k}''} \models \tilde{\Psi}_{s,r}$)).
   We have employed the correspondance between disjuncts of $hist_{i-1}$ and branches, where $k(\bar{D})$ corresponds to $\bar{D}$.
6. (exists $\tilde{\Psi}_s$)($\tilde{\Psi}_s \in sec_\emptyset$ and (for all $\bar{k}''$)(for all "non-contradictory"$\bar{D} \in \mathscr{D}_{i-1}$) (exists $\tilde{\Psi}_{s,r}^{\bar{D}}$)($\tilde{\Psi}_{s,r} \in \tilde{\Psi}_s^{\bar{D}}$ and $\chi_{\bar{k}''} \models \tilde{\Psi}_{s,r}^{\bar{D}}$)).
   Here $\tilde{\Psi}_s^{\bar{D}}$ is the version of $\tilde{\Psi}_s$ in the branch $sec[\bar{D}]$. The simplifications of the adaption subprotocol preserve the applicability of the efficient implication check, as stated in Prop. 2. Bascially, this kind of assertion is checked by the violation subprotocol of the policy-adaption approach. □

3.3 Efficiency of Policy Adaption

Without restrictions the worst-case complexity of policy adaption is inevitably determined by the complexity of the decision problems for propositional logic and thus expected to be exponential. Exponential efforts might also be hidden in transforming sentences into disjunctive forms or even determining all prime implicants. However, queries or negated queries that consist of strict disjunctions or generate strict disjunctions, respectively, are the *sole cause of branching* and thus of an exponential explosion of the size of an adapted policy. Besides these general remarks, analytical complexity results on "average"-case complexity appear to be hardly obtainable and are beyond the scope of this paper. It is left open to future work to implement a prototype and to set up practical experiments. If we then aim at empirically comparing policy adaption and view generation for special cases, we will be challenged to identify the best available optimization techniques for each of the two approaches.

If we restrict on queries that are single literals and then inspect such a literal, we have to determine whether and how the atom involved occurs in one of the implicants in the current policy data. To generalize the data structure exemplified in Fig. 1, we could maintain an efficiently searchable structure of all relevant atoms, together with the set structure comprising all current implicants (then including single literals), linking an atom with all pertinent implicants.

4 Related Work, Extensions and Conclusions

Though the policy-adaption based approach is innovative for inference control by means of Controlled Query Evaluation, some of the underlying ideas are already implicitly present in various previous work. First of all, we observe that a mechanism for enforcing inference control can be seen as an *automaton* that is basically specified by its set of *internal states*, its *state transition function* and its output or *reaction function*. In principle, for Controlled Query Evaluation a state has to reflect both a user's history and the confidentiality policy suitably. Accordingly, in a straightforward approach, a state can just be formed by a combination of two components: a current log of the user's history and a current version of the policy. In fact, the view-based approach explicitly maintains these two components. In contrast, the policy-adaption based approach aims at representing both of the needed features within one component.

All work on state-dependent control is somehow related to our contribution, as can be seen from the following examples. The works on "enforceable security properties" [10,9] treat states as abstract objects, without indicating implementations. Advanced discretionary access control based on logic programming, like the Flexible Authorization Framework [8] maintains a special "done-predicate", which can be seen as a kind of a user log or as a kind of a dynamic component of the access control policy, depending on the point of view. The Dynamic Authorization Framework [3] additionally selects a current model as a dynamic policy component to determine the current semantics. Dynamic mandatory access control [2] offers to adapt security labels assigned to objects as a classification like "high-water marks", where classifications can be seen as a part of the access control policy. Many further examples stem from the dynamic control of workflows. Control of probabilistic inferences [7] uses a Bayesian network, which is updated after returning some piece of information to a user; the current network reflects the confidentiality requirements still to be enforced.

We demonstrated in detail that the proposed policy-adaption approach can be employed *effectively* for a specific situation of Controlled Query Evaluation, and we also indicated how to implement this approach such that inference control can be performed *efficiently* for special cases. It would be worthwhile to also consider more expressive situations, including incomplete instances and open queries. Such extensions will challenge us to transfer the current considerations to the more complex modal first-order logic. Seen from a even more general perspective, the ultimate goal of further efforts should be the following: We should aim at finding suitable combinations of the view-based approach and the policy-adaption based appraoch, in order to achieve the best possible efficiency for specific situations; and maybe we could further aim at constructing an optimizer that automatically recognizes the best combination for a current situation.

References

1. Abiteboul, S., Hull, R., Vianu, V.: Foundations of Databases. Addison-Wesley, Reading (1995)
2. Bell, D.E., LaPadula, L.J.: Secure computer systems: A mathematical model, volume II. Journal of Computer Security 4(2/3), 229–263 (1996); reprint of MITRE Corporation (1974)
3. Bertino, E., Buccafurri, F., Ferrari, E., Rullo, P.: A logic-based approach for enforcing access control. Journal of Computer Security 8(2/3) (2000)
4. Biskup, J.: Security in Computing Systems – Challenges, Approaches and Solutions. Springer, Heidelberg (2009)
5. Biskup, J.: Usability confinement of server reactions: Maintaining inference-proof client views by controlled interaction execution. In: Kikuchi, S., Sachdeva, S., Bhalla, S. (eds.) DNIS 2010. LNCS, vol. 5999, pp. 80–106. Springer, Heidelberg (2010)
6. Biskup, J., Bonatti, P.A.: Controlled query evaluation for enforcing confidentiality in complete information systems. Int. J. Inf. Sec. 3(1), 14–27 (2004)
7. Chen, Y., Chu, W.W.: Protection of database security via collaborative inference detection. IEEE Trans. Knowl. Data Eng. 20(8), 1013–1027 (2008)
8. Jajodia, S., Samarati, P., Sapino, M.L., Subrahmanian, V.S.: Flexible support for multiple access control policies. ACM Trans. Database Syst. 26(2), 214–260 (2001)
9. Ligatti, J., Reddy, S.: A theory of runtime enforcement, with results. In: Gritzalis, D., Preneel, B., Theoharidou, M. (eds.) ESORICS 2010. LNCS, vol. 6345, pp. 87–100. Springer, Heidelberg (2010)
10. Schneider, F.B.: Enforceable security policies. ACM Trans. Inf. Syst. Secur. 3(1), 30–50 (2000)
11. Sicherman, G.L., de Jonge, W., van de Riet, R.P.: Answering queries without revealing secrets. ACM Trans. Database Syst. 8(1), 41–59 (1983)

Multilevel Secure Data Stream Processing

Raman Adaikkalavan[1,⋆], Indrakshi Ray[2], and Xing Xie[2]

[1] Computer and Information Science, Indiana University South Bend
raman@cs.iusb.edu
[2] Computer Science, Colorado State University
{iray,xing}@cs.colostate.edu

Abstract. With sensors and mobile devices becoming ubiquitous, situation monitoring applications are becoming a reality. Data Stream Management Systems (DSMSs) have been proposed to address the data processing needs of such applications that require collection of high-speed data, computing results on-the-fly, and taking actions in real-time. Although a lot of work appears in the area of DSMS, not much has been done in multilevel secure (MLS) DSMS making the technology unsuitable for highly sensitive applications such as battlefield monitoring. An MLS DSMS should ensure the absence of illegal information flow in a DSMS and more importantly provide the performance needed to handle continuous queries. We investigate the issues important in an MLS DSMS and propose an architecture that best meets the goals of MLS DSMS. We discuss how continuous queries can be executed in such a system and sharing across queries accomplished for maximum performance benefits.

Keywords: Multilevel Security, DSMS, Continuous Query Processing.

1 Introduction

With the advancement of smart technologies and ubiquitous availability of sensor and mobile devices, situation monitoring applications are becoming a reality. Such applications require collecting high-speed data, processing them, computing results on-the-fly, and taking actions in real-time. Data Stream Management Systems (DSMSs) [7,14,4,9,1,5,16] have been proposed for such applications that allow processing of streaming data and execution of continuous queries. One potential use of this technology is for military applications where DSMS receives information from various devices and sensors, not all of which belong to the same security level. In such applications, users and information are classified into the various security levels and mandatory rules govern the information flow across security levels. DSMSs need to execute queries based on live streaming data classified at various levels in response to request from users at different security levels without causing illegal information flow. Our work attempts to extend an existing DSMS to support such capabilities.

Researchers have worked on secure data and query processing in the context of DSMSs. However, almost all of these works focus on providing access control [15,11] to streaming data [21,13,22,12,3]. However, controlling access is not enough to prevent

⋆ This work was supported, in part, by IU South Bend Research Grant.

Y. Li (Ed.): Data and Applications Security and Privacy XXV, LNCS 6818, pp. 122–137, 2011.

security breaches in the above mentioned applications where illegal information flow can occur across security levels. For instance, the existence of covert and overt channels can cause information to be passed from a more sensitive level to a lesser one. Multilevel security (MLS) not only prevents unauthorized access but also ensures the absence of such illegal information flow.

Designing an MLS DSMS requires us to address several research issues. We need to provide a continuous query language for expressing real-world MLS DSMS queries. The formalization of such a language will allow us to determine query equivalence and facilitate query optimization. Note that, traditional notions of query equivalence will not work because the same query issued by users at different security levels will return different results. Moreover, query processing should be efficient to meet the QoS requirements of a DSMS. This necessitates sharing query plans of multiple queries to reduce query execution time without causing illegal information flow. In order to process MLS continuous queries in a secure manner, it is therefore necessary to completely redesign or make major modifications to the components of a DSMS.

In this work, we propose a suitable architecture for processing MLS continuous queries. We also formalize MLS continuous query processing and discuss how such queries can be executed in our proposed architecture. We discuss how query plans can reuse plans from existing queries. We augment the approaches proposed by the Stanford STREAM [4], Aurora [9], and Borealis [1] projects and allow sharing of query plans submitted by different users not all of which have been submitted at the same time. This not only allows good resource utilization but also helps achieve the quality-of-service (QoS) critical to stream processing applications.

The rest of the paper is organized as follows. In Section 2, we define a MLS formalization model for stream data applications where data sources, data streams, queries, and other components in DSMS are assigned with security levels with proper accessing rules. In Section 3, we propose a replicated architecture to address MLS stream applications. In order to accelerate processing rates, we explore different sharing approaches between continuous queries in Section 4. We discuss related work in section 5. In Section 6, conclusions and future work are discussed.

2 Multilevel Security Formalization Model

We begin by presenting our *model* for multilevel secure (MLS) DSMS system. An MLS DSMS is associated with a security structure that is a partial order, $(\mathbf{L}, <)$. $\mathbf{L}$ is a set of security levels, and $<$ is the dominance relation between levels. If $L_1 < L_2$, then L_2 is said to strictly dominate L_1 and L_1 is said to be strictly dominated by L_2. If $L_1 = L_2$, then the two levels are said to be equal. $L_1 < L_2$ or $L_1 = L_2$ is denoted by $L_1 \leq L_2$. If $L_1 \leq L_2$, then L_2 is said to dominate L_1 and L_1 is said to be dominated by L_2. Two levels L_1 and L_2 are said to be incomparable if neither $L_1 \leq L_2$ nor $L_2 \leq L_1$. We assume the existence of a level U, that corresponds to the level unclassified or public knowledge. The level U is the greatest lower bound of all the levels in $\mathbf{L}$. Any data object classified at level U is accessible to all the users of the MLS DSMS. Each MLS DSMS object $x \in \mathbf{D}$ is associated with exactly one security level which we denote as $L(x)$ where $L(x) \in \mathbf{L}$. (The function L maps entities to security levels.) We assume that the security level of an object remains fixed for the entire lifetime of the object.

The users of the system are cleared to different security levels. We denote the *security clearance* of user U_i by $L(U_i)$. Consider a setting consisting of two security levels: High (H) and Low (L), where $L < H$. The user Jane Doe has the security clearance of High. That is, $L(JaneDoe) = H$. Each user has one or more associated *principals*. The number of principals associated with the user depends on their security clearance; it equals the number of levels dominated by the user's security clearance. In our example Jane Doe has two principals: $JaneDoe.H$ and $JaneDoe.L$. During each session, the user logs in as one of the principals. All processes that the user initiates in that session inherit security level of the corresponding principal.

Each continuous query Q_i is associated with exactly one security level. The level of the query remains fixed for the entire execution. The security level of the query is the level of the principal who has submitted the query. For example, if Jane Doe logs in as $JaneDoe.L$, all queries initiated by Jane Doe during that session will have the level Low (L). A continuous query Q_i consists of one or more operators OP_i, where the operators inherit the level of the query. We require a query Q_i to obey the simple security property and the restricted $\star$-property of the Bell-LaPadula model [10].

1. An operator OP_i with $L(OP_i) = C$ can read an object x only if $L(x) \leq C$.
2. An operator OP_i with $L(OP_i) = C$ can write an object x only if $L(x) = C$.

In general, multilevel security can be supported at three *granularities*: attribute, tuple, or stream. Though stream level enforcement (i.e., single level streams within the DSMS) may be the easiest way of supporting multilevel security, it does not work for many MLS applications. We have analyzed stream applications from various domains (e.g., battlefield monitoring, infrastructure security). In such applications, streams containing tuples having different levels are often input to the DSMS. Thus, providing stream level security would not be beneficial to such applications. In this research work, we do security enforcement at tuple level (i.e., we assign level to each tuple). Thus, we do not consider the security level of the attributes individually, in this paper.

We do not present a separate attack model in this paper. Like all MLS systems, our goal is to allow information flow only from the dominated levels to the dominating ones. All other information flow, either overtly or covertly, should be disallowed by our architecture.

3 Multilevel Stream Processing Architecture

In this section, we begin by discussing a general DSMS architecture and describe how it can be adapted to process MLS continuous queries.

3.1 General DSMS Architecture

A typical DSMS [7,14,16] architecture (based on the STREAM system [4]) is shown in Figure 1. A Continuous Query (CQ) can be defined using specification languages [5], or as query plans [14]. The CQs defined using specification languages are processed by the input processor, which generates a query plan. Each *query plan* is a directed graph of operators (e.g., Select, Project, Join, Aggregate). Each operator is associated with one or more input *queues*[1] and an output queue. One or more *synopses*[2] [5] are associated with each operator (e.g., Join) that needs to maintain the current state of the tuples for future evaluation of the operator. The generated query plans are then instantiated, and query operators are put in to the ready state so that they can be executed. Based on a scheduling strategy (e.g., round robin) [16,6], the scheduler picks a query, an operator, or a path, and starts the execution. The run-time optimizer monitors the system, and initiates load shedding [16,25,8] as and when required. Both these QoS delivery mechanisms minimize resource usage (e.g., queue size) and maximize performance and throughput. Each stream has a stream shepherd operator in the DSMS which handles all the tuples arriving in that stream. Seq window operator reads the tuples from the shepherd operator and propagates to leaf nodes of queries. This operator is shared by all the queries that use that stream. In the directed graph of operators, the data tuples are propagated from the leaf operator to the root operator. Each operator produces a stream (can also be a relation) of tuples. After a processed tuple exits the query plan, the output manager sends it to the query creators (or users).

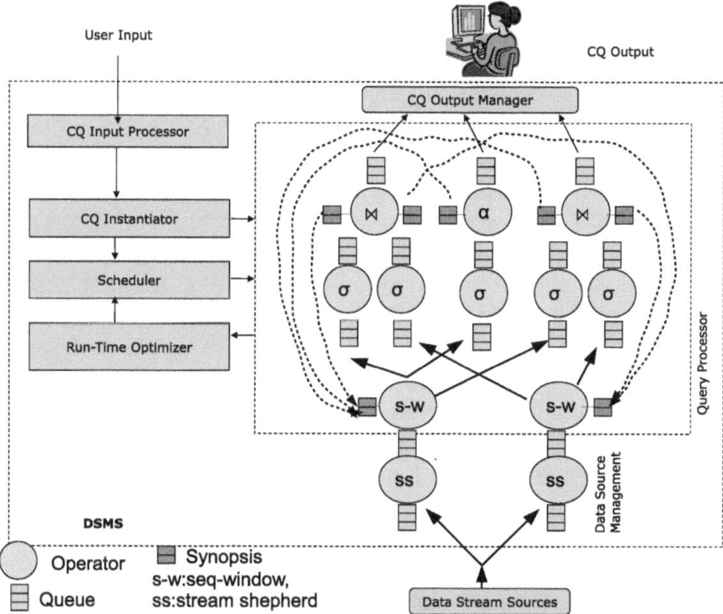

Fig. 1. Data Stream Management System (DSMS)

1 Queues are used by the operators to propagate tuples.

2 Synopses are temporary storage structures used by the operators (e.g., Join) that need to maintain a state. In this paper, we use synopses and *windows*, alternatively.

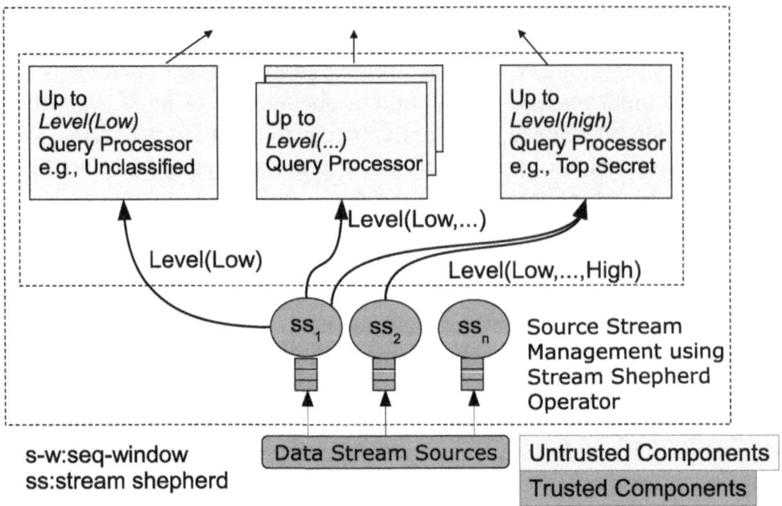

Fig. 2. Replicated MLS DSMS Architecture

3.2 MLS DSMS Architecture

In this section, we discuss how we can adapt the general DSMS architecture to process MLS continuous queries. We focus our attention to the query processor component of the architecture presented in Figure 1. The query processor of an MLS DSMS can have various types of architecture depending on how logical isolation is achieved across the different security levels. We borrow our ideas in this regard from the various architectures (trusted, kernelized, and replicated) that have been proposed in MLS DBMS literature [15,18,2]. We choose the replicated architecture as the first step and plan to propose other alternatives as part of our future work.

Our architecture is based on the replicated model where each level L stores not only the tuples with classification L but also those whose classification is dominated by L. We present one example of a replicated query processor in Figure 2, although many variations are possible.

The query processors are untrusted and replicated at various security levels. Each query processor runs at a security level (L) and is responsible for executing queries submitted by the users who have logged on at the same level. The response to a query may involve data belonging to one or multiple security levels; however, the level of all the tuples returned in the response must be dominated by the query level.

The stream shepherd operator must be redefined to ensure that only tuples at the dominated level are passed on to the dominating level. All the other operators are untrusted and are replicated at various levels. The input queues carrying data at dominated levels are replicated at the dominating levels as well. Sequential-Window operators and synopses used for processing blocking operators such as join and aggregation are created as needed for the query processors at that level. In the next section, we discuss query processing in more details.

4 Shared Query Processing in Replicated DSMS

In this section, first we discuss MLS CQL queries informally, and then discuss shared query processing.

4.1 MLS CQL Queries

Consider the following data streams (Vitals and Position) and continuous query `Q` written using the CQL language [5]. Query `Q` joins tuples from two streams. The sliding windows maintain the last 100 tuples for computations.

```
Vitals (soldier id (sid), blood pressure (bp), pulse rate (pr));
Position (soldier id (sid), latitude (lat), longitude (lon));
```

```
Q: SELECT AVG(bp), AVG(pr) FROM Vitals[ROWS 100], Position[ROWS 100]
   WHERE Vitals.sid = Position.sid
```

To support MLS, stream and query definitions have to be modified to include security levels. Below, we discuss MLS CQL briefly as a complete discussion is outside the scope of this paper. An MLS CQL query can include the LEVEL attribute in the WHERE clause, SELECT clause, and window specification. Let us consider the following examples.

```
SELECT AVG(bp) WHERE LEVEL = "S" FROM Vitals [ROWS 100]
SELECT AVG(bp) FROM Vitals [ROWS 100 LEVEL = "S"]
SELECT AVG(bp) FROM Vitals [ROWS 100] WHERE LEVEL = "S"
```

In the first query the WHERE clause conditions are applied before a tuple enters a window. In the second query, the window keeps only tuples based on the condition specified. In the third query, the window maintains 100 tuples, but the WHERE clause is applied during AVG calculation. The first and second queries are equivalent. Note that, for these queries, we have simple selections and we do not have any join conditions. If the WHERE clause specifies a join condition, this condition can only be checked in the join operator which is processed after the window selection. Our algorithms, presented in this paper, address all three types of queries. However, due to space constraints, our examples are based on the first type of query which processes the WHERE conditions except the join condition before window selection.

We consider only tuple-based (e.g., query `Q`) and partitioned by windows [5]. In the query shown below, the partitioned window maintains two different partitions (as it gets only tuples with level S or TS), and the average is calculated for each partition.

```
SELECT AVG(bp) WHERE LEVEL = "S" OR "TS"
FROM Vitals [PARTITIONED BY LEVEL ROWS 100]
```

Processing each MLS query involves several steps. First, the selection condition of the query is written in conjunctive normal form. Second, the query must be rewritten to add a where clause that says the level of tuples returned must be dominated by the level of the user. Subsequently, we generate the query plan. In this work, we represent a query plan in the form of a tree which we refer to as an *operator tree*. Note that, many operator

Table 1. Continuous Queries

Query	User	Login Level	Query Specification
Q_1/Q'_1	Ann/Bob	H	SELECT AVG(bp) FROM Vitals [PARTITIONED BY LEVEL ROWS 20]
Q_2	Carl	H	SELECT AVG(bp) WHERE LEVEL = "L" FROM Vitals [ROWS 20]
Q_3	Dan	H	SELECT AVG(bp) WHERE bp > 50 FROM Vitals [PARTITIONED BY LEVEL ROWS 5]
Q_4	Dan	H	SELECT AVG(pr) WHERE V.sid = P.sid AND bp > 120 AND lon = "4E" FROM Vitals [ROWS 10] V, Position [ROWS 10] P
Q_5	Ellen	H	SELECT V.sid, pr WHERE V.sid = P.sid AND bp > 120 AND lon = "4E" FROM Vitals [ROWS 10] V, Position [ROWS 10] P
Q_6	Frank	H	SELECT sid, bp WHERE bp > 120 FROM Vitals
Q_7	Gail	H	SELECT sid, bp, pr WHERE LEVEL = "L" AND bp > 120 FROM Vitals
Q_8	John	H	SELECT sid WHERE pr > 100 FROM Vitals

trees may be associated with a query corresponding to the different plans. However, we show just one such tree for each query. The formal definition of an operator tree appears below.

Definition 1. *[Operator Tree] An* operator tree *for a query Q_x is represented in the form of OPT (Q_x) consists of a set of nodes N_{Q_x} and a set of edges E_{Q_x}. Each node N_i corresponds to some operator in the query Q_x. Each edge (i, j) in this tree connecting node N_i with node N_j signifies that the output of node N_i is the input to node N_j. Each node N_i is labeled with the name of the operator $N_i.op$, its parameters $N_i.parm$, the synopses $N_i.syn$ (for blocking operators), and input queues $N_i.inputQueue$ which are used for its computation. The label of node N_i also includes the output produced by the node, denoted by $N_i.outputQueue$, that can be used by other nodes or sent as response to the users.*

Operator trees for queries Q_6 and Q_7 defined in Table 1 appear in Figures 3(a) and 3(b), respectively. An operator tree has all the information needed for processing the query. Specifically, the labels on the node indicate how the computation is to be done for evaluating that operator, where an operator is the basic unit of data processing in a DSMS. The name component specifies the type of the operator, such as, *SELECT*, *PROJECT*, *AVG*, etc. The parameter is denoted as a set. For the *SELECT* operator, parameter is the set of conjuncts in the selection condition. For the *PROJECT* operator it is the set of attributes. The synopsis is needed for the blocking operators, such as, join and aggregate operations and has type (e.g., tuple-based, partitioned by) and size as its attributes. The input queues are derived from the streams (or relations) needed by the operator.

We use the streams (Vitals and Position) and continuous queries shown in Table 1 to discuss query processing. We also assume the tuples sent by soldiers involved in a highly classified mission to be classified as high (H) and other missions to be classified as low (L). Medics or users can login in at different levels and submit queries. Also note that in Table 1 all queries are issued in high (H) level. The main reason to choose one level is that all queries issued by a user logged in at that level is processed by a query processor running at that level. Hence we use examples from H level to introduce and discuss various sharing methods. All these queries are executed by one query processor at level high, shown in Figure 2.

Queries Q_1 and Q'_1, issued by Ann and Bob respectively, compute the average blood pressure of the last 20 tuples at each level in Vitals stream. Query Q_2 computes the average blood pressure of the last 20 tuples having level L. Query Q_3 computes the average blood pressure for the last 5 tuples at each level where the pressure is greater than 50. In queries Q_4 and Q_5, the last 10 tuples that satisfy the selection conditions are maintained in the synopses and are joined. Average and projection are computed over the results from the join. In queries Q_6 to Q_8, there are only selection conditions and projection (duplicate preserving) operations. Query Q_7 selects level L tuples that have $bp > 120$ and projects three attributes.

4.2 Query Sharing

Typically, in a DSMS there can be several queries that are being executed concurrently. Query sharing will increase the efficiency of these queries. Query sharing obviates the need for evaluating the same operator(s) multiple times if different queries need it. In such a case, the operator trees of different queries can be merged. Figure 3(c) shows the merging of operator trees of queries Q_6 and Q_7 shown in Figures 3(a) and 3(b), respectively. In the Figure 4, we show how the operator trees of Q_4 and Q_5 can be merged. Later we will formalize how such sharing can be done.

In our replicated MLS DSMS query processing architecture, we focus on sharing queries to save resources such as CPU cycles and memory usage. In our architecture, we share queries that are submitted by users with the same principal security level as all these queries run in the same query processor. Since queries shared have the same security level, our replicated MLS DSMS query processor avoids security violations like covert channel during sharing.

We next formalize basic operations that are used for comparing the nodes belonging to different operator trees. Such operations are needed to evaluate whether sharing is possible or not between queries. We begin with the equivalence operator. If nodes belonging to different operator trees are equivalent, then only one node needs to be computing for evaluating the queries corresponding to these different operator trees.

Definition 2. *[Equivalence of Nodes] Node $N_i \in N_{Q_x}$ is said to be* equivalent *to node $N_j \in N_{Q_y}$, denoted by $N_i \equiv N_j$, where N_i, N_j are in the operator trees $OPT(Q_x)$, $OPT(Q_y)$ respectively, if the following condition holds: $N_i.op = N_j.op \wedge N_i.parm = N_j.parm \wedge N_i.syn = N_j.syn \wedge N_i.inputQueue = N_j.inputQueue$*

In some cases, for evaluating node N_i belonging to operator tree $OPT(Q_x)$, we may be able to reuse the results of evaluating node N_j belonging to operator tree $OPT(Q_y)$.

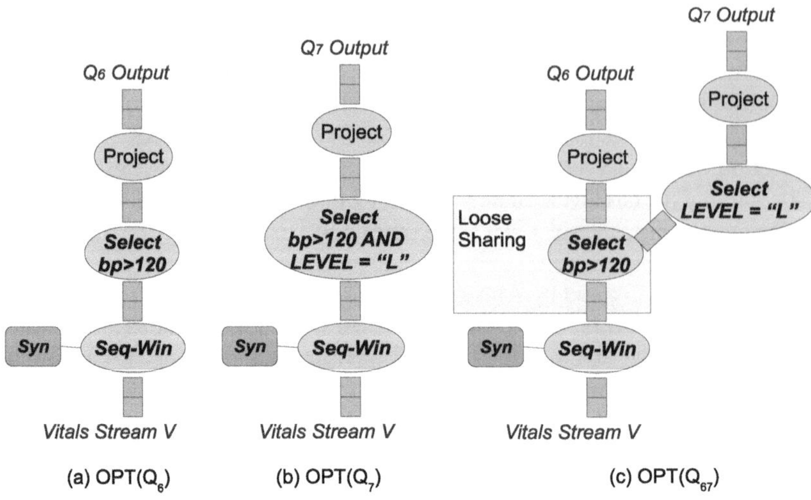

Fig. 3. Operator Tree for Q_6, Q_7, and Loose Partial Sharing of Q_6 and Q_7

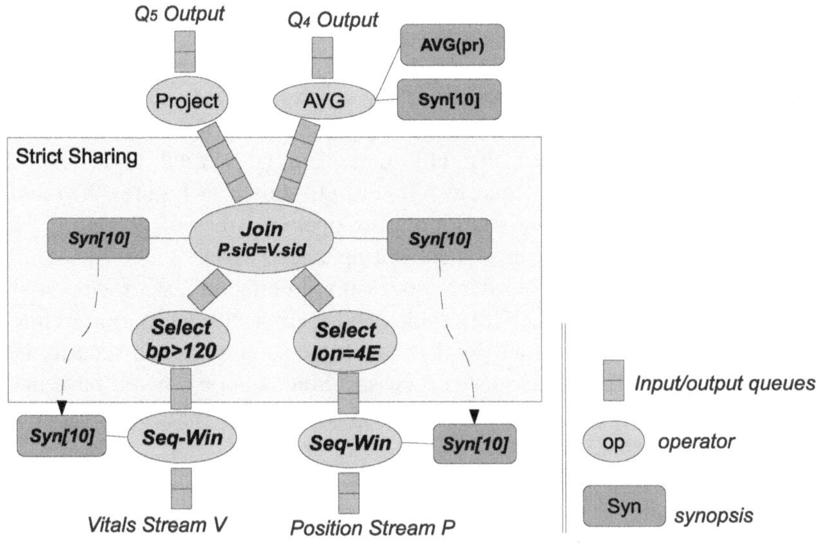

Fig. 4. Strict Partial Sharing Operator Tree for Q_4 and Q_5

This is possible if the nodes are related by the subsumes relationship defined below. Such relationship is possible when the operators match and are non-blocking and the operator parameters are related by a subset relation.

Definition 3. *[Subsume Relation of Nodes] Node $N_i \in N_{Q_x}$ is said to be* subsumed *by node $N_j \in N_{Q_y}$, denoted by $N_i \subseteq N_j$, where N_i, N_j are in the operator trees $OPT(Q_x)$,*

$OPT(Q_y)$ and are referred to as subsumed node, subsuming node *respectively, if the following conditions hold:*

1. *Condition 1:*
   - *Case 1 [$N_i.op = PROJECT$]:*
     $N_i.op = N_j.op \wedge N_i.parm \subseteq N_j.parm \wedge N_i.inputQueue = N_j.inputQueue$.
   - *Case 2 [$N_i.op = SELECT$]:*
     $N_i.op = N_j.op \wedge N_j.parm \subseteq N_i.parm \wedge N_i.inputQueue = N_j.inputQueue$.
2. *Condition 2: $N_i.op$ is a non-blocking operator.*

Consider the SELECT nodes of the operator trees of queries Q_6 and Q_7 shown in Figure 3, where the SELECT node of Q_7 is subsumed by the SELECT node of Q_6. We have different forms of sharing that are possible in our architecture which we now discuss.

Complete Sharing

The best form of sharing is complete sharing where no additional work is needed for processing a new query. However, in order to have complete sharing, the two queries must have equivalent operator trees. The notion of equivalence of operator trees is given below.

Definition 4. *[Equivalence of Operator Trees] Two operator trees $OPT(Q_x)$ and $OPT(Q_y)$ are said to be equivalent, denoted by $OPT(Q_x) \equiv OPT(Q_y)$ if the following conditions hold.*

1. *for each node $N_i \in N_{Q_x}$, there exists a node $N_j \in N_{Q_y}$, such that $N_i \equiv N_j$.*
2. *for each node $N_p \in N_{Q_y}$, there exists a node $N_r \in N_{Q_x}$, such that $N_p \equiv N_r$.*

The formal definition of complete sharing appears below.

Definition 5. *[Complete Sharing] Query Q_x can be* completely shared *with an ongoing query Q_y submitted by a user at the same security level only if $OPT(Q_i) \equiv OPT(Q_j)$.*

Complete sharing is possible only when the queries are equivalent. For example, queries Q_1 and Q_1' have identical operator trees and can be completely shared. In such cases, we do not need to do anything else for processing the new query. However, this may not happen often in practice.

Partial Sharing

We next define partial sharing which allows multiple queries to share the processing of one or more nodes, if they are related by the equivalence or subsume relation.

Definition 6. *[Partial Sharing] Query Q_x can be* partially shared *with an ongoing query Q_y submitted at the same security level only if the following conditions hold*

1. *$OPT(Q_x) \not\equiv OPT(Q_y)$*
2. *there exists $N_i \in N_{Q_x}$ and $N_j \in N_{Q_y}$, such that one of the following holds: $N_i \equiv N_j$, $N_i \subseteq N_j$ or $N_j \subseteq N_i$.*

We have two forms of partial sharing which we describe below. The main motivation is the sharing of blocking operators have to be handled differently from non-blocking operators. The sharing of blocking operators is more restrictive in which the conditions for join operator, for example, must exactly match the other query's join operator. On the other hand, with non-blocking operators they can be subsumed. The formal definition of these two forms of sharing appears below.

Definition 7. *[Strict Partial Sharing] Query Q_x can be* strict partially shared *with an ongoing query Q_y submitted at the same security level only if the following conditions hold*

1. $OPT(Q_x) \not\equiv OPT(Q_y)$
2. *there exists* $N_i \in N_{Q_x}$ *and* $N_j \in N_{Q_y}$*, such that* $N_i \equiv N_j$
3. *there does not exist* $N_i \in N_{Q_x}$ *and* $N_j \in N_{Q_y}$*, such that* $N_i \subseteq N_j$ *or* $N_j \subseteq N_i$*.*

Definition 8. *[Loose Partial Sharing] Query Q_x can be* loose partially shared *with an ongoing query Q_y submitted at the same security level only if the following conditions hold*

1. $OPT(Q_x) \not\equiv OPT(Q_y)$
2. *there exists* $N_i \in N_{Q_x}$ *and* $N_j \in N_{Q_y}$*, such that* $N_i \subseteq N_j$*.*

In the loose partial sharing, we will have a node on the ongoing query that subsumes a node of an incoming query. When nodes are related by subsume relation, then it is possible to decompose the subsumed nodes. The decomposition tries to make use of operator evaluation of the subsuming node in order to evaluate the subsumed node. The decomposition is formalized below.

Definition 9. *[Decomposition of Subsumed Nodes] Let $N_i \subseteq N_j$ where $N_i \in OPT(Q_x)$ and $N_j \in OPT(Q_y)$. Node N_i can be decomposed into two nodes N_i' and N_i'' in the following manner.*

Node N_i'
1. $N_i'.op = N_j.op$
2. $N_i'.inputQueue = N_j.inputQueue$
3. $N_i'.parm = N_j.parm$

Node N_i''
1. $N_i''.op = N_i.op$
2. $N_i''.inputQueue = N_i'.outputQueue$
3. $N_i''.parm = N_i.parm - N_i'.parm (if\ N_i.op = SELECT)$
   $N_i''.parm = N_i'.parm - N_i.parm (if\ N_i.op = PROJECT)$

Consider the SELECT nodes of the operator trees of query Q_6 and Q_7 shown in Figure 3. In this case, the SELECT node of Q_7 is subsumed by the SELECT node of Q_6. Select node of Q_7 which is the subsumed by the select node of Q_6 can be decomposed into two select nodes. One of these new nodes mirror Q_6 and the other is also a select node that checks for the additional select condition. Partial sharing is possible because of the overlap of operator trees.

Algorithm 1. Merge Operator Trees

INPUT: $OPT(Q_x)$ and $OPT(Q_y)$
OUTPUT: $OPT(Q_{xy})$ representing the merged operator tree
Initialize $N_{Q_{xy}} = \{\}$
Initialize $E_{Q_{xy}} = \{\}$
foreach *node* $N_i \in N_{Q_x}$ **do**
  $N_{Q_{xy}} = N_{Q_{xy}} \cup N_i$
end
foreach *edge* $(i, j) \in E_{Q_x}$ **do**
  $E_{Q_{xy}} = E_{Q_{xy}} \cup edge\,(i, j)$
end
foreach *node* $N_i \in N_{Q_y}$ **do**
  if $\nexists N_j \in N_{Q_x}$ *such that* $N_i \equiv N_j$ **then**
    $N_{Q_{xy}} = N_{Q_{xy}} \cup N_i$
  end
end
foreach *edge* $(i, j) \in E_{Q_y}$ **do**
  if *edge* $(i, j) \notin E_{Q_{xy}}$ **then**
    $E_{Q_{xy}} = E_{Q_{xy}} \cup edge\,(i, j)$
  end
end

Definition 10. *[Overlap of Operator Trees] Two operator trees $OPT(Q_x)$ and $OPT(Q_y)$ are said to* overlap *if $OPT(Q_x) \not\equiv OPT(Q_y)$ and there exists a pair of nodes N_i and N_j where $N_i \in N_{Q_x}$ and $N_j \in N_{Q_y}$ such that $N_i \equiv N_j$.*

When operator trees corresponding to two queries overlap, we can generate the merged operator tree using Algorithm 1. The merged operator tree signifies the processing of the partially shared queries.

Figure 4 illustrates the strict sharing of $OPT(Q_4)$ and $OPT(Q_5)$. As shown, we share select and join operators. The result of the join is processed by duplicate preserving project and aggregation operators. On the other hand, seq-window operator is common to all queries using a stream. Figures 3 (a) and (b) show the $OPT(Q_6)$ and $OPT(Q_7)$, respectively. Figure 3 (c) illustrates the $OPT(Q_{67})$ which shares both the query operations using the loose partial sharing approach. In this case, the query Q_7 is subsumed by Q_6 according to subsume relation definition. Based on Definition 9 (decomposition of subsumed nodes), we split Q_7 select condition into two ($bp > 120$ and level = "L") nodes and then share the $bp > 120$ node with Q_6.

5 Related Work

Though there has been a lot of research on multilevel security, to the best of our knowledge, ours is the first work in multilevel secure data stream processing systems. In this section, we will discuss works from closely related areas: DSMS, DSMS security, and MLS in real-time systems.

Data Stream Management Systems (DSMSs): Most of the works carried out in DSMSs address various problems ranging from theoretical results to implementing comprehensive prototypes on how to handle data streams and produce near real-time response without affecting the quality of service. There have been lots of works on developing QoS delivery mechanisms such as scheduling strategies [16,6] and load shedding techniques [16,25,8]. Some of the research prototypes include: Stanford STREAM Data Manager [7,4], Aurora [9], Borealis [1,17], and MavStream [20].

DSMS Sharing: In general DSMSs like STREAM [7,4], Aurora [9], and Borealis [1,17], queries issued by the same user at the same time can share the Seq-window operators and synopses. In the STREAM system, Seq-window operators are reused by queries. Instead of sharing plans, Aurora research focus on providing better scheduling of large number queries, by batching operators as atomic execution unit. In the Borealis project, information on input data criteria from executing queries can be shared and modified by new incoming queries. Here the execution of operators will be the same but the input data criteria can be revised. Even though many approaches target on better QoS in terms of scheduling and revising, sharing execution and computation among queries submitted at different times by the same user or at the same time between different users are not supported in general DSMS. Besides sharing common source Seq-window operators, sharing intermediate computations will result in big performance gains.

DSMS Security: There has been several recent works on securing DSMSs [21,13,22,12,3] by providing role-based access control. Though these systems support secure processing they do not prevent illegal information flows. In addition, in MLS systems we need to classify each component of the DSMS as opposed to access control support. Punctuation-based enforcement of RBAC over data streams is proposed in [22]. Access control policies are transmitted every time using one or more security punctuations before the actual data tuple is transmitted. Query punctuations define the privileges for a CQ. Both punctuations are processed by a special filter operator (stream shield) that is part of the query plan. Secure shared continuous query processing is proposed in [3]. The authors present a three-stage framework to enforce access control without introducing special operators, rewriting query plans, or affecting QoS delivery mechanisms. Supporting role-based access control via query rewriting techniques is proposed in [13,12]. To enforce access control policies, query plans are rewritten and policies are mapped to a set of map and filter operations. When a query is activated, the privileges of the query submitter are used to produce the resultant query plan. The architecture proposed in [21] uses a post-query filter to enforce stream level access control policies. The filter applies security policies after query processing but before a user receives the results from the DSMS.

MLS in Real Time Systems: In MLS real-time database system, research focuses on designing a DBMS where transactions having timing constraint deadlines executes in serialization order without data conflicts and security violations. Issues like security breach and task scheduling are similar to our MLS DSMS. Covert channel issues must be addressed due to sharing data among transactions from different levels in real-time DBMS. Many concurrent control protocols, like 2PL high priority, OPT-Sacrifice, and OPT-WAIT [19], deal with the high level transactions by suspending or restarting them if they conflict with low level transactions. However, the starvation on high level transactions becomes serious if there are too many conflicts in the system. S2PL [24] provides a better way on balancing the security and performance among conflicting transactions: high level transactions should wait for the commit of conflicting low level transactions only once then executed. Real-time DBMSs also need proper scheduling strategy in order to satisfy the various transaction deadlines. There are many priority selection algorithms like arrival timestamp, early-deadline-first, least-slack-time-first, etc [23], which impact the scheduling strategies in DSMS research. Although a large number of theories have been proposed on real-time system design, we cannot use them directly into MLS DSMS because of the differences between real-time and data stream systems. For the execution unit in the system, real-time DBMS uses transient transactions while DSMS handles continuous queries. In order to cause a security breach, transactions might set up inference or covert channel via accessing the same data item while continuous queries try to manipulate the response time. Scheduling strategy in MLS real-time transaction processing must address security, serialization and transaction deadlines, whereas scheduling in CQ must address security and query response time and throughput.

6 Conclusions and Future Work

Data Stream Management Systems (DSMSs) have been developed to address the data processing needs of situation monitoring applications. However, many situation monitoring applications, such as battlefield monitoring, emergency threat and resource management, involve data that are classified at various security levels. Existing DSMSs must be redesigned to ensure that illegal information flow do not occur in such applications. Towards this end, we developed an architecture for MLS DSMS and showed how MLS continuous queries can be executed in such systems. We have also shown how query plans can be shared across queries submitted by possibly different users to maximize resource utilization and improve performance. Our approach does not have security violations and can be used to process MLS data streams.

We plan to implement a prototype and study the overhead that is being caused due to MLS processing. We plan to investigate MLS DSMS query processing for kernelized and trusted architectures as well and develop prototypes. In the trusted architecture, it may be possible to share query plans across security levels and the performance improved. We plan to do a comparative study of the different architectures to find out which approach is the most suitable for processing MLS DSMS queries.

Currently, we have used simple extensions to CQL to express MLS continuous-queries. In future, we plan to extend CQL completely so that we can express more complex MLS continuous queries. In our work, when a user submits a query, we check whether the plans for the existing queries can be reused to improve the performance. Note that, such verification must be carried out dynamically. Towards this end, we plan to see how existing constraint solvers can be used to check for query equivalences. We also plan to evaluate the performance impact of dynamic plan generation and equivalence evaluation. We also plan to investigate more on building other components such as scheduling and load shedding for MLS DSMS.

References

1. Abadi, D.J., Ahmad, Y., Balazinska, M., Çetintemel, U., Cherniack, M., Hwang, J., Lindner, W., Maskey, A., Rasin, A., Ryvkina, E., Tatbul, N., Xing, Y., Zdonik, S.B.: The design of the borealis stream processing engine. In: Proc. of the CIDR, pp. 277–289 (2005)
2. Abrams, M.D., Jajodia, S.G., Podell, H.J. (eds.): Information Security: An Integrated Collection of Essays, 1st edn. IEEE Computer Society Press, Los Alamitos (1995)
3. Adaikkalavan, R., Perez, T.: Secure Shared Continuous Query Processing. In: Proc. of the ACM SAC (Data Streams Track), Taiwan, pp. 1005–1011 (March 2011)
4. Arasu, A., Babcock, B., Babu, S., Cieslewicz, J., Datar, M., Ito, K., Motwani, R., Srivastava, U., Widom, J.: Stream: The stanford data stream management system. Technical Report 2004-20, Stanford InfoLab (2004)
5. Arasu, A., Babu, S., Widom, J.: The CQL continuous query language: semantic foundations and query execution. VLDB Journal 15(2), 121–142 (2006)
6. Babcock, B., Babu, S., Datar, M., Motwani, R., Thomas, D.: Operator scheduling in data stream systems. VLDB Journal 13(4), 333–353 (2004)
7. Babcock, B., Babu, S., Datar, M., Motwani, R., Widom, J.: Models and issues in data stream systems. In: Proc. of the PODS, pp. 1–16 (June 2002)
8. Babcock, B., Datar, M., Motwani, R.: Load shedding for aggregation queries over data streams. In: Proc. of the ICDE, pp. 350–361 (March 2004)
9. Balakrishnan, H., Balazinska, M., Carney, D., Çetintemel, U., Cherniack, M., Convey, C., Galvez, E., Salz, J., Stonebraker, M., Tatbul, N., Tibbetts, R., Zdonik, S.B.: Retrospective on aurora. VLDB Journal: Special Issue on Data Stream Processing 13(4), 370–383 (2004)
10. Bell, D.E., LaPadula, L.J.: Secure Computer System: Unified Exposition and MULTICS Interpretation. Technical Report MTR-2997 Rev. 1 and ESD-TR-75-306, rev. 1, The MITRE Corporation, Bedford, MA 01730 (March 1976)
11. Bishop, M.: Computer Security: Art and Science. Addison-Wesley, Reading (2002)
12. Cao, J., Carminati, B., Ferrari, E., Tan, K.: Acstream: Enforcing access control over data streams. In: Proc. of the ICDE, pp. 1495–1498 (2009)
13. Carminati, B., Ferrari, E., Tan, K.L.: Enforcing access control over data streams. In: Proc. of the ACM SACMAT, pp. 21–30 (2007)
14. Carney, D., Çetintemel, U., Cherniack, M., Convey, C., Lee, S., Seidman, G., Stonebraker, M., Tatbul, N., Zdonik, S.B.: Monitoring Streams - A New Class of Data Management Applications. In: Proc. of the VLDB, pp. 215–226 (August 2002)
15. Castano, S., Fugini, M.G., Martella, G., Samarati, P.: Database Security (ACM Press Book). Addison-Wesley, Reading (1994)
16. Chakravarthy, S., Jiang, Q.: Stream Data Processing: A Quality of Service Perspective Modeling, Scheduling, Load Shedding, and Complex Event Processing. Advances in Database Systems 36 (2009)
17. Cherniack, M., Balakrishnan, H., Balazinska, M., Carney, D., Çetintemel, U., Xing, Y., Zdonik, S.B.: Scalable distributed stream processing. In: Proc. of the CIDR (2003)
18. Committee on Multilevel Data Management Security, Air Force Studies Board, Commission on Engineering and Technical Systems. National Research Council, National Academy Press, Washington D.C. (March 1983); Multilevel data management security
19. George, B., Haritsa, J.R.: Secure Concurrency Control in Firm Real-Time Databases. Distributed and Parallel Databases 5, 275–320 (1997)
20. Jiang, Q., Chakravarthy, S.: Anatomy of a Data Stream Management System. In: ADBIS Research Communications (2006)
21. Lindner, W., Meier, J.: Securing the borealis data stream engine. In: IDEAS, pp. 137–147 (2006)

22. Nehme, R.V., Rundensteiner, E.A., Bertino, E.: A security punctuation framework for enforcing access control on streaming data. In: Proc. of the ICDE, pp. 406–415 (2008)
23. Ozsoyoglu, G., Snodgrass, R.T.: Temporal and real-time databases: A survey. IEEE Knowledge and Data Engineering 7(4), 513–532 (1995)
24. Son, S.H., David, R.: Design and analysis of a secure two-phase locking protocol. In: Proc. of the CSAC, pp. 374–379 (November 1994)
25. Tatbul, N., Çetintemel, U., Zdonik, S.B., Cherniack, M., Stonebraker, M.: Load Shedding in a Data Stream Manager. In: Proc. of the VLDB, pp. 309–320 (September 2003)

A Query Sharing

Table 2 shows the ways in which queries Q1 to Q8 defined in Table 1 can be shared. For example, when Q5 is executing and Q4 is the newly issued query then they both can be strict shared.

Table 2. Query Sharing

Incoming / Executing	Q1	Q2	Q3	Q4	Q5	Q6	Q7	Q8
Q1	*Complete*	-	-	-	-	-	-	-
Q2	-	*Complete*	-	-	-	-	*Loose* Select (LEVEL)	-
Q3	-	-	*Complete*	-	-	-	-	-
Q4	-	-	-	*Complete*	*Strict* Select(bp), Select(lon), Join	*Loose* Select(bp)	*Loose* Select(bp)	-
Q5	-	-	-	*Strict* Select(bp), Select(lon), Join	*Complete*	*Loose* Select(bp)	*Loose* Select(bp)	-
Q6	-	-	-	*Loose* Select(bp)	*Loose* Select(bp)	*Complete*	*Loose* Select(bp)	-
Q7	-	-	-	-	-	-	*Complete*	-
Q8	-	-	-	-	-	-	-	*Complete*

Query Processing in Private Data Outsourcing Using Anonymization

Ahmet Erhan Nergiz and Chris Clifton

Purdue University, West Lafayette, IN 47907
{anergiz,clifton}@cs.purdue.edu

Abstract. We present a query processing scheme in a private data outsourcing model. We assume data is divided into identifying and sensitive data using an anatomy approach[20]; only the client is able to reconstruct the original identifiable data. The key contribution of this paper is a relational query processor that minimizes the client-side computation while ensuring the server learns nothing violating the privacy constraints.

Keywords: privacy, anonymization, data outsourcing, anatomy model.

1 Introduction

Data outsourcing is a growing business. Cloud computing developments such as Amazon Relational Database Service promise further reduced cost. However, use of such a service can be constrained by privacy laws, requiring specialized service agreements and data protection that could reduce economies of scale and dramatically increase costs.

Most privacy laws apply to data "relating to an identified or identifiable natural person"[6], data that cannot be directly or indirectly linked to an individual is not restricted. Some laws are even more specific; the U.S. Healthcare laws apply only to identifiable *health information*[10]. We propose a private data outsourcing approach where the link between identifying information and sensitive (protected) information is encrypted, with the ability to decrypt this link residing only with the client. As the server no longer has access to *individually identifiable* protected information, it is not subject to privacy laws, and can offer a service that does not need to be customized to the needs of each country- or sector-specific requirements; any risk of violating privacy through releasing sensitive information tied to an individual remains with the client.

We admit that the legal and privacy issues of this model are open to debate (although some laws suggest the appropriateness of this model; U.S. laws applying to educational institutions specifically allow disclosure of "directory information" on an opt-out basis [7]); such debate is not in the scope of this paper. We propose a data model based on *anatomization*[20]. This divides data into *anatomy groups*, separates identifying and sensitive data into two tables, and provides a join key at the group level (see Figure 2.) We add an encrypted key that does allow reconstructing the record, but the ability to decrypt and reconstruct resides only at the client. Note that this model can support a variety of privacy

Y. Li (Ed.): Data and Applications Security and Privacy XXV, LNCS 6818, pp. 138–153, 2011.

constraints, including k-anonymity[18, 19], discernibility/l-diversity[17, 14], and t-closeness[13]. While the original anatomization paper just considered a single table, extending this to a full relational database has been explored[16].

This paper presents a relational query processor operating within this model. The goal is to minimize communication and client-side computation, while ensuring that the privacy constraints captured in the anatomization are maintained. At first glance, this is straightforward: standard relational query processing at the server, except that any joins involving the encrypted key must be done at the client; an appropriate distributed query optimizer should do a reasonably good job of this. However, two issues arise that confound this simple approach:

1. By making use of the anatomy groups, and the knowledge that there is an one-to-one mapping (unknown to the server) between tuples in such groups, we can perform portions of the join between identifying and sensitive information at the server without violating privacy constraints, and
2. Performing joins at the client and sending results back to the server for further processing (as might be recommended by a distributed query optimizer) can violate privacy constraints.

We first give the threat model and related work in consequent subsections and then provide definitions and notations for an anatomized database in Section 2. In Section 3, we show how standard relational algebra operations can be performed to lower client-side cost using issue 1. We conclude our paper with Section 4.

1.1 Threat Model

In our private data outsourcing model, a data owner (i.e., client) first anonymizes the database such that individually identifiable links are encrypted besides the anonymization of such links. The data owner sends the modified database to a semi-honest third party (i.e., server) to delegate most of the query processing. The server is only allowed to try to infer additional information than that is allowed by the anonymization technique we use and it is assumed not to return incorrect or/and incomplete result, or alter the protocol in an attempt to gain information. Moreover, the server does not modify the database that the data owner sends at the beginning of the protocol.

1.2 Related Work

Private data outsourcing also known as database-as-a-service model was first introduced by Hacigumus et al. [9]. They used bucketization over encrypted database that allows the server to partially execute queries on the behalf of the client. There is a yet unmeasured trade-off between efficiency of the system and the privacy of individuals directly related to the size and the contents of each bucket of encrypted values. Although, there has been an effort to address the optimization of this trade-off in [11], no privacy measurement showing the amount of information leakage is given. However, Damiani et al. [4] proposed another technique that uses hashing for bucketization and encrypted B+ trees for indexing. They give an aggregate metric showing the exposure of the database contents in various adversarial models. However, we note that an aggregate exposure metric fails to ensure the privacy of each individual's identity.

Instead of using encryption, Aggarwal et al. [1] proposed vertical fragmentation to hide functional dependencies from an adversary. They require two non-colluding servers to send each fragment. Another approach described in [3] is to fragment the tables into partitions and have the client store a small partition storing the sensitive values. The rest is stored in the server in plaintext. They prove that finding the optimal partitioning is NP-hard and give a heuristic solution instead.

As far as we know the closest idea to ours is in [12]. They give an l-diverse partitioning scheme based on anatomization[20] for a single table having multiple sensitive attributes. Our work is orthogonal to their work such that we give detailed query evaluation strategies given such an l-diverse partitioning scheme exists for multirelational databases.

2 Data Outsourcing Using Anatomy

As stated before, we assume use of the anatomy model[20] to meet privacy constraints. Making this work for multiple tables does demand extra thought; a solution for this is given in [16]. This paper assumes an anatomized database meeting privacy constraints; we now present relevant definitions and notations (based on [16]) that we will use in describing query processing.

2.1 Definitions and Notations

Definition 2.1 (Equivalence class/QI-group). *An equivalence class, E_j, is a subset of tuples in table T such that $T = \bigcup_{j=1}^{m} E_j$ and for any pair, (E_{j_1}, E_{j_2}) where $1 \leq j_1 \neq j_2 \leq m$, $E_{j_1} \cap E_{j_2} = \emptyset$.*

Definition 2.2 (l-diversity). *A set of equivalence classes is said to be* **l-diverse**, *if each equivalence class, E_j where $1 \leq j \leq m$, satisfies*

$$\forall v \in \pi_S E_j,\ f(v, E_j)/|E_j| \leq 1/l$$

where S is the sensitive attribute in T, $f(v, E_j)$ returns the frequency of v in E_j and $|E_j|$ is the number of tuples in E_j.

We use a variation of the definition of Anatomy in [20].

Definition 2.3 (Anatomy). *Given a table T partitioned into m equivalence classes using l-diversity without generalization, anatomy produces a quasi-identifier table (QIT) and a sensitive table (SNT) as follows. QIT has schema*

$$(A_1, \ldots, A_d, GID, SEQ)$$

Doctor	*Gender*	*Patient*
Alice	Female	Ike
Carol	Female	Eric
Bob	Male	Olga
Dave	Male	Kelly
Carol	Female	Faye
Alice	Female	Mike
Dave	Male	Jason
Carol	Female	Max

(a) Physician

Patient	*Age*	*City*	*Disease*
Ike	41	Dayton	Cold
Eric	22	Richmond	Fever
Olga	30	Lafayette	Flu
Kelly	35	Lafayette	Cough
Faye	24	Richmond	Flu
Mike	47	Richmond	Fever
Jason	45	Lafayette	Cough
Max	31	Lafayette	Flu

(b) Patient

Fig. 1. Original Database

where $A_i \in Q_T$ *for* $1 \leq i \leq d = |Q_T|$, Q_T *is the set of identifying attributes in* T, *GID is the group id of the equivalence class and SEQ is the unique sequence number for a tuple. For each* $E_j \in T$ *and each tuple* $t \in E_j$, *QIT has a tuple of the form:*

$$(t[1], \ldots, t[d], j, s)$$

The SNT has schema

$$(HSEQ, GID, A_{d+1})$$

where A_{d+1} *is the sensitive attribute in* T, *GID is the group id of the equivalence class and HSEQ contains the outputs of* $\mathrm{H}_{\bar{k}}(s)$ *defined as in Definition 2.4 where* s *is the corresponding unique sequence number in QIT for a tuple. For each* $E_j \in T$ *and each tuple* $t \in E_j$, *SNT has a tuple of the form:*

$$(\mathrm{H}_{\bar{k}}(s), j, v)$$

For instance, the anatomy anonymization of person specific tables *Physician* and *Patient* in Figure 1 is shown Figure 2.

Note that we show a (keyed) hash as the "join key" between the two subtables. We use HMAC [2] for hiding the join links due to the efficiency of cryptographic hash functions; one could also encrypt the key using a standard mechanism (with nonces) or a Probabilistic Encryption method [8] to achieve semantic security. We formally describe this problem below.

Definition 2.4 (Hiding Join Link). *Given two tables* T_1 *and* T_2 *having the same cardinality and a joining attribute, SEQ in domain* D, *mapping* T_1 *1:1 to* T_2, *a function* $\mathrm{H} : \bar{k} \times D \rightarrow D'$ *is said to hide the join link, SEQ, once each value* v *in* T_2*.SEQ is updated with* $\mathrm{H}_{\bar{k}}(v)$ *if*

- *Without knowing the secret* $\bar{k}$ *used in* H, *it is hard to join* T_1 *with* T_2 *on attribute SEQ.*
- *In case* H *can be applied to inputs with unbounded length, it is hard to encounter two values,* v_1 *and* v_2, *such that* $\mathrm{H}_{\bar{k}}(v_1) = \mathrm{H}_{\bar{k}}(v_2)$.

Doctor	*Gender*	*GID*	*SEQ*
Alice	Female	1	1
Carol	Female	1	2
Bob	Male	2	3
Dave	Male	2	4
Carol	Female	3	5
Alice	Female	3	6
Dave	Male	4	7
Carol	Female	4	8

(a) $\text{Physician}_{\text{QIT}}$

HSEQ	*GID*	*Patient*
$\text{H}_{\bar{k}_1}(1)$	1	Ike
$\text{H}_{\bar{k}_1}(2)$	1	Eric
$\text{H}_{\bar{k}_1}(3)$	2	Olga
$\text{H}_{\bar{k}_1}(4)$	2	Kelly
$\text{H}_{\bar{k}_1}(5)$	3	Faye
$\text{H}_{\bar{k}_1}(6)$	3	Mike
$\text{H}_{\bar{k}_1}(7)$	4	Jason
$\text{H}_{\bar{k}_1}(8)$	4	Max

(b) $\text{Physician}_{\text{SNT}}$

Patient	*Age*	*City*	*GID*	*SEQ*
Ike	41	Dayton	1	1
Eric	22	Richmond	1	2
Olga	30	Lafayette	2	3
Kelly	35	Lafayette	2	4
Faye	24	Richmond	3	5
Mike	47	Richmond	3	6
Jason	45	Lafayette	4	7
Max	31	Lafayette	4	8

(c) $\text{Patient}_{\text{QIT}}$

HSEQ	*GID*	*Disease*
$\text{H}_{\bar{k}_2}(1)$	1	Cold
$\text{H}_{\bar{k}_2}(2)$	1	Fever
$\text{H}_{\bar{k}_2}(3)$	2	Flu
$\text{H}_{\bar{k}_2}(4)$	2	Cough
$\text{H}_{\bar{k}_2}(5)$	3	Flu
$\text{H}_{\bar{k}_2}(6)$	3	Fever
$\text{H}_{\bar{k}_2}(7)$	4	Cough
$\text{H}_{\bar{k}_2}(8)$	4	Flu

(d) $\text{Patient}_{\text{SNT}}$

Fig. 2. Anatomized Database

Remark 1. When HMAC used, one needs to apply HMAC to the attribute $T_1.SEQ$ to join T_1 and T_2 since HMAC is hard to invert even the used key $\bar{k}$ is known whereas when encryption is used, one needs to decrypt each $\text{H}_{\bar{k}}(v)$ in T_2 and then T_1 and T_2 can be joined since the strategy used in HMAC cannot be used in randomized encryptions where encrypting the same value each time results in a different ciphertext based on the random used during the encryption process.

In Theorem 2.1, we show that the probability of having a collision in the hash values of any equivalence group is negligible which in return proves our model is correct with overwhelming probability.

Theorem 2.1 (Correctness). *Given QIT, SNT tables each having n tuples and structured as in Definition 2.3, and HMAC with l-bit outputs used for hiding the actual join link between QIT and SNT; one can construct the original table T by joining $QIT_{updated}$ and SNT with overwhelming probability if $2^l \gg n$ where $QIT_{updated}$ is computed by updating each value v in $QIT.SEQ$ with $\text{H}_{\bar{k}}(v)$ value.*

Proof. T can only be constructed if $\langle t_1.GID, t_1.SEQ\rangle$ pair matches with exactly one tuple t_2 of SNT for each tuple t_1 of $QIT_{updated}$. Hence the pair $\langle t_1.GID, t_1.SEQ\rangle$ needs to be unique across the tuples of $QIT_{updated}$. The same is also true for $\langle t_2.HSEQ, t_2.GID\rangle$ in SNT. Since all sequence values in QIT.SEQ is unique, the only case that there are more than one same $\langle t_1.GID, t_1.SEQ\rangle$

value is when there is a collision in one of the equivalence class. Recall that $T = \bigcup_{j=1}^{m} E_j$ and let c be $max(|E_1|, \ldots, |E_m|)$. Then the probability, $\mathcal{P}$, of not having the same $\mathrm{H}_{\bar{k}}(v)$ value for any v in any equivalence class in $QIT_{updated}$ or SNT can be approximated by using the birthday problem analysis [5].

$$\mathcal{P} \approx \left(e^{-\binom{c}{2}/2^{l}}\right)^{m} \approx \left(e^{-cn/2^{l+1}}\right)$$

Considering the current world population and having a tuple for each person in the world, the largest database can hold at most 2^{33} tuples. When $l = 160$ and $n = 2^{33}$ and assuming c is a small constant, $\mathcal{P} \approx 1$.

2.2 Privacy Preservation

Given QIT and SNT, a semi-honest adversary can only associate each individual to a sensitive attribute with some probability based on the size of an equivalence class. Lemma 2.1 gives the formulation for this probability.

Lemma 2.1. *Given $\mathrm{H}_{\bar{k}}(.)$ is a cryptographic hash function, the probability that a tuple in QIT, $(t[1], \ldots, t[d], j, s)$, matches with a tuple in SNT $(\mathrm{H}_{\bar{k}}(s'), j, v)$ is*

$$\mathcal{P}((t[1], \ldots, t[d], v) \in T) = f(v, E_j)/|E_j|$$

where $f(v, E_j)$ returns the frequency of v in E_j, $|E_j|$ is the number of tuples in E_j and $\bar{k}$ is the unknown key for the cryptographic hash function, $\mathrm{H}_{\bar{k}}(.)$.

Proof. Each tuple belonging to some equivalence class E_j^{QIT} in QIT, joins with every tuple in the corresponding equivalence class, E_j^{SNT}, in SNT due to the same GID, j. Thus for a tuple $t \in E_j^{QIT}$, $\{t\} \times E_j^{SNT}$ is the set of all the tuples that t contributes to $QIT \bowtie SNT$. Therefore the sample space for t's possible matching sensitive value v is $|\{t\} \times E_j^{SNT}| = |E_j^{SNT}| = |E_j|$. However there exists only one tuple, t', such that $t' \in \{t\} \times E_j^{SNT}$ and $t' \in T$ by Definition 2.3. Due to the first property of function H in Definition 2.4, it is infeasible to guess t' correctly out of $\{t\} \times E_j^{SNT}$ tuples without knowing the key $\bar{k}$ in H to get HSEQ values. Thus, the probability that t matches with sensitive value v in E_j^{SNT} is the count of v in E_j^{SNT} divided by the sample space (i.e., $|E_j|$).

For instance, the probability of the individual represented by the first tuple in $\mathrm{Patient}_{\mathrm{QIT}}$ in Figure 2, $\langle Ike, 41, Dayton\rangle$, having *Cold* is 1/2 since $|E_1| = 2$ and the frequency of *Cold* in E_1 is 1 (i.e., $f(Cold, E_1) = 1$).

Theorem 2.2. *The client cannot safely send any information resulting from a join between identifying and sensitive information back to the server, unless such information would provide no benefit to further join processing.*

Proof. Let QIT and SNT be the anatomization of T such that $\forall t_1 \in QIT$; $\exists t_2 \in SNT$, $(t = t_1 \bowtie t_2) \in T$ and the probability, $\mathcal{P}'$, of finding each tuple t from QIT and SNT is $1/k$. Then each equivalence class has k items and there are n/k number of equivalence classes in both QIT and SNT where n is the number of tuples in T. Hence there are $(k!)^{n/k}$ possible tables that can be derived from QIT and SNT and at least one of these tables corresponds to the original table T. Let T_i^j denote each of these possible tables where $1 \leq i \leq (k!)^{n/k-1}$ and $1 \leq j \leq k!$; and $\bar{T}$ denote the set of all T_i^j's. Then T^j denotes all possible tables where an equivalence class, E, has a fixed permutation (i.e., j^{th} permutation of equivalence class, E) and T_i denotes all possible tables where all equivalence classes except E has a fixed permutation (i.e. i^{th} permutation of all equivalence classes except E). Then we get the probability formulas,

$$\mathcal{P}\left\{T_i^j = T \mid T \in T_i\right\} = \frac{1}{k!}$$

$$\mathcal{P}\left\{T \in T^j\right\} = \sum_{i=1}^{(k!)^{n/k-1}} \mathcal{P}\left\{T_i^j = T \mid T \in T_i\right\} \mathcal{P}\left\{T \in T_i\right\} = \frac{1}{k!}$$

Assume a query q' that is $q'(q(T) \bowtie C)$ where C is another table and the client sends the intermediate result $q(T)$ to the server for improved evaluation of q'. If $\forall T_i^j \in \bar{T}\ q(T_i^j) = q(T)$, sending the result of $q(T)$ does not give any benefit to the server since it can compute $q(T)$ by itself. If $q(T_i^j) \neq q(T)$ for some $T_i^j \in \bar{T}$, sending the result of $q(T)$ violates the privacy since $\mathcal{P}\{T \in T^j\} < 1/k!$ due to the fact that $\mathcal{P}\{T_i^j = T\} = 0$. If $\mathcal{P}\{T \in T^j\} < 1/k!$, there is at least one j' such that $\mathcal{P}\{T \in T^{j'}\} > 1/k!$ and therefore $\mathcal{P}'$ is not $1/k$ for all the tuples in E.

$$\mathcal{P}\left\{T \in T^j\right\} = ((k!)^{n/k-1} - 1) \times \frac{1}{(k!)^{n/k}} < \frac{1}{k!}$$

3 Query Operators

Query processing that operates on only the QIT or SNT sub-tables can be performed at the server without raising privacy issues; it is when these must be combined that we must take care. A simple solution is to operate on each independently, then send the results to the client to decrypt and combine. However, we can often do better. We now detail how relational query operations can be performed in ways that minimize the computation performed on the client. Interested reader may refer to our technical report [15] in which we include all proofs and algorithms that we omit in this paper due to the page limit.

3.1 Selection

Selection on a single table T anonymized into QIT and SNT can be broken into selection on QIT, selection on SNT, and selection criteria requiring the join of the two. The single sub-table selections are performed first. The resulting tables are then queried to determine where an anatomization group contains values that could satisfy the cross-subtable criterion. If so, all possible matching tuples from each group are passed to the client, which can decrypt, join, and complete the selection.

Definition 3.1 (CNF Predicates). *A set of predicate, P, being in CNF form with respect to a table T anonymized as two tables QIT and SNT, has the following form:*

$$P = \bigwedge_{1 \leq i \leq n} \left(\bigvee_{1 \leq j \leq m_i} P_i^j \right)$$

where P_i^j is a single-literal clause having a form att op value *or* att op att. *Without losing generality, each set of P_i's are defined further as*

$$P_{QIT} = P_1 \wedge \ldots \wedge P_\alpha, \quad P_{SNT} = P_{\alpha+1} \wedge \ldots \wedge P_\beta, \quad P_{QS} = P_{\beta+1} \wedge \ldots \wedge P_n$$

where P_{QIT} and P_{SNT} are only applicable to attributes of QIT and SNT respectively. P_{QS} contains predicates applicable to both QIT and SNT in each its disjunctions. Let P_i^T be the ith disjunction of single-literal clauses in P_{QS} that is only applicable to the attributes of table T. Then P_{QS} is defined as

$$P_{QS} = \bigwedge_{\beta < i \leq n} \left(P_i^{QIT} \vee P_i^{SNT} \right)$$

Definition 3.2 (Server-side Selection Query). *Given QIT and SNT tables derived from a table T using Anatomy model anonymization and a set of predicates P in conjunctive normal form defined as in Definition 3.1, a selection query written as $\sigma_P(QIT, SNT)$ returns two tables, QIT'' and SNT'':*

$$\begin{aligned}
QIT' &= (\sigma_{P_{QIT}}(QIT)) \ltimes (\sigma_{P_{SNT}}(SNT)) \\
SNT' &= (\sigma_{P_{SNT}}(SNT)) \ltimes (\sigma_{P_{QIT}}(QIT)) \\
S_{GID} &= \bigcap_{i=\beta+1}^{n} \left(\pi_{GID}(\sigma_{P_i^{QIT}} QIT') \cup \pi_{GID}(\sigma_{P_i^{SNT}} SNT') \right) \\
QIT'' &= QIT' \bowtie S_{GID} \\
SNT'' &= SNT' \bowtie S_{GID}
\end{aligned}$$

Lemma 3.1. *Given table QIT, and SNT along with a predicate P defined as in Definition 3.1, and tables QIT'' and SNT'' calculated with the steps defined in Definition 3.2; the following property holds*

$$\sigma_{P_{QS}}(QIT'' \bowtie SNT'') = \sigma_P(QIT \bowtie SNT)$$

Definition 3.3 (Client-side Selection Query). *Given QIT'' and SNT'' tables computed by the server and a predicate P_{QS} in conjunctive normal form defined as in Definition 3.1 where each P_i in P_{QS} checks at least one attribute from each QIT and SNT table, the client updates each tuple of QIT'' by replacing the values of SEQ attribute with their corresponding keyed hash value (i.e., $s \rightarrow \mathrm{H}_{\bar{k}}(s)$). Then the final selection query is written as*

$$R = \sigma_{P_{QS}}(QIT''_{updated} \bowtie SNT'')$$

Theorem 3.1. *Given P as in Definition 3.1, QIT, and SNT; R derived according to Definition 3.2 and 3.3 is equal to $\sigma_P(T)$ if the pair $\langle QIT, SNT\rangle$ is an anatomization of table T according to Definition 2.3.*

Example 1. According to Definition 3.2 and 3.3, given query

$$\sigma_{(Age>40)\wedge(Disease=Flu \text{ or } Cough)\wedge(Disease=Cough \vee Age<3)}(\text{Patient}_{\text{QIT}}, \text{Patient}_{\text{SNT}})$$

$P_{QIT} = (Age > 40)$, $P_{SNT} = (Disease = Flu \vee Disease = Cough)$, and $P_{QS} = (Disease = Fever \vee Age < 3)$. QIT' has the 6th and 7th tuples of table $\text{Patient}_{\text{QIT}}$ based on P_{QIT}. 1st tuple is not included since the corresponding group of $\text{Patient}_{\text{SNT}}$ doesn't satisfy the P_{SNT} (which is ensured with semi-join). SNT' has 5th, 7th and 8th tuples of table $\text{Patient}_{\text{SNT}}$. And $S_{GID} = \{4\}$ since none of the tuples in group 3 satisfies the predicate P_{QS}. Then QIT'' has 7th tuple of $\text{Patient}_{\text{QIT}}$ and SNT'' has 7th and 8th tuples of $\text{Patient}_{\text{SNT}}$. After server sends these intermediate results to the client, client updates the SEQ field of QIT'' and computes $R = \langle Jason, 45, Lafayette, 4, \text{H}_{\bar{k}_2}(7), \text{H}_{\bar{k}_2}(7), 4, Cough\rangle$

Cross sub-table correlation. The reader may have noticed an apparent issue: This process potentially returns a single value from the QIT and SNT from the server to the client, implying to the server that these are linked. The key is to remember that it is quite possible that these values do not join; the query result could be empty. This only becomes a problem if 1) attributes in QIT are correlated with attributes in SNT, and 2) the server knows of this correlation.

If attributes are not correlated, then the chance that a single tuple selected from a group in QIT based on a query matches a single tuple from the same group in SNT is $1/k$, and the server cannot infer that they match. Even if the values are correlated, if the server does not know of that correlation it must assume the match probability is $1/k$. If the server knows of the correlation, then it can infer that the two values match based on the QIT and SNT values alone, without even processing a query.

An issue arises when the server does not know of the correlation, but repeated queries suggest such a correlation. However, these issues are with the decision on how to anatomize the table, not with the query processing mechanism itself – the proposed query processing mechanism reveals only linkages that the server could discover from only the data, queries, and knowledge of correlations.

3.2 Projection

Projection is at first glance straightforward, as removing attributes can be done independently on each sub-table. The difficulty comes in removing duplicates: two tuples may be identical in all non-encrypted attributes in QIT (or SNT), but not be a duplicate in the join.

There is an exception when all values in an anatomy group become identical under projection; then only a single tuple representing the entire group needs to be returned. However, this only works if no selection is performed on "projected out" attributes prior to the projection.

We show how projection operator, denoted by π, is processed in case of eliminating duplicates. We also use π^d throughout the paper to denote that the projection operator does not eliminate duplicates. Since calculating π^d is straightforward, we show the processing of π instead.

Definition 3.4 (Server-side Projection Query). *Given QIT and SNT tables derived from a table T using Anatomy model anonymization and a set of attributes A', projection query without duplicates written as*

$$\pi_{A'}(QIT, SNT),\ A' = A'_{QIT} \cup A'_{SNT} \text{ and } SEQ, GID, HSEQ \notin A'$$

returns a set of tables, R:

$$R = \begin{cases} \{R', T'_{QIT}, T'_{SNT}\} & \text{if } A'_{QIT} \neq \emptyset \text{ and } A'_{SNT} \neq \emptyset \\ \pi_{A'_{QIT}}(QIT) & \text{if } A'_{QIT} \neq \emptyset \text{ and } A'_{SNT} = \emptyset \\ \pi_{A'_{SNT}}(SNT) & \text{if } A'_{QIT} = \emptyset \text{ and } A'_{SNT} \neq \emptyset \end{cases}$$

where $R' = \pi_{A'}\left(\sigma_{GID \notin S}\left(R'_{QIT} \bowtie R'_{SNT}\right)\right)$, $T'_{QIT} = \pi^d_{A'_{QIT},SEQ}\left(\sigma_{GID \in S} QIT\right)$, *and* $T'_{SNT} = \pi^d_{A'_{SNT},HSEQ}\left(\sigma_{GID \in S} SNT\right)$*; and where* $R'_{QIT} = \pi_{A'_{QIT},GID}\left(QIT\right)$, $R'_{SNT} = \pi_{A'_{SNT},GID}\left(SNT\right)$, *and S is defined as*

$$S = \left\{i : \left|\sigma_{GID=i}\left(R'_{QIT}\right)\right| > 1 \wedge \left|\sigma_{GID=i}\left(R'_{SNT}\right)\right| > 1\right\}$$

Lemma 3.2. *Given* R' *and S as in Definition 3.4,*

$$R' = \pi_{A'}\left(\sigma_{GID \notin S}\left(R'_{QIT} \bowtie R'_{SNT}\right)\right) = \pi_{A'}\left(\sigma_{GID \notin S}\left(QIT_{updated} \bowtie SNT\right)\right)$$

Definition 3.5 (Client-side Projection Query). *Given the set of tables, R, computed by the server; if* $|R| = 1$ *then the client outputs the only table in R without any processing. Otherwise, the client updates each tuple of* T'_{QIT} *by replacing the values of SEQ attribute with their corresponding keyed hash value (i.e.,* $s \rightarrow \mathrm{H}_{\bar{k}}(s)$*). Then the final result is computed by*

$$R'' = \pi_{A'}\left(R' \cup \pi_{A'}\left(T'_{QIT_{updated}} \bowtie T'_{SNT}\right)\right)$$

Theorem 3.2. *Given* $A' = A'_{QIT} \cup A'_{SNT}$, *QIT, and SNT;* R'' *derived according to Definition 3.4 and 3.5 is equal to* $\pi_{A'}(T)$ *if the pair* $\langle QIT, SNT \rangle$ *is an anatomization of table T according to Definition 2.3.*

Example 2. Given query $\pi_{City,Disease}(\text{Patient}_{\text{QIT}}, \text{Patient}_{\text{SNT}})$; $S = \{1\}$ since neither $\pi_{City}(\text{Patient}_{\text{QIT}})$ nor $\pi_{Disease}(\text{Patient}_{\text{SNT}})$ have only one element when $GID = 1$. However all other groups (i.e., $\{2, 3, 4\}$) can be projected without the knowledge of actual link between $\text{Patient}_{\text{QIT}}$, $\text{Patient}_{\text{SNT}}$. Intermediate tables are shown in Figure 3.

City	*Disease*
Lafayette	Cough
Lafayette	Flu
Richmond	Fever
Richmond	Flu

(a) R'

City	*SEQ*
Dayton	1
Richmond	2

(b) T'_{QIT}

City	*SEQ*
$\mathrm{H}_{\bar{k}_2}(1)$	Cold
$\mathrm{H}_{\bar{k}_2}(2)$	Fever

(c) T'_{SNT}

City	*Disease*
Dayton	Cold
Lafayette	Cough
Lafayette	Flu
Richmond	Fever
Richmond	Flu

(d) R''

Fig. 3. Intermediate tables in Example 2

3.3 Join

Join is problematic, as it can be an expensive operation. We detail below a natural join. The key is to push join as late as possible, as it only results in reduction on the sub-tables containing the join criterion (e.g., the *QIT* sub-tables); the other sub-tables can only be reduced to the extent that the join eliminates complete anatomization groups.

Definition 3.6 (Server-side Join Query). *Given* $Z_1 = QIT_1$, $Z_2 = QIT_2$ *and their corresponding sensitive attribute tables,* $Z_3 = SNT_1$ *and* $Z_4 = SNT_2$, *derived from table* T_1 *and* T_2 *respectively using anatomization, join query written as* $(QIT_1, SNT_1) \bowtie (QIT_2, SNT_2)$ *returns three tables*

$$\langle R_1, R_2, R_3 \rangle = \langle Z_i \bowtie Z_j, Z_k, Z_l \rangle$$

where $\exists a : a \in A_{Z_i} \cap A_{Z_j}$ *and* $1 \leq i \neq j \neq k \neq l \leq 4$.

Definition 3.7 (Client-side Join Query). *Given* $\langle R_1, R_2, R_3 \rangle$ *tables computed by the server; for every* R_i *having attribute* SEQ_j *the client updates each tuple of* R_i *by replacing the value of* SEQ_j *attribute with its corresponding keyed hash value (i.e.,* $s_j \rightarrow \mathrm{H}_{\bar{k}_j}(s_j)$*) where* $1 \leq i \leq 3$ *and* $1 \leq j \leq 2$. *Then the final join query would be computed as*

$$R = R_1 \bowtie R_2 \bowtie R_3$$

Theorem 3.3. *Given* QIT_1, QIT_2, SNT_1 *and* SNT_2; R *derived according to Definition 3.6 and 3.7 is equal to* $T_1 \bowtie T_2$ *if the pairs,* $\langle QIT_1, SNT_1 \rangle$ *and* $\langle QIT_2, SNT_2 \rangle$, *are anatomizations of table* T_1 *and* T_2 *respectively.*

3.4 Group-By

Group-by is challenging, as it is also an expensive operation, but can in some cases be done largely at the server. This is dependent on the type of aggregate being computed. In some cases, an anatomization group may be contained entirely in a group-by group; if so, an aggregate such as MAX need only return a single value for that anatomization group. However, if the values in an anatomization group are split across multiple group-by groups, all tuples must be returned, as the server has no way of knowing which tuple goes in which group.

We now show how to apply this optimization (when all tuples in an anatomization group are in the same group-by group) for several classes of aggregates.

Definition 3.8 (Aggregate Function Set). *Given a three sets of attributes, X_{QIT}, X_{SNT} and X^*, defined as a subset of A_{QIT}, A_{SNT}, and $\{*\}$ respectively; a group-by aggregate function set, F, consists of individual functions (e.g., COUNT, AVG) each defined on one of the attributes of X.*

$$F(X) = \{f_1(x_1), f_2(x_2), \ldots, f_k(x_k)\} \quad \text{where } X = X_{QIT} \cup X_{SNT} \cup X^*$$

Definition 3.9 (Auxiliary Function Set). *Given an aggregate function set F defined as in Definition 3.8 along with its input set X, an auxiliary function set F' is defined such that*

- *if $AVG(x_i) \in F(X)$ then also $COUNT(x_i) \in F(X) \cup F'(X)$*
- *if $S(x_i) \in F(X)$ then both $COUNT(x_i)$ and $AVG(x_i)$ are also in $F(X) \cup F'(X)$ where S could be STDEV, VAR, STDEVP, or VARP.*

Definition 3.10 ($\dot{\bowtie}$ operator). *Given two tables QIT and SNT derived from T by anonymization based on Anatomy model, $QIT \dot{\bowtie} SNT$ merges the two tables vertically such that each tuple of QIT in each group is joined with only one of the tuples in the same group of SNT without taking SEQ and $HSEQ$ into account.*

Definition 3.11 (Server-side Group-By Query). *Given QIT and SNT tables derived from a table T using Anatomy model anonymization, a set of attributes for the grouping, A', and a set of aggregate functions defined as in Definition 3.8; a group-by query is written as*

$$_{A'}\gamma_{F(X)}(QIT, SNT)$$

where $A' = A'_{QIT} \cup A'_{SNT}$. The above group-by query returns a set of tables R based on the grouping attributes A',

$$R = \begin{cases} \{R', T'_{QIT}, T'_{SNT}\} & \text{if } A'_{QIT} \neq \emptyset \text{ and } A'_{SNT} \neq \emptyset \\ _{A'}\gamma_{F(X)}(QIT) & \text{if } A'_{QIT} \neq \emptyset \text{ and } A'_{SNT} = \emptyset \text{ and } X_{SNT} = \emptyset \\ _{A'}\gamma_{F(X)}(SNT) & \text{if } A'_{QIT} = \emptyset \text{ and } A'_{SNT} \neq \emptyset \text{ and } X_{QIT} = \emptyset \end{cases}$$

where tables R', T'_{QIT}, and T'_{SNT}; defined as

$$\begin{aligned} R' &= {}_{A'}\gamma_{F(X),F'(X)}\left(\sigma_{GID \in S}\left(R'_{QIT} \dot{\bowtie} R'_{SNT}\right)\right) \\ T'_{QIT} &= \pi_{A'_{QIT}, SEQ, X_{QIT}}\left(\sigma_{GID \notin S} QIT\right) \\ T'_{SNT} &= \pi_{A'_{SNT}, HSEQ, X_{SNT}}\left(\sigma_{GID \notin S} SNT\right) \end{aligned}$$

where F' is as in Definition 3.9 and R'_{QIT}, R'_{SNT}, and S; are defined as

$$R'_{QIT} = \pi^d_{A'_{QIT},GID,X_{QIT}}(QIT)$$
$$R'_{SNT} = \pi^d_{A'_{SNT},GID,X_{SNT}}(SNT)$$
$$S = \left\{i : |\sigma_{GID=i}(\pi_{A'_{QIT},GID}R'_{QIT})| = 1 \wedge |\sigma_{GID=i}(\pi_{A'_{SNT},GID}R'_{SNT})| = 1\right\}$$
$$\cup \left\{i : \left|\sigma_{GID=i}\left(distinct(R'_{QIT})\right)\right| = 1 \vee |\sigma_{GID=i}\left(distinct(R'_{SNT})\right)| = 1\right\}$$

Lemma 3.3. *Given R' and S defined in Definition 3.11,*

$$R' = {}_{A'}\gamma_{F(X),F'(X)}\left(\sigma_{GID \in S}\left(QIT_{updated} \bowtie SNT\right)\right)$$

Definition 3.12 ($\dot\cup$ operator). *Given two disjoint tables T_1 and T_2 having identical schemas, $\dot\cup$ operator merges two group-by query results:*

$$g'(T_1)\dot\cup g'(T_2) = g(T_1 \cup T_2)$$

where $g' : T \mapsto {}_{A'}\gamma_{F(X),F'(X)}T$ and $g : T \mapsto {}_{A'}\gamma_{F(X)}T$ for some set of attributes, A', and a set of aggregate functions defined as in Definition 3.8 and 3.9.

Remark 2. There are three types of aggregate functions:

1. Functions having the property $f(f(X), f(Y)) = f(X, Y)$ where X and Y are single valued datasets. Hence the results of such functions can be combined to get a single result for multiple datasets (e.g., MAX, MIN, SUM, COUNT).
2. Functions not having the above property since they require every single value in the dataset to evaluate the result (e.g., CHECKSUM, MEDIAN). The whole dataset should be given as an input to this type of functions.
3. Functions not having the above property unless there is some auxiliary information given about the dataset. For instance, the results of average function of multiple dataset cannot be combined unless the count of values in each dataset is also given. Similarly standard deviation or variation results can be combined when both average and count of values in each dataset is given.

The $\dot\cup$ operator in Definition 3.12 is general such that it covers both the first and third type of functions. If the aggregate functions are only of the first type, there is no need to include an auxiliary function set, $F'(X)$, in the formulation.

In Algorithm 1, we present an algorithm that calculates the $\dot\cup$ operator.

Definition 3.13 (Client-side Group-By Query). *Given the set of tables, R, computed by the server; if $|R| = 1$ then the client outputs the only table in R without any processing. Otherwise, the client updates each tuple of T'_{QIT} by replacing the values of SEQ attribute with their corresponding keyed hash value (i.e., $s \rightarrow \mathrm{H}_{\bar{k}}(s)$). Then the final result of group-by query is computed by using special $\dot\cup$ operator in Definition 3.12,*

$$R'' = R'\dot\cup\left({}_{A'}\gamma_{F(X),F'(X)}\left(T'_{QIT_{updated}} \bowtie T'_{SNT}\right)\right)$$

Algorithm 1. The algorithm for $\dot{\cup}$ operation

input : Tables, $T_1' = {}_{A'}\gamma_{F(X),F'(X)}T_1$ and $T_2' = {}_{A'}\gamma_{F(X),F'(X)}T_2$
output: Table $T = T_1'\dot{\cup}T_2'$
sort T_1' and T_2' on attribute list A' if they are not sorted already;
$b_1 \leftarrow 1$; $b_2 \leftarrow 1$;
while *T_1' and T_2' has more tuples* **do**
  if $b_1 = 1$ **then** $t_1 \leftarrow$ the next tuple in T_1';
  if $b_2 = 1$ **then** $t_2 \leftarrow$ the next tuple in T_2';
  if $t_1.A' < t_2.A'$ **then** write t_1 into table T, $b_1 \leftarrow 1$, $b_2 \leftarrow 0$;
  else if $t_2.A' < t_1.A'$ **then** write t_2 into table T, $b_2 \leftarrow 1$, $b_1 \leftarrow 0$;
  else
    $t.A' \leftarrow t_1.A'$;
    foreach $f_i(x_i) \in F(X)$ **do**
      if *$f_i(\cdot)$ is type 1* **then** $t.f_i(x_i) \leftarrow f_i(t_1.f_i(x_i), t_2.f_i(x_i))$;
      else if *$f_i(\cdot)$ is type 2* **then** $t.f_i(x_i) \leftarrow$ undefined;
      else if *$f_i(\cdot)$ is type 3* **then**
        $\exists\text{COUNT}(x_i) \in F(X) \cup F'(X)$;
        $AVG_{x_i} \leftarrow \frac{\sum_{j=1}^{2} t_j.\text{AVG}(x_i)\times t_j.\text{COUNT}(x_i)}{\sum_{j=1}^{2} t_j.\text{COUNT}(x_i)}$;
        if $f_i(\cdot) = AVG$ **then** $t.f_i(x_i) \leftarrow AVG_{x_i}$;
        else if $f_i(\cdot) = STDEV$ **then**
          $\exists\text{AVG}(x_i) \in F(X) \cup F'(X)$;
          $t.f_i(x_i) \leftarrow$
          $\sqrt{\frac{\sum_{j=1}^{2}(t_j.\text{AVG}(x_i)^2 + t_j.\text{STDEV}(x_i)^2)\times t_j.\text{COUNT}(x_i)}{\sum_{j=1}^{2} t_j.\text{COUNT}(x_i)} - AVG_{x_i}^2}$;
        else if $f_i(\cdot) = VAR$ **then**
          $\exists\text{AVG}(x_i) \in F(X) \cup F'(X)$;
          $t.f_i(x_i) \leftarrow$
          $\frac{\sum_{j=1}^{2}\left(t_j.\text{AVG}(x_i)^2 + t_j.\text{VAR}(x_i)\right)\times t_j.\text{COUNT}(x_i)}{\sum_{j=1}^{2} t_j.\text{COUNT}(x_i)} - AVG_{x_i}^2$;
    write t into table T; $b_1 \leftarrow 1$; $b_2 \leftarrow 1$;
write all remaining tuples of T_1' and T_2' into T;

Theorem 3.4. *Given QIT, SNT, a set of attributes, A', for grouping and aggregate functions f_1 through f_k along with their inputs x_1 through x_k; R'' derived according to Definition 3.11, 3.12 and 3.13 is equal to ${}_{A'}\gamma_{F(X)}T$ if the pair $\langle QIT, SNT\rangle$ is an anonymization of table T based on Anatomy model.*

Example 3. According to Definition 3.11 and 3.13, given query

$$ {}_{Gender,City}\gamma_{AVG(AGE)}(\text{Physician}_{\text{QIT}}, \text{Physician}_{\text{SNT}} \bowtie \text{Patient}_{\text{QIT}}) $$

all groups in $S = \{1, 2, 3\}$ can be projected without knowing the link between $\text{Physician}_{\text{QIT}}$ and $\text{Physician}_{\text{SNT}}$. Intermediate tables are shown in Figure 4.

Gender	*City*	*AVG(AGE)*	*COUNT(*)*
Female	Dayton	41	1
Female	Richmond	31	3
Male	Lafayette	32.5	2

(a) R'

Gender	*SEQ*
Male	7
Female	8

(b) T'_{QIT}

HSEQ	*Age*	*City*
$H_{\bar{k}_1}(7)$	45	Lafayette
$H_{\bar{k}_1}(8)$	30	Lafayette

(c) T'_{SNT}

Gender	*City*	*AVG(AGE)*
Female	Dayton	41
Female	Lafayette	30
Female	Richmond	31
Male	Lafayette	32

(d) R''

Fig. 4. Intermediate tables in Example 3

4 Conclusions and Further Work

We have shown how given an anatomization of a database that meets privacy constraints, we can store that database at an untrusted (semi-honest) server and perform queries that minimize the load on the client. This frees the server from constraints imposed by privacy law, allowing it to provide a service while avoiding concerns over privacy.

There has been extensive work on storing and processing *encrypted* data. Our approach is to minimize the encryption, while still satisfying privacy constraints. This provides not only significant performance advantages, but also allows the server to provide "value-added" services. Such services could include address correction and normalization (cleaning individual data) as well as data analysis. Such services provide a more compelling business case for private data outsourcing than an "encrypt everything" approach, while still ensuring that outsourcing does not pose a privacy risk.

As a future work, we will implement the presented query operators and evaluate the performance of our system in a real anatomized database. Moreover, this paper looks only at a fixed database and read-only queries. Insert, update, and delete pose additional challenges, and are also left as future work. Another challenge that arises is data modeling: given a database and privacy constraints, what is the appropriate normalization for an anatomized database?

Acknowledgments. This publication was made possible by the support of an NPRP grant from the QNRF. The statements made herein are solely the responsibility of the author. Partial support for this work was provided by MURI award FA9550-08-1-0265 from the Air Force Office of Scientific Research.

References

[1] Aggarwal, G., Bawa, M., Ganesan, P., Garcia-molina, H., Kenthapadi, K., Motwani, R., Srivastava, U., Thomas, D., Xu, Y.: Two can keep a secret: A distributed architecture for secure database services. In: Proc. CIDR (2005)

[2] Bellare, M., Canetti, R., Krawczyk, H.: Keying hash functions for message authentication. In: Koblitz, N. (ed.) CRYPTO 1996. LNCS, vol. 1109, pp. 1–15. Springer, Heidelberg (1996)
[3] Ciriani, V., De Capitani Di Vimercati, S., Foresti, S., Jajodia, S., Paraboschi, S., Samarati, P.: Keep a few: outsourcing data while maintaining confidentiality. In: Backes, M., Ning, P. (eds.) ESORICS 2009. LNCS, vol. 5789, pp. 440–455. Springer, Heidelberg (2009)
[4] Damiani, E., Vimercati, S.D.C., Jajodia, S., Paraboschi, S., Samarati, P.: Balancing confidentiality and efficiency in untrusted relational dbmss. In: ACM CCS 2003, Washington D.C., USA, pp. 93–102 (2003)
[5] DasGupta, A.: The birthday and matching problems. In: Fundamentals of Probability: A First Course. Springer Texts in Statistics, pp. 23–28. Springer, NY (2010)
[6] Directive 95/46/EC of the European Parliament and of the Council of 24 October 1995 on the protection of individuals with regard to the processing of personal data and on the free movement of such data. Official Journal of the European Communities I(281), 31–50 (1995)
[7] Family educational rights and privacy act of 1974. Congressional Record 120, 39862–39866 (1974), http://www2.ed.gov/policy/gen/guid/fpco/ferpa/
[8] Goldwasser, S., Micali, S.: Probabilistic encryption & how to play mental poker keeping secret all partial information. In: Procs. of the 14th ACM Symposium on Theory of Computing, STOC 1982, pp. 365–377. ACM, New York (1982)
[9] Hacıgümüş, H., Iyer, B.R., Mehrotra, S.: Executing SQL over encrypted data in the database-service-provider model. In: Proc. of ACM SIGMOD Int. Conf. on Management of Data, Madison, Wisconsin, pp. 216–227 (2002)
[10] Standard for privacy of individually identifiable health information. Federal Register 67(157), 53181–53273 (2002), http://www.hhs.gov/ocr/privacy/hipaa/administrative/privacyrule/index.html
[11] : A privacy-preserving index for range queries. In: Proc. of the 30th Int. Conf. on Very Large Data Bases, VLDB 2004. VLDB Endowment, vol. 30, pp. 720–731 (2004)
[12] Jiang, X., Gao, J., Wang, T., Yang, D.: Multiple sensitive association protection in the outsourced database. In: Kitagawa, H., Ishikawa, Y., Li, Q., Watanabe, C. (eds.) DASFAA 2010. LNCS, vol. 5982, pp. 123–137. Springer, Heidelberg (2010)
[13] Li, N., Li, T.: t-closeness: Privacy beyond k-anonymity and l-diversity. In: Proc. of the 23rd Int. Conf. on Data Engineering (ICDE 2007), Istanbul, Turkey (2007)
[14] Machanavajjhala, A., Gehrke, J., Kifer, D., Venkitasubramaniam, M.: l-diversity: Privacy beyond k-anonymity. ACM Trans. on Know. Discovery from Data (TKDD) (1) (2007)
[15] Nergiz, A.E., Clifton, C.: Query processing in private data outsourcing using anonymization. Tech. Rep. 11-004, CS, Purdue University, http://www.cs.purdue.edu/research/technical_reports/2011/TRf
[16] Nergiz, M.E., Clifton, C., Nergiz, A.E.: Multirelational k-anonymity. IEEE Transactions on Knowledge and Data Engineering 21(8), 1104–1117 (2009)
[17] Øhrn, A., Ohno-Machado, L.: Using boolean reasoning to anonymize databases. Artificial Intelligence in Medicine 15(3), 235–254 (1999)
[18] Samarati, P.: Protecting respondent's privacy in microdata release. IEEE Transactions on Knowledge and Data Engineering 13(6), 1010–1027 (2001)
[19] Sweeney, L.: k-anonymity: a model for protecting privacy. International Journal on Uncertainty, Fuzziness and Knowledge-based Systems (5), 557–570 (2002)
[20] Xiao, X., Tao, Y.: Anatomy: Simple and effective privacy preservation. In: Proc. of 32nd Int. Conf. on Very Large Data Bases (VLDB), Seoul, Korea (2006)

Private Database Search with Sublinear Query Time

Keith B. Frikken and Boyang Li

Department of Computer Science and Software Engineering
Miami University, Oxford, OH 45056
{frikkekb, lib}@muohio.edu

Abstract. The problem of private database search has been well studied. The notion of privacy considered is twofold: i) the querier only learns the result of the query (and things that can be deduced from it), and ii) the server learns nothing (in a computational sense) about the query. A fundamental drawback with prior approaches is that the query computation is linear in the dataset. We overcome this drawback by making the following assumption: the server has its dataset ahead of time and is able to perform linear precomputation for each query. This new model, which we call the precomputation model, is appropriate in circumstances where it is crucial that queries are answered efficiently once they become available. Our main contribution is a precomputed search protocol that requires linear precomputation time but that allows logarithmic search time. Using this protocol, we then show how to answer the following types of queries with sublinear query computation in this precomputation model: i) point existence queries, ii) rank queries, iii) lookup queries, and iv) one-dimensional range queries.

Keywords: Private Database Search, Secure Two-party Computation, and Precomputation.

1 Introduction

There are many privacy/confidentiality concerns when querying a database about personal information. For example, if a user is querying information about a medical condition, religious beliefs, or political leanings then the query should remain private. Furthermore, a corporation asking a query may fear that revealing the query is a risk to their competitive advantage. Furthermore, even if the database owner is trusted, there is always the fear that a corrupt insider at the database owner's organization would leak the query information. The desire to protect the queries is not only a concern of the querying entity, but the database owner might not want this information due to liability concerns. One way to mitigate these concerns is to make the database publicly available, but this is not always an option. For example, if the database contains information about individuals, then revealing this information publicly may not be legal. Also, if the database owner wants to charge for queries, then revealing the information publicly is not a option. Example 1 gives a more detailed example that demonstrates the need for private querying.

Example 1. A federal agency wants the ability to query a transaction database to determine if a suspect (for which the agency has a warrant) is contained in the database.

Y. Li (Ed.): Data and Applications Security and Privacy XXV, LNCS 6818, pp. 154–169, 2011.

Furthermore, the federal agency wants to keep the identity of the suspect private, because: i) revealing this information might compromise the investigation, and ii) to avoid possible litigation if the suspect is innocent. The owner of the database wants to help the agency, but does not want to violate the privacy rights of the other people in the database.

Any secure function evaluation/secure multi-party computation, such as [17], can be used to solve this private database querying problem. Unfortunately, these solutions require the server and the client to perform computation and communication that is linear in the size of the dataset. Overcoming this linear bound appears impossible. If the server doesn't "touch" every item in the dataset, then the server learns some information about the query. To overcome this linear bound, we introduce a new model, which we call the precomputation model. In this model, queries are divided into the following two phases:

1. *Precomputation Phase:* In this phase the server does computation on its dataset. Furthermore, the server generates a message that is sent to the client. This phase assumes that the server's information is known, but that the query is unknown, and this phase is allowed to require linear complexity. The precomputation message can be sent (perhaps on a DVD) to the client before the query is known.
2. *Query Phase:* After the query is made available, this phase captures the interaction between the client and the server.

The two main goals of a protocol in this precomputation model are: i) that the computation/communication of the interactive query phase and the client computation phase is sublinear in the size of the dataset, and ii) that the total computation/communication is "close" to that required by the general solutions. Returning to Example 1 the database owner may be willing to precompute information, so that when the query becomes available the federal agency will be able to obtain its result as quickly as possible. Furthermore, the owner might compute several messages and send the information to the federal agency before the query is being asked.

The rest of this manuscript is organized as follows: Section 2 introduces the problems which can be solved by our protocol and the contribution of this paper. Section 3 and 4 introduce the building blocks and new tools used in the remainder of the manuscript. In section 5, a protocol for the private database search problem in the precomputation model is given. Section 6 gives a sketch of the security analysis. In section 7, we present experiments and results of comparison between naive scheme and our protocol. Finally, Section 8 describes related work and Section 9 concludes the paper and gives future work.

2 Problem Definition and Contributions

We consider the following general database search problem

$SEARCH(s_0, \ldots, s_n, m_1, \ldots, m_{2n-1}\ ;\ q)$: where the server has a sorted sequence of points $s_0, s_1, \ldots, s_n$ and a sequence of messages $m_1, \ldots, m_{2n-1}$; furthermore a client has a query point q. Without loss of generality we assume $s_0 = -\infty$ and $s_n = \infty$

(this can be accomplished by padding the list with values that are smaller/larger than any q value). At the end of the protocol the client obtains message m_ℓ where: i) $\ell = 2i$ if $s_i = q$ and ii) $\ell = 2i - 1$ if $s_{i-1} < q < s_i$. That is, if the query point is in the server's dataset, then the client learns the corresponding message, and otherwise the client learns a message that is assigned to values between two search keys. The security requirement is that the server should learn nothing (computationally) about the query point, and the client should learn nothing other than the message. For example, the client should not learn if the query is an exact match or an in-between match, unless the messages reveals this information. Furthermore, the protocol should be secure against a semi-honest server and a malicious client.

This private database search problem can be used to solve the following types of common database queries in a private manner:

1. *Existence:* The server has a set $S = \{s_1, \ldots, s_{n-1}\}$ and the client has a query point q. The boundary of all elements in S and q is (s_0, s_n). At the end of the query the client should learn whether $q \in S$. Let Π be the permutation that sorts S and let $m_i = 1$ if i is even and otherwise let $m_i = 0$. The existence problem is solved by $SEARCH(s_0, s_{\Pi(1)}, \ldots, s_{\Pi(n-1)}, s_n, m_1, \ldots, m_{2n-1}\ ;\ q)$.
2. *Message Lookup:* Suppose that the server has a set of tuples where the first element is a key and the second element is a message associated with that key, i.e., $S = \{(s_1, m_1), \ldots, (s_{n-1}, m_{n-1})\}$, and that the client wants to lookup the message associated with key q. The boundary of the keys and q is (s_0, s_n). More formally, the client wants to learn m_i such that $s_i = q$ and if no such match exists then the client should learn $\perp$. Let Π be the permutation that sorts $\{s_1, \ldots, s_{n-1}\}$ and let $m_i = m_{\Pi(i)}$ if i is even and otherwise let $m_i = \perp$. The message lookup problem is solved by $SEARCH(s_0, s_{\Pi(1)}, \ldots, s_{\Pi(n-1)}, s_n, m_1, \ldots, m_{2n-1}\ ;\ q)$.
3. *Rank:* Another variation is for the client to learn the rank of its query in the set. That is, the server has a sorted sequence $s_1, \ldots, s_{n-1}$, the client has a query q, and the answer to the query is the value $|\{s_i : q > s_i\}|$. The boundary of all elements in S and q is (s_0, s_n). If we let $m_i = \lfloor \frac{i-1}{2} \rfloor$, then this is easily solved by $SEARCH(s_0, s_{\Pi(1)}, \ldots, s_{\Pi(n-1)}, s_n, m_1, \ldots, m_{2n-1}\ ;\ q)$.
4. *One-dimensional range query:* Suppose that the server has a set of points $S = \{s_1, \ldots, s_{n-1}\}$ and the client has a query interval $[a, b)$. Also, the boundary of a, b, and all elements in S is (s_0, s_n). The desired output of this protocol is $|\{s_i : a \leq s_i < b\}|$. This can be solved with two calls to search, but we postpone the discussion of this solution until section 3.4.

In this paper we are interested in solving the private database search problem in the precomputation model. In this model, the server is allowed to perform precomputation on the values for each query. Furthermore, the server is allowed to send the client a single message before the protocol begins. While this assumption is unreasonable in some environments, it is applicable in some situations (for example in the database search problems considered in the introduction). The goal of such a protocol is to minimize the time it takes to answer the query once the client's query is known. Moreover, the goals of the protocol are:

1. The precomputation phase should require at most linear computation.
2. The message should be at most linear in the size of the database.
3. The query phase of the protocol should require sublinear computation and communication. Also, the client should perform at most linear computation.

In this paper we introduce a new protocol for private database search that requires the server to perform $O(n)$ work in the precomputation phase and $O(1)$ modular exponentiations in the query phase. Furthermore, the size of the precomputation message is $O(n)$. The client and server perform $O(1)$ communication in the query phase and the client performs $O(1)$ modular exponentiations. Finally, the client performs only $O(\log n)$ computation during the query phase.

A related problem is that of keyword search [4]. This problem is identical to the message lookup protocol described above. While keyword search is less flexible, then the problem described above it is still useful to compare the efficiency of these two approaches for message lookup. In the keyword search protocol described in [4], the total communication is $O(polylogN)$ and the client performs only $O(\log N)$ modular exponentiations. However, in this protocol the server must perform $O(N)$ modular exponentiations and the query still requires $O(N)$ computation. Thus while the communication of this scheme is lower than the communication required by our scheme, our protocol has significantly more efficient query processing in the precomputation model. Table 1 compares the performance of the keyword search protocol for message lookup.

Table 1 also compares our scheme versus the standard naive scheme admitted by traditional SFE solutions (such as [17]). More specifically, this naive solution would be a circuit that performed $O(N)$ equality comparisons followed by a logical or of the results of theses comparisons. In this naive scheme, during the precomputation phase the server would compute the circuit and this garbled circuit would constitute the precomputation message. Note that the performance of these schemes is asymptotically the same in all aspects except client computation and query computation. Notice that our new scheme achieves a significant performance improvement in the query phase, which is the main motivation for the precomputation model.

Table 1. Performance Comparison

Category	Our Scheme	Naive Scheme	Keyword Search
Server Comp	$O(N)$	$O(N)$	$O(N)$
Server Mod Exps	$O(1)$	$O(1)$	$O(N)$
Client Comp	$O(\log N)$	$O(N)$	$O(\log N)$
Client Mod Exps	$O(1)$	$O(1)$	$O(\log N)$
Precomp Message Size	$O(N)$	$O(N)$	0
Query Comm	$O(1)$	$O(1)$	$O(polylog(N))$
Query Phase Comp	$O(\log N)$	$O(N)$	$O(N)$

3 Building Blocks

3.1 Notational Conventions

For $i \in \{0,1\}^b$, the binary representation of i is denoted by $i[b]i[b-1]\cdots i[1]$ where $i[b]$ is the most significant bit. The symbol $||$ is used to represent concatenation. When a value is used in a superscript and is surrounded by () then this corresponds to a string label and not the value itself. When given a boolean value B, the value $\overline{B}$ is the complement of B. When specifying a protocol with two parties, the two parties inputs are separated by a semi-colon.

3.2 Oblivious Transfer

A well-known building block for privacy-preserving computations is chosen 1-out-of-k OT. In this protocol the sender inputs k values $v_0, \ldots, v_{k-1}$, the chooser inputs a choice $\sigma \in [0, k-1]$, and at the end of the protocol the chooser learns v_σ. Furthermore, the chooser should not learn anything about any values other than v_σ and the sender should not learn anything about σ. The OT functionality is defined as $((v_0, \ldots, v_{k-1}); \sigma) \mapsto (\perp\ ;\ v_\sigma)$ where $\perp$ is the empty string. In the remainder of this paper we only utilize the case where $k = 2$ and denote the OT protocol as $OT(v_0, v_1\ ;\ \sigma)$. An efficient two-message protocol for OT was given in [13]. In this protocol the chooser and sender must perform $O(1)$ computation, modular exponentiations, and communication to achieve chosen 1-out-of-2 OT.

3.3 Permuted Encodings

A method, introduced in [17], for splitting a Boolean value, v, between two parties so that neither knows the value is as follows: one party chooses two encodings for the value w_0 and w_1 which are randomly chosen from a large domain[1]. The other party obtains the encoding w_v. The first party knows the meaning of the encodings, but does not know the actual value, and the second party knows the actual encoding value but does not know what it means. We use the variation, introduced in [14], which is: the first party chooses a permutation value λ, and the other party learns the values $v \oplus \lambda$ and w_v. This extra piece of information is useful to improve the efficiency of the underlying scheme. When given a b-bit value v, we use $ENCODE(v, \{(\lambda_i, w_0^i, w_1^i) : i \in [1,b]\})$ to denote the permuted encodings of each bit of v (i.e., $\{(v[i] \oplus \lambda_i, w_{v[i]}^i) : i \in [1,b]\}$). We use $EGEN(1^\kappa)$ to denote the process of generating a permuted encoding given a security parameter κ; that is, $EGEN(1^\kappa)$ produces a set of values $\{\lambda, e_0, e_1\}$ which are a permutation bit, a zero-encoding, and a one-encoding.

3.4 Scrambled Circuit Evaluation

Yao's scrambled circuit evaluation [17] allows for the computation of any function in a privacy-preserving manner. At a high level this approach works by creating a circuit that computes the desired function, and then one party, the generator, scrambles the circuit,

[1] The domain must be large enough to prevent guessing.

and the other party, the evaluator, evaluates the scrambled circuit. The specific version of Yao's protocol that is used in this paper was described in [14]. This version of Yao's protocol was implemented in the Fairplay system [12] and was shown to be efficient for some problems. Recently, this technique has been proven secure in [11]. As this paper utilizes Yao's protocol extensively we review it next (we refer the reader to [14,11] for a full description).

1. The generator creates the scrambled circuit as follows:
   (a) For each wire of the circuit, the generator chooses a permutation and two encodings (one for each possible value) of the wire.
   (b) For each gate of the circuit, the generator creates a PEGLT that will allow the user to obtain the permuted encoding of the output wire based on the permuted encodings of the two input wires.
2. The generator sends the gates' PEGLTs to the evaluator along with the permuted encoding values for all of the wires corresponding to generator inputs.
3. The generator and evaluator engage in a 1-out-of-2 OT protocol for each of the wires corresponding to evaluator inputs, where the evaluator learns the permuted encodings for these wires.
4. The evaluator uses the PEGLTs and the encodings of the input wires to obtain the permuted encodings for all wires of the circuit.
5. The result of the computation can either remain split or can be revealed to either participant. For example, to reveal the result to the evaluator, the generator simply sends the permutation bit for each output wire.

In the remainder of the manuscript we use the following notations:

– $CGEN_b(\circ, \{(\lambda_i, e_0^i, e_1^i) : i \in [1, b]\}, \{(\lambda'_i, f_0^i, f_1^i) : i \in [1, b]\}, \{\lambda, g_0, g_1\})$ denotes the process of generating a circuit that compares to values with $x \circ y$ over b-bit values where $\circ \in \{=, \leq\}$. Furthermore, the permuted encodings for x and y are $\{(\lambda_i, e_0^i, e_1^i) : i \in [1, b]\}$ and $\{(\lambda'_i, f_0^i, f_1^i) : i \in [1, b]\}$ respectively. Finally, the set of permuted encodings for the output wire is $\{\lambda, g_0, g_1\})$. As output this creates the gate gadgets (i.e., the PEGLTs) for the circuit computing operation $\circ$.
– $CEVAL_b(C, \{(x[i] \oplus \lambda_i, e_{x[i]}^i) : i \in [1, b]\}, \{(y[i] \oplus \lambda'_i, f_{y[i]}^i) : i \in [1, b]\}$ evaluates the scrambled circuit C given the encodings for x and y. If C was generated for operation $\circ$, then the result of this evaluation is $r \oplus \lambda, g_r$ where r is the value of the predicate $x \circ y$. That is, this returns the permuted encoding of the result of the circuit.

Achieving One-dimensional Range Querying. A tool for private database search can be used in conjunction with scrambled circuit evaluation to answer one-dimensional range queries. That is, suppose that the server has a set of points $S = \{s_1, \ldots, s_n\}$, the client has a query interval $[a, b)$, and the desired client output of this protocol is $|\{s_i : a \leq s_i < b\}|$. This can be computed by computing $rank_S(b) - rank_S(a)$ where $rank_S(x)$ is the rank of x in S. Thus to compute the result securely, the server can create a subtraction circuit, and then use two private database searches. In the first search the client can obtain the encodings used in the subtraction circuit for $rank_S(a)$ and in the second search the client can learn the encodings in the subtraction circuit for $rank_S(b)$. Then the client can evaluate the circuit to obtain the desired result without revealing either $rank_S(a)$ or $rank_S(b)$.

4 New Tool: Chained PEGLTs

In this section we present a generalization of the gate gadget that is used in Yao's SFE [17] called Permuted Encrypted Garbled Lookup Tables (PEGLT). In this protocol the two parties have b bits split between them using permuted encodings. That is for Boolean values $v_1, \ldots, v_b$, the server has a set of encodings $\{(\lambda_i, e_0^i, e_1^i) : i \in [1, b]\}$ and the client has the corresponding values $\{(\lambda_i \oplus v_i, e_{v_i}^i) : i \in [1, b]\}$. Furthermore, the server has a set of messages $\{M_i : i \in \{0,1\}^b\}$ where each message is m bits long (in what follows we assume that $m = O(1)$). At the end of the protocol, the client should learn $M_{v_1 v_2 \cdots v_b}$ and nothing else, and the server should not learn anything about the split value.

Due to page constraints we do not give the protocol for a traditional PEGLT, but instead give a variation of PEGLTs where the client and server engage in n different PEGLTs where each PEGLT uses the same encodings as the previous PEGLT but has an additional encoding. That is the servers inputs in the successive protocols are $\{(\lambda_i, e_0^i, e_1^i) : i \in [1, 1]\}, \{(\lambda_i, e_0^i, e_1^i) : i \in [1, 2]\}, \ldots, \{(\lambda_i, e_0^i, e_1^i) : i \in [1, n]\}$ and the clients inputs are $\{(\lambda_i \oplus v_i, e_{v_i}^i) : i \in [1, 1]\}, \ldots, \{(\lambda_i \oplus v_i, e_{v_i}^i) : i \in [1, n]\}$. Furthermore, the server's messages are the sets $\{M_i^1 : i \in \{0,1\}^1\}, \{M_i^2 : i \in \{0,1\}^2\}, \ldots, \{M_i^n : i \in \{0,1\}^n\}$. Another requirement is that the server should be able to generate all of the lookup tables at the same time without interaction from the client, and the correctness and security requirements are the same as those in the previous section.

The main idea of this protocol is that server will choose $n+1$ sets of keys, denoted by $K_0, \ldots, K_n$ where $K_j = \{k_i^j : i \in \{0,1\}^j\}$. Now, these keys will be appended to the end of the messages used in the scheme; that is, for each $j \in [1, n]$ and $i \in \{0,1\}^j$, $\hat{M}_i^j = M_i^j || k_i^j$. At the jth PEGLT, the client will learn a single modified message from the set $\{\hat{M}_i^j : i \in \{0,1\}^j\}$, and thus will learn a single key from K_j. The key k_i^j will be used with the appropriate encoding to encrypt the messages $\hat{M}_{i0}^{j+1}$ and $\hat{M}_{i1}^{j+1}$. Essentially, key k_i^j is a compressed form of the encodings $e_{i_1}^1, \ldots, e_{i_j}^j$ in that client will be able to learn k_i^j if and only if it has $e_{i_1}^1, \ldots, e_{i_j}^j$. Thus the j PRF evaluations that were done for these encodings in the $(j+1)$st table can be replaced by a single PRF using this key.

In Figure 1 we describe the details of the table generation phase of chained PEGLT. In this scheme the server generates all n lookup tables, without interacting with the client.

To help clarify this protocol we do an example with $n = 2$. In this case the server has inputs $\{(\lambda_1, e_0^1, e_1^1), (\lambda_2, e_0^2, e_1^2), M_0, M_1, M_{00}, M_{01}, M_{10}, M_{11}\}$. For the sake of an example assume that $\lambda_1 = 0$ and $\lambda_2 = 1$. The server will generate three sets of keys from $\{0,1\}^\kappa$; denote these by $K_0 = \{k_\perp^0\}$, $K_1 = \{k_0^1, k_1^1\}$, and $K_2 = \{k_{00}^2, k_{01}^2, k_{10}^2, k_{11}^2\}$. Now the server creates two tables, the first of which is the ordered

1. For $\ell = 0$ to n create a key set $K_\ell = \{k_i^\ell : i \in \{0,1\}^\ell\}$ where each k_i^ℓ is chosen uniformly from $\{0,1\}^\kappa$.
2. For $j = 1$ to n do the following steps:
   (a) For all $i = i_1 \cdots i_j \in \{0,1\}^j$, the server chooses $r_i \leftarrow \{0,1\}^\kappa$ and computes $i' = i'_1 \cdots i'_j = i_1 \oplus \lambda_1 || \ldots || i_j \oplus \lambda_i$. The server also creates a message $\hat{M}_i^j = M_{i'}^j || k_{i'}^j$. Then the server then computes $C_i^j = (r_i, F_{e^j_{i'_j}}(r_i) \oplus F_{k_h^{j-1}}(r_i) \oplus \hat{M}_i^j)$ where F is a pseudorandom function mapping $\{0,1\}^\kappa \times \{0,1\}^\kappa \to \{0,1\}^{m+\kappa}$ and $h = i'_1 \cdots i'_{j-1}$.
   (b) Create table $T_j = \{C_\ell^j : \ell \in \{0,1\}^j\}$.
3. Return the message $k_\perp^0, T_1, \ldots, T_n$.

Fig. 1. $GENTAB_n(\{(\lambda_i, e_0^i, e_1^i) : i \in [1,n]\}, \{\{M_i^j : i \in \{0,1\}^j\} : j \in [1,n]\}, 1^\kappa)$

1. Let $\ell = (v_1 \oplus \lambda_1) || \cdots || (v_b \oplus \lambda_b)$ and lookup $C_\ell = (r_\ell, D_\ell)$ from table T_j.
2. Compute $\hat{M}_\ell = D_\ell \oplus F_{k^{j-1}_{v_1 \cdots v_{j-1}}}(r_\ell) \oplus F_{e^j_{v_j}}(r_\ell)$. Parse $\hat{M}_\ell$ into $M^j_{v_1 \ldots v_j}$ and $k^j_{v_1 \ldots v_j}$ and return these values.

Fig. 2. $LOOKUP_j(T_j, k^{j-1}_{v_1 \cdots v_{j-1}}, \{(v_\ell \oplus \lambda_\ell, e^\ell_{v_\ell}) : \ell \in [1,j]\})$

set $\{(r_0, F_{k_\perp^0}(r_0) \oplus F_{e_0^1}(r_0) \oplus (M_0^1 || k_0^1)), (r_1, F_{k_\perp^0}(r_1) \oplus F_{e_1^1}(r_1) \oplus (M_1^1 || k_1^1))\}$. The second table (which is the more interesting table) will be the ordered set (recall that $\lambda_1 = 0$ and $\lambda_2 = 1$):

$$\{(r_{00}, F_{k_0^1}(r_{00}) \oplus F_{e_1^2}(r_{00}) \oplus (M_{01}^2 || k_{01}^2)), (r_{01}, F_{k_0^1}(r_{01}) \oplus F_{e_0^2}(r_{01}) \oplus (M_{00}^2 || k_{00}^2)),$$
$$(r_{10}, F_{k_1^1}(r_{10}) \oplus F_{e_1^2}(r_{10}) \oplus (M_{11}^2 || k_{11}^2)), (r_{11}, F_{k_1^1}(r_{11}) \oplus F_{e_0^2}(r_{11}) \oplus (M_{10}^2 || k_{10}^2))\}$$

In the table lookup phase, the client will have the message $k_\perp^0, T_1, \ldots, T_n$ and it will sequentially obtain the permuted encodings for the value v. In Figure 2 we describe the details of the protocol for the jth lookup (where the user will learn a message and a key).

Returning to the example suppose that $v = 01$, and thus the client should obtain M_0^1 and M_{01}^2 from the first and second table lookup respectively. In the first table lookup the client has $k_\perp^0$, $v_1 \oplus \lambda_1 = 0$, and $e_{v_1}^1 = e_0^1$. The client takes entry 0 in T_1 (i.e., $(r_0, F_{k_\perp^0}(r_0) \oplus F_{e_0^1}(r_0) \oplus (M_0^1 || k_0^1))$) and computes $M_0^1 || k_0^1$, which is the correct message. Now in the second table lookup the client uses k_0^1 and $v_2 \oplus \lambda_2 = 0$ and $e_{v_2}^2 = e_1^2$ to decrypt entry 00 in the table T_2. That is, the client decrypts $(r_{00}, F_{k_0^1}(r_{00}) \oplus F_{e_1^2}(r_{00}) \oplus (M_{01}^2 || k_{01}^2))$ to obtain $M_{01}^2 || k_{01}^2$, which is what is expected.

In chained PEGLT server needs to perform only $O(1)$ pseudorandom functions per table entry. Since there are only $O(2^n)$ entries in all n tables, the server needs to perform $O(2^n)$ computation. Furthermore, the client only performs $O(1)$ PRF evaluations per lookup, and thus performs only $O(n)$ computation. Finally, the efficiency of the above scheme can be improved slightly by removing the first encryption key and the last encryption key (i.e., keys is K_0 and K_n). However, this improvement does not change the asymptotic complexity of the protocol.

5 Private Database Search Protocol

In this section, the main result of this paper is presented. Specifically, a protocol for the private database search problem in the precomputation model is given that requires the client only perform sublinear (in the size of the database) computation and communication. In the private database search problem the server has a sorted sequence of points $s_1, s_2, \ldots, s_N$ (where each $s_i \in \{0,1\}^b$) and a sequence of messages $m_1, \ldots, m_{2N+1}$; furthermore the client has a query point $q \in \{0,1\}^b$. For ease of presentation we assume[2] that N is a power of 2 and denote $n = \log N$.

The main idea of this protocol is to use a standard binary search to achieve computation and communications that is logarithmic in the dataset size. We often refer to the binary search as a navigation through a complete binary search tree where the leaf nodes of the tree are the values in the server's set in sorted order. The difficulty with performing a private binary search is that the path of the search (i.e., whether the search goes left or right at a specific node) must be hidden from both the client and the server. This path cannot be revealed to the server because it would reveal a small range that contains the query, and the path cannot be revealed to the client, because this would reveal the rank of the query. Neither of these things are revealed by the result alone. To hide the search path, we utilize the well known technique of permuted encodings for these values. These permuted encodings are used in scrambled circuit evaluations to perform the comparison at each node on the search path, and chained PEGLTs are used to obtain the encodings for the nodes in the search tree. To make this discussion more concrete we present some formal notation.

We organize the values into a complete binary search tree, where the root node is denoted by T, and the intermediate nodes are denoted by $T_{i_1 i_2 \cdots i_m}$ where all i values are in $\{0,1\}$ and $m \in [1,n]$. The intermediate nodes are organized such that the left (resp. right) child of $T_{i_1 i_2 \cdots i_j}$ is $T_{i_1 i_2 \cdots i_j 0}$ (resp. $T_{i_1 i_2 \cdots i_j 1}$). The value of node $T_{i_1 i_2 \cdots i_j}$ is denoted by $v_{i_1 i_2 \cdots i_j}$. Note that the leaf nodes of the tree contain the values in set S is sorted order; that is, $v_i = s_i$ for all $i \in \{0,1\}^n$. The levels of the tree are denoted by $L_0, L_1, \ldots, L_n$ where L_0 is the root level of the tree and L_n is the leaf level. When performing a binary search on the tree, a comparison is made between q and a specific value at each level of the tree. We denote the result of the comparison at level L_j as R_j, where R_j is 0 (resp. 1) if q is less than or equal to (resp. greater than or equal to) the value at level L_j. Finally, note that the comparison at level L_j is between q and $v_{R_0 R_1 \cdots R_{j-1}}$.

The querier will obtain three types of permuted encodings in our scheme, including:

1. *Querier's value:* These correspond to the permuted encodings for the value q. The permutation, zero encoding, and one encoding for bit $q[i]$ are denoted respectively by $\lambda^{(q),i}$, $e_0^{(q),i}$, and $e_1^{(q),i}$. The set of these values $\{(\lambda^{(q),i}, e_0^{(q),i}, e_1^{(q),i}) : i \in [1,b]\}$ is denoted by $PE^{(q)}$.

[2] It is straightforward to remove this assumption through padding.

2. *Level L_j value:* These correspond to the permuted encodings for the server's value at the node for level L_j. The permutation, zero encoding, and one encoding for bit $L_j[i]$ are denoted respectively by $\lambda^{(L),j,i}$, $e_0^{(L),j,i}$, and $e_1^{(L),j,i}$. The set of values corresponding to level L_j, i.e., $\{(\lambda^{(L),j,i}, e_0^{(L),j,i}, e_1^{(L),j,i}) : i \in [1, b]\}$ is denoted by $PE^{(L),j}$.
3. *Comparison Results:* These correspond to the permuted encoding for R_j. The permutation, zero encoding, and one encoding for R_j are denoted respectively by $\lambda^{(R),j}$, $e_0^{(R),j}$, and $e_1^{(R),j}$. The set of these values corresponding to a specific level L_j, i.e., $\{\lambda^{(R),j}, e_0^{(R),j}, e_1^{(R),j}\}$, is denoted by as $PE^{(R),j}$.

Now that the notation has been defined, a more concrete view of our protocol is possible. The major steps of the protocol are as follows:

1. To bootstrap the system, the client and server engage in an OT protocol where the client learns the permuted encodings for q, the server sends the client the permuted encodings corresponding to v (the value at the root of the tree). These encodings are input into a scrambled comparison circuit which will split the value of R_0 in a permuted encoded format.
2. At each non-leaf level, L_j, a chained PEGLT is used to reveal the permuted encodings for $v_{R_0 R_1 \cdots R_{j-1}}$ to the client. These new encodings are then used in a scrambled comparison circuit to compare the value $v_{R_0 R_1 \cdots R_{j-1}}$ to q to obtain the permuted encoding for R_j.
3. When the leaf level is reached, a chained PEGLT is used to reveal the permuted encodings for $v_{R_0 R_1 \cdots R_{n-1}}$ to the client. These encodings are used along with the encodings for q in a scrambled circuit to reveal encodings for where q is less than, greater than, or equal to $v_{R_0 R_1 \cdots R_{n-1}}$. These two bits are used in the PEGLT to reveal the corresponding message.

5.1 Precomputation Phase

As input to the precomputation phase, the server inputs its set $S = \{s_1, \ldots, s_n\}$, a set of messages $m_1, \ldots, m_{2n+1}$, and a security parameter 1^κ. The full details of the precomputation phase are given in Figure 3.

5.2 Query Phase

In the query phase the client first performs a series of oblivious transfers that reveal to the client the permuted encodings of the query value q. Then, the client uses those encodings and the precomputation message to compute the result. Essentially, this phase uses the circuit at each level of the search tree to compare q and the current value of the node on the search path. The results of this comparison are used with the lookup tables from the precomputation phase to obtain the permuted encodings for the next node in the tree (see Figure 4).

1. *Choose permuted encodings/Setup:* Using $Egen(1^\kappa)$, the server chooses the following sets of permuted encodings: $\{(\lambda^{(q),i}, e_0^{(q),i}, e_1^{(q),i}) : i \in [1,b]\}$, $\{(\lambda^{(L),j,i}, e_0^{(L),j,i}, e_1^{(L),j,i}) : j \in [0,n], i \in [1,b]\}$ and $\{(\lambda^{(R),j}, e_0^{(R),j}, e_1^{(R),j}) : j \in [0,n]\}$. The server also creates a tree T that contains the values of S.
2. *Generate comparison circuits:* For $j \in [0, n-1]$ the server creates a scrambled comparison circuit that will be used to compare q and $v_{R_0 R_1 \cdots R_{j-1}}$ by using $C_j = CGEN(\leq, PE^{(q)}, PE^{(L),j}, PE^{(R),j})$.
3. The server creates a scrambled equality circuit for the last level of the tree that will be used to compare q and $v_{R_0 R_1 \cdots R_{n-1}}$ by using
$C_n = CGEN((=), PE^{(q)}, PE^{(L),n}, PE^{(R),n})$.
4. *Generate PEGLTs:* Using chained PEGLT, the server creates a mechanism to use the R encodings to obtain the encodings for the values on the search path of q and for the server messages. That is for $j \in [1, n-1]$ let $M_i^j = v_{i_1,\ldots,i_j}$ and let $M_i^n = m_i$, then the server computes $LT = GENTAB_n(\{PE^{(R),i} : i \in [1,n]\}, \{\{M_i^j : i \in \{0,1\}^j\} : j \in [1,n]\}, 1^\kappa)$.
5. *Create message:* Form a message, we call it PM in the remainder of this section, consisting of the following elements and return it: $\{C_i : i \in [0,n]\}, LT, ENCODE(v, PE^{(L),0})$.

Fig. 3. Precomputation Phase$(1^\kappa, S)$

1. The client and server engage in b 1-out-of-2 OTs as follows : $OT(q[i] \ ; \ \lambda^{(q),i} \| e_0^{(q),i}, \overline{\lambda^{(q),i}} \| e_1^{(q),i})$ for all $i \in [1,b]$ where the client is the chooser and the server is the sender. The client gets $ENCODE(q, PR^{(q)})$.
2. For $i = 0$ to $n-1$ the client does the following:
   (a) $E_i = R_i \oplus \lambda^{(R),i} \| e_{R_i}^{(R),i} = CEVAL(C_i, A, B_i)$ where $A = ENCODE(q, PR^{(q)})$ and $B_i = ENCODE(v_{R_0 \cdots R_{i-1}}, PE^{(L),i})$.
   (b) The client learns $ENCODE(v_{R_0 \cdots R_i}, PE^{(L),i})$ and $k_{v_1 \ldots v_{i+1}}^{i+1}$ by doing: $LOOKUP_{i+1}(T_{i+1}, k_{v_1 \ldots v_{i+1}}^i, E_i)$.
3. For the leaf level, the client does the following: $E_n = R_n \oplus \lambda^{(R),n} \| e_{R_n}^{(R),n} = CEVAL(C_n, A, B_n)$ where $A = ENCODE(q, PR^{(q)})$ and
$B_n = ENCODE(v_{R_0 \cdots R_{n-1}}, PE^{(L),n})$.
4. The client uses $R_n \oplus \lambda^{(R),n}$ and $\lambda^{(R),n}$ to learn the value of R_n which is the desired result.

Fig. 4. Query Phase$(PM, q \ ; \ PE^{(q)})$)

5.3 Performance Analysis

Assume that $b = O(1)$, then in the precomputation phase the server creates $O(\log N)$ circuits each with size $O(1)$. The chained PEGLT will require $O(n)$ computation. In the interactive phase the scheme requires $O(1)$ 1-out-of-2 OTs each of which requires $O(1)$ computations/modular exponentiations. Hence, the query phase requires each party to perform $O(1)$ modular exponentiations, and since these can be done in parallel, this phase requires $O(1)$ rounds. Finally, in the query phase the client has to evaluate $O(\log N)$ circuits each with $O(1)$ gates, and thus this requires $O(\log N)$ computation.

The client also has to do the chained PEGLT lookup which requires $O(\log N)$ computation for all lookups. Thus the total query computation is $O(\log N)$. We summarize the performance of our scheme in Table 1 (in section 2).

6 Proof of Security

Due to page constraints we give only a sketch of the security analysis. This protocol is secure in the honest-but-curious adversary model[3]. The standard definition for security states that there should be a probabilistic polynomial time simulator that can produce a transcript that is computationally indistinguishable from the client's (resp server's) view of the real protocol when given the client's (resp. server's) input and output. For a formal definition see [7]. When proving the security of a protocol, the composition theorem of [2] is useful. This theorem states that if the protocol is proven secure when the protocol's building blocks are replaced by a version of those building blocks that utilize a trusted third party, then the protocol that results from the building blocks being replaced by secure implementations is also secure. Now, the server's view consists the results of the oblivious transfer during the interactive query phase where the server plays the part of the sender. In OT the sender does not have any output, and hence security against a dishonest server is straightforwad. To demonstrate client-side security, notice that all of the building blocks (OT, scrambled circuits, and PEGLT) reveal only permuted encodings to the client. Hence, these intermediate results are trivially simulateable.

7 Experiments

In this section, we present experiments and results of a comparison between the naive scheme and our protocol. The experiments are on a *Intel(R) Core(TM)2 Duo CPU E6750 @ 2.66GHz 2.67GHz* CPU and *2.00 GB* RAM. The operating system is Windows7 Enterprise (x64). The implementations are written in Java.

In this experiment, we implement the protocols solving the point existence queries problem, which is the server inputs a set of numbers S and the client inputs a number q to learn whether $q \in S$. We varied server's input size form 100 to 3000 in step of 100. For each input size we run each experiment 20 times and report the mean performance. The bit size of input number is 16.

Precomputation time (cf. Figure 5). Our experiments shows the naive scheme costs linear time in the precomputation phase. Since only little time is needed in small input size by using our scheme, the performance for our scheme is not very obvious here. Clearly, our scheme is much faster than naive scheme in the precomputation phase. The reason is that our scheme generates less circuits than naive scheme and generating Chained-PEGLT is faster than generating circuits.

Communication size (cf. Figure 6). Both schemes require linear communication size. The data jumps in certain number of input for our scheme. That's because the size of message depends on the height of the search tree.

[3] Recall that an adversary is honest but curious if the adversary will follow the protocol, but will try to learn additional information.

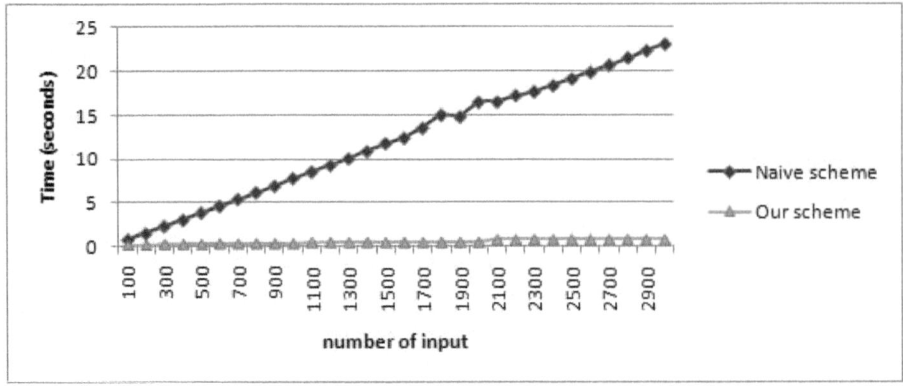

Fig. 5. Precomputation time

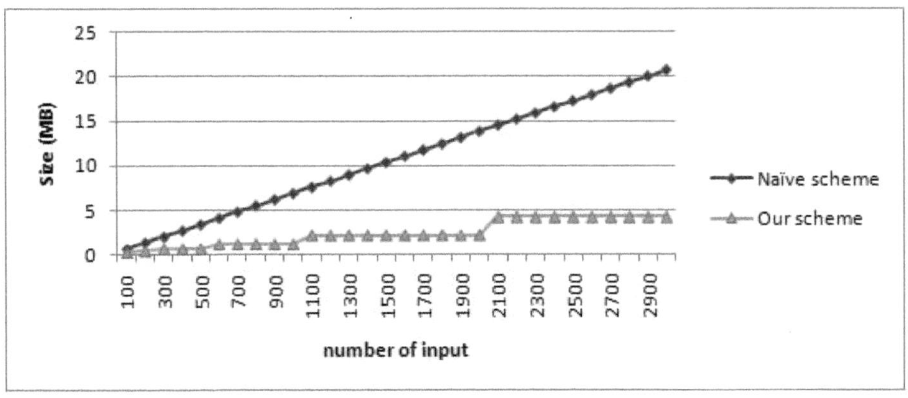

Fig. 6. Communication size

OT time. There is no difference between our scheme and naive scheme in OT time, because the client does same OT in both scheme for its input. Due to page constraints we do not provide the comparison figure.

Evaluation time (cf. Figure 7). Our scheme significantly improves the performance in evaluation time. In further experiments, the evaluation time for our solution is still under 0.002 seconds even server's input size increases to 50000.

8 Related Work

Secure Multiparty Computation (SMC) is the problem of creating a privacy-preserving protocol for any function f[4]; that is, creating a protocol that computes f over distributed inputs while revealing only the result and inferences that can be made from this result. General results state that any function can be computed in such a secure manner. The first constructions for secure two-party SMC were given in [16,17]; these

[4] We are assuming that f can be computed in polynomial time when given all of the inputs.

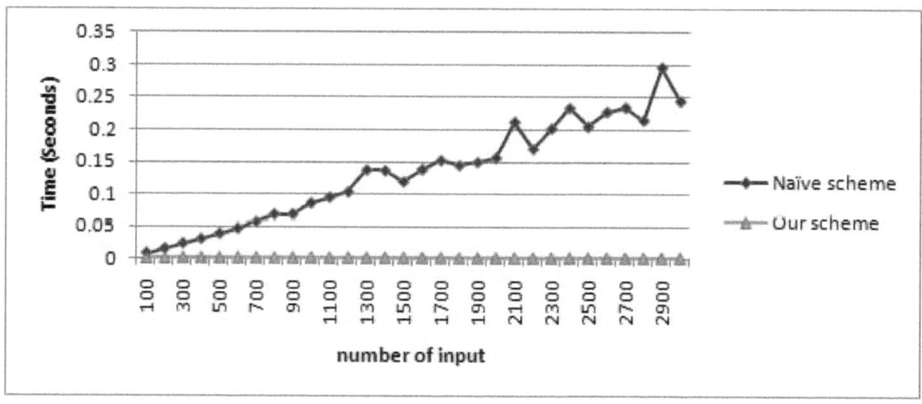

Fig. 7. Evaluation time

assumed that the adversary of the protocol was honest-but-curious (HBC) in that the adversary will follow the protocol exactly but will attempt to make additional inferences. Later a construction was given for multiple parties [8] in the malicious adversary model (where the adversary deviates arbitrarily from the protocol) assuming that a majority of the participants are honest. There have also been many other papers attempting to improve the efficiency of these protocols to make the general results practical. However, to our knowledge all of these protocols require linear computation and/or communication when solving the private data querying problem.

An area that is related is private information retrieval (PIR) [3,10,1]. In PIR, the server has a sequence of bits $v_1, \ldots, v_N$ and the client has a specific index $i \in N$. The goal of PIR is that the client should learn v_i without revealing anything about the index to the serve, while requiring only sublinear communication. While PIR is related to accessing a database in a private manner, there are important differences between PIR and the work in this manuscript. First, it is not clear how PIR could be used to solve the problems solved in this manuscript. That is, PIR allows the client to access a specific bit, but this doesn't appear to solve problems like message lookup and range queries. Secondly, PIR requires linear computation, whereas the goal of this paper is to have sublinear computation in the query phase.

Another related problem is the area of oblivious RAM [9]. In oblivious RAM, a data owner wants to access a dataset but desires to hide the access pattern from an adversary that holds the data. Techniques have been developed which allow an access cost that requires sublinear computation and communication (in an amortized sense). Furthermore, recent results [15] have shown that these schemes can be practical. However, the oblivious RAM model does not apply to the problems considered in this paper, because the Oblivious RAM model assumes that the accessing party has all of the data. In our case this would correspond to the client having all of the data and querying its own data.

9 Conclusions/Future Work

In summary, in this paper we introduce the precomputation model for privately accessing a database. In this model, the database owner performs linear precomputation on the dataset for each query, but this step can be completed without the query being fixed. We also present several protocols in this model where the query time is sublinear based on a new building block of a private database search. As future work we propose the following problems: A limitation of the current approach is that the precomputation must be done for each query. It would be interesting if the precomputation information could be shared for multiple queries. Perhaps the current techniques could be combined with the approach in [5] that uses fully homomorphic encryption [6]. Also, the current approach only works for the honest but curious model. An interesting extension would be to extend this to the malicious adversary model.

Acknowledgement

The authors would like to thank the anonymous reviewers for their comments and useful suggestions. Portions of this work were supported by Grant CNS-0915843 from the National Science Foundation.

References

1. Cachin, C., Micali, S., Stadler, M.: Computationally private information retrieval with polylogarithmic communication. In: Stern, J. (ed.) EUROCRYPT 1999. LNCS, vol. 1592, pp. 402–414. Springer, Heidelberg (1999)
2. Canetti, R.: Security and composition of multiparty cryptographic protocols. Journal of Cryptology 13(1), 143–202 (2000)
3. Chor, B., Kushilevitz, E., Goldreich, O., Sudan, M.: Private information retrieval. J. ACM 45(6), 965–981 (1998)
4. Freedman, M.J., Ishai, Y., Pinkas, B., Reingold, O.: Keyword search and oblivious pseudorandom functions. In: Kilian, J. (ed.) TCC 2005. LNCS, vol. 3378, pp. 303–324. Springer, Heidelberg (2005)
5. Gennaro, R., Gentry, C., Parno, B.: Non-interactive verifiable computing: Outsourcing computation to untrusted workers. In: Rabin, T. (ed.) CRYPTO 2010. LNCS, vol. 6223, pp. 465–482. Springer, Heidelberg (2010)
6. Gentry, C.: Fully homomorphic encryption using ideal lattices. In: STOC 2009: Proceedings of the 41st Annual ACM Symposium on Theory of Computing, pp. 169–178. ACM, New York (2009)
7. Goldreich, O.: Foundations of Cryptography. Basic Application, vol. II. Cambridge University Press, Cambridge (2004)
8. Goldreich, O., Micali, S., Wigderson, A.: How to play any mental game. In: Proceedings of the Nineteenth Annual ACM Conference on Theory of Computing, pp. 218–229 (May 1987)
9. Goldreich, O., Ostrovsky, R.: Software protection and simulation on oblivious rams. J. ACM 43(3), 431–473 (1996)
10. Kushilevitz, E., Ostrovsky, R.: Replication is not needed: single database, computationally-private information retrieval. In: FOCS 1997: Proceedings of the 38th Annual Symposium on Foundations of Computer Science (FOCS 1997), pp. 364–373. IEEE Computer Society, Los Alamitos (1997)

11. Lindelll, Y., Pinkas, B.: A proof of yao's protocol for secure two-party computation. Journal of Cryptology 22(2), 161–188 (2009)
12. Malkhi, D., Nisan, N., Pinkas, B., Sella, Y.: Fairplay—a secure two-party computation system. In: SSYM 2004: Proceedings of the 13th Conference on USENIX Security Symposium, p. 20. USENIX Association, Berkeley (2004)
13. Naor, M., Pinkas, B.: Efficient oblivious transfer protocols. In: Proceedings of the Twelfth Annual ACM-SIAM Symposium on Discrete Algorithms, pp. 448–457. Society for Industrial and Applied Mathematics (2001)
14. Naor, M., Pinkas, B., Sumner, R.: Privacy preserving auctions and mechanism design. In: EC 1999: Proceedings of the 1st ACM Conference on Electronic Commerce, pp. 129–139. ACM, New York (1999)
15. Williams, P., Sion, R., Carbunar, B.: Building castles out of mud: practical access pattern privacy and correctness on untrusted storage. In: CCS 2008: Proceedings of the 15th ACM Conference on Computer and Communications Security, pp. 139–148. ACM, New York (2008)
16. Yao, A.C.: Protocols for secure computation. In: Proceedings of the 23rd Annual IEEE Symposium on Foundations of Computer Science, pp. 160–164 (1982)
17. Yao, A.C.: How to generate and exchange secrets. In: Proceedings of the 27th Annual IEEE Symposium on Foundations of Computer Science, pp. 162–167 (1986)

Efficient Distributed Linear Programming with Limited Disclosure*

Yuan Hong, Jaideep Vaidya, and Haibing Lu

MSIS Department and CIMIC, Rutgers University, NJ, USA
{yhong,jsvaidya,haibing}@cimic.rutgers.edu

Abstract. In today's networked world, resource providers and consumers are distributed globally and locally. However, with resource constraints, optimization is necessary to ensure the best possible usage of such scarce resources. *Distributed linear programming (DisLP)* problems allow collaborative agents to jointly maximize profits (or minimize costs) with a linear objective function while conforming to several shared as well as local linear constraints. Since each agent's share of the global constraints and the local constraints generally refer to its private limitations or capacities, serious privacy problems may arise if such information is revealed. While there have been some solutions proposed that allow secure computation of such problems, they typically rely on inefficient protocols with enormous communication cost. In this paper, we present a secure and extremely efficient protocol to solve DisLP problems where constraints are arbitrarily partitioned and no variable is shared between agents. In the entire protocol, each agent learns only a partial solution (about its variables), but learns nothing about the private input/output of other agents, assuming semi-honest behavior. We present a rigorous security proof and communication cost analysis for our protocol and experimentally validate the costs, demonstrating its robustness.

1 Introduction

Optimization is a fundamental problem found in all industries. As an essential subclass of optimization, linear programming models are widely applicable to solving numerous profit-maximizing or cost-minimizing problems in various fields such as transportation, commodities, airlines and communication.

For instance, in the packaged goods industry, delivery trucks are empty 25% of the time. Just four years ago, Land O'Lakes truckers spent much of their time shuttling empty trucks down slow-moving highways, wasting several million dollars annually. By using a web based collaborative logistics service (Nistevo.com), to merge loads from different companies (even competitors) bound to the same destination, huge savings were realized (freight costs were cut by 15%, for an annual savings of $2 million[1]). This required sending all information to a central site. Such complete sharing of data may often be impossible for many corporations, and thus result in great loss of possible efficiencies. Since this is a transportation problem which can be modeled through linear programming, a *Distributed linear programming* (DisLP) solution that tightly limits

* This work is supported in part by the National Science Foundation under Grant No. CNS-0746943.

Y. Li (Ed.): Data and Applications Security and Privacy XXV, LNCS 6818, pp. 170–185, 2011.

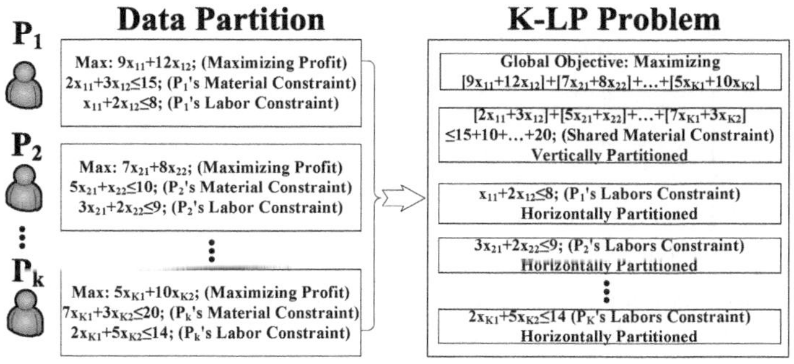

Fig. 1. Distributed LP Problem Formulation (Example 1)

the information disclosure would make this possible without the release of proprietary information. Specifically, DisLP problems can facilitate collaborative agents to jointly maximize global profits (or minimize costs) while satisfying several (global or local) linear constraints. Since each agent's share of the global constraints and the local constraints generally refer to its private limitations or capacities and the optimal solution represents its decision, limited disclosure should prevent revealing such information in this distributed computing scenario.

While completely arbitrary partitioning of constraints and variables is possible, in many realistic DisLP problems, each company holds its own variables: the values for which together constitute the global optimum decision. Variables are generally not shared between companies because collaborators may have their own operations w.r.t. a maximized profit or minimized cost. Consider the following example:

Example 1. K Companies $P_1 \dots P_K$ share some raw materials for production (maximizing profits): the amount of company P_i's ($i \in [1, K]$) product j to be manufactured are denoted as x_{ij}, thus P_i holds $x_i = \{\forall j, x_{ij}\}$.

In the collaborative production problem above, the constraints are arbitrarily partitioned. On one hand, $P_1 \dots P_K$ should have some local constraints (i.e. each company's local labor constraint) that is only known to each company. On the other hand, there may be some global constraints (i.e. the total quantity of the shared raw materials). Figure 1 demonstrates a simple example of this. K companies jointly manufacture products (two for each company) using a shared material where P_1, P_2, ..., P_K have the amount 15, 10, ..., 20, respectively (The sum of the global profits can be increased by this collaboration since the combined resources are better utilized). They also have their local constraints, i.e. the total labor for producing each company's products are bounded with constraints 8, 9 and 14 respectively. After solving this DisLP problem, each company should know the (global) optimal production amount for only its products but should not learn anything about the private constraints and solution of other companies. To simplify the notation, we formally define it as below:

Definition 1 (K-Agent LP Problem (K-LP)). *An LP problem is solved by K distributed agents where each agent P_i holds n_i variables x_i, share of the objective c_i, its local constraints $B_i x_i \bowtie_i b_i$, and the matrix/vector A_i/b_0^i in the global constraints $\sum_{i=1}^{K} A_i x_i \bowtie_0 b_0$ (as shown in Equation 1*[1,2,3]*)($i \in [1, K]$ and $\sum_{i=1}^{K} b_0^i = b_0$).*

$$\max \quad c_1^T x_1 + c_2^T x_2 + \cdots + c_K^T x_K$$
$$s.t. \begin{cases} x_1 \in \mathbb{R}^{n_1} \\ x_2 \in \mathbb{R}^{n_2} \\ \vdots \\ x_K \in \mathbb{R}^{n_K} \end{cases} : \begin{pmatrix} A_1 \dots A_K \\ B_1 & & \\ & \ddots & \\ & & B_K \end{pmatrix} \begin{pmatrix} x_1 \\ x_2 \\ \vdots \\ x_K \end{pmatrix} \begin{matrix} \bowtie_0 \\ \bowtie_1 \\ \vdots \\ \bowtie_K \end{matrix} \begin{pmatrix} b_0 \\ b_1 \\ \vdots \\ b_K \end{pmatrix} \quad (1)$$

Indeed, besides collaborative production, K-LP problems occur very frequently in reality, i.e. collaborative delivery of goods for different companies to save transportation cost, selling the goods in bundles for distributed agents to maximize the global profits, and determining profit-maximized travel packages for hotels, airlines and car rental companies.

We intend to introduce a secure and efficient distributed computing solution to the K-LP problem. Thus, our key contributions are: 1) to propose a privacy-preserving transformation for the K-LP problem; 2) to propose a secure protocol robust against honest-but-curious adversaries (semi-honest model: assuming that all the agents follow our protocol) that is fair to all agents, and 3) to experimentally validate the cost of the proposed protocol.

The rest of this paper is structured as follows. Section 2 reviews some related work. Section 3 introduces some preliminaries for our approach. Section 4 presents the transformation process (for security purpose) and shows that how to derive the optimal solution for each agent after solving the transformed problem. In Section 5, we present the secure protocol with security proof and computation cost analysis. Finally, we experimentally validate the protocol in Section 6 and conclude the paper in Section 7.

2 Literature Review

Optimization problems occur in all walks of real life. There is work in distributed optimization that aims to achieve a global objective using only local information. Distributed Constraint Satisfaction was formalized by Yokoo[2] to solve naturally distributed constraint satisfaction problems. These problems are divided between agents, who then have to communicate among themselves to solve them. ADOPT[3] is a backtracking based bound propagation mechanism. It operates completely decentralized, and asynchronously. The downside is that it may require a very large number of messages, thus producing big communication overheads.

However, in general, the work in distributed optimization has concentrated on reducing communication costs and has paid little or no attention to security constraints. Thus, some of the summaries may reveal significant information. In particular, the rigor of security proofs has not been applied much in this area. There is some work in secure optimization. Silaghi and Rajeshirke [4] show that a secure combinatorial problem solver must necessarily pick the result randomly among optimal solutions to be really

---

[1] $\bowtie$ denotes $\leq, =$ or $\geq$.

[2] Due to $\{\min : c^T x \equiv \max : -c^T x\}$, we model $\max : c^T x$.

[3] size: $\forall i \in [1, K]$, $\{A_i : m_0 \times n_i\}$, $\{B_i : m_i \times n_i\}$, $\{c_i : n_i\}$, $\{b_0 : m_0\}$ and $\{b_i : m_i\}$

secure. Silaghi and Mitra [5] propose arithmetic circuits for solving constraint optimization problems that are exponential in the number of variables for any constraint graph. A significantly more efficient optimization protocol specialized on generalized Vickrey auctions and based on dynamic programming is proposed by Suzuki and Yokoo [6]. However, much of this work is still based on generic solutions and not quite ready for practical use. Even so, some of this work can definitely be leveraged to advance the state of the art by building general transformations or privacy-preserving variants of well known methods.

Privacy-preserving linear programming problem has been introduced to solve the LP problem with limited information disclosure between two agents [7][8][9][10]. Nevertheless, several shortcomings can be discovered in their work. First, neither of them is applicable to solving multi-agent (more than two) distributed LP problems. Second, the secure protocols require enormous computation costs: even if the computational cost of Li et al.'s work [8] and Vaidya's work [7][9] includes a polynomial number of homomorphic encryptions, it still requires considerable time complexity for the total encryption. The efficiency should be greatly declined for large DisLP problems. Mangasarian [11]proposed a privacy-preserving formulation of a linear program over vertically partitioned constraint matrix while our approach is introduced to privately solve arbitrarily partitioned LP problems in this paper, and no formal security analysis is given in [11]. A secure third-party based protocol for LP was proposed by Du [10], however the LP problem is not addressed fully or formally and an optimal solution is not guaranteed. We will propose a secure and efficient DisLP approach to resolve the above limitations.

3 Preliminaries

In this section, we briefly review some definitions and properties related to LP problems.

3.1 Polyhedra

From the geometrical point of view, LP problems can be represented as polyhedra. We thus present some geometrical definitions for LP problems.

Definition 2 (Polyhedron of Linear Constraints). *A polyhedron $P \subseteq \mathbb{R}^n$ is the set of points that satisfy a finite number (m) of linear constraints $P = \{x \in \mathbb{R}^n : Ax \bowtie b\}$ where A is an $m \times n$ constraint matrix.*

Definition 3 (Convex Combination). *A point $x \in \mathbb{R}^n$ is a convex combination of a set $S \subseteq \mathbb{R}^n$ if x can be expressed as $x = \sum_i \lambda_i x^i$ for a finite subset $\{x^i\}$ of S and $\lambda > 0$ with $\sum_i \lambda_i = 1$.*

Definition 4 (Vertex). *A point $x^e \in P$ is a vertex of $P = \{x \in \mathbb{R}^n : Ax \bowtie b\}$ if it cannot be represented as a convex combination of two other points $x^i, x^j \in P$.*

Definition 5 (Ray in Polyhedron). *Given a non-empty polyhedron $P = \{x \in \mathbb{R}^n : Ax \bowtie b\}$, a vector $r \in \mathbb{R}^n, r \neq 0$ is a ray if $Ar \bowtie 0$.*

Definition 6 (Extreme Ray). *A ray r is an extreme ray of $P = \{x \in \mathbb{R}^n : Ax \bowtie b\}$ if there does not exist two distinct rays r^i and r^j of P such that $r = \frac{1}{2}(r^i + r^j)$.*

3.2 Dantzig-Wolfe Decomposition

Assume that we let x^i (size n vector) represent a vertex or extreme ray in the LP problem. Hence, every point inside the polyhedron can be represented by all the vertices and/or extreme rays using convexity combination (Minkowski's Representation Theorem [12]). Thus, a polyhedron P can be represented by another polyhedron $P' = \{\lambda \in \mathbb{R}^{|E|} : \sum_{i \in E} \delta_i \lambda_i = 1; \lambda \leq 0\}$ where

$$\delta_i = \begin{cases} 1 \text{ if } x^i \text{ is a vertex} \\ 0 \text{ if } x^i \text{ is an extreme ray} \end{cases} \tag{2}$$

Hence, the original LP problem (Equation 1) can be transformed to a master problem (Equation 3) using Dantzig-Wolfe Decomposition [12]. Assuming that x_i^j represents the extreme point or ray associated with λ_{ij}.

$$max \quad \sum_j c_1^T x_1^j \lambda_{1j} + \cdots + \sum_j c_K^T x_K^j \lambda_{Kj}$$

$$s.t. \begin{cases} \sum_j A_1 x_1^j \lambda_{1j} + \cdots + \sum_j A_K x_K^j \lambda_{Kj} \bowtie b_0 \\ \sum_j \delta_{1j} \lambda_{1j} \qquad\qquad\qquad\qquad = 1 \\ \qquad\qquad \ddots \\ \qquad\qquad\qquad \sum_j \delta_{Kj} \lambda_{Kj} = 1 \\ \lambda_1 \in \mathbb{R}^{|E_1|}, \ldots, \lambda_K \in \mathbb{R}^{|E_K|}, \delta_{ij} \in \{0,1\}, i \in [1, K] \end{cases} \tag{3}$$

As proven in [12], primal feasible points, optimal primal points, an unbounded rays, dual feasible points, optimal dual points and certificate of infeasibility in the *master problem* are equivalent to the *original problem*.

4 Revised Dantzig-Wolfe Decomposition

As shown in Equation 1, K-LP problem has a typical Block-angular structure, though the number of global constraints can be significantly larger than each agent's local constraints. Hence, we can solve the K-LP problem using Dantzig-Wolfe decomposition. In this section, we transform our K-LP problem to an anonymized (block-angular) format that preserves each agent's private input/output. We also show that the optimal solution for each agent's variables can be derived after solving the transformed problem.

4.1 K-LP Transformation

Du [13][10] and Vaidya [7] proposed a transformation approach for solving two-agent DisLP problems: transforming an $m \times n$ constraint matrix M (the objective vector c^T) to another $m \times n$ matrix $M' = MQ$ ($c'^T = c^T Q$) by post-multiplying an $n \times n$ matrix Q, solving the transformed problem and deriving the original solution. Meanwhile, Bednarz et al. [14] showed how to select transformation matrix Q. Following them, we let each agent P_i ($i \in [1, K]$) transform its local constraints B_i, its share of the global constraints A_i and its objective vector c_i using its own transformation matrix Q_i.

We let K agents transform A_i and B_i by Q_i individually for the following reason. Essentially, we extend a revised version of Dantzig-Wolfe decomposition to solve K-LP and ensures that the protocol is secure. Thus, an arbitrary agent should be chosen as the master problem solver whereas all agents (including the master problem solving agent) should solve the pricing problems. For transformed K-LP problem (Equation 4), we can let $\forall P_i$ $(i \in [1, K])$ send its transformed matrices/vector A_iQ_i, B_iQ_i, $c_i^TQ_i$ to another agent P_j $(j \in [1, K], j \neq i)$ and let P_j solve P_i's transformed pricing problems. In this case, we can show that no private information can be learnt while solving the problems (The attack specified in [14] can be eliminated in our secure K-LP problem). Otherwise, if each agent solves its pricing problem, since each agent knows its transformation matrix, additional information might be disclosed from master solver to pricing problem solvers (this is further discussed in Section 5).

$$\max \quad \sum_{i=1}^{K} c_i^T Q_i y_i$$
$$s.t. \begin{cases} y_1 \in \mathbb{R}^{n_1} \\ y_2 \in \mathbb{R}^{n_2} \\ \vdots \\ y_K \in \mathbb{R}^{n_K} \end{cases} \begin{pmatrix} A_1Q_1 \dots A_KQ_K \\ B_1Q_1 & & \\ & \ddots & \\ & & B_KQ_K \end{pmatrix} \begin{pmatrix} y_1 \\ y_2 \\ \vdots \\ y_K \end{pmatrix} \begin{matrix} \bowtie_0 \\ \bowtie_1 \\ \vdots \\ \bowtie_K \end{matrix} \begin{pmatrix} b_0 \\ b_1 \\ \vdots \\ b_K \end{pmatrix} \tag{4}$$

The K-LP problem can be transformed to another block-angular structured LP problem as shown in Equation 4. We can derive the original solution from the solution of the transformed K-LP problem using the following theorem.

Theorem 1. *Given the optimal solution of the transformed K-LP problem $y^* = (y_1^*, y_2^*, \dots, y_K^*)$, the solution $x^* = (Q_1y_1^*, Q_2y_2^*, \dots, Q_Ky_K^*)$ should be the optimal solution of the original K-LP problem.*

Proof. Suppose $x^* = (Q_1y_1^*, Q_2y_2^*, \dots, Q_Ky_K^*)$ is not the optimal solution of the original vertical LP problem. In this case, we have another vector $x' = (x_1', x_2', \dots, x_K')$ such that $c^Tx' > c^Tx^* \implies c_1^Tx_1' + \dots + c_K^Tx_K' > c_1^Tx_1^* + \dots + c_K^Tx_K^*$ where $Mx' \bowtie b$ and $x' \geq 0$. Let $y' = (y_1', \dots, y_K') = (Q_1^{-1}x_1', \dots, Q_K^{-1}x_K')$, thus we have $c_1^TQ_1y_1' + \dots + c_K^TQ_Ky_K' = c_1^TQ_1Q_1^{-1}x_1' + \dots + c_K^TQ_KQ_K^{-1}x_K' = c_1^Tx_1' + \dots + c_K^Tx_K'$.

Thus, $c_1^Tx_1' + \dots + c_K^Tx_K' = c_1^TQ_1y_1' + \dots + c_K^TQ_Ky_K' > c_1^Tx_1^* + \dots + c_K^Tx_K^* \implies c_1^TQ_1y_1' + \dots + c_K^TQ_Ky_K' > c_1^TQ_1Q_1^{-1}x_1^* + \dots + c_K^TQ_KQ_K^{-1}x_K^* \implies c_1^TQ_1y_1' + \dots + c_K^TQ_Ky_K' > c_1^TQ_1y_1^* + \dots + c_K^TQ_Ky_K^*$ (since $Q_1^{-1}x_1^* = y_1^*, \dots, Q_K^{-1}x_K^* = y_K^*$)

Hence, y' is a better solution than y^* which is a contradiction to that y^* is the optimal solution. Thus, Theorem 1 has been proven.

4.2 Righthand-Side Value b Anonymization Algorithm

Besides protecting each party's share of the global constraint matrix A_i, B_i, solving the LP problems also requires the righthand side constants b in the constraints. Since b sometimes refers to the amount of limited resources (i.e. labors, materials) or some demands (i.e. the amount of one product should be no less than 10, $x_{ij} \geq 10$), they should not be revealed. We can anonymize b for each agent before transforming the constraint matrix and sending them to other agents.

Specifically, each agent P_i ($i \in [1, K]$) has two distinct constant vectors in the global and local constraints: b_0^i and b_i where $b_0 = \sum_{i=1}^{K} b_0^i$. Indeed, we can create artificial variables and equations to anonymize either b_0^i or b_i. For anonymizing b_0^i in the global constraints $\sum_{i=1}^{K} A_i x_i \bowtie_0 b_0^i$, each agent P_i can create a new artificial variable $s_{ij} = \eta_{ij}$ (fixed value) for the jth row ($j \in [1, m_0]$) of A_i. Hence, $m_0 \times n_i$ matrix A_i is expanded to a greater $m_0 \times (n_i + m_0)$ matrix as shown in Equation 5 ($A_i^1, \ldots, A_i^{m_0}$ denote the rows of matrix A_i).

$$A_i = \begin{pmatrix} A_i^1 \\ A_i^2 \\ \vdots \\ A_i^{m_0} \end{pmatrix} \Longrightarrow A_i' = \begin{pmatrix} A_i^1 & s_{i1} & 0 & \ldots & 0 \\ A_i^2 & 0 & s_{i2} & \ldots & 0 \\ \vdots & \vdots & \vdots & \ddots & \vdots \\ A_i^{m_0} & 0 & 0 & \ldots & s_{im_0} \end{pmatrix} \tag{5}$$

Algorithm 1. Righthand-side Value b Anonymization

Input : K honest-but-curious agents $P_1, \ldots, P_K$ where P_i ($i \in [1, K]$) holds a set of variables x_i, $A_i(m_0 \times n_i$ matrix), $B_i(m_i \times n_i$ matrix), vectors b_i (size m_i), b_0^i(size m_0), and c_i (size n_i)
Output: anonymized $b' = \{b_0', b_1', \ldots, b_K'\}$ (size $m_0, m_1', \ldots, m_K'$) where A_i, B_i, c_i are updated to $A_i'(m_0 \times n_i'$ matrix), $B_i'(m_i' \times n_i'$ matrix), c_i' (size n_i') ($i \in [1, K]$)

/* A_i^j and B_i^j denote the jth row of A_i and B_i */
forall *agent* $P_i, i \in \{1, 2, \ldots, K\}$ **do**
  generates a m_0-dimensional random vector η_i ;
  initializes m_0 new variables $s_i = \{s_{i1}, \ldots, s_{im_0}\}$ where $s_i = \eta_i$;
  $(b_0^i)' \leftarrow b_0^i + \eta_i$;
  for *the jth global constraint* ($j \in [1, m_0]$) **do**
    $A_i^j x_i \leftarrow A_i^j x_i + s_{ij}$;
    $(b_0^i)_j \leftarrow (b_0^i)_j'$;
  forall *constraint* $B_i^j x_i \bowtie_i^j b_i^j$ *in* $B_i x_i \bowtie_i b_i$ **do**
    generates a linear equation using $\forall s_{ij} \in s_i$: $\sum_{\forall h} h_{ij} s_{ij} = \sum_{\forall j} h_{ij} \eta_{ij}$ where h_{ij} is a random number;
    $B_i^j x_i \bowtie_i^j b_i^j \leftarrow B_i^j x_i + \sum_{\forall j} h_{ij} s_{ij} \bowtie_i^j b_i^j + \sum_{\forall j} h_{ij} \eta_{ij}$;
  generates m_0 linear independent equations: $\sum_{\forall j} r_{ij} s_{ij} = \sum_{\forall j} r_{ij} \eta_{ij}$ where random numbers $\forall r_{ij}$ guarantee linear independence;
  update them into local constraints: $B_i' x_i' \bowtie_i b_i' \leftarrow B_i x_i \bowtie_i b_i' \cup \sum_{\forall j} r_{ij} s_{ij} = \sum_{\forall j} r_{ij} \eta_{ij}$;
  /* permutate the variables and generate more artificial variables if necessary */

We thus have $(b_0^i)' \leftarrow b_0^i + \eta_i$ where $\eta_i = \{\forall j, \eta_{ij}\}$ (can be negative) is a random m_0-dimensional vector generated by agent P_i. Finally, each agent P_i creates additional m_0 linear independent local constraints $\sum_{\forall j} r_{ij} s_{ij} = \sum_{\forall j} r_{ij} \eta_{ij}$ using variables $\{\forall j, s_{ij}\}$ and associate them with constraints in $B_i x_i \bowtie_i b_i$ that ensure $s_i = \eta_i$ where $s_i = \{\forall j, s_{ij}\}$. Therefore, we have:

- the jth global constraint should be converted to $\sum_{i=1}^{K} A_i^j x_i + \sum_{i=1}^{K} s_{ij} \bowtie_0^j \sum_{i=1}^{K} (b_0^i)_j'$ where $(b_0^i)_j'$ represents the jth number in $(b_0^i)'$.
- additional local constraints ensure $\sum_{i=1}^{K} A_i x_i \bowtie_0 \sum_{i=1}^{K} b_0^i$ for a feasible K-LP problem since $\forall i, s_i = \eta_i$.

Besides b_0^i, we can anonymize b_i using a similar approach. P_i can use the same set of artificial variables s_i to anonymize b_i. By generating linear combination (not required to be linear independent) of the variables $s_i = \{\forall j, s_{ij}\}$, the left-hand side of the jth constraint in $B_i x_i \bowtie_i b_i$ can be updated: $B_i^j x_i \leftarrow B_i^j x_i + \sum_{\forall j} h_{ij} s_{ij}$ where h_{ij} is a random number. (the jth value in b_i is updated by $b_i^j \leftarrow b_i^j + \sum_{\forall j} h_{ij}\eta_{ij}$. If anonymizing b_i as above, adversaries may guess m_0 additional (linear independent) local constraints out of $m_i + m_0$ constraints from P_i's sub-polyhedron. The probability of guessing out m_0 linear independent constraints and calculating the values of the artificial variables is $\frac{m_0! m_i!}{(m_i+m_0)!}$ (if we standardize all the operational symbols $\bowtie_i$, guessing equations is choosing m_0 from $(m_i + m_0)$ constraints). However, the anonymization process should be prior to the matrix multiplication transformation, thus those m_0 equations include $n_i + m_0$ variables (coefficients of the non-artificial variables in these equations is transformed to non-zero). Hence, although the adversary knows m_0 linear independent equations, it is also impossible to figure out values η_i. Hence, b_i and b_0^i can be secure against adversaries. Algorithm 1 introduces the detailed steps of anonymizing b. Note: if any agent P_i requires higher privacy guarantee, P_i can generate more artificial variables for both b_0^i and b_i (A typical tradeoff between privacy and efficiency).

4.3 Revised Dantzig-Wolfe Decomposition

Dantzig-Wolfe decomposition was originally utilized to solve large-scale block-angular structured LP problems. However, for all the K-LP problems, we can appropriately partition the constraints into block-angular structure. Specifically, we can consider each agent's local constraints as the constraints of its pricing problems. By contrast, any constraint that is shared by at least two agents is regarded as the global constraint. Even if A_i may have more rows than B_i, the constraints are still block-angular partitioned.

Furthermore, after locally anonymizing b and transforming the blocks, each agent still has its local constraints block $B_i' Q_i$ and the global constraints share $A_i' Q_i$. Hence, we can solve the transformed K-LP problem using Dantzig-Wolfe decomposition. We thus denote the entire process as Revised Dantzig-Wolfe Decomposition:

Definition 7 (Revised Dantzig-Wolfe Decomposition). *A secure and efficient approach to solving K-LP problems that includes the following stages: anonymizing b by each agent, transforming blocks by each agent and solving the transformed K-LP problem using Dantzig-Wolfe Decomposition.*

According to Equation 3, the Dantzig-Wolfe representation of the transformed K-LP problem is:

$$max \quad \sum_j c_1'^T Q_1 y_1^j \lambda_{1j} + \cdots + \sum_j c_K'^T Q_K y_K^j \lambda_{Kj}$$

$$s.t. \begin{cases} \sum_{\forall j} A_1' Q_1 y_1^j \lambda_{1j} + \cdots + \sum_{\forall j} A_K' Q_K y_K^j \lambda_{Kj} \bowtie_0 b_0' \\ \sum_{\forall j} \delta_{1j} \lambda_{1j} \qquad\qquad\qquad = 1 \\ \qquad\qquad \ddots \\ \qquad\qquad\qquad \sum_{\forall j} \delta_{Kj} \lambda_{Kj} = 1 \\ \lambda_1 \in \mathbb{R}^{|E_1'|}, \ldots, \lambda_K \in \mathbb{R}^{|E_K'|}, \delta_{ij} \in \{0,1\}, i \in [1, K] \end{cases} \tag{6}$$

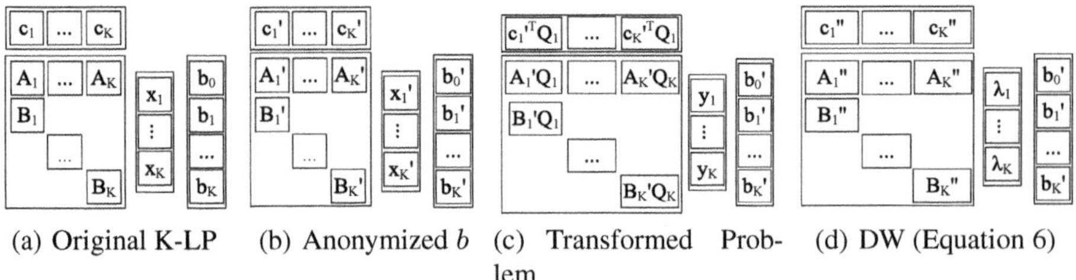

(a) Original K-LP (b) Anonymized b (c) Transformed Problem (d) DW (Equation 6)

Fig. 2. Revised Dantzig-Wolfe Decomposition for K-LP Problem

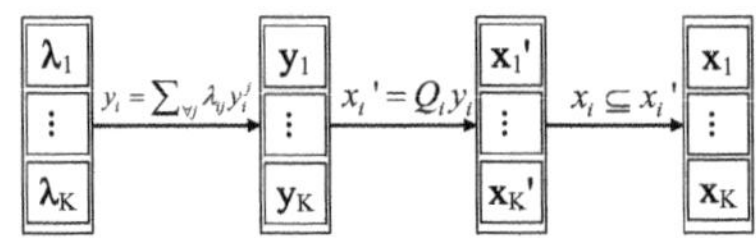

Fig. 3. Solution Transformation After Solving K-LP Problem

where $\forall i \in [1, K], c_i \subseteq c_i', A_i \subseteq A_i', B_i \subseteq B_i'$ (c_i', A_i', B_i' are expanded from c_i, A_i, B_i for anonymizing b).

Figure 2 presents the three steps of Revised Dantzig-Wolfe Decomposition. Furthermore, after solving the problem, each agent P_i should obtain an optimal solution $\lambda_i = \{\forall j, \lambda_{ij}\}$. Figure 3 shows the process of deriving each agent's optimal solution for the original K-LP problem. Specifically, in step 1, the optimal solutions for each agent's transformed problem can be derived by computing the convexity combination of all vertices/extreme rays y_i^j: $y_i = \sum_{\forall j} \lambda_{ij} y_i^j$. In step 2 ($x_i' = Q_i y_i$)[4], the optimal solution of the original problem with anonymized b can be derived by left multiply Q_i for each agent (Theorem 1). In step 3, each agent can extract its individual optimal solution in the K-LP problem by excluding the artificial variables (for anonymizing b) from the optimal solution of x_i'.

The advantages of this sort of decomposition are: the pricing problems can be solved independently; the master problem solver does not need to get into the details on how the proposals are generated; if the subproblems have special structure (e.g., perhaps one is a transportation problem) then those specialized solution techniques can be used. This also makes it easier to preserve privacy if the large problem could be solved without knowing the precise solutions of the pricing problems. Particularly, we can let an arbitrary agent formulate and solve the transformed master problem (Equation 6). However, the efficiency and security is not good enough for large-scale problems since the number of vertices/extreme rays are $\frac{n_i'!}{m_i'!(n_i'-m_i')!}$ for each agent and all the variables should be sent to the master problem solver (assuming that the K-LP problem is standardized with slack variables before transformation). In Section 5, the K-agent Column

[4] Apparently, if $y_i = 0$ and we have $x_i' = Q_i y_i$, x_i' should be 0 and revealed to other agents. However, y_i includes some transformed variables that is originally the value-fixed but unknown artificial variables for anonymizing b. Hence, x_i' cannot be computed due to unknown Q_i and non-zero y_i (the situation when the optimal solution in y_i is 0, is not known to the holder other than P_i), and this possible privacy leakage can be resolved.

Generation Protocol can handle this problem and the detailed security proof and communication costs are also given there.

5 Secure Column Generation Protocol for K-LP Problems

While solving K-LP by revised Dantzig-Wolfe decomposition, it is fair to all K agents. Hence, we assume that an arbitrary agent can be the master problem solver. Each agent's subproblems can be solved by another agent while the problem is iteratively solving (the pricing problems and the solvers can be randomly permutated). To simplify the notation, we assume that P_1 solves the restricted master problems (RMP), P_i sends $A_i'Q_i$, $B_i'Q_i$, $c_i'^T Q_i$, $(b_0^i)'$ and b_i' to P_{i+1} that solves P_i's pricing problems (P_1 solves P_K's pricing problems). In this section, we present our K-agent column generation protocol with security proof and computation cost analysis.

5.1 Solving RMP by an Arbitrary Agent

As mentioned in Section 4, the full master problem in the revised Dantzig-wolfe decomposition includes $\sum_{i=1}^{K} \frac{n_i'!}{m_i'!(n_i'-m_i')!}$ variables. However, it is not necessary to involve all the vertices/extreme rays simply because a fairly small number of constraints in the master problem might result in many non-basis variables in the full master problem. Hence, restricted master problem (RMP) of the transformed K-LP problem is introduced to improve efficiency.

We let $[c_i] = (\forall j \in [1, \frac{n_i'!}{m_i'!(n_i'-m_i')!}], c_i'^T Q_i y_i^j)$ and $[A_i] = (\forall j \in [1, \frac{n_i'!}{m_i'!(n_i'-m_i')!}], A_i' Q_i y_i^j)$. For RMP, we denote the coefficients in the master problem restricted to $\mathbb{R}^{|\widehat{E_1}|}, \ldots, \mathbb{R}^{|\widehat{E_K}|}$ as $\widehat{c_i}$, $\widehat{A_i}$, $\widehat{y_i}$, $\widehat{\delta}$ and $\widehat{\lambda}$. Specifically, some of the variables λ for all agents are initialized to non-basis 0. τ_i denotes the number of vertices in P_i's pricing problem that has been proposed to the master solver where $\forall i \in [1, K], \tau_i \leq \frac{n_i'!}{m_i'!(n_i'-m_i')!}$. Hence, we represent the RMP as below:

$$
\begin{aligned}
& max \quad \widehat{c_1}^T \widehat{\lambda_1} + \cdots + \widehat{c_K}^T \widehat{\lambda_K} \\
& s.t. \begin{cases}
\widehat{A_1 \lambda_1} + \cdots + \widehat{A_K \lambda_K} \bowtie_0 b_0' \\
\sum_{j=1}^{\tau_1} \delta_{1j} \lambda_{1j} \quad = 1 \\
\vdots \\
\sum_{j=1}^{\tau_K} \delta_{Kj} \lambda_{Kj} = 1 \\
\lambda_1 \in \mathbb{R}^{|\widehat{E_1}|}, \ldots, \lambda_K \in \mathbb{R}^{|\widehat{E_K}|}, \delta_{ij} \in \{0,1\}, i \in [1,K]
\end{cases}
\end{aligned}
\tag{7}
$$

Lemma 1. *Solving the RMP of a K-LP problem Reveals only:*

- *the revised DW representation of the K-LP problem;*
- *the optimal solution of the revised DW representation;*
- *the total payoff (optimal value) of each agent;*

Proof. RMP is a special case of the full master problem where some variables in $\forall i, \lambda_i$ are fixed to be non-basis (not sent to the RMP solver P_1). Hence, the worse case is that all the columns of the master problem are required to formulate the RMP. We thus discuss the privacy leakage in this case.

We look at the matrices/vectors that are acquired by P_1 from all other agents P_i where $\forall i \in [1, K]$. Specifically, $[c_i] = (\forall j \in [1, \frac{n'_i!}{m'_i!(n'_i-m'_i)!}], c_i'^T Q_i y_i^j)$ and $[A_i] = (\forall j \in [1, \frac{n'_i!}{m'_i!(n'_i-m'_i)!}], A'_i Q_i y_i^j)$ should be sent to P_1. At this time, $[c_i]$ is a vector with size $\frac{n'_i!}{m'_i!(n'_i-m'_i)!}$ and $[A_i]$ is an $m_0 \times \frac{n'_i!}{m'_i!(n'_i-m'_i)!}$ matrix. The jth value in $[c_i]$ is equal to $c_i'^T Q_i y_i^j$, and the jth column in matrix $[A_i]$ is equal to $A'_i Q_i y_i^j$.

Since P_1 does not know y_i^j and Q_i, it is impossible to calculate or estimate the (size n'_i) vector c'_i and sub-matrices A_i and B_i. Specifically, even if P_1 can construct $(m_0 + 1) \cdot \frac{n'_i!}{m'_i!(n'_i-m'_i)!}$ non-linear equations based on the elements from $[c_i]$ and $[A_i]$, the number of unknown variables in the equations (from c'_i, A'_i, Q_i[5] and $\forall j \in [1, \frac{n'_i!}{m'_i!(n'_i-m'_i)!}]$, y_i^j) should be $n'_i + m_0 n'_i + n'_i + n'_i \cdot \frac{n'_i!}{m'_i!(n'_i-m'_i)!}$. Due to $n'_i >> m_0$ in linear programs, we have $n'_i + m_0 n'_i + n'_i + n'_i \cdot \frac{n'_i!}{m'_i!(n'_i-m'_i)!} >> (m_0 + 1) \cdot \frac{n'_i!}{m'_i!(n'_i-m'_i)!}$. Thus, those unknown variables in c'_i, A'_i, Q_i and $\forall j \in [1, \frac{n'_i!}{m'_i!(n'_i-m'_i)!}], y_i^j$ cannot be derived from the non-linear equations. As a result, P_1 learns nothing about A_i, c_i, b_0^i (anonymized) and $B_i x_i \bowtie_i b_i$ (since vertices/extreme rays $\forall j, y_i^j$ are unknown) from any agent P_i.

By contrast, while solving the problem, P_1 formulates and solves the RMPs. P_1 thus knows the primal and dual solution of the RMP. In addition, anonymizing b and transforming c_i, A_i and B_i does not change the total payoff (optimal value) of each agent, the payoffs of all values are revealed to P_1 as well (Vaidya's protocol [7] also reveals this payoff). Nevertheless, the private constraints and the optimal solution cannot be inferred based on this limited disclosure.

Hence, solving the RMPs is secure.

5.2 Solving Pricing Problems by Peer-Agent

While solving the K-LP problem by the column generation algorithm(CGA), in every iteration, each agent's pricing problem might be formulated to test that whether any column of the master problem (vertex/extreme ray of the corresponding agent) should be proposed to the master problem solver or not. If any agent's pricing problem cannot propose column to the master solver in the previous iterations, no pricing problem is required for this agent anymore. As discussed in Section 4.1, we permutate the pricing problem owners and the pricing problem solvers where private information can be protected via transformation. We now introduce the details of solving pricing problems and analyze the potential privacy loss.

Assuming that an honest-but-curious agent $P_{i+1} (i \in [1, K])$ has received agent P_i's (if $i = K \implies i+1 = 1$) variables y_i, transformed matrices/vector $A'_i Q_i, B'_i Q_i, c_i'^T Q_i$

[5] As described in [14], Q_i should be a monomial matrix, thus Q_i has n'_i unknown variables located in $n_i'^2$ unknown positions.

and the anonymized vectors b'_i, $(b^i_0)'$ (as shown in Figure 2(c)). Agent P_{i+1} thus formulates and solves agent P_i's pricing problem.

In every iteration, after solving RMP (by P_1), P_1 sends the optimal dual solution $\{\pi, \mu_i\}$ to P_{i+1} ($\mu_i = \{\forall j, (\mu_i)_j\}$) if the RMP is feasible. The reduced cost d_{ij} of variable λ_{ij} for agent P_i can be derived as:

$$d_{ij} = (c_i'^T Q_i - \pi A_i' Q_i) y_i^j - \begin{cases} (\mu_i)_j & \text{if } y_i^j \text{ is a vertex} \\ 0 & \text{if } y_i^j \text{ is an extreme ray} \end{cases} \tag{8}$$

Therefore, P_{i+1} formulates P_i's pricing problem as:

$$\begin{aligned} max \quad & (c_i'^T Q_i - \pi A_i' Q_i) y_i \\ s.t. & \begin{cases} B_i' Q_i y_i \bowtie b_i' \\ y_i \in \mathbb{R}^{n_i'} \end{cases} \end{aligned} \tag{9}$$

Lemma 2. *If P_{i+1} solves P_i's transformed pricing problems, P_{i+1} learns only:*

- *the feasibility of P_i' block sub-polyhedron $B_i x_i \bowtie_i b_i$;*
- *dual optimal values (π, μ_i) of the RMP for transformed K-LP;*

Proof. Since we can let another arbitrary peer-agent solve any agent's pricing problems (fairness property): assuming that P_{i+1} solves P_i's pricing problem ($i = K \implies i + 1 = 1$). Similarly, we first look at the matrices/vectors acquired by P_{i+1} from P_i: size n_i' vector $c_i'^T Q$, $m_i' \times n_i'$ matrix $B_i' Q_i$ and $m_0 \times n_i'$ matrix $A_i' Q_i$. The jth value in $c_i'^T Q_i$ is equal to $c_i'^T Q_i^j$ (Q_i^j denotes the jth column of Q_i), and the value of the kth row and the jth column in $A_i' Q_i$ (or $B_i' Q_i$) is equal to the scalar product of the kth row of A_i' (or B_i') and Q_i^j.

Since P_{i+1} does not know Q_i, it is impossible to calculate or estimate the (size n_i') vector c_i' and matrices A_i' (or A_i) and B_i' (or B_i). Specifically, even if P_{i+1} can construct $(m_0 + m_i' + 1)n_i'$ non-linear equations based on the elements from $c_i'^T Q_i$, $A_i' Q_i$ and $B_i' Q_i$, the number of unknown variables in the equations (from c_i', A_i', B_i and Q_i) should be $n_i' + m_0 n_i' + m_i' n_i' + n_i'$. Due to $n_i' >> 0$ in linear programs, we have $n_i' + m_0 n_i' + m_i' n_i' + n_i' >> (m_0 + m_i' + 1)n_i'$. Thus, those unknown variables in c_i', A_i', B_i and Q_i cannot be derived from the non-linear equations[6].

Hence, P_{i+1} learns nothing about A_i, B_i, c_i, b^i_0 (anonymized) and b_i (anonymized) from P_i if P_{i+1} solves P_i's pricing problems.

By contrast, before solving the pricing problem, P_{i+1} should acquire the some dual optimal values of the RMP (only π and μ_i). P_{i+1} thus knows the dual optimal solution of the RMP related to the convexity combination represented global constraints

[6] Note: Bednarz et al. [14] proposed a possible attack on inferring Q with the known transformed and original objective vectors ($C^T Q$ and C^T) along with the known optimal solutions of the transformed problem and the original problem ($y*$ and $x* = Qy*$). However, this attack only applies to the special case of DisLP in Vaidya's work [7] where one party holds the objective function while the other party holds the constraints. In our protocol, P_i sends $C_i'^T Q_i$ to P_{i+1}, but $C_i'^T$ is unknown to P_{i+1}, hence it is impossible to compute all the possibilities of Q_i by P_{i+1} in terms of Bednarz's approach. In addition, the original solution is not revealed as well. It is impossible to verify the exact Q_i by P_{i+1} following the approach in [14].

(π) and the constraints $\sum_{\forall j} \delta_{ij}\lambda_{ij} = 1$ (μ_i). However, P_{i+1} cannot learn the actual pricing problem since everything in the K-LP is transformed in the RMP. Furthermore, if the polyhedron $B_i'Q_iy_i \bowtie_i b_i'$ is infeasible, we have: polyhedron $B_i'x_i \bowtie_i b_i'$ is also infeasible (Theorem 2). Hence, the specific agent with the infeasible local constraints should be spotted (Actually, this should be revealed in any case). However, the private constraints and the meanings of the concrete variables cannot be inferred with this information. (For more rigorous privacy protection, we can randomly permutate the agents.)

Hence, solving the Pricing Problems by another arbitrary agent is secure.

Theorem 2. *The polyhedra $B_ix_i \bowtie_i b_i$ and $B_iQ_iy_i \bowtie_i b_i$ have the same feasibility where $i \in [1, K]$.*

Proof. We prove this equivalence in two facts:

First, suppose that the polyhedron $B_ix_i \bowtie_i b_i$ is feasible and one of its feasible solutions is x_i. Now, we have all the constraints (equalities or inequalities) in B_i that satisfy $B_ix_i \bowtie_i b_i$. Let $x_i = Q_iy_i$, hence $B_iQ_iy_i \bowtie_i b_i$ are all satisfied and the polyhedron $B_iQ_iy_i \bowtie_i b_i$ is feasible.

On the contrary, suppose that the polyhedron $B_iQ_iy_i \bowtie_i b_i$ is feasible and one of its feasible solutions is y_i. Now, we have all the constraints (equalities or inequalities) in B_iQ_i that satisfy $B_iQ_iy_i \bowtie_i b_i$. Let $y_i = Q_i^{-1}x_i$, hence $B_ix_i \bowtie_i b_i$ are all satisfied and the polyhedron $B_ix_i \bowtie_i b_i$ is feasible.

Thus, Theorem 2 has been proven.

5.3 Secure K-agent Column Generation Algorithm (SCGA)

In the standard column generation algorithm [12], the RMP solver will ask the pricing problem solvers for proposals and choose a combination of proposals that maximizes global profits while meeting all the constraints in the RMP. Figure 4 demonstrates our secure K-agent column generation protocol where the steps represent:

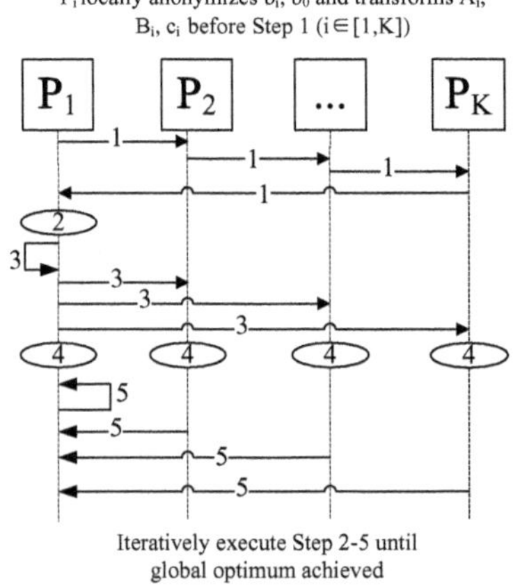

Fig. 4. Secure K-agent Column Generation Protocol

1. $\forall i \in [1,k]$, P_i sends $A_i'Q_i$, $B_i'Q_i$, $(b_0^i)'$, b_i' and $c_i'^T Q_i$ to P_{i+1}.
2. P_1 solves a RMP problem.
3. P_1 distributes dual values (π, μ_i) to P_{i+1}.
4. P_{i+1} solves P_i's pricing problems.
5. P_{i+1} proposes P_i's column to P_1 if necessary.

Practically, the main drawback of this approach is in possible convergence problems. Normally, this method gets very good answers quickly, but it requires a lot of time to find the optimal solution. The subproblems may continue to generate proposals only slightly better than the ones before. Thus, we might have to stop with a near-optimal solution for efficiency reasons if necessary [12]. Specifically, if the RMP is feasible and the pricing problems are all feasible and bounded, P_1 can calculate a new upper bound (dual value) of the master problem $\hat{z} = z^* + \sum_{i=1}^{K}(z_i^* - \mu_i)$. If $\hat{z} < \bar{z}^*$, update the best known dual value $\bar{z}^* \leftarrow \hat{z}$. P_1 thus compute the optimal gap $d = \bar{z}^* - z^*$ and the relative optimal gap $d' = \frac{d}{1+|z^*|}$. If the gap is tolerable, we stop the protocol where the optimal solution of the current RMP is near-optimal. In case of near-optimal tolerance, all the optimal values of the pricing problems $\forall i \in [1,K]$, z_i^* should be sent to P_1 along with the proposed column. However, the protocol is still secure in semi-honest model.

Theorem 3. *The K-agent Column Generation Protocol is secure in Semi-honest model.*

Proof. As proven in Lemma 1 and 2, solving RMPs and pricing problems is secure for all K honest-but-curious agents. Since our K-agent Column Generation Protocol the repeated steps of solving transformed RMPs and pricing problems, it is straightforward to show that the protocol is secure against semi-honest adversaries.

5.4 Communication Cost Analysis

Our secure column generation protocol is mainly based on local transformation rather than cryptographic encryption that dominates the cost in current privacy-preserving DisLP techniques[10][8][7][9]. Hence, our approach significantly outperforms the above work on communication costs, especially in large-scale problems. Specifically, the size of the constraints matrix (all the constraints) should be $(m_0 + \sum_{i=1}^{K} m_i) \times \sum_{i=1}^{K} n_i$. After anonymizing b, the constraint matrix is enlarged to $(m_0 + \sum_{i=1}^{K} m_i') \times \sum_{i=1}^{K} n_i'$. Each pair of matrices A_i', B_i' is locally transformed. Besides solving the LP problem, only one-time $(m_0 + m_i' + 1)n_i'$ scalar product computation (transforming c', A_i', B_i') is required for each agent since anonymizing b does take ignorable computational cost (generating random numbers and equations). For large-scale block-angular structured problems, column generation algorithm has been proven to be more efficient than some standard methods (i.e. simplex or revised simplex algorithm)[15][12]. As discussed in Section 1, K-LP problem is a typical block-angular structured LP problem (distributed among K agents). Hence, the communication cost of our secure column generation algorithm is tiny and negligible.

6 Experiments

We implemented the secure column generation algorithm (SCGA) for solving K-LP problems. Specifically, we present two groups of results: 1. the performance comparison

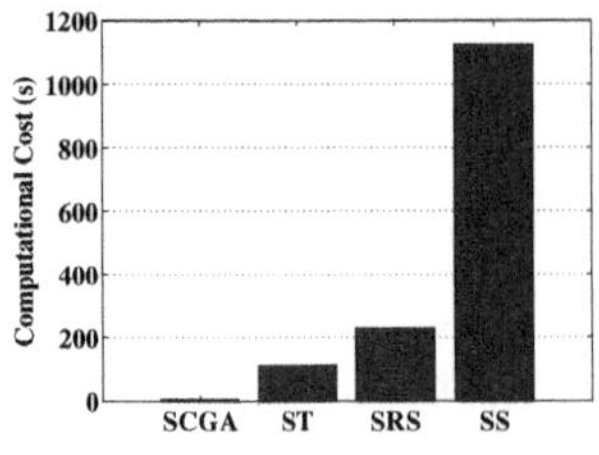

(a) Secure (Two-agent) DisLP Methods

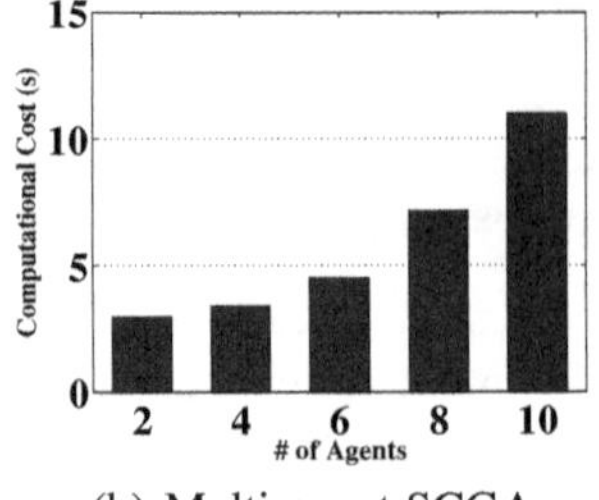

(b) Multi-agent SCGA

Fig. 5. Experimental Results (Near-optimal Tolerance Parameter=10^{-6})

for all secure (two-agent) DisLP methods. 2. the performance of SCGA on varying number of agents where each agent has 15 variables. All the experiments were carried on an HP machine with Intel Core 2 Duo CPU 3GHz and 3G RAM.

To compare all secure DisLP methods, we generate 10 LP problems with 50 variables and 30×50 constraint matrix (not very dense) and run 4 algorithms for all 10 problems. Specifically, we assume that two agents collaboratively solve the LP problems where each agent holds 25 distinct variables. The number of local constraints for each agent and the number of global constraints are determined by the structure of 10 different 30×50 constraint matrix (we guarantee that every agent has at least one local constraints via the density of the constraint matrix). Before collaboratively solving the problem, each agent anonymizes the right-hand value and transforms the matrices/vector (the LP problems should be expanded a little bit). Figure 5(a) demonstrates the average runtime (10 LP problems) of SCGA, Secure Transformation (ST)[7], Secure Revised Simplex Method (SRS)[9] and Secure Simplex Method (SS) [8]. It is quite clear that the efficiency of SCGA significantly outperforms other algorithms in secure K-LP problems.

Furthermore, we run another group of experiments for validating the performance of SCGA on multiple agents. We generate different size of K-LP problems by assuming that each agent holds 15 variables and 5 local constraints. We let the number of global constraints be 10, thus the constraint matrix becomes $(5K + 10) \times 15K$. Hence, we run SCGA for different number of agents $K \in \{2, 4, 6, 8, 10\}$. The total computational cost (including anonymization, transformation and solving the problems) on varying K is shown in Figure 5(b). Thus, our SCGA exhibits great scalability for securely solving increasing scale of K-LP problems.

7 Conclusion and Future Work

DisLP problems allow collaborative agents to improve their global maximum profit (or save their global minimum cost). However, the private constraints (input) and solutions (output) of distributed agents might be revealed among them while solving the DisLP problem. In this paper, we have introduced an extremely efficient protocol to solve

K-agent DisLP problems with limited disclosure. Our protocol is robust against semi-honest adversaries and is fair to all agents. In the future, we also plan to make the protocol resilient to malicious adversaries by making it incentive compatible.

References

1. Turban, E., Rainer, R.K., Potter, R.E.: Introduction to information technology, chapter 2nd, information technologies: Concepts and management, 3rd edn. John Wiley and Sons, Chichester
2. Yokoo, M., Durfee, E.H., Ishida, T., Kuwabar, K.: Distributed constraint satisfaction for formalizing distributed problem solving. In: Proceedings of International Conference on Distributed Computing Systems, pp. 614–621 (1992)
3. Modi, P.J., Shen, W.-M., Tambe, M., Yokoo, M.: An asynchronous complete method for distributed constraint optimization. In: AAMAS 2003: Proceedings of the Second International Joint Conference on Autonomous Agents and Multiagent Systems, pp. 161–168. ACM Press, New York (2003)
4. Silaghi, M.-C., Rajeshirke, V.: The effect of policies for selecting the solution of a discsp on privacy loss. In: AAMAS 2004: Proceedings of the Third International Joint Conference on Autonomous Agents and Multiagent Systems, pp. 1396–1397 (2004)
5. Silaghi, M.C., Mitra, D.: Distributed constraint satisfaction and optimization with privacy enforcement. Iat 00, 531–535 (2004)
6. Suzuki, K., Yokoo, M.: Secure generalized vickrey auction using homomorphic encryption. In: Wright, R.N. (ed.) FC 2003. LNCS, vol. 2742, pp. 239–249. Springer, Heidelberg (2003)
7. Vaidya, J.: Privacy-preserving linear programming. In: SAC, pp. 2002–2007 (2009)
8. Li, J., Atallah, M.J.: Secure and private collaborative linear programming. In: International Conference on Collaborative Computing: Networking, Applications and Worksharing, CollaborateCom 2006, pp. 1–8 (2006)
9. Vaidya, J.: A secure revised simplex algorithm for privacy-preserving linear programming. In: AINA 2009: Proceedings of the 23rd IEEE International Conference on Advanced Information Networking and Applications (2009)
10. Du, W.: A Study of Several Specific Secure Two-party Computation Problems. PhD thesis, Purdue University, West Lafayette, Indiana (2001)
11. Mangasarian, O.L.: Privacy-preserving linear programming. Optimization Letters 5(1), 28–34 (2010)
12. Tebboth, J.R.: A Computational Study of Dantzig-Wolfe Decomposition. PhD thesis, University of Buckingham (2001)
13. Du, W., Atallah, M.J.: Privacy-preserving cooperative scientific computations. In: Proceedings of the 14th IEEE Computer Security Foundations Workshop, pp. 273–282 (2001)
14. Bednarz, A., Bean, N., Roughan, M.: Hiccups on the road to privacy-preserving linear programming. In: Proceedings of the 8th ACM Workshop on Privacy in the Electronic Society, WPES 2009, pp. 117–120. ACM, New York (2009)
15. Nemhauser, G.L., Wolsey, L.A.: Integer and combinatorial optimization. Wiley-Interscience, New York (1988)

Privacy-Preserving Data Mining: A Game-Theoretic Approach

Atsuko Miyaji and Mohammad Shahriar Rahman

School of Information Science, Japan Advanced Institute of Science and Technology
1-1 Asahidai, Nomi, Ishikawa, Japan 923-1292
{miyaji,mohammad}@jaist.ac.jp

Abstract. Privacy-preserving data mining has been an active research area in recent years due to privacy concerns in many distributed data mining settings. Protocols for privacy-preserving data mining have considered semi-honest, malicious, and covert adversarial models in cryptographic settings, whereby an adversary is assumed to follow, arbitrarily deviate from the protocol, or behaving somewhere in between these two, respectively. Semi-honest model provides weak security requiring small amount of computation, on the other hand, malicious and covert models provide strong security requiring expensive computations like homomorphic encryptions. However, game theory allows us to design protocols where parties are neither honest nor malicious but are instead viewed as rational and are assumed (only) to act in their own self-interest. In this paper, we build efficient and secure set-intersection protocol in game-theoretic setting using cryptographic primitives. Our construction avoids the use of expensive tools like homomorphic encryption and oblivious transfer. We also show that our protocol satisfies computational versions of strict Nash equilibrium and stability with respect to trembles.

Keywords: Privacy-preserving data mining, Set-intersection, Game theory, Computational strict Nash equilibrium, Stability with respect to trembles.

1 Introduction

A key utility of large databases today is scientific or economic research. Despite the potential gain, this is often not possible due to the confidentiality issues which arise, leading to concerns over privacy infringement while performing the data mining operations. The need for privacy is sometimes due to law (e.g., for medical databases) or can be motivated by business interests. To address the privacy problem, several privacy-preserving data mining protocols using cryptographic techniques have been suggested. Depending on the adversarial behavior assumptions, those protocols use different models. Classically, two main categories of adversaries have been considered:

Semi-honest adversaries: Following Goldreich's definition [11], protocols secure in the presence of semi-honest adversaries (or honest-but-curious) assume

Y. Li (Ed.): Data and Applications Security and Privacy XXV, LNCS 6818, pp. 186–200, 2011.

that parties faithfully follow all protocol specifications and do not misrepresent any information related to their inputs, e.g., set size and content. However, during or after protocol execution, any party might (passively) attempt to infer additional information about the other party's input. This model is formalized by requiring that each party does not learn more information that it would in an ideal implementation relying on a trusted third party (TTP).

Malicious adversaries: Security in the presence of malicious parties allows arbitrary deviations from the protocol. In general, however, it does not prevent parties from refusing to participate in the protocol, modifying their private input sets, or prematurely aborting the protocol. Security in the malicious model is achieved if the adversary (interacting in the real protocol, without the TTP) can learn no more information than it could in the ideal scenario.

A new type of adversarial model, named covert adversary, has been proposed recently by Aumann et al. [3].

Covert Adversaries: These adversaries are somewhere in between the semi-honest and malicious models. In many real-world settings, parties are willing to actively cheat (not semi-honest), but only if they are not caught (not arbitrarily malicious). Covert adversarial behavior accurately models many real-world situations. It explicitly models the probability of catching adversarial behavior; a probability that can be tuned to the specific circumstances of the problem. In particular, it is not assumed that adversaries are only willing to risk being caught with negligible probability, but rather allow for much higher probabilities.

In the above models, a secure protocol emulates (in its real execution) the ideal execution that includes a TTP. This notion is formulated by requiring the existence of adversaries in the ideal execution model that can simulate adversarial behavior in the real execution model. In other words, the implicit assumption in the original formulation of the problem is that each party is either honest or corrupt, and honest parties are all willing to cooperate when reconstruction of the secret is desired. However, the assumption of semi-honest behavior may be unrealistic in some settings. In such cases, participating parties may prefer to use a protocol that is secure against malicious behavior. It is clear that the protocols secure in the malicious model offer more security. Regarding malicious adversaries, it has been shown that, under suitable cryptographic assumptions, any multi-party probabilistic polynomial time functionality (PPT) can be securely computed for any number of malicious corrupted parties. However, these are not efficient enough to be used in practice. Most of these constructions use general zero-knowledge proofs for fully malicious multi-party computation (MPC) protocols. These zero-knowledge compilers lead to rather inefficient constructions [31]. In typical cryptographic MPC protocols, parties are allowed to abort when they can find some malicious behavior from other parties. This means that the parties have to start the protocol from the scratch which is undesirable for operations on huge data sets.

Since the work of Halpern and Teague [14], protocols for some cryptographic tasks (e.g., secret sharing, multi-party computation) have begun to be re-evaluated in a game-theoretic light (see [7,20] for an overview of work in this direction). In this setting, parties are neither honest nor corrupt but are instead viewed as rational and are assumed (only) to act in their own self-interest. This feature is particularly interesting for data mining operations where huge collection of data is used, since parties will not deviate (i.e., abort) as there is no incentive to do so. In many real-world settings, parties are willing to actively deviate/cheat, but only if they are not caught. This is the case in many business, financial, political and diplomatic settings, where honest behavior cannot be assumed, but where the companies, institutions and individuals involved cannot afford the embarrassment, loss of reputation, and negative press associated with being caught cheating, hence having smaller incentive.

In data mining area, private set-intersection and set-union protocols allow two parties interact on their respective input sets. These protocols address several realistic privacy issues. Typical application examples include:

1. Business Interest: Companies may want to decide whether to make a business alliance by the percentage of customers shared among them, without publishing their customer databases including the shared customers among them. This can be treated as an intersection cardinality problem. As another example, to determine which customers appear on a do-not-receive-advertisements list, a store must perform a set-intersection operation between its private customer list and the producers list.

2. Aviation Security: The Department of Homeland Security (DHS) of the U.S. needs to check whether any passenger on each flight from/to the United States must be denied boarding, based on some passenger watch list. For this purpose, airlines submit their entire list of passengers to DHS, together with other sensitive information, such as credit card numbers. This poses liability issues with regard to innocent passengers' data and concerns about potential data losses. In practice, information only related to the passengers on the list should obtained by DHS without disclosing any information to the airlines.

3. Healthcare: Insurance companies often need to obtain information about their insured patients from other parties, such as other insurance carriers or hospitals. The insurance carriers cannot disclose the identity of inquired patients, whereas, the hospitals cannot provide any information on other patients.

1.1 Related Work

Cryptographic techniques have been used to design many different distributed privacy-preserving data mining algorithms. In general, there are two types of assumptions on data distribution: vertical and horizontal partitioning. In the case of horizontally partitioned data, different sites collect the same set of information about different entities. For example, different credit card companies may collect credit card transactions of different individuals. Secure distributed protocols have been developed for horizontally partitioned data for mining decision trees [25], k-means clustering [24], k-nn classifiers [18]. In the case of vertically partitioned data, it is assumed that different sites collect information about the same set of entities but they collect different feature sets. For example, both a university and a hospital may collect information about a student. Again, secure protocols for the vertically partitioned case have been developed for mining association rules [35], and k-means clusters [16,34]. All of those previous protocols claimed to be secure only in the semi-honest model. In [9,19], authors present two-party secure protocols in the malicious model for data mining. They follow the generic malicious model definitions from the cryptographic literature, and also focus on the security issues in the malicious model, and provide the malicious versions of the subprotocols commonly used in previous privacy-preserving data mining algorithms. Assuming that at least one party behaves in semi-honest model, they use threshold homomorphic encryption for malicious adversaries presented by Cramer et al. [5]. Recently, Miyaji et al. presented a new adversarial model named covert adversaries [31] for performing data mining algorithms. They show that protocols under covert adversarial model behave in between semi-honest and malicious models. Oblivious transfer (OT) and homomorphic encryption have been used as the building blocks in [31]. Since homomorphic encryption is considered too expensive [27] and oblivious transfer is often the most expensive part of cryptographic protocols [26], the protocols proposed in malicious and covert adversarial models are not very practical for operations on large data items. Game theory and data mining, in general, have been combined in [17,32] for constructing various data mining algorithms. Rational adversaries have also been considered in privacy-preserving set operations [36,2]. These protocols consider Nash equilibrium to analyze the rational behavior of the participating entities. As discussed by Kol and Naor in [23], using Nash equilibrium is not suitable in many cases, since many bad strategies are not ruled out by it. Instead, they suggest the stronger notion of strict Nash equilibrium in the information-theoretic setting, in which every player's strategy is a strict best response. Due to the restrictive nature of this notion, it is regarded as a sufficient condition and not as a necessary one. As in all of cryptography, computational relaxations are meaningful and should be considered; doing so allows us to get around the limitations of the information-theoretic setting. So, analyzing set operations from the viewpoint of computational strict Nash equilibrium is interesting, since it gives a more realistic results. There have been several works on game theory based MPC/secret sharing schemes [1,14,22,29,10,33,15]. But [14,33] require the continual involvement of the dealer even after the initial shares have been distributed or assume that sufficiently many parties behave honestly during the computation phase. Some schemes [1,22,29] rely on multiple invocations of protocols. Other work [15] relies on physical assumptions such as secure envelopes and ballot boxes. [10] proposed efficient protocols for rational secret sharing. But secret sharing schemes cannot be directly used for our purpose since they require the existence of TTP and their set up is different.

1.2 Our Contribution

In this work, we build two-party secure set-intersection protocol in game-theoretic setting using cryptographic primitives. It is assumed that parties are neither honest nor corrupt but are instead rational and are assumed to act only in their own self-interest. Our construction avoids the use of expensive tools like homomorphic encryption and oblivious transfer. We have used verifiable random functions as the underlying cryptographic primitive which is simple and efficient. It is also possible to use our protocol for computing set-union operations. We also show that our protocol satisfies computational versions of strict Nash equilibrium and stability with respect to trembles, defined by Fuchsbauer et al. [10].

Organization of the paper: The remainder of the paper is organized as follows: Section 2 presents the background and preliminaries. Section 3 describes the protocol model. Section 4 includes protocol construction. In Section 5, we analyze the protocol formally. We give some concluding remarks in Section 6.

2 Background and Preliminary

2.1 Cryptographic Considerations in Game Theory

Achieving a secure protocol is the objective in the cryptographic setting. Eliminating the trusted party is one of the main tasks while maintaining the privacy. On the other hand, in game theory, some particular equilibrium is defined to achieve stability. The existence of the trusted party/mediator is a parameter setting resulting in a more desirable, but harder to implement equilibrium concept for rational behaviors. Thus, privacy is a goal in the cryptographic setting while in the game theory setting it is a means to an end.

Games are treated in a modified way with a differently defined equilibrium notions in a cryptographic setting with. Katz, in [20], gives some examples of how this might be done for the specific case of parties running a protocol in the cryptographic setting. A security parameter n is introduced which is provided to all parties at the beginning of the game. The action of a player P_j now corresponds to running an interactive Turing Machine (TM) T_j. The T_j takes the current state and messages received from the other party as the input, and outputs message of player P_j along with updated state. The message m_j is sent to the other party. In a computational sense, it is required that T_j runs in PPT meaning that the function is computed in time polynomial in n. T_j is thus allowed to run for an unbounded number of rounds and, it can be added that the expected number of rounds is also polynomial for which T_j runs. The security parameter n is given as input to the utility functions. Utility functions map transcripts of a protocol execution to the reals that can be computed in time polynomial in n. Let Δ be a computational game in which the actions of each player correspond to the PPT TMs. Also, the utilities of each player are computed in time polynomial in n. Thus, mixed strategies are no longer needed to be considered, since a polynomial time mixed strategy corresponds to a pure strategy (since pure strategies correspond to randomized TMs) [20]. The parties are not assumed to be curious in negligible changes in their utilities, and this is an important difference between the cryptographic setting and the setting that has been considered here.

2.2 Definitions

In this section, we will state the definitions of computational strict Nash equilibrium and computational strict Nash equilibrium w.r.t. trembles introduced in [10]. A protocol is in Nash equilibrium if no deviations are advantageous; it is in strict Nash equilibrium if all deviations are disadvantageous. In other words, there is no incentive to deviate in the case of a Nash equilibrium whereas there is an incentive not to deviate for a strict Nash equilibrium. Another advantage of strict Nash is that protocols satisfying this notion inhibit subliminal communication. A party who tries to use protocol messages as a covert channel has the risks to lose utility if there is any reasonable probability that the other player is following the protocol, since any detectable deviation by a party from the protocol results in lower utility while the other party follows the protocol. The computational version of strict Nash equilibrium is intuitively close to strict Nash considering the computational limitations. Moreover, our protocol satisfies a strong condition that each party can send a unique legal message that at every point in the protocol. Our protocol thus rules out subliminal communication in a strong sense. We denote the security parameter by n. A function ϵ is negligible if for all $c > 0$ there is a $n_c > 0$ such that $\epsilon(n) < 1/n^c$ for all $n > n_c$; let $negl$ denote a generic negligible function. We say ϵ is noticeable if there exist c, n_c such that $\epsilon(n) > 1/n^c$ for all $n > n_c$.

We consider the strategies in our work as the PPT interactive Turing machines. Given a vector of strategies $\boldsymbol{\sigma}$ for two parties in the computation phase, let $u_j(\boldsymbol{\sigma})$ denote the expected utility of P_j, where the expected utility is a function of the security parameter n. This expectation is taken over the randomness of the players' strategies. Following the standard game-theoretic notation, $(\sigma'_j, \boldsymbol{\sigma}_{-j})$ denotes the strategy vector $\boldsymbol{\sigma}$ with P_j's strategy changed to σ'_j.

Definition 1. *Π induces a computational Nash equilibrium if for any PPT strategy σ'_1 of P_1 we have $u_1(\sigma'_1, \sigma_2) \leq u_1(\sigma_1, \sigma_2) + negl(n)$, and similarly for P_2.*

The computational notion of stability with respect to trembles models players' uncertainty about other parties' behavior, and guarantees that even if a party P_i believes that other parties might play some arbitrary strategy with small probability δ (but follow the protocol with probability $1 - \delta$), there is still no better strategy for P_i than to follow the protocol. The following definition is stated for the case of a deviating P_1 (definition for a deviating P_2 is analogous). Let P_1 and P_2 interact, following σ_1 and σ_2, respectively. Let mes denote the messages sent by P_1, but not including any messages sent by P_1 after it writes to its (write-once) output tape. Then $view_2^{\Pi}$ includes the information given by the trusted party to P_2, the random coins of P_2, and the (partial) transcript mes. We fix a strategy γ_1 and an algorithm A. Now, let P_1 and P_2 interact, following γ_1 and σ_2, respectively. Given the entire view of P_1, algorithm A outputs an arbitrary part mes' of mes. Then $view_2^{A,\gamma_1}$ includes the information given by the trusted party to P_2, the random coins of P_2, and the (partial) transcript mes'.

Definition 2. *Strategy γ_1 yields equivalent play with respect to Π, denoted $\gamma_1 \approx \Pi$, if there exists a PPT algorithm A such that for all PPT distinguishers D*
$| Pr[D(1^n, view_2^{A,\gamma_1}) = 1] - Pr[D(1^n, view_2^{\Pi}) = 1] | \leq negl(n)$

Definition 3. *Π induces a computational strict Nash equilibrium if*
1. Π induces a computational Nash equilibrium;
2. For any PPT strategy $\sigma_1' \not\approx \Pi$, there is a $c > 0$ such that $u_1(\sigma_1, \sigma_2) \leq u_1(\sigma_1', \sigma_2) + 1/n^c$ for infinitely many values of n .

In stability with respect to trembles, we say that γ_i is δ-close to σ_j if with probability $1-\delta$ party P_j plays σ_j, while with probability δ it follows an arbitrary PPT strategy σ_j'. In fact, a pair of strategies (σ_1, σ_2) is stable with respect to trembles if σ_1 (resp., σ_2) remains the best response even if the other party plays a strategy other than σ_2 (resp., σ_1) with some small (but noticeable) probability δ. The fact that the prescribed strategies are in Nash equilibrium ensures that any (polynomial-time) local computation performed by either party is of no benefit as long as the other party follows the protocol. Stated differently, even if a party P_j believes that the other party might play a different strategy with some small probability δ, there is still no better strategy for P_j than to outwardly follow the protocol.

Definition 4. *Π induces a computational strict Nash equilibrium that is stable with respect to trembles if*
1. Π induces a computational Nash equilibrium;
2. There is a noticeable function δ such that for any PPT strategy γ_2 that is δ-close to σ_2, and any PPT strategy γ_1, there exists a PPT strategy $\sigma_1' \approx \Pi$ such that $u_1(\gamma_1, \gamma_2) \leq u_1(\sigma_1', \gamma_2) + negl(n)$

Verifiable Random Functions (VRFs): A VRF is a keyed function whose output is random-looking but can still be verified as correct, given an associated proof. The notion was introduced by Micali et al. [30], and various efficient constructions in the standard model are known [6,8,28]. It has been shown in [28] that efficient VRFs can be constructed without relying on zero-knowledge proofs[1]. A verifiable random function (VRF) with range $R = \{R_n\}$ is a tuple of PPT algorithms $(Gen, Eval, Prove, Verify)$ such that: $G(1^n)$ generates the key pair (pk, sk). $Eval_{sk}(x)$ computes the value $y = F_{pk}(x)$; $Prove_{sk}(x)$ computes the proof z that $y = F_{pk}(x)$; and $Verify_{pk}(x, y, z)$ verifies that $y = F_{pk}(x)$ using the proof z. For such a VRF, the following hold:

Correctness: For all n, the algorithm $Eval_{sk}$ maps n-bit input to a set R_n. Furthermore, for any $x \in \{0,1\}^n$ we have $Verify_{pk}(x, Eval_{sk}(x), Prove_{sk}(x)) = 1$.

Verifiability: For all (pk, sk) output by $Gen(1^n)$, there does not exist a tuple (x, y, y', z, z') with $y \neq y'$ and $Verify_{pk}(x, y, z) = 1 = Verify_{pk}(x, y', z')$.

[1] The VRF gives us computational security. However, it is also possible to design our protocol with information-theoretic security using information-theoretically secure MACs. The details will appear in the full version.

Unique proofs: For all (pk, sk) output by $Gen(1^n)$, there does not exist a tuple (x, y, z, z') with $z \neq z'$ and $Verify_{pk}(x, y, z) = 1 = Verify_{pk}(x, y, z')$.

Pseudorandomness: Let $\mathcal{A}$ be a PPT adversary in the following game:

1. Generate $(pk, sk) \leftarrow Gen(1^n)$ and give pk to $\mathcal{A}$. $\mathcal{A}$ queries a sequence of strings $x_1, \ldots x_l \in \{0,1\}^n$ and is given $y_i = Eval_{sk}(x_i)$ and $z_i = Prove_{sk}(x_i)$ in response.

2. $\mathcal{A}$ outputs a string $x \in \{0,1\}^n$ s.t. $x \notin \{x_1, \ldots x_l\} \in \{0,1\}^n$.

3. $\mathcal{A}$ chooses a random $b \in \{0,1\}$. If $b = 0$ then $\mathcal{A}$ is given $y = Eval_{sk}(x)$; if $b = 1$ then $\mathcal{A}$ is given a random $y \in R_n$.

4. $\mathcal{A}$ makes queries as in step 2, as long as none of these queries is equal to x.

5. $\mathcal{A}$ outputs b' and succeeds if $b' = b$ at the end of the experiment.

We require that the success probability of any PPT adversary $\mathcal{A}$ is $1/2 + negl(n)$.

3 Model

In a typical protocol, parties are viewed as either honest or semi-honest/malicious. To model rationality, we consider players' utilities. Here we assume that $\mathcal{F} = \{f : X \times Y \rightarrow Z\}$ is a functionality where $\mid X \mid = \mid Y \mid$ and their domain is polynomial in size $(poly(n))$. Let $\mathcal{D}$ be the domain of output which is polynomial in size. The function returns a vector I that represents the set-intersection where I_t is set to one if item t is in the set-intersection. In other words, for all the data items of the parties (i.e., X and Y), we will compute $X \cap Y$, and we get I as the output of the function. Clearly for calculating set-intersection, we need to calculate $x_e \wedge y_e$ for each e where $x_e \in X$ and $y_e \in Y$. Similarly, for set-union, we need to calculate $x_e \vee y_e$ for all e. This can be rewritten as $\neg(\neg x_e \wedge \neg y_e)$. Computing the set-union is thus straight forward.

Given that j parties are active during the computation phase, let the outcome o of the computation phase be a vector of length j with $o_j = 1$ iff the output of P_j is equal to the exact intersection (i.e., P_j learns the correct output). Let $\nu_j(o)$ be the utility of player P_j for the outcome o. Following [14,10], we make the following assumptions about the utility functions of the players:

- If $o_j > o'_j$, then $\nu(o_j) > \nu(o'_j)$
- If $o_j = o'_j$ and $\sum_j o_j < \sum_j o'_j$, then $\nu(o_j) > \nu(o'_j)$

In other words, player P_j first prefers outcomes in which he learns the output; otherwise, P_j prefers strategies in which the fewest number of other players learn the result (in our two-party case, the other player learns). From the point of view of P_j, we consider the following three cases of utilities for the outcome o where $U^* > U > U'$:

- If only P_j learns the output, then $\nu_j(o) = U^*$.
- If P_j learns the output and the other player does also, then $\nu_j(o) = U$.
- If P_j does not learn the output, then $\nu_j(o) = U'$.

So, we have the expected utility of a party who outputs a random guess for the output[2] (assuming other party aborts without any output, or with the wrong output) as follows: $U_{rand} = \frac{1}{|\mathcal{D}|} \cdot U^* + (1 - \frac{1}{|\mathcal{D}|}) \cdot U'$.

Also, we assume that $U > U_{rand}$; else players have almost no incentive to run the computation phase at all. As in [10], we make no distinction between outputting the wrong secret and outputting a special 'don't know' symbol- both are considered as a failure to output the correct output.

To complete the protocol, we need to provide a way for parties to identify the real iteration. Some work [1,12,22,29] allows parties to identify the real iteration as soon as it occurs. This approach could be used in our protocol if we assume simultaneous channels. But, this approach is vulnerable to an obvious rushing strategy when simultaneous channels are not available. To avoid this, we follow the approach shown in [10]: delay the signal indicating whether a given iteration is real or fake until the following iteration. In this case, until being sure of the occurance of real iteration, a party cannot risk aborting. Moreover, once a party learns that the real iteration occurred, the real iteration is over and all parties can compute the real output. Simultaneous channels are thus not needed in this process at the price of adding only a single round.

4 Rational Set-Intersection Protocol

4.1 An Overview of the Protocol

Let x denote the input of P_1, let y denote the input of P_2, and let f denote the set-intersection function they are trying to compute. We follow the same high-level approach as in [14,12,29,1,22,23]. Our intersection computation protocol proceeds in a sequence of 'fake' iterations followed by a single 'real' iteration. As in [13,21,10], our protocol is composed of two stages, where the first stage can be viewed as a pre-processing stage and the second stage that computes the intersection takes place in a sequence of $r = r(n)$ iterations. Briefly speaking, the stages have the following form:

Pre-processing stage:

- A value $i^* \in \{1, \ldots, r\}$ is chosen according to some geometric distribution $0 < \alpha < 1$ where α depends on the players' utilities (discussed later in Section 5). This represents the iteration, in which parties will learn the 'true output'.
- For $i < i^*$, $\{a_i\} = \{a_1, \ldots, a_r\}$ (resp.,$\{b_i\} = \{b_1, \ldots, b_r\}$) are chosen according to some distribution that is independent of y (resp., x). For $i \geq i^*$, $a_i = b_i = f(x, y)$.
- Each a_i is randomly divided into shares $a_i^{(1)}$, $a_i^{(2)}$ with $a_i^{(1)} \oplus a_i^{(2)} = a_i$ (and similarly for each b_i). The stage concludes with P_1 being given $a_1^{(1)}$,

[2] We do not consider U''- the utility when neither party learns the output, since 'not learning the output' is not the target of a rational adversary in practice.

$b_1^{(1)}, \ldots, a_r^{(1)}, b_r^{(1)}$, and P_2 being given $a_1^{(2)}, b_1^{(2)}, \ldots, a_r^{(2)}, b_r^{(2)}$ alongside the VRFs [3] (*ShareGen*$_r$ provides the parties with VRFs so that if a malicious party modifies the share it sends to the other party, then the other party will almost certainly detect this due to the property of VRFs. It will be treated as an abort if such manipulation is detected.).

After this stage, each party has a set of random shares that reveal nothing about the other party's input.

Intersection Computation Phase:

In each iteration i, for $i = 1, \ldots, r$, the parties do the following: First, P_2 sends $a_i^{(2)}$ to P_1 who reconstructs a_i; then P_1 sends $b_i^{(1)}$ to P_2 who reconstructs b_i. (Parties also checks the VRF but we omit this here.) If a party aborts in some iteration i, then the other party outputs the value reconstructed in the previous iteration. Otherwise, after reaching iteration r the parties output a_r and b_r, respectively. To compute the correct intersection, parties run a sequence of iterations until the real iteration is identified, and both parties output the result at that point. If some party fails to follow the protocol, the other party aborts. In fact, it is rational for P_j to follow the protocol as long as the expected gain of deviating is positive only if P_j aborts exactly in iteration i^*; and is outweighed by the expected loss if P_j aborts before iteration i^*. The intersection computation phase proceeds in a series of iterations, where each iteration consists of one message sent by each party. Since we want to avoid simultaneous communication, we simply require P_2 to communicate first in each iteration.

When X and Y (the domains of f) are polynomial size, we follow [13,21] and set $a_i = f(x, \hat{y})$ for $\hat{y}$ chosen uniformly from Y , and set $b_i = f(\hat{x}, y)$ for $\hat{x}$ chosen uniformly (and independently) from X. Note that a_i (resp., b_i) is independent of y (resp., x), as desired.

4.2 Protocol Construction

As described above, our protocol Π consists of two stages. Let p be an arbitrary polynomial, and set $r = p \cdot \mid Y \mid$. We implement the first stage of Π using a subprotocol π for computing a randomized functionality *ShareGen*$_r$ (parameterized by a polynomial r) defined in Figure 1. This functionality returns shares to each party, alongside r-time VRF $(Gen, Eval, Prove, Verify)$. In the second stage of Π, the parties exchange these shares in a sequence of r iterations as described in Figure 2. The protocol returns I at the end of the operations on all the data items.

[3] It is the parties' own interest that they input the correct values for *ShareGen*$_r$. Otherwise, they will receive incorrect shares that will give them no chance to compute the correct intersection result, which will only enable them of having smaller incentives.

Input: Let the inputs to $ShareGen_r$ be $x \in X_n$ and $y \in Y_n$. (If one of the received inputs is not in the correct domain, a default input is substituted.)

Computation:

- Define values $a_1, \ldots, a_r$ and $b_1, \ldots, b_r$ in the following way:
  - Choose i^* according to some geometric distribution α
  - For $i < i^*$ do,
    - Choose $\hat{y} \leftarrow Y_n$ and set $a_i = f_n(x, \hat{y})$
    - Choose $\hat{x} \leftarrow X_n$ and set $b_i = f_n(\hat{x}, y)$
  - For $i = i^*$, set $a_i = b_i = q = f_n(x, y)$.
  - For $i > i^*$, set $a_i = b_i = NULL$
- For all iteration i, choose $(a_i^{(1)}, a_i^{(2)})$ and $(b_i^{(1)}, b_i^{(2)})$ as random secret shares of a_i and b_i, respectively. (I.e., $a_i^{(1)} \oplus a_i^{(2)} = a_i$, $b_i^{(1)} \oplus b_i^{(2)} = b_i$)
- Let $\mathcal{D} = \{0,1\}^l$ be the domain of the output. Let $(Gen, Eval, Prove, Verify)$ and $(Gen', Eval', Prove', Verify')$ be VRFs with range $\{0,1\}^l$ and $\{0,1\}^n$, respectively. Compute (pk_1, sk_1), $(pk_2, sk_2) \leftarrow Gen(1^n)$ and (pk_1', sk_1'), $(pk_2', sk_2') \leftarrow Gen'(1^n)$. For all i, compute $share1_i = Eval_{sk_2}(i \| b_i^{(1)})$ and $share2_i = Eval_{sk_1}(i \| a_i^{(1)})$. Also compute $signal1 = Eval'_{sk_2'}(i^* + 1)$ and $signal2 = Eval'_{sk_1'}(i^* + 1)$

Output:

- Send to P_1 the values $(sk_1, sk_1', pk_2, pk_2', a_1^{(1)}, \ldots, a_r^{(1)}, (b_1^{(1)}, share1_1), \ldots, (b_r^{(1)}, share1_r), signal1)$.
- Send to P_2 the values $(sk_2, sk_2', pk_1, pk_1', b_1^{(1)}, \ldots, b_r^{(1)}, (a_1^{(1)}, share2_1), \ldots, (a_r^{(1)}, share2_r), signal2)$.

Fig. 1. Functionality $ShareGen_r$

5 Protocol Analysis

Here we will give some intuition as to why the reconstruction phase of Π is a computational Nash equilibrium for an appropriate choice of α. Let us assume that P_2 follows the protocol, and P_1 deviates from the protocol. (It is easier to analyze the deviations by P_2 since P_2 starts in every iteration.) As soon as it receives $z_2^{(i)} = signal1$, P_1 can abort in iteration $i = i^* + 1$, or it can abort in some iteration $i < i^* + 1$. While aborting in $i = i^* + 1$, P_1 'knows' that it learned the correct output in the preceding iteration (iteration i^*) and can thus output the correct result; however, P_2 will output the correct result as well since it sent the $z_2^{(i)} = signal1$ value to P_1. So P_1 does not increase its utility beyond what it would achieve by following the protocol. In the second case, when P_1 aborts in some iteration $i < i^* + 1$, the best strategy P_1 can adopt is to output $a_1^{(i)}$ hoping that $i = i^*$. Thus, following this strategy, the expected utility that P_1 obtains can be calculated as follows:

Input: Party P_1 has input x and party P_2 has input y.

Computation:

- Preliminary phase:
  1. P_1 chooses $\hat{y} \in Y_n$ uniformly at random, and sets $a_0 = f_n(x, \hat{y})$. Similarly, P_2 chooses $\hat{x} \in X_n$ uniformly at random, and sets $b_0 = f_n(\hat{x}, y)$.
  2. Parties P_1 and P_2 run a protocol π to compute $ShareGen$, , using their inputs x and y.
  3. If P_2 receives $\perp$ from the above computation, it outputs b_0 and halts. Otherwise, the parties proceed to the next step.
  4. Denote the output of P_1 from π by $(sk_1, sk'_1, pk_2, pk'_2, a_1^{(1)}, \ldots, a_r^{(1)}, (b_1^{(1)}, share1_1), \ldots, (b_r^{(1)}, share1_r), signal1)$.
  5. Denote the output of P_2 from π by $(sk_2, sk'_2, pk_1, pk'_1, b_1^{(1)}, \ldots, b_r^{(1)}, (a_1^{(1)}, share2_1), \ldots, (a_r^{(1)}, share2_r), signal2)$.
- Intersection Computation Phase

  For all i do:

  P_2 sends message to P_1:
  1. P_2 computes $y_2^{(i)} = Prove_{sk_2}(i \| a_i^{(2)}), z_2^{(i)} = Eval'_{sk'_2}(i), \bar{z}_2^{(i)} = Prove'_{sk'_2}(i)$. It sends $(a_i^{(2)}, share2_i, y_2^{(i)}, z_2^{(i)}, \bar{z}_2^{(i)})$ to P_1.
  2. If P_2 does not send anything to P_1, then P_1 outputs a_{i-1} and halts. P_2 sends $(a_i^{(2)}, share2_i, y_2^{(i)}, z_2^{(i)}, \bar{z}_2^{(i)})$ to P_1. If $Verify_{pk_2}(i \| a_i^{(2)}, share2_i, y_2^{(i)}) = 0$ or $Verify'_{pk'_2}(i, z_2^{(i)}, \bar{z}_2^{(i)}) = 0$, then P_1 outputs a_{i-1} and halts. If $signal1 \neq z_2^{(i)}$ then P_1 outputs a_{i-1}, sends its iteration-i message to P_2, and halts.
  3. If $Verify_{pk_2}(i \| a_i^{(2)}, share2_i, y_2^{(i)}) = 1$ and $a_i^{(1)} \oplus a_i^{(2)} \neq NULL$ (i.e., $x = x_i$), then P_1 sets $a_i = a_i^{(1)} \oplus a_i^{(2)}$, and continues running the protocol.

  P_1 sends message to P_2:
  1. P_1 computes $y_1^{(i)} = Prove_{sk_1}(i \| b_i^{(1)}), z_1^{(i)} = Eval'_{sk'_1}(i), \bar{z}_1^{(i)} = Prove'_{sk'_1}(i)$. It sends $(b_i^{(1)}, share1_i, y_1^{(i)}, z_1^{(i)}, \bar{z}_1^{(i)})$ to P_2.
  2. If P_1 does not send anything, then P_2 outputs b_{i-1} and halts. P_1 sends $(b_i^{(1)}, share1_i, y_1^{(i)}, z_1^{(i)}, \bar{z}_1^{(i)})$ to P_2. If $Verify_{pk_1}(i \| b_i^{(1)}, share1_i, y_1^{(i)}) = 0$ or $Verify'_{pk'_1}(i, z_1^{(i)}, \bar{z}_1^{(i)}) = 0$, then P_2 outputs b_{i-1} and halts. If $signal2 \neq z_1^{(i)}$ then P_2 outputs b_{i-1}, sends its iteration-i message to P_1, and halts.
  3. If $Verify_{pk_1}(i \| b_i^{(1)}, share1_i, y_1^{(i)}) = 1$ and $b_i^{(1)} \oplus b_i^{(2)} \neq NULL$ (i.e., $y = y_i$), then P_2 sets $b_i = b_i^{(1)} \oplus b_i^{(2)}$, and continues running the protocol.

Output: If all r iterations have been run, party P_1 outputs a_r and party P_2 outputs b_r.

Fig. 2. Protocol for computing the functionality for set-intersection

- P_1 aborts exactly in iteration $i = i^*$. In this case, the utility that P_1 gets is at most U^*.
- When $i < i^*$, P_1 has 'no information' about correct a_r and so the best it can do is guess. In this case, the expected utility of P_1 is at most U_{rand}.

Considering the above, P_1's expected utility of following this strategy is at most:

$$\alpha \times U^* + (1 - \alpha) \times U_{rand}$$

Now, it is possible to set the value of α such that the expected utility of this strategy is strictly less than U, since $U_{rand} < U$ by assumption. In such a case, P_1 has no incentive to deviate. Since there is always a unique valid message a party can send and anything else is treated as an abort, it follows that the protocol Π induces a strict computational Nash equilibrium which is stable with respect to trembles.

The detailed proof of the following propositions will be given in the full version of the paper.

Proposition 1. *The protocol Π induces a computational Nash equilibrium given that $0 < \alpha < 1$, $U > \alpha \times U^* + (1 - \alpha) \times U_{rand}$, and the pseudorandomness of VRFs.*

Proposition 2. *If $0 < \alpha < 1$, $U > \alpha \times U^* + (1 - \alpha) \times U_{rand}$, VRFs are pseudorandom, and there is always a unique valid message each party can send, then the protocol Π induces a computational strict Nash equilibrium.*

Proposition 3. *The protocol Π is stable with respect to trembles given that $0 < \alpha < 1$ and $U > \alpha \times U^* + (1 - \alpha) \times U_{rand}$.*

According to the above propositions and their proofs, we give the theorem as follows:

Theorem 1. *If $0 < \alpha < 1$, $U > \alpha \times U^* + (1 - \alpha) \times U_{rand}$, and VRFs are pseudorandom, then Π induces a computational strict Nash equilibrium that is stable with respect to trembles.*

6 Conclusion

In this paper, we have proposed a privacy-preserving set-intersection protocol in two-party settings from the game-theoretic perspective. We have used verifiable random functions as the underlying cryptographic primitive which is simple and efficient. It is also possible to use our protocol for computing set-union operations. We also show that our protocol satisfies computational versions of strict Nash equilibrium and stability with respect to trembles. Applying game-theoretic approach for multi-party setting where parties are allowed to collude is an interesting open problem.

References

1. Abraham, I., Dolev, D., Gonen, R., Halpern, J.: Distributed Computing Meets Game Theory: Robust Mechanisms for Rational Secret Sharing and Multi-party Computation. In: 25th ACM Symposium Annual on Principles of Distributed Computing, pp. 53–62 (2006)

2. Agrawal, R., Terzi, E.: On Honesty in Sovereign Information Sharing. In: Ioannidis, Y., Scholl, M.H., Schmidt, J.W., Matthes, F., Hatzopoulos, M., Böhm, K., Kemper, A., Grust, T., Böhm, C. (eds.) EDBT 2006. LNCS, vol. 3896, pp. 240–256. Springer, Heidelberg (2006)
3. Aumann, Y., Lindell, Y.: Security Against Covert Adversaries: Efficient Protocols for Realistic Adversaries. In: Vadhan, S.P. (ed.) TCC 2007. LNCS, vol. 4392, pp. 137–156. Springer, Heidelberg (2007)
4. Bellare, M., Micali, S.: Non-interactive Oblivious Transfer and Applications. In: Brassard, G. (ed.) CRYPTO 1989. LNCS, vol. 435, pp. 547–557. Springer, Heidelberg (1990)
5. Cramer, R., Damgard, I., Nielsen, J.B.: Multi-party Computation from Threshold Homomorphic Encryption. In: Pfitzmann, B. (ed.) EUROCRYPT 2001. LNCS, vol. 2045, pp. 280–299. Springer, Heidelberg (2001)
6. Dodis, Y.: Efficient Construction of (distributed) Verifiable Random Functions. In: Desmedt, Y.G. (ed.) PKC 2003. LNCS, vol. 2567, pp. 1–17. Springer, Heidelberg (2002)
7. Dodis, Y., Rabin, T.: Cryptography and Game Theory. In: Nisan, N., Roughgarden, T., Tardos, E., Vazirani, V. (eds.) Algorithmic Game Theory, pp. 181–207. Cambridge University Press, Cambridge (2007)
8. Dodis, Y., Yampolskiy, A.: A Verifiable Random Function with Short Proofs and Keys. In: Vaudenay, S. (ed.) PKC 2005. LNCS, vol. 3386, pp. 416–431. Springer, Heidelberg (2005)
9. Emura, K., Miyaji, A., Rahman, M.S.: Efficient Privacy-Preserving Data Mining in Malicious Model. In: Cao, L., Feng, Y., Zhong, J. (eds.) ADMA 2010, Part I. LNCS, vol. 6440, pp. 370–382. Springer, Heidelberg (2010)
10. Fuchsbauer, G., Katz, J., Naccache, D.: Efficient Rational Secret Sharing in Standard Communication Networks. In: Micciancio, D. (ed.) TCC 2010. LNCS, vol. 5978, pp. 419–436. Springer, Heidelberg (2010)
11. Goldreich, O.: Foundations of cryptography: Basic applications. Cambridge Univ. Press, Cambridge (2004)
12. Gordon, S.D., Katz, J.: Rational Secret Sharing, Revisited. In: De Prisco, R., Yung, M. (eds.) SCN 2006. LNCS, vol. 4116, pp. 229–241. Springer, Heidelberg (2006)
13. Gordon, S.D., Hazay, C., Katz, J., Lindell, Y.: Complete Fairness in Secure Two-party Computation. In: 40th Annual ACM Symposium on Theory of Computing, STOC 2008, pp. 413–422 (2008)
14. Halpern, J., Teague, V.: Rational Secret Sharing and Multi-party Computation: Extended abstract. In: 36th Annual ACM Symposium on Theory of Computing, STOC 2004, pp. 623–632 (2004)
15. Izmalkov, S., Micali, S., Lepinski, M.: Rational Secure Computation and Ideal Mechanism Design. In: 46th Annual Symposium on Foundations of Computer Science, FOCS 2005, pp. 585–595 (2005)
16. Jagannathan, G., Wright, R.N.: Privacy-preserving Distributed k-means Clustering over Arbitrarily Partitioned Data. In: ACM SIGKDD International Conference on Knowledge Discovery and Data Mining, KDD 2005, pp. 593–599 (2005)
17. Jiang, W., Clifton, C., Kantarcioglu, M.: Transforming Semi-Honest Protocols to Ensure Accountability. Data and Knowledge Engineering (DKE) 65(1), 57–74 (2008)
18. Kantarcioglu, M., Clifton, C.: Privately Computing a Distributed k-nn Classifier. In: Boulicaut, J.-F., Esposito, F., Giannotti, F., Pedreschi, D. (eds.) PKDD 2004. LNCS (LNAI), vol. 3202, pp. 279–290. Springer, Heidelberg (2004)

19. Kantarcioglu, M., Kardes, O.: Privacy-preserving Data Mining in the Malicious model. International Journal of Information and Computer Security 2(4), 353–375 (2008)
20. Katz, J.: Bridging Game Theory and Cryptography: Recent Results and Future Directions. In: Canetti, R. (ed.) TCC 2008. LNCS, vol. 4948, pp. 251–272. Springer, Heidelberg (2008)
21. Katz, J.: On Achieving the Best of Both Worlds in Secure Multi-party Computation. In: 39th Annual ACM Symposium on Theory of Computing, STOC 2007, pp. 11–20 (2007)
22. Kol, G., Naor, M.: Cryptography and Game Theory: Designing Protocols for Exchanging Information. In: Canetti, R. (ed.) TCC 2008. LNCS, vol. 4948, pp. 320–339. Springer, Heidelberg (2008)
23. Kol, G., Naor, M.: Games for Exchanging Information. In: 40th Annual ACM Symposium on Theory of Computing, STOC 2008, pp. 423–432 (2008)
24. Lin, X., Clifton, C., Zhu, M.: Privacy-preserving Clustering with Distributed EM Mixture Modeling. Knowledge and Information Systems 8(1), 68–81 (2005)
25. Lindell, Y., Pinkas, B.: Privacy-preserving Data Mining. In: Bellare, M. (ed.) CRYPTO 2000. LNCS, vol. 1880, pp. 36–54. Springer, Heidelberg (2000)
26. Lipmaa, H.: Verifiable Homomorphic Oblivious Transfer and Private Equality Test. In: Laih, C.-S. (ed.) ASIACRYPT 2003. LNCS, vol. 2894, pp. 416–433. Springer, Heidelberg (2003)
27. Liu, J., Lu, Y.H., Koh, C.K.: Performance Analysis of Arithmetic Operations in Homomorphic Encryption. In: ECE Technical Reports, Purdue University (2010)
28. Lysyanskaya, A.: Unique Signatures and Verifiable Random Functions from the DH-DDH Separation. In: Yung, M. (ed.) CRYPTO 2002. LNCS, vol. 2442, pp. 597–612. Springer, Heidelberg (2002)
29. Lysyanskaya, A., Triandopoulos, N.: Rationality and Adversarial behavior in Multi-party computation. In: Dwork, C. (ed.) CRYPTO 2006. LNCS, vol. 4117, pp. 180–197. Springer, Heidelberg (2006)
30. Micali, S., Rabin, M.O., Vadhan, S.P.: Verifiable Random Functions. In: 40th Annual Symposium on Foundations of Computer Science, FOCS 1999, pp. 120–130 (1999)
31. Miyaji, A., Rahman, M.S.: Privacy-preserving Data Mining in Presence of Covert Adversaries. In: Cao, L., Feng, Y., Zhong, J. (eds.) ADMA 2010, Part I. LNCS, vol. 6440, pp. 429–440. Springer, Heidelberg (2010)
32. Nix, R., Kantarcioglu, M.: Incentive Compatible Distributed Data Mining. In: IEEE International Conference on Privacy, Security, Risk and Trust, pp. 735–742 (2010)
33. Ong, S.J., Parkes, D., Rosen, A., Vadhan, S.: Fairness with an Honest Minority and a Rational Majority. In: Reingold, O. (ed.) TCC 2009. LNCS, vol. 5444, pp. 36–53. Springer, Heidelberg (2009)
34. Su, C., Bao, F., Zhou, J., Takagi, T., Sakurai, K.: Security and Correctness Analysis on Privacy-Preserving k-Means Clustering Schemes. IEICE Trans. Fundamentals E92-A(4), 1246–1250 (2009)
35. Vaidya, J., Clifton, C.: Privacy Preserving Association Rule Mining in Vertically Partitioned Data. In: ACM SIGKDD International Conference on Knowledge Discovery and Data Mining, KDD 2002, pp. 639–644 (2002)
36. Zhang, N., Zhao, W.: Distributed Privacy-preserving Information Sharing. In: The 31st International Conference on Very Large Data Bases, VLDB 2005, pp. 889–900 (2005)

Enhancing CardSpace Authentication Using a Mobile Device

Haitham S. Al-Sinani and Chris J. Mitchell

Information Security Group
Royal Holloway, University of London
{Haitham.Al-Sinani.2009,C.Mitchell}@rhul.ac.uk
http://www.isg.rhul.ac.uk

Abstract. In this paper we propose a simple, novel scheme for using a mobile device to enhance CardSpace authentication. During the process of user authentication on a PC using CardSpace, a random and short-lived one-time password is sent to the user's mobile device; this must then be entered into the PC by the user when prompted. The scheme does not require any changes to login servers, the CardSpace identity selector, or to the mobile device itself. We specify the scheme and give details of a proof-of-concept prototype. Security and operational analyses are also provided.

Keywords: CardSpace, OTP, mobile device, authentication.

1 Introduction

In line with the continuing increase in the number of on-line services requiring authentication, there has been a proportional rise in the number of digital identities needed for authentication purposes. This has contributed to the recent rapid growth in identity-oriented attacks, such as phishing, pharming, etc. In an attempt to mitigate such attacks, Microsoft has introduced an identity management system called CardSpace.

CardSpace is a user-friendly tool supporting user authentication. To sign on to a website, a CardSpace user selects a virtual card, known as an information card (InfoCard), from an interface provided by the CardSpace identity selector (CIdS), instead of providing a username and password.

One fundamental limitation of CardSpace is that anyone with access to a Windows user account can also access and use the InfoCards. By default, CardSpace does not provide access protection for the CIdS. To address this issue, CardSpace allows individual InfoCards to be PIN-protected. Also, the entire Windows user account could, of course, be password-protected. Whilst the use of passwords and PINs for InfoCard protection can help, it does not completely solve the problem, not least because one of the fundamental design goals of CardSpace is to reduce reliance on password authentication.

We address this limitation through the introduction of a second authentication factor to be used in conjunction with CardSpace authentication. This additional

Y. Li (Ed.): Data and Applications Security and Privacy XXV, LNCS 6818, pp. 201–216, 2011.

means of user authentication involves a one-time password (OTP) supplied to the user by a standard mobile device capable of receiving SMS messages. Such devices are ubiquitous, making the system almost universally applicable. The system also provides two-factor authentication, the first factor being possession of the PC containing the InfoCard and the second factor being possession of the appropriate mobile phone. Two factor authentication is typically considered 'strong authentication' [1].

The wide use of Windows, recent versions of which incorporate CardSpace, means that any enhancement to CardSpace security is likely to be of significance for large numbers of identity management users and service providers. In addition, the use of a mobile phone to enhance CardSpace-based authentication is attractive since users are neither required to remember any new passwords nor obliged to use any additional hardware. Furthermore, many RPs may not accept the burden of supporting a second authentication factor (e.g. SMS-based authentication), unless there is a significant financial incentive or if forced to do so for legal or regulatory reasons. As a result, a client-side technique for supporting SMS authentication for CardSpace-enabled RPs could be practically useful. Such a technique avoids any impact on the performance of the server, since the additional overhead is handled by the client.

The remainder of the paper is organised as follows. Section 2 gives an overview of CardSpace, and section 3 presents the proposed scheme. In section 4 we discuss implementation issues, and in section 5 we provide a security analysis. In section 6 we describe a prototype realisation, and section 7 highlights possible areas for related work. Finally, section 8 concludes the paper.

2 CardSpace

2.1 Introduction

CardSpace provides a secure and consistent way for users to control and manage personal data, to review personal data before sending it to a website, and to verify the identity of visited websites. It enables websites to obtain data from users, e.g. to support user authentication and authorisation.

Digital identities are represented to users as Information Cards (or InfoCards). There are two types of InfoCards: personal (self-issued) cards, and managed cards issued by remote IdPs. Personal cards are created by users themselves, and the claims listed in such an InfoCard are asserted by the self-issued identity provider (SIP) that co-exists with the CardSpace identity selector (CIdS) on the user machine. InfoCards, personal or managed, do not contain sensitive information, but instead carry metadata indicating the types of personal data associated with this identity, and from where assertions regarding this data can be obtained. The data referred to by personal cards is stored on the user machine, whereas the data referred to by a managed card is held by the identity provider (IdP) that issued it [2,3,4,5].

The proposed scheme can operate with both managed and personal cards. However, in this paper we only describe its operation with personal cards because the security risks associated with such cards are much greater; any adversary who has access to a logged-in Windows machine can use any of the personal cards unless they are PIN-protected, which is not the default case. By contrast, use of a managed card typically involves authentication by the issuing IdP. The use of personal cards is described below; the use of managed cards is covered in the relevant specifications [2,3,6,7].

By default, CardSpace is supported by Internet Explorer (IE) from version 7 onwards. Extensions to other browsers, such as Firefox[1] and Safari[2], also exist. An updated version, CardSpace 2.0 Beta 2, was released, although Microsoft announced in early 2011 that it will not ship; instead Microsoft has released a technology preview of U-Prove[3]. In this paper we refer throughout to the CardSpace version that is shipped by default as part of Windows Vista and Windows 7, that is available as a free download for XP and Server 2003, and which has been approved as an OASIS standard [7].

2.2 Personal Cards

The CIdS allows a user to create a personal card and populate its fields with self-asserted claims. CardSpace restricts the contents of personal cards to non-sensitive data. Prerequisites for use of a personal card include a CardSpace-enabled relying party (RP) and a CardSpace-enabled user agent, e.g. a web browser capable of invoking the CIdS. At the time that an InfoCard is created, a card-specific ID and master key are also created and stored by the SIP (which also stores the values of the claims for this card).

Using Personal Cards. When using personal cards, CardSpace adopts the following protocol. We describe the protocol for the case where the RP does not employ a security token service (STS), a software component responsible for security policy and token management within an IdP and, optionally, within an RP [6].

1. User agent → RP. HTTP/S request: GET (login page).
2. RP → user agent. HTTP/S response. A login page is returned containing the CardSpace-enabling tags in which the RP security policy is embedded.
3. User → user agent. The RP web page offers the option to use CardSpace; selecting this option activates the CIdS, which is passed the RP security policy. Note that if this is the first time that this RP has been contacted, the CIdS will display the identity of the RP and give the user the option to either proceed or abort the protocol.

[1] `https://addons.mozilla.org/en-US/firefox/addon/openinfocard-identity-selector/`

[2] `http://www.hccp.org/safari-plug-in.html`

[3] `http://blogs.msdn.com/b/card/archive/2011/02/15/beyond-windows-cardspace.aspx`

4. CIdS → InfoCards. The CIdS, after evaluating the RP security policy, highlights those InfoCards matching the policy and greys out the rest. InfoCards previously used for this RP are displayed in the upper half of the selector screen.
5. User → CIdS. The user chooses a personal card. (Alternatively, the user could create and choose a new personal card). The user can preview the card (with its associated claims) to ensure that they are willing to release the claim values. Of the claims specified in an InfoCard, only those requested in the RP policy will be passed to the requesting RP.
6. CIdS ⇌ SIP. The CIdS creates and sends a SAML-based Request Security Token (RST) to the SIP, which responds with a SAML-based Request Security Token Response (RSTR).
7. CIdS → user agent → RP. The RSTR is passed to the user agent, which forwards it to the RP.
8. RP → user agent. The RP validates the token, and, if satisfied, grants access.

Private Personal Identifiers (PPIDs). The PPID is an identifier linking a specific InfoCard to a particular RP [2]. When a user first uses a personal card at a particular RP, CardSpace generates a site-specific PPID by combining the card ID with data taken from the RP certificate, and a site-specific signature key pair by combining the card master key with data taken from the RP certificate. In both cases, the domain name and/or IP address of the RP is used if no RP certificate is available. After generation, the PPID and key pair are stored by the SIP for use in future interactions with this RP.

Since the PPID and key pair are RP-specific, the PPID does not function as a global user identifier, helping to enhance user privacy and reduce the impact of PPID compromise. The CIdS displays a shortened version of the PPID to protect against social engineering attacks and improve readability.

When a user first interacts with an RP using CardSpace, the RP retrieves the PPID and the public key from the received SAML security token, and stores them. If a personal InfoCard is re-used at a site, the supplied security token will contain the same PPID and public key as used previously, and will be signed using the corresponding private key. The RP compares the received PPID and public key with its stored values, and verifies the digital signature.

The PPID could be used on its own as a shared secret to authenticate a user to an RP. However, it is recommended that the associated (public) signature verification key, as held by the RP, should always be used to verify the signed security token to provide a more robust authentication method [2].

3 The Scheme

We next give an overview of the novel scheme, covering relevant operational aspects.

3.1 Entities Involved

The entities involved are:

- a CardSpace-enabled RP (with which the user must have an account);
- a CardSpace-enabled user agent (e.g. a suitable web browser such as IE);
- a handheld device capable of receiving SMS[4] messages (e.g. a mobile phone); and
- software installed on the user PC (referred to throughout as the 'adaptor') implementing the scheme described below.

The adaptor could be implemented as a browser extension[5], which must be able to read, inspect and modify browser-rendered web pages, and must also be able to intercept CardSpace-issued RSTR tokens. In addition, it must be able to generate and send a random, short-lived OTP to the user's mobile phone, and provide a means for the user to enter the OTP. Prior to use of the protocol, the browser extension must be installed and provided with the phone number of the user's mobile phone.

3.2 Operation

The system operates as follows; a summary of the protocol is shown in figures 1 and 2. Steps 1, 2, 4–7, and 10 are the same as steps 1, 2, 3–6, and 8, respectively, of the CardSpace personal card protocol given in section 2.2.

3. Adaptor → user agent. The adaptor scans the login page to detect whether the RP website supports CardSpace. If so, it proceeds; otherwise it terminates.
8. Unlike in the 'standard' case, the RSTR does not reach the RP; instead the adaptor performs the following steps.
   (a) CIdS → adaptor: RSTR. The adaptor intercepts the RSTR and temporarily stores it.
   (b) Adaptor: generates OTP. The adaptor computes (and temporarily stores) a random, short-lived OTP.
   (c) Adaptor → mobile phone: OTP. The adaptor sends the OTP to the user's mobile phone in an SMS message, sent via an HTTPS-protected connection to the SMS Centre or SMS gateway of a wireless carrier or SMS service provider. This method is adopted because it does not require a special application to be installed on the user's mobile phone, which

[4] SMS (Short Messaging Service) allows mobile phones to exchange short messages of at most 160 Latin characters; this service is supported by all GSM and 3G handsets.

[5] Note that if the adaptor is implemented as a browser extension, then the CardSpace-enabled RP must not employ an STS. Instead, the RP must express its security policy using HTML/XHTML, and interactions between the CIdS and the RP must be based on HTTP/S via a web browser (a simpler and probably more common scenario for RP interactions). This is because a (JavaScript-based) browser extension is by itself incapable of managing the necessary communications with an RP STS.

3. A → UA, where A is the adaptor and UA is the user agent.
8. CIdS → [A: generates OTP] → M, where M is the mobile device.
   More specifically:
   a. CIdS → A: RSTR;
   b. A: generates OTP; and
   c. A → M: OTP.
9. U → UA: OTP, where U is the user.

Fig. 1. Summary of the Protocol

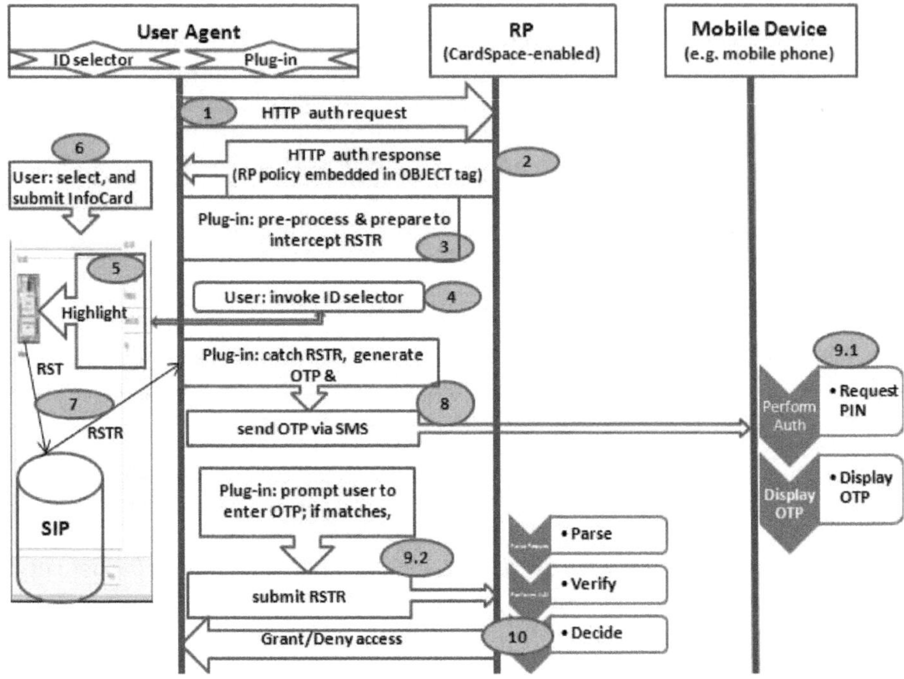

Fig. 2. Protocol exchanges

may not be possible in non-smart phones. In addition such an approach has a better transmission rate than other methods such as Bluetooth or infrared (see section 4.2).

9. User ⇌ user agent. The adaptor prompts the user to enter the OTP, and the user reads it from the phone display[6]. The adaptor verifies that the entered OTP matches the one it just generated. The OTP must be entered within a defined interval, e.g. of 10 minutes, after its generation; otherwise the adaptor will delete the RSTR and provide an error message to the user.

[6] Note that if the mobile phone and/or the SIM card are PIN-protected, then the user must first enter the correct PIN(s).

4 Discussion

We now consider implementation issues, possible variants and potential advantages of the scheme.

4.1 Implementation Issues

The length of the OTP must be carefully chosen to achieve an acceptable balance between security and usability. To maximise usability and avoid confusion, we propose the use of a 4-character OTP made up of lower case letters and digits (excluding 0, i, j and o). This gives a total of 32^4 possible OTPs (i.e. just over a million), which is roughly 100 times the number of possible 4-digit PINs commonly used for bank cards.

4.2 Variants of the Scheme

OTP Transmission. In the scheme described above, the OTP is sent from the client to the mobile device in an SMS message. Whilst convenient, this has cost implications and may also involve a delay of a few seconds. Possible alternatives include sending it via Bluetooth, infrared or a USB/serial cable. Such approaches have the advantage of avoiding the SMS messaging costs but require both devices to support the relevant technologies. The main disadvantage of such approaches is the need to install a special application on the phone; this will rule out non-smart phones, and significantly increase the complexity of setting up the scheme.

A further alternative would be to use a messaging service other than SMS for the OTP transfer (e.g. instant messaging or email); like the use of the SMS service, such an approach would avoid the need to install any new applications on the phone.

OTP Entry. In the scheme as described above, the user manually enters the OTP, which is potentially inconvenient and time-consuming (although the use of a 4-digit PIN, as described in section 4.1, should minimise inconvenience). An alternative would be to send the OTP back automatically, e.g. via an SMS message sent to the SMS gateway, from where the adaptor could retrieve it. Whilst convenient, such a process could be costly, since use of the SMS gateway would incur additional messaging costs.

RSTR. As part of step 9 of section 3.2 the adaptor could create a new SAML token containing the RSTR produced by the SIP and an additional SAML field indicating that the user has been authenticated using an SMS-transmitted OTP. Of course, the RP would need to be modified to be able to process such a token, although this would be straightforward. This authentication statement would give the RP added assurance of user authenticity.

4.3 Advantages

Like other OTP-based authentication systems, the proposed scheme reduces exposure to shoulder-surfing attacks and also helps to thwart key loggers.

The scheme does not require users to remember new passwords for each new account; this could reduce the risk of password re-use, writing passwords down in insecure ways, and use of easily-guessable passwords.

In addition to strengthening user authentication, the scheme could also serve as an intrusion detector. If the user receives an unexpected OTP, then it could be deduced that there is a security breach.

Finally, the scheme operates transparently to external parties, and hence does not require any changes to RPs or identity selectors.

5 Security Analysis

5.1 Threats to the Mobile Device

If an unprotected mobile phone or SIM is lost, stolen or borrowed, then it might be possible to access an OTP from the SMS inbox. However, this will be of no value without access to the corresponding PC (and the OTP will expire a short time after generation). Moreover, a lost phone or SIM is likely to be reported by its owner, causing the SIM to be deactivated, which means that the usefulness of such a stolen device for impersonating a user will be very limited.

5.2 Threats to the Supporting Infrastructure

An attacker with temporary access to the PC but without the mobile phone could attempt to intercept the OTP whilst it is being transmitted from the PC to the phone. However, the communication link between the SMS gateway and the PC is protected using HTTPS, and the connection between the visited mobile network and the mobile phone is protected by the air interface encryption mechanism of the mobile network [8,9]. This leaves the SMS gateway and the SMS network itself as the only sources of such a threat, and routinely compromising either the gateway or the SMS network for such a purpose seems unlikely to be realistic in practice.

5.3 Threats to the PC

Exhausting the User's SMS Credit. An adversary who has access to the user's PC but does not possess the user's mobile phone could cause the system to repeatedly send SMS messages, resulting in exhaustion of the user's SIM credit at the SMS gateway. This risk can be mitigated in the following ways.

1. If a user receives an unexpected SMS containing an OTP, the user should immediately change their password at the SMS gateway. This will deny the adversary the ability to send any further SMS messages from the user's PC.
2. The browser extension could implement a simple, client-based, lock-out mechanism using cookies. That is, if the correct OTP is not entered within three attempts, the browser extension could write a persistent[7] cookie to the client

[7] Persistent cookies can survive across a number of sessions, including after exiting the browser and/or after a machine reboot. Such cookies have an expiry date; if a cookie expires it is deleted.

PC which will cause the current attempt to log in to the RP to be terminated. The browser extension would then generate a special lock-out OTP and send it to the user's mobile phone. The next time that the user attempts to log in to the same domain, the browser extension (before invoking the CIdS) would prompt the user to enter the lock-out OTP, and would only proceed if the correct OTP is entered. Although this solution may help to discourage an attacker, it is not foolproof since cookies could be manually deleted on the client machine, and an attacker could arrange for OTP-bearing SMSs to be sent to a large number of different domains.

Disabling the Browser Extension. If the system is configured so that it is possible to disable the OTP adaptor, then a knowledgeable intruder could defeat the protection provided by the scheme. Therefore, a robust implementation of the scheme proposed in section 3.2 must not allow an adversary to disable it. That is, the system must be configured to oblige users to use CardSpace coupled with the OTP adaptor.

Browser extensions can be enabled/disabled at will by anyone who has access to a Windows user account. So an adversary with access to InfoCards could simply disable the browser extension to cause CardSpace to operate normally.

It may be possible to remove this threat, at least partially, by installing the browser extension so that administrator privileges are required to disable it, and also persuading the PC owner to log in using a non-administrator account. It may also be possible to make use of UAC[8] (User Account Control), so that disabling a browser extension causes Windows to prompt the user for an administrator password.

Ultimately, it would be desirable to implement the scheme described in section 3.2 as an integral part of CardSpace, thereby negating this threat. In such a scenario, each InfoCard might be given a selectable field to indicate whether SMS-based authentication is required. A user could thus choose to SMS-protect an important InfoCard by simply selecting the appropriate field.

Exploiting CardSpace Backup Facilities. The CardSpace backup facilities could be exploited to allow an InfoCard to be exported from one PC to another. An attacker could, for example, export a personal card to a USB memory stick, and then reload the card on his or her own PC in order to impersonate the card owner. An exported card could also be transferred as an email attachment. This risk could be mitigated using countermeasures similar to those discussed above.

6 Prototype Realisation

We next give details of a prototype implementation of the scheme. The prototype is coded in JavaScript, chosen because its wide adoption should simplify the task of porting the prototype to a range of other browsers. It uses the Document Object Model (DOM) to inspect and manipulate HTML pages and XML

[8] `http://technet.microsoft.com/en-us/library/cc709691(WS.10).aspx#BKMK_S1`

documents. The JavaScript code is executed using a C#-driven browser helper object (BHO), a DLL (Dynamic-Link Library) module designed as a plug-in for IE. Once installed, the BHO attaches itself to IE, thus gaining access to the current page's DOM. Note that the scheme operates with both the CardSpace and the Higgins[9] identity selectors without any modification.

6.1 User Registration

Prior to use, the prototype user must have accounts with a CardSpace RP and an SMS gateway service provider, e.g. Clickatell (`clickatell.com`). The prototype provides step-by-step instructions in order to assist the user in inserting their mobile phone number and their SMS account login details (e.g. username and password) into the plug-in source code.

6.2 Prototype Operation

In this section we consider specific operational aspects of the prototype. We refer throughout to the numbered protocol steps given in section 3.2 (see also figure 2).

In step 3 the plug-in uses the DOM to perform the following processes.

3.1 It scans the web page in the following way[10].
   (a) It searches through the HTML elements of the web page to detect whether any HTML forms are present. If so, it searches each form, scanning through each of its child elements for an HTML object tag.
   (b) If an object tag is found, it retrieves and examines its type. If it is of type 'application/x-informationCard' (which indicates website support for CardSpace), it continues; otherwise it aborts.
   (c) It retrieves and stores in a cookie the name attribute of the CardSpace object tag. This is important since the RP server will use this name to retrieve the token from the HTTP POST array.

3.2 It embeds a JavaScript function in the head section of the HTML page to intercept the RSTR.

3.3 It obtains the action attribute of the CardSpace HTML form and stores it in a cookie. This attribute specifies the URL of the CardSpace RP server to which the RSTR must be forwarded for processing. If the attribute is not a fully qualified domain name address, the JavaScript inherent properties, e.g. *document.location.protocol* and/or *document.location.host*, are used to help reconstruct the full URL address.

3.4 It changes the current action attribute of the CardSpace HTML form to point to the newly created 'interception' function (see step 3.2 above).

---

[9] `http://wiki.eclipse.org/GTK_Selector_1.1-Win`

[10] The CardSpace user guide [6] specifies two HTML extension formats that can be used to invoke the CIdS from a web page, both of which involve placing the CardSpace object tag inside an HTML form. This motivates the choice of the web page search method (see also [4,10]).

In step 8 the plug-in uses the DOM to perform the following steps.

8.1 It intercepts the RSTR sent by the CIdS using the added function.
8.2 It generates a 4-character, random OTP (see section 4.1). It also starts a 10-minute time counter.
8.3 It builds an HTTPS-based URL, inserting the user's mobile phone number, the user's account login details, and the OTP.
8.4 It automatically invokes the URL in a new, small browser window. This process will cause the OTP to be sent to the SMS gateway via a secure TLS/SSL channel. On receipt of the OTP, the SMS gateway delivers it to the user's mobile phone in an SMS message.
8.5 It prompts the user to enter the OTP, using a JavaScript pop-up box.
8.6 It verifies the user-entered OTP by comparing it with the version it previously generated (in step 8.2), ensuring that the OTP has been entered within the 10-minute time window. If the verification succeeds it proceeds to the next step. If the verification fails, the user is allowed to try again. However, if the verification fails for three successive OTP entry attempts, the plug-in terminates the login process and writes a persistent cookie to prevent the user from logging into this RP using the same browser for a defined time period, e.g. 24 hours. This process operates as follows.

    On the first occasion that the system is used with a particular RP, or if the previously written cookie has expired and been deleted, the plug-in writes a persistent cookie containing the number of failed OTP entry attempts for this RP (i.e. either zero if the attempt is successful or one if the attempt fails) and with a lifetime of 24 hours. Whenever the system is used subsequently the presence of this cookie is checked; if it is present then the current number of failed OTP entry attempts it records is checked — if it is equal to three then no SMS is sent and the RSTR is blocked, i.e. the system is locked out and can only be unlocked if the user enters the special lockout OTP. If it is less than three then the system proceeds. If the OTP entry attempt succeeds then a new cookie is written containing the value zero; if the OTP entry attempt fails, then a new cookie is written containing a value one larger than the previous value.
8.7 It creates an 'invisible' HTML form with method attribute set to 'POST'.
8.8 It writes the entire RSTR message into the invisible HTML form as a hidden variable, with the name attribute of this variable set to the CardSpace object tag's name (see step 3.1.c).
8.9 It writes the end-point URL of the CardSpace-enabled RP into the action attribute of the invisible form (see step 3.3).
8.10 Finally, it auto-submits the HTML form (transparently to the user), using the JavaScript inherent method 'submit'.

6.3 Practical Issues

The plug-in must scan every HTML web page to check whether it supports CardSpace, and this may affect system performance. However, informal tests on the prototype suggest that this is not a serious issue. In addition, the plug-in can be configured so that it only operates with certain websites.

If the web browser is compromised, then an adversary could steal the RSTR and the OTP, block the user-RP connection, and submit the token, thus impersonating the user. If the RP does not use https, then the RSTR will not be encrypted. Assuming that the web browser is not a secure environment, then it may be possible for a malicious plug-in or some other type of malware to get access to sensitive information disclosed by the plaintext RSTR. However, the same risks apply when manually entering credentials (e.g. username-password) into the browser [11].

Finally note that some older browsers (or browsers with scripting disabled) may not be able to run the prototype plug-in, as it was built using JavaScript. However, most modern browsers support JavaScript (or ECMAscript), and hence building the prototype in JavaScript is not a major usability obstacle.

7 Related Work

Using a mobile device as a means of user authentication is attractive because of the ubiquity of mobile phones, and many such schemes have been proposed. Examples of schemes in which a mobile phone is used to authenticate a user to a remote server include the following.

- Hart et al. [11] proposed a scheme in which user credentials (i.e. username and password) are stored in a Java-enabled SIM card. When the user visits a website, the browser extension requests the site's user credentials from an SMS gateway, which then sends a specially formatted SMS message to the appropriate SIM card. The SIM card responds with another SMS message containing the requested credentials, and the SMS gateway forwards them to the browser extension via an HTTPS channel. The browser extension then auto-submits them to the visited site. The scheme requires the user to possess a SIM capable of hosting an application, and for the user to load an appropriate application into it. It also has an SMS messaging cost at least twice that of the scheme described in this paper.
- Wu et al. [12] and Jammalamadaka et al. [13] proposed schemes involving a combination of a third party proxy, which stores the user credentials, and a mobile phone. The schemes are designed for use in cases where an untrusted PC, e.g. in an Internet kiosk, is used to access a remote website, and they avoid the need for the user to enter long-term secret credentials into such a PC (see also [14]). The phone is used to explicitly authorise the proxy to release the credentials to the remote website. Unfortunately, not only is the use of a proxy a potential security and reliability threat, but the PC must be configured to use the proxy. This latter requirement is not only potentially inconvenient, but in some cases may be impossible to meet since the user may not have the necessary permissions to change the browser settings.
- Florêncio and Herley proposed 'URRSA' [15], an OTP-enhanced service (based on a reverse proxy [16]) that allows users to access password-protected

websites. The URRSA service does not require changes to login servers. A list of 10 different encrypted copies of a long-term user password (effectively OTPs) is generated and sent to the user's mobile phone using SMS; the corresponding decryption keys are stored at the URRSA server. A user wishing to access a protected site first navigates to the URRSA site and enters the URL and userID of the account to be accessed. The user then enters the appropriate OTP from the current list, allowing the URRSA server to decrypt and temporarily store the real password. The URRSA server then fetches the previously registered login page and prompts the user to click the submit button; the login process then proceeds. The user process for this scheme is relatively complex, and new lists will need to be downloaded fairly frequently, increasing the burden on the user.
- Aloul et al. [17] proposed a system that involves using a PIN-protected mobile phone as a token for OTP generation. Additionally, an SMS-based mechanism is implemented as both a backup mechanism for retrieving the OTP and as a possible means of client-server synchronisation. This method requires both the client and server to pay to send SMS messages. Unlike the scheme described here, the mobile phone must be J2ME-enabled, and, prior to use, the user must install a special application in the phone.
- Mannan et al. [18] and Alqattan et al. [19] proposed similar schemes in which the entry of user authentication credentials is accomplished using a trusted handheld device, e.g. a PIN-protected mobile phone. For instance, in the 'MP-Auth' scheme [18], the mobile device encrypts the password using the end server's public key before passing it via an untrusted machine to the remote server. However, unlike the scheme described in this paper, these schemes require changes to login servers and also require users to possess J2ME-enabled mobile phones.
- Schuba et al. [20] proposed the 'Internet ID' approach, in which a mobile phone is used to provide user authentication to a Liberty IdP. We outline the variant most similar to the scheme described above. A Liberty IdP generates a random sequence of symbols, and sends them to the user's mobile phone in an SMS message. Simultaneously, these symbols are shown on the PC browser, and the user is required to confirm to the phone that the browser-displayed symbols are the same as those in the SMS message, e.g. by clicking a link on the WAP page on the mobile phone. Although this system does not require the user to type anything, it does require changes to the operation of Liberty IdPs.
- Jørstad et al. [21] proposed a scheme which supports interoperation between CardSpace and Liberty. It uses a mobile phone for user authentication to the IdP; the IdP sends an SMS message to the user, and, in order to be authenticated, the user must confirm receipt of the message. Much like the 'Internet ID' approach [20], this method requires changes to the operation of the IdP.

Examples of schemes in which a mobile phone is used to authenticate the user to a local PC include the following.

- Lach [1] proposed 'MOTH', a scheme in which a workstation and a mobile device communicate using Bluetooth, and authentication is realised using digital signatures. Unlike in our scheme, the mobile device in the MOTH system must be able to run Java midlets. To avoid an attacker bypassing the scheme, a MOTH-conformant PC must be configured to only use the MOTH service for authentication, and not to fall back to password authentication. Similarly, the scheme described in this paper must be configured to oblige the use of the adaptor with CardSpace (see section 5.3). In MOTH, binding a user to a public key remains a challenge.
- Abdulhameed et al. [22] proposed a method which uses a Bluetooth-enabled mobile phone. The user's PC communicates with the phone via a Bluetooth link, and public key cryptographic techniques are used to provide mutual authentication between the PC and the phone. The PC periodically senses the phone to ensure that the user is still present; if the mobile phone moves out of range, the PC is configured to take certain measures to raise the security level. It is unclear from the paper whether this form of authentication could be disabled by an attacker so that the PC reverts to password-based user authentication, a possible means of circumventing the scheme. Not only must the mobile phone be Bluetooth-enabled, but it must also support Java to provide certain cryptographic and authentication services.

Finally note that the scheme proposed in this paper falls somewhere in between the two classes described above, in that it provides authentication to a local PC in such a way that it enables authentication to a remote site to continue in a more secure way.

8 Conclusions and Future Work

In this paper we have proposed a simple and novel scheme for using a mobile device to enhance CardSpace authentication. During the process of user authentication on a PC using CardSpace, a random and short-lived one-time password is sent to the mobile device; this must then be entered into the PC by the user. The scheme does not require any changes to login servers, the CardSpace identity selector, or to the mobile device itself. We have given details of a proof-of-concept prototype. Security and operational analyses have also been provided.

Planned future work includes exploring the possibility of extending the scheme to operate with other client-enabled identity management systems, including password managers. We also plan to develop the prototype in various ways, including:

- preventing it being disabled by an unauthorised PC user;
- providing support for OTP transfer to the mobile via Bluetooth and/or infrared; and
- supporting automated OTP entry from the mobile.

Acknowledgements

The first author is sponsored by the Diwan of Royal Court, Sultanate of Oman. The helpful comments provided by anonymous referees are gratefully acknowledged.

References

1. Lach, J.: Using Mobile Devices for User Authentication. In: Kwiecień, A., Gaj, P., Stera, P. (eds.) CN 2010. Communications in Computer and Information Science, vol. 79, pp. 263–268. Springer, Heidelberg (2010)
2. Bertocci, V., Serack, G., Baker, C.: Understanding Windows CardSpace: An Introduction to the Concepts and Challenges of Digital Identities. Addison-Wesley, Reading (2008)
3. Mercuri, M.: Beginning Information Cards and CardSpace: From Novice to Professional. Apress, New York (2007)
4. Al-Sinani, H.S., Mitchell, C.J.: Using CardSpace as a Password Manager. In: de Leeuw, E., Fischer-Hübner, S., Fritsch, L. (eds.) IDMAN 2010. IFIP Advances in Information and Communication Technology, vol. 343, pp. 18–30. Springer, Heidelberg (2010)
5. Al-Sinani, H.S., Alrodhan, W.A., Mitchell, C.J.: CardSpace-Liberty integration for CardSpace users. In: Klingenstein, K., Ellison, C.M. (eds.) Proceedings of the 9th Symposium on Identity and Trust on the Internet (IDtrust 2010), Gaithersburg, Maryland, USA, April 13-15, pp. 12–25. ACM, New York (2010)
6. Jones, M.B.: A Guide to Using the Identity Selector Interoperability Profile V1.5 within Web Applications and Browsers. Microsoft Corporation (2008)
7. Jones, M.B., McIntosh, M. (eds.): Identity Metasystem Interoperability Version 1.0 (IMI 1.0). OASIS Standard (2009), http://docs.oasis-open.org/imi/identity/v1.0/identity.html
8. Guthery, S.B., Cronin, M.J.: Mobile Application Development with SMS and SIM Toolkit. McGraw-Hill, New York (2002)
9. Le Bodic, G.: Mobile Messaging Technologies and Services SMS, EMS and MMS. Wiley, Chichester (2003)
10. Al-Sinani, H.S., Mitchell, C.J.: Implementing PassCard — a CardSpace-based Password Manager. Technical Report: RHUL–MA–2010–15 (Department of Mathematics, Royal Holloway, University of London) (2010), http://www.ma.rhul.ac.uk/static/techrep/2010/RHUL-MA-2010-15.pdf
11. Hart, J., Markantonakis, K., Mayes, K.: Website Credential Storage and Two-Factor Web Authentication with a Java SIM. In: Samarati, P., Tunstall, M., Posegga, J., Markantonakis, K., Sauveron, D. (eds.) WISTP 2010. LNCS, vol. 6033, pp. 229–236. Springer, Heidelberg (2010)
12. Wu, M., Garfinkel, S., Miller, R.: Secure web authentication with mobile phones. In: DIMACS Workshop on Usable Privacy and Security Systems (2004), http://homepages.mcs.vuw.ac.nz/~ian/shared/papers/secureweb.pdf
13. Jammalamadaka, R., van der Horst, T., Mehrotra, S., Seamons, K., Venkasubramanian, N.: Delegate: A proxy based architecture for secure website access from an untrusted machine. In: ACSAC 2006: Proceedings of the 22nd Annual Computer Security Applications Conference, pp. 57–66. IEEE Computer Society, Washington (2006)

14. Pashalidis, A., Mitchell, C.J.: Impostor: A single sign-on system for use from untrusted devices. In: Proceedings of IEEE Globecom 2004, Global Telecommunications Conference, Dallas, Texas, USA, vol. 4, pp. 2191–2195. IEEE Press, Los Alamitos (2004)
15. Florêncio, D., Herley, C.: One-time password access to any server without changing the server. In: Wu, T.-C., Lei, C.-L., Rijmen, V., Lee, D.-T. (eds.) ISC 2008. LNCS, vol. 5222, pp. 401–420. Springer, Heidelberg (2008)
16. Luotonen, A.: Web Proxy Servers. Prentice Hall PTR, New Jersey (1997)
17. Aloul, F., Zahidi, S., El-Hajj, W.: Two factor authentication using mobile phones. In: AICCSA 2009: Proceedings of the IEEE/ACS International Conference on Computer Systems and Applications, Rabat, Morroco, pp. 641–644. IEEE, Los Alamitos (2009)
18. Mannan, M., Oorschot, P.V.: Using a personal device to strengthen password authentication from an untrusted computer. In: Dietrich, S., Dhamija, R. (eds.) FC 2007 and USEC 2007. LNCS, vol. 4886, pp. 88–103. Springer, Heidelberg (2007)
19. Alqattan, A., Kaviani, N., Lewis, P., Pearson, N.: A two-Factor Authentication System using Mobile Devices to Protect against Untrusted Public Computers. University of British Columbia, Canada (2007), http://courses.ece.ubc.ca/412/term_project/reports/2007-fall/A_Two-Factor_Authentication_System_Using_Mobile%20_Devices_to_Protect_against_Untrusted_Public_Computers.pdf
20. Schuba, M., Gerstenberger, V., Lahaije, P.: Internet ID — Flexible Re-use of Mobile Phone Authentication Security for Service Access (2004), http://www.ericsson.com/res/thecompany/docs/journal_conference_papers/service_layer/internet_id_nordsec.pdf
21. Jørstad, I., Van Thuan, D., Jønvik, T., Van Thanh, D.: Bridging CardSpace and Liberty Alliance with SIM authentication. In: Proceedings of the 10th International Conference on Intelligence in Next Generation Networks (ICIN 2007), Adera, Pessac, pp. 8–13 (2007)
22. Abdelhameed, R., Khatun, S., Ali, B., Ramli, A.: Authentication model based bluetooth-enabled mobile phone. Journal of Computer Science 1(2), 200–203 (2005)

Verifiable Secret Sharing with Comprehensive and Efficient Public Verification

Kun Peng

Institute for Infocomm Research
1 Fusionopolis Way, Singapore
dr.kun.peng@gmail.com

Abstract. VSS (verifiable secret sharing) is an important security protection tool in distributed systems. When VSS is employed in publicly verifiable applications, it needs to achieve public verifiability and be upgraded to PVSS (publicly verifiable secret sharing). Besides the two basic security properties, bindingness and hidingness, PVSS concentrates on public verifiability of validity all the operations in VSS so that there is no doubt about any operation and any dispute can be publicly solved. The existing PVSS schemes achieve security and public verifiability at a high cost. Moreover, their public verification operations are not defined and specified comprehensively and in complete details. In addition, most of them are vulnerable to an attack called simple plaintext attack. To overcome those drawbacks in PVSS, a new PVSS protocol is proposed in this paper. It defines public verifiability of VSS in a comprehensive and formal security model, which describes every verification operation in details and can publicly solve any dispute. All the public verification operations are efficiently implemented in the new PVSS protocol, which is more efficient than the existing PVSS schemes. It prevents simple plaintext attack in an efficient way.

1 Introduction

The first threshold secret sharing technique is Shamir's t-out-of-n secret sharing [14]. It is one of the most basic tools in distributed computing systems. A dealer holds a secret and shares it among n distributed share holders. Any t distributed share holders can put their shares together to reconstruct the secret, while no information about the secret is obtained if the number of available distributed shares is less than t. In practical applications, sometimes the share holders do not trust the dealer and want to verify that their shares are valid such that any t of them reconstruct the same secret. So VSS [4,12,8,6,12,3,1,5,9,10,11] is proposed, in which there is a verification mechanism for each share holder to verify validity of his share. In VSS, the share verification mechanism cannot reveal any information about the secret or any of its shares. In [13], this property is called hidingness, while in other schemes it has other names like zero knowledge, indistinguishability, confidentiality and privacy. We inherit the name hidingness and define it in a simulation-based formal model, which is popular in formal analysis

Y. Li (Ed.): Data and Applications Security and Privacy XXV, LNCS 6818, pp. 217–230, 2011.

of privacy. Another important security property in VSS is bindingness, which is called soundness or consistency in some other places. A VSS protocol is binding if its verification mechanism guarantees that each share is generated from the same secret.

In some applications of VSS, validity of sharing and reconstruction of the secret need to be publicly verified or checked. So PVSS is designed. The existing PVSS schemes [15,2,7,13,11] have some drawbacks. Firstly, they are complex and inefficient, especially in computation. Moreover, public verification operations are not comprehensively defined and specified in them. Most of them only focus on proof of validity of encryption in terms of the shares, while other public verification operations like public dispute solution and public verification of reconstruction are not specified in details. In addition, most of them [15,2,13][1] publish a deterministic commitment of the secret and so are vulnerable to an attack called simple plaintext attack detailed in Section 2. The attack prevents application of the PVSS schemes in some environments. Although the attack can be prevented by replacing their commitment algorithms with probabilistic commitment algorithms, the countermeasure leads to more complex commitment, proof and verification operations, so further deteriorates efficiency of the PVSS schemes.

In this paper, a new PVSS protocol is designed. It achieves comprehensive public verifiability defined in complete details and in a formal security model. It is much more efficient than the existing PVSS schemes in both computation and communication. It is inherently invulnerable to the simple plaintext attack and does not need any additional cost to prevent it. The rest of this paper is arranged as follows. PVSS and its security properties, especially public verifiability, are formally and comprehensively defined and modeled in Section 2. The new PVSS protocol is proposed in Section 3. It is analysed in security and efficiency and compared with the existing PVSS schemes in Section 4. The paper is concluded in Section 5.

2 Security Model

In Shamir's t-out-of-n secret sharing [14], a dealer A uses the following procedure to share a secret s among n distributed share holders $P_1, P_2, \ldots, P_n$.

1. A builds a polynomial $f(x) = \sum_{j=0}^{t-1} a_j x^j$ where $a_0 = s$ and a_i for $j = 1, 2, \ldots, t-1$ are random integers.
2. A sends $s_i = f(i)$ as a share to P_i for $i = 1, 2, \ldots, n$.
3. Any t share holders can reconstruct the secret: $s = \sum_{i \in V} s_i w_i$ where $w_i = \prod_{j \in V, j \neq i} \frac{j}{j-i}$ and V is the set containing the indexes of the t shares. Any group of less than t share holders get no information about the secret.

[1] A method is mentioned in [13] to prevent simple plaintext attack. However, it needs additional operations and approximately doubles the computational cost. In comparison with our much more efficient countermeasure against the attack, it is not good enough.

If the dealer is not trusted and the share holders want to verify validity of the shares, VSS is needed, which must satisfy the following two properties.

- Bindingness: there is a unique secret such that if the ith share passes the validity verification, it is the ith share of the unique secret.
- Hidingness: the verification mechanism does not reveal any information about the secret.

VSS and its security properties are formally defined as follows.

Definition 1. *(VSS) In a t-out-of-n VSS protocol, there exist explicitly or implicitly committed (to be detailed in Definition 2) integers* $a_0, a_1, \ldots, a_{t-1}$ *such that any share holder* P_i *can verify* $s_i = \sum_{j=0}^{t-1} a_j i^j$.

Definition 2. *An integer is explicitly committed to if its commitment is published. An integer is implicitly committed to if its unique existence can be proved such that successful verification of the proof with an overwhelmingly large probability guarantees that it is uniquely determined by the proof.*

Definition 3. *(Bindingness) In a t-out-of-n binding VSS protocol, if* P_i*'s verification of validity of* s_i *is passed with a non-negligible probability, it is guaranteed that* $s_i = \sum_{j=0}^{t-1} a_j i^j$ *where integers* $a_0, a_1, \ldots, a_{t-1}$ *are publicly committed to or extracted from the dealer's proof as defined in Definition 2.*

Definition 4. *(Hidingness) A VSS protocol is hiding if the information revealed in its verification mechanism can be simulated without any difference by a party without any knowledge of the secret or any of its share.*

In applications of secret sharing requiring public verifiability, apart from the normal functionality of VSS, the following publicly verifiable operations are needed to publicly detect and handle various misbehaviors.

- Share distribution must be public. Namely, the dealer must publicly show that it really send a secret share to every share holder.
- Validity of shares should be publicly verified against a public commitment of the secret. If the public verification is passed, any share holder's knowledge of a valid share can be publicly recognised and he cannot complain of receiving an invalid share later.
- When the public verification of a share fails, there must be a public mechanism to detect whether the corresponding share holder or the dealer is cheating.
- When the secret is reconstructed, it can be publicly verified to be correct against the public commitment of the secret.
- When secret reconstruction fails, it can be publicly detected which share holder provides an invalid share and should be responsible.

These five operations are called public share distribution, public verification of share validity against public commitment, public solution to dispute in sharing, public verification of reconstruction and public detection of invalid share. More formally, in applications requiring public verifiability, PVSS is needed and Definitions 1, 3 and 4 should be extended to Definitions 5, 6 and 7 respectively.

Definition 5. *In a t-out-of-n PVSS protocol, encryptions of the shares are published. Moreover, there is a public commitment of the secret denoted as C. The following public proofs and verifications are necessary.*

- *(Public verification of share validity against public commitment) Any share s_i can be publicly verified through a proof and verification operation*

$$A\ (a_0, a_1, \dots, a_{t-1}, \dots) \longrightarrow \alpha$$
$$P_i\ (s_i, \dots) \longrightarrow \beta_i$$

  where $P\ (\theta) \longrightarrow \gamma$ means that a party P with secret input θ outputs public information γ and "..." means that additional secret information may be used. The verification returns a public result

$$T(\alpha, \beta_i) = \begin{cases} TRUE \implies s_i \text{ is valid;} \\ FALSE \implies s_i \text{ is invalid.} \end{cases} \tag{1}$$

  There exist explicitly or implicitly committed (as defined in Definition 2) integers $a_0, a_1, \dots, a_{t-1}$ such that if the verification result is $TRUE$ for any s_i it is guaranteed $s_i = \sum_{j=0}^{t-1} a_j i^j$ where a_0 is the secret committed in C.
- *(Public solution to dispute in sharing) When (1) returns $FALSE$, P_i has to publicly prove his honesty through a proof*

$$Proof_{(sk_i)}(C, E_i, \alpha, \beta_i)$$

  where sk_i denotes P_i's private key, E_i denotes the public encryption of P_i's share and $Proof_{(\tau)}(\delta)$ denote a proof using secret information τ against public information δ. If the proof is successful, the dealer is cheating; otherwise P_i is cheating.
- *(Public verification of reconstruction) The reconstructed secret ς, which includes s and perhaps other reconstruction results, can be publicly verified against C in*

$$Test\ (\varsigma, C, \alpha) \tag{2}$$

  If the test is successful, s is publicly accepted as the secret committed in C. Otherwise, ς is invalid and some share used to reconstruct s must be invalid.
- *(Public detection of invalid share) When (2) fails, each share holder P_i having participated in the reconstruction proves validity of the share he provides through a proof*

$$Proof_{(sk_i)}(E_i, \alpha, \beta_i)$$

  If the proof is successful, P_i is honest; otherwise P_i is cheating.

Definition 6. *(Bindingness in PVSS) If (1) returns $TRUE$ with a non-negligible probability, it is publicly guaranteed that $s_i = \sum_{j=0}^{t-1} a_j i^j$ where integers $a_0, a_1, \dots, a_{t-1}$ are publicly committed to or extracted from the dealer's proof as defined in Definition 2.*

Definition 7. *(Hidingness in PVSS) Before any share is published, the published information can be simulated in a indistinguishable way by a party without any knowledge of the secret or any of its share. In PVSS, commitment of the secret is usually published. So a special attack against privacy defined in Definition 8 cannot be ignored.*

Definition 8. *(Simple plaintext attack) Given a message s' and C, the public commitment of the shared secret, a polynomial attacker wants to test whether s' is committed in C and thus is the shared secret. The game can be more formally described as follows.*

1. *A randomly choose a bit b. If $b = 0$, he sets $s' = s$; if $b = 1$, he randomly chooses s' from Z_q.*
2. *A sends s' and C to the attacker.*
3. *The attacker has to guess b.*

If the probability that the polynomial attacker can correctly guess b is non-negligible, the simple plaintext attack is successful.

In most applications of PVSS (e.g. e-voting) the message space contains some readable plaintexts with sensible meaning in a not-very-large range. So the simple plaintext attack is harmful. For example, by repeating it in a brute-force attack, an attacker can find the secret. When the attacker has some additional information about the secret, the attack is especially effective. So the PVSS schemes vulnerable to this attack [15,2,13] have limited applications.

Besides higher formality and comprehensiveness and awareness of simple plaintext attack, our definition has a novelty: the integers used to generate the shares (denoted as $a_0, a_1, \ldots, a_{t-1}$ in our definition) are not necessary to be explicitly committed to. As will be illustrated in Section 3, our design of PVSS takes advantage of this novel property to improve efficiency. As unlike in the existing PVSS schemes it is not necessary to make explicit commitment to $a_0, a_1, \ldots, a_{t-1}$ and publish their commitments, efficiency in computation, communication and storage can be greatly improved. In our design, the dealer proves his knowledge of the integers used to generate the shares such that when his proof can succeed with a non-negligible probability $a_0, a_1, \ldots, a_{t-1}$ can be uniquely extracted from his proof. As shown in Section 3.1, this novel mechanism in general works well in VSS, which only enables the share holders to verify their own shares and usually does not have a compulsory need to publish an explicit commitment of the secret. As sometimes in applications of PVSS an explicit public commitment of the secret is needed (especially when an application employs the PVSS mechanism and then securely handles the shared secret in a publicly verifiable manner), an explicit commitment of the secret (denoted as C) is still included in Definition 5. However, in comparison with the public and explicit commitment to t or $2t$ integers in the existing PVSS schemes, our design only explicitly commits to two integers and is much more efficient.

3 The New PVSS Protocol

The new PVSS protocol is proposed in this section. Firstly, its main idea is introduced. Then a detailed description is present.

3.1 The Main Idea

The main idea of the new PVSS technique is to specify VSS efficiently and then make all the operations publicly verifiable. VSS is designed in a novel way. After a secret is shared among some share holders, the dealer shares an additional random secret among them if they require verification of their shares. Then shares of the two secrets are combined by a random linear relation. Validity of the combined shares can be verified through Lagrange Interpolation. Verification of validity of the original shares is passed if and only if the combined shares are valid. The sharing and verification operations are as follows.

1. Setting:
   A large prime q is chosen. It must be at least larger than any possible secret to share.
2. Sharing:
   A builds a polynomial $F(x) = \sum_{j=0}^{t-1} a_j x^j$ where $a_0 = s$ and a_j for $j = 1, 2, \ldots, t-1$ are random integers chosen from Z_q. A sends $s_i = F(i) \bmod q$ as a share to P_i for $i = 1, 2, \ldots, n$.
3. Verification:
   If verification of validity of the shares are required, the following proof and verification procedure is run.
   (a) A randomly chooses an additional secret k in Z_q.
   (b) A builds a polynomial $G(x) = \sum_{j=0}^{t-1} b_j x^j$ where $b_0 = k$ and b_j for $j = 1, 2, \ldots, t-1$ are random integers chosen from Z_q.
   (c) A sends $k_i = G(i) \bmod q$ to P_i for $i = 1, 2, \ldots, n$.
   (d) A random integer r is chosen in some way (to be detailed in Section 3.2) in Z_q as a public challenge to A.
   (e) A publishes $c_j = b_j + r a_j \bmod q$ for $j = 0, 1, \ldots, t-1$.
   (f) Any P_i can verify
   $$k_i + r s_i = \sum_{j=0}^{t-1} c_j i^j \bmod q \tag{3}$$
   if he doubts validity of his share. He accepts validity of s_i if and only if the equation holds.
4. Reconstruction
   A set with at least t share holders can reconstruct the secret: $s = \sum_{i \in V} s_i w_i \bmod q$ where $w_i = \prod_{j \in V, j \neq i} \frac{j}{j-i} \bmod q$ and V is the set containing the indexes of the t shares.

To achieve public verifiability, commitment of the secret and encryption of the shares should be published, so that the four proof and verification operations defined in Definition 5 can be publicly implemented against them. Especially, a much simpler and more efficient commitment mechanism is employed in our new design than in the existing PVSS schemes. The advantages of the new idea is that it can achieve high efficiency in both computation and communication.

3.2 Detailed Description

The basic operations of the new PVSS protocol are described in Figure 1, while its proof and verification operations to support public verification as required in Definition 5 are described in Figure 2. Note that in comparison with the existing PVSS schemes we employ much more efficient symmetric cipher to encrypt the shares when distributing them and much more efficient commitment operations when committing to the secret.

1. Public commitment
   The dealer publicly publishes a commitment of his secret.
   (a) p and q are large primes such that $p = 2q + 1$. G is the cyclic subgroup of Z_p^* with order q. g and h are two generators of G such that $\log_g h$ is secret.
   (b) A has a secret s in Z_q to share. He randomly chooses an additional secret k in Z_q.
   (c) A publishes $u = g^s h^x \bmod p$ and $v = g^k h^y \bmod p$ where x and y are randomly chosen from Z_q.
2. Public share distribution
   The dealer encrypts the shares and publicly sends them to the share holders. Unlike the existing PVSS schemes, which employ costly asymmetric encryption algorithms, our new solution can employ a much more efficient symmetric encryption algorithm to encrypt the shares. However, for fairness in comparison with the existing PVSS schemes, we include distribution of the symmetric keys through asymmetric cipher in our share distribution procedure. The dealer publicly distributes the shares of secret s as follows.
   (a) A builds a polynomial $G(x) = \sum_{j=0}^{t-1} b_j x^j$ where $b_0 = k$ and b_j for $j = 1, 2, \ldots, t-1$ are random integers chosen from Z_q.
   (b) A calculates $k_i = G(i) \bmod q$ and publishes $d_i = E_i(k_i)$ for each P_i where $E_i()$ denotes encryption using P_i's public key and an asymmetric encryption algorithm (e.g. RSA or ElGamal).
   (c) A builds a polynomial $F(x) = \sum_{j=0}^{t-1} a_j x^j$ where $a_0 = s$ and a_j for $j = 1, 2, \ldots, t-1$ are random integers chosen from Z_q.
   (d) A calculates $s_i = F(i) \bmod q$ and publishes $e_i = E_{k_i}(s_i)$ for each P_i where $E_{k_i}()$ denotes symmetric encryption using session key k_i and an symmetric encryption algorithm (e.g. AES).
3. Reconstruction
   If at least t share holders submit their shares s_i, the secret s is reconstructed:

$$s = \sum_{i \in V} s_i w_i \bmod q \text{ where } w_i = \prod_{j \in V, j \neq i} \frac{j}{j-i} \bmod q$$

   and V is the set containing the indexes of the t shares.

Fig. 1. Basic Operations of PVSS

– Public verification of share validity against public commitment
  1. $r = H(d_1, d_2, \ldots, d_n, e_1, e_2, \ldots, e_n)$ is generated where $H()$ is a one-way and collision-resistent hash function with an image domain Z_q.
  2. An P_i requesting public verification of his share decrypts d_i and obtains k_i, which is then used to decrypt e_i into s_i.
  3. P_i publishes $h_i = H(k_i + rs_i)$.
  4. A publishes $c_j = b_j + ra_j \bmod q$ for $j = 0, 1, \ldots, t-1$
     $z = y + rx \bmod q$.
  5. P_i publishes $z_i = k_i + rs_i \bmod q$.
  6. It is publicly verified

$$g^{c_0} h^z = u^r v \bmod p \quad (4)$$

$$z_i = \sum_{j=0}^{t-1} c_j i^j \bmod q \quad (5)$$

$$h_i = H(z_i) \quad (6)$$

  Validity of s_i is accepted if and only if all the three equations (4) , (5) and (6) are satisfied. Their satisfaction publicly guarantees that P_i knows the ith share of the secret committed in u. If (4) fails, the dealer is dishonest and must have cheated. If (6) fails, P_i is dishonest and must have cheated. If (5) fails, there is a dispute between the dealer and P_i about validity of s_i, which can be solved in the next proof and verification operation.

– Public solution to dispute in sharing
  If (5) fails, P_i has to publish k_i and s_i. Any one can verify

$$k_i + rs_i \neq \sum_{j=0}^{t-1} c_j i^j \bmod q$$

$$e_i = E_{k_i}(s_i)$$

$$d_i = E_i(k_i)$$

  If they are satisfied, P_i is honest and the dealer must have given him an invalid share. Otherwise P_i is dishonest and must have tampered with his share.

– Public verification of reconstruction
  1. k is reconstructed: $k = \sum_{i \in V} k_i w_i \bmod q$ where $w_i = \prod_{j \in V, j \neq i} \frac{j}{j-i} \bmod q$
  2. It is publicly verified

$$(u/g^s)^r (v/g^k) = h^z \bmod p. \quad (7)$$

  s passes the verification for its validity only if (7) is satisfied. Note that if necessary a new r in Z_q can be randomly chosen (or generated by a hash function) and a new z can be calculated as $z = y + rx \bmod q$.

– Public detection of invalid share
  If (7) is not satisfied, the reconstructed s is invalid and some invalid share must have been used in the reconstruction. So for each s_i used in the reconstruction

$$k_i + rs_i = \sum_{j=0}^{t-1} c_j i^j \bmod q$$

$$e_i = E_{k_i}(s_i)$$

$$d_i = E_i(k_i)$$

  are publicly verified. If any of the three equation fails for an s_i, the corresponding P_i must have given an invalid share and should be responsible for failure of the reconstruction.

Fig. 2. Proof and Verification Operations in PVSS

4 Analysis and Comparison

The four proof and verification operations in Figure 2 satisfy the security requirements in Definition 5, Definition 6 and Definition 7. Firstly, Theorem 1 illustrates that the "public verification of share validity against public commitment" operation implements public verification of validity of the shares. Secondly, it is straightforward that the "public solution to dispute in sharing" operation can publicly solve any dispute between the dealer and any share holder about validity of any share. Thirdly, Theorem 2 illustrates that the "public verification of reconstruction" operation publicly guarantees that the reconstructed secret s is committed in u. Fourthly, it is straightforward that the "public detection of invalid share" operation can publicly detect any invalid share provided by any share holder. So the new PVSS protocol is binding and improves public verifiability. Hidingness of the new PVSS protocol is proved in Theorem 3, which guarantees that the secret and its shares are not revealed and especially formally guarantees that the new PVSS protocol is invulnerable to the simple plaintext attack.

Theorem 1. *The new PVSS protocol can publicly guarantee validity of the shares against a public commitment of the secret. More precisely, if (4), (5) and (6) are satisfied with a probability larger than $1/q$, s_i is publicly guaranteed to be the ith share of the secret explicitly committed in u and generated by a polynomial determined by a set of implicitly committed integers $a_0, a_1, \ldots, a_{t-1}$ as defined in Definition 5 and Definition 6.*

Proof: As (4), (5) and (6) are satisfied with a probability larger than $1/q$, there must exist two different integers r and r' in Z_q such that A and P_i can provide $z, c_0, c_1, \ldots, c_{t-1}, z_i$ and $z', c'_0, c'_1, \ldots, c'_{t-1}, z'_i$ respectively to satisfy

$$z_i = \sum_{j=0}^{t-1} c_j i^j \bmod q \quad (8)$$

$$z'_i = \sum_{j=0}^{t-1} c'_j i^j \bmod q \quad (9)$$

$$g^{c_0} h^z = u^r v \bmod p \quad (10)$$

$$g^{c'_0} h^{z'} = u^{r'} v \bmod p. \quad (11)$$

Otherwise, there is at most one r in Z_q for A and P_i to provide $z, c_0, c_1, \ldots, c_{t-1}$ and z_i to satisfy (4), (5) and (6) and the probability that they are satisfied is no larger than $1/q$, which is a contradiction.

Integers $s_i, k_i, a_0, a_1, \ldots, a_{t-1}$ and $b_0, b_1, \ldots, b_{t-1}$ to satisfy

$$z_i = r s_i + k_i \bmod q \quad (12)$$

$$z'_i = r' s_i + k_i \bmod q \quad (13)$$

$$c_j = r a_j + b_j \bmod q \text{ for } j = 0, 1, \ldots, t-1 \quad (14)$$

$$c'_j = r' a_j + b_j \bmod q \text{ for } j = 0, 1, \ldots, t-1 \quad (15)$$

can be calculated as

$$\begin{pmatrix} s_i \\ k_i \end{pmatrix} = \begin{pmatrix} r & 1 \\ r' & 1 \end{pmatrix}^{-1} \begin{pmatrix} z_i \\ z'_i \end{pmatrix}$$

$$\begin{pmatrix} a_j \\ b_j \end{pmatrix} = \begin{pmatrix} r & 1 \\ r' & 1 \end{pmatrix}^{-1} \begin{pmatrix} c_j \\ c'_j \end{pmatrix} \text{ for } j = 0, 1, \ldots, t-1.$$

where the calculations in the matrices are performed modulo q. Note that (8), (12) and (14) imply

$$k_i + rs_i = \sum_{j=0}^{t-1}(ra_j + b_j)i^j \bmod q; \tag{16}$$

(9), (13) and (15) imply

$$k_i + r's_i = \sum_{j=0}^{t-1}(r'a_j + b_j)i^j \bmod q; \tag{17}$$

10) and (14) imply

$$g^{ra_0+b_0}h^z = u^r v \bmod p; \tag{18}$$

and 11) and (15) imply

$$g^{r'a_0+b_0}h^{z'} = u^{r'} v \bmod p. \tag{19}$$

Moreover, (16)-(17) yields

$$(r - r')s_i = \sum_{j=0}^{t-1}(r - r')a_j i^j \bmod q; \tag{20}$$

while (18)/(19) yields

$$g^{(r-r')a_0}h^{z-z'} = u^{r-r'} \bmod p. \tag{21}$$

Also note that r and r' are different integers in Z_q and q is a prime and thus $r - r' \neq 0 \bmod q$. So (20) implies

$$s_i = \sum_{j=0}^{t-1} a_j i^j \bmod q$$

and (21) implies

$$g^{a_0}h^{(z-z')/(r-r')} = u \bmod p.$$

Therefore, s_i is the ith share of a_0, which is publicly committed in u. □

Theorem 2. *If (7) is satisfied with a probability larger than $1/q$, the reconstructed secret s is committed to by the dealer in u.*

Proof: As (7) is satisfied with a probability larger than $1/q$, there must exist two different integers in Z_q, r and r', such that given them A can return z and z' respectively to satisfy

$$(u/g^s)^r(v/g^k) = h^z \bmod p \tag{22}$$
$$(u/g^s)^{r'}(v/g^k) = h^{z'} \bmod p \tag{23}$$

Otherwise, there is at most one r in Z_q for A to produce a z to satisfy (7) and the probability that (7) is satisfied is no larger than $1/q$, which is a contradiction.
(22)/(23) yields

$$(u/g^s)^{r-r'} = h^{z-z'} \bmod p \tag{24}$$

If the dealer commits to an integer other than s in u, he must know integers s' and x' such that

$$u = g^{s'} h^{x'} \bmod p \tag{25}$$

and $s \neq s' \bmod q$. Note that
(24) and (25) imply

$$g^{(s'-s)(r-r')} = h^{z-z'-x'(r-r')} \bmod p.$$

Also note that r and r' are different integers in Z_q and q is a prime and thus $r - r' \neq 0 \bmod q$. So

$$\log_g h = (z - z' - x'(r - r'))/((s' - s)(r - r')) \bmod q$$

can be calculated in polynomial time, which is contradictory to the assumption that $\log_g h$ is secret and the DL problem is hard. Therefore, the reconstructed secret s is committed in u. □

Theorem 3. *The new PVSS protocol is hiding.*

Proof: We firstly show that the basic operations and one of the proof and verifications operations is hiding and then illustrate that the other three proof and verification operations dose not compromise hidingness although they need to publish some shares. The basic operations and one of the proof and verification operations "public verification of share validity against public commitment" have a transcript $u, v, d_1, d_2, \ldots, d_n, e_1, e_2, \ldots, e_n, r, c_0, c_1, \ldots, c_{t-1}, z, z_1, z_2, \ldots, z_n, h_1, h_2, \ldots, h_n$. Security of the employed encryption algorithm guarantees that it is difficult to extract the shares from $d_1, d_2, \ldots, d_n, e_1, e_2, \ldots, e_n$. The other variables in the transcript can be simulated by a party without any knowledge of any secret as follows.

1. He randomly chooses integers $r, z, c_0, c_1, \ldots, c_{t-1}$ from Z_q.
2. He calculates $z_i = \sum_{j=0}^{t-1} c_j i^j \bmod q$ and $h_i = H(z_i)$ for $i = 1, 2, \ldots, n$.
3. He randomly chooses integers s and x from Z_q and calculates $u = g^s h^x \bmod p$.
4. He calculates $k = c_0 - rs \bmod q$, $y = z - rx \bmod q$ and $v = g^k h^y \bmod p$.

In the random oracle model, distribution of r in the simulated transcript and in the real transcript are indistinguishable. Distribution of the simulated transcript and that of the real transcript of $u, v, c_0, c_1, \ldots, c_{t-1}, z, z_1, z_2, \ldots, z_n, h_1, h_2, \ldots, h_n$ are the same as follows.

- Each of $c_0, c_1, \ldots, c_{t-1}, z, z_1, z_2, \ldots, z_n$ is uniformly distributed in Z_q.
- Each of u and v is uniformly distributed in G.
- Each of $h_1, h_2, \ldots, h_n$ has a distribution $D\ \{h \mid h = H(Z),\ Z$ is uniformly distributed in $Z_q\}$ where $D\ \{\mu \mid \nu\}$ denote distribution of a variable μ determined by condition ν.
- The variables satisfy

$$g^{c_0} h^z = u^r v \bmod p$$
$$z_i = \sum_{j=0}^{t-1} c_j i^j \bmod q$$
$$h_i = H(z_i).$$

So no secret information is revealed from $u, v, r, c_0, c_1, \ldots, c_{t-1}, z, z_1, z_2, \ldots, z_n$, $h_1, h_2, \ldots, h_n$.

In "public solution to dispute in sharing", a share claimed to be invalid by its holder is published. If the share is really invalid, it is unrelated with the secret, so does not reveal any secret information. What if a malicious share holder takes this chance of disputing his share to reveal a valid share? Does such a revealing compromise hidingness of PVSS? Our answer is that if a share holder wants to reveal his share, he can do it anytime using any chance and the revealing cannot be prevented at all. So if a procedure is used by a malicious share holder as a chance to reveal his share, the procedure is not to blame. Actually, a basic assumption for any secret sharing technique to work is that each share holders will not reveal his share unless in the secret reconstruction phase. In "public verification of reconstruction", the secret has been reconstructed, so there is no secret information to be revealed. In "public detection of invalid share", the shares are published. Do the published valid shares violate privacy of PVSS? Our answer is that they do not as the PVSS protocol has passed the reconstruction phase when they are published. In the reconstruction phase the secret should be recovered and it is senseless to conceal its shares afterwards.

Therefore, none of the operations in the new PVSS protocol violates hidingness. □

The new PVSS protocol and the existing PVSS protocols are compared in Table 1. Neither the new PVSS protocol nor the existing PVSS protocols employs extensive communication, so communication is not compared although the new extended VSS is slightly more efficient in total communication including publishing encrypted shares and commitment values and transferring proof transcripts. We focus our comparison on computational cost, the bottleneck of PVSS. Our estimation of computational cost is comprehensive and takes into account the exponentiations needed in all the operations. When estimating computational cost of our new PVSS protocol, we have an observation: exponentiations with small bases and exponents like i^j is much less costly than an exponentiation usually used in asymmetric crypto, which has a base in a large cyclic group and a large exponent only limited by the order of the cyclic group. So, in efficiency analysis of threshold secret sharing (e.g. [9,13]), an exponentiation used in Lagrange Interpolation is usually not treated like an exponentiation in the asymmetric crypto operations,

Table 1. Comparison of PVSS Schemes

scheme	encry--ption	commit-ment	decryption and recon--struction	PV1	PV2	PV3	PV4	simple plaintext attack
[7]	n	$2t$	n	$n+t$ $+38$	0	t	0	no
DL based [15]	$2n$	t	$2n$	$t+7K$	0	1	2	yes
e^{th} root based [15]	$2n$	t	$2n$	$t+6$	0	1	2	yes
[2]	n	t	n	$t+15$	0	1	1	yes
[13]	n	t	$2n$	$t+8$	0	t	2	yes
new PVSS	n	4	n	3	1	4	1	no

but counted as a small number of multiplications. Therefore, the number of all the modulo exponentiations in large cyclic groups (with bases and exponents usually hundreds of bits long) are counted in our estimation, while exponentiations with small bases and exponents (like i^j in Lagrange Interpolation where i and j are no larger than indexes of the share holders) are ignored. In [15], K is the time a proof and verification primitive with 1-bit challenge has to be repeated to guarantee soundness with a probability $1 - 2^{-K}$. For fairness of the comparison, when any implementation detail of the new PVSS protocol (e.g. choice of parameters or underlying algorithms) is not explicitly determined, it is assumed to be the same as that in most of the existing PVSS schemes. The four proof and verification operations defined in Definition 5 are denoted as PV1, PV2, PV3 and PV4. In PV1, PV2 and PV4, cost for a share is counted. Except for [7], the existing PVSS schemes employ deterministic commitment algorithms for public commitment of the secret. So they are vulnerable to the simple plaintext attack. As stated before, overcoming the vulnerability is costly and further deteriorates their efficiency. The comparison demonstrates that the new PVSS scheme achieves stronger security and higher efficiency than the existing PVSS schemes.

5 Conclusion

The new PVSS protocol improves efficiency and security of PVSS. It achieves comprehensive and complete public verifiability and is more efficient than the existing PVSS schemes. Moreover, it is inherently invulnerable to the simple plaintext attack.

References

1. Benaloh, C.: Secret sharing homomorphisms: Keeping shares of a secret secret. In: Odlyzko, A.M. (ed.) CRYPTO 1986. LNCS, vol. 263, pp. 251–260. Springer, Heidelberg (1987)
2. Boudot, F., Traore, J.: Efficient publicly verifiable secret sharing schemes with fast or delayed recovery. In: Varadharajan, V., Mu, Y. (eds.) ICICS 1999. LNCS, vol. 1726, pp. 87–102. Springer, Heidelberg (1999)

3. Cachin, C., Kursawe, K., Lysyanskaya, A., Strobl, R.: Asynchronous verifiable secret sharing and proactive cryptosystems. In: ACM CCS 2002, pp. 88–97 (2002)
4. Chaum, D., Crepeau, C., Damgård, I.: Multiparty unconditionally secure protocols (extended abstract). In: Proceedings of the Twentieth Annual ACM Symposium on Theory of Computing, STOC 1988, pp. 11–19 (1988)
5. Feldman, P.: A practical scheme for non-interactive verifiable secret sharing. In: FOCS 1987, pp. 427–437 (1987)
6. Fitzi, M., Garay, J., Gollakota, S., Rangan, C., Srinathan, K.: Round-optimal and efficient verifiable secret sharing. In: Halevi, S., Rabin, T. (eds.) TCC 2006. LNCS, vol. 3876, pp. 329–342. Springer, Heidelberg (2006)
7. Fujisaki, E., Okamoto, T.: A practical and provably secure scheme for publicly verifiable secret sharing and its applications. In: Nyberg, K. (ed.) EUROCRYPT 1998. LNCS, vol. 1403, pp. 32–46. Springer, Heidelberg (1998)
8. Gennaro, R., Micali, S.: Verifiable secret sharing as secure computation. In: Guillou, L.C., Quisquater, J.-J. (eds.) EUROCRYPT 1995. LNCS, vol. 921, pp. 168–182. Springer, Heidelberg (1995)
9. Pedersen, T.: Distributed provers with applications to undeniable signatures. In: Davies, D.W. (ed.) EUROCRYPT 1991. LNCS, vol. 547, pp. 221–242. Springer, Heidelberg (1991)
10. Pedersen, T.: Non-interactive and information-theoretic secure verifiable secret sharing. In: Feigenbaum, J. (ed.) CRYPTO 1991. LNCS, vol. 576, pp. 129–140. Springer, Heidelberg (1992)
11. Peng, K., Bao, F.: Efficient publicly verifiable secret sharing with correctness. In: Youm, H.Y., Yung, M. (eds.) WISA 2009. LNCS, vol. 5932, pp. 118–132. Springer, Heidelberg (2009)
12. Rabin, T., Ben-Or, M.: Verifiable secret sharing and multiparty protocols with honest majority. In: ACM STOC 1989, pp. 73–85 (1989)
13. Schoenmakers, B.: A simple publicly verifiable secret sharing scheme and its application to electronic voting. In: Wiener, M. (ed.) CRYPTO 1999. LNCS, vol. 1666, pp. 148–164. Springer, Heidelberg (1999)
14. Shamir, A.: How to share a secret. Communication of the ACM 22(11), 612–613 (1979)
15. Stadler, M.: Publicly verifiable secret sharing. In: Maurer, U.M. (ed.) EUROCRYPT 1996. LNCS, vol. 1070, pp. 190–199. Springer, Heidelberg (1996)

A Robust Remote User Authentication Scheme against Smart Card Security Breach

Chun-Ta Li[1], Cheng-Chi Lee[2,3,⋆], Chen-Ju Liu[1], and Chin-Wen Lee[1]

[1] Department of Information Management, Tainan University of Technology
529 Zhongzheng Road, Tainan City 71002, Taiwan (R.O.C.)
th0040@mail.tut.edu.tw

[2] Department of Library and Information Science, Fu Jen Catholic University
510 Jhongjheng Road, New Taipei City 24205, Taiwan (R.O.C.)
cclee@mail.fju.edu.tw

[3] Department of Photonics and Communication Engineering, Asia University
500 Lioufeng Road, Taichung City 41354, Taiwan (R.O.C.)

Abstract. Remote user authentication is important to identify whether communicating parties are genuine and trustworthy using the password and the smart card between a login user and a remote server. Recently, we find that Kim et al.'s password-based authentication scheme [1] assume that the attacker cannot extract the secret information of the smart card. However, in reality, the authors in [2,8] show that the secrets stored in the card can be extracted by monitoring its power consumption. Therefore, Kim et al.'s scheme fail to resist smart card security breach. As the main contribution of this paper, a robust remote user authentication scheme against smart card security breach is presented, while keeping the merits of the well-known smart card based authentication schemes.

Keywords: Cryptanalysis; Network security; Password; Remote user authentication; Smart card.

1 Introduction

With the significant advances in communication networks over the last couple of decades, remote user authentication based on passwords [1,3,6,7] or biometrics [4,5] over insecure networks is the conventional method of authentication and has already been accepted warmly. Typically a network of remote servers are responsible for managing and supplying network services to login users for which user authentication protocols have been provided during a login procedure.

Recently, Liao et al. [7] proposed nine requirements for rating performance of a new password authentication scheme in terms of security, friendliness and efficiency. A new password authentication scheme using smart cards should satisfy the following requirements: (1) without maintaining verification tables; (2) users can freely choose and update passwords; (3) resistance to password disclosure to the server; (4) prevention of masquerade attacks; (5) resistance to replay,

⋆ Corresponding author.

Y. Li (Ed.): Data and Applications Security and Privacy XXV, LNCS 6818, pp. 231–238, 2011.

modification, parallel session and stolen-verifier attacks; (6) a easy-to-remember password; (7) low communication cost and computation complexity; (8) achieve mutual authentication between login users and remote servers; (9) resistance to guessing attacks even if the smart card is lost or stolen by attackers. Besides requirements stated in reference [7], we list three additional requirements to solve all problems in smart card-based authentication schemes, including: (10) session key agreement; (11) resistance to insider attacks; (12) prevention of smart card security breach attacks. For Requirement (12), it is important to note that secret information stored in a smart card can be extracted by analyzing and monitoring its power consumption [2,8]. Obviously, if a legal user's smart card is lost and it is picked up by a malicious attacker or an attacker steals user's smart card, the user's sensitive password may be derived out by an attacker. After that, there is no way to prevent the attacker from masquerading as the legal user. In this paper, we focus on the security of password authentication schemes for the merit that the design scheme achieves Requirement (12) and we will propose a robust remote user authentication scheme with better security strength while keeping the above-mentioned requirements.

The remainder of the paper is organized as follows. Section 2 is a brief review of Kim et al.'s authentication scheme and we show their security weaknesses in Section 3. The new remote user authentication scheme against smart card security breach is proposed in Section 4. Security analysis of the proposed scheme is presented in Section 5 and Section 6 concludes the paper.

2 A Review of Kim et al.'s Scheme

In this section, we review Kim et al.'s password-based remote authentication scheme [1] and their scheme is composed of three phases, registration, authentication and password update. For convenience of description, terminology and notations used in the paper are summarized as follows:

- U_i: The login user.
- (ID_i, PW_i, SC_i): The identity, password and the smart card of U_i.
- S: The remote server.
- X: The master secret key, which is kept secret and only known by S.
- N: The number of times U_i re-registers to S.
- SK: The common session key.
- $\oplus$: The bitwise XOR operation.
- $H(\cdot)$: A collision free one-way hash function.
- $||$: String concatenation.
- $E_K(.)/D_K(.)$: The symmetric encryption/decryption function with key K.
- $\Longrightarrow$: A secure channel.
- $\longrightarrow$: A public channel.

2.1 Registration Phase

(R.1) $U_i \Longrightarrow S : ID_i, PW_i$

U_i choose his/her identity ID_i and password PW_i and submits $\{ID_i, PW_i\}$ to the remote authentication server S.

(R.2) $S \Longrightarrow SC_i : K_1, K_2, R, H(\cdot)$
Upon receiving U_i's login request, S computes $K_1 = H(ID_i \oplus X) \oplus b$, $K_2 = H(ID_i \oplus X \oplus b) \oplus H(PW_i \oplus H(PW_i))$, and $R = K_1 \oplus H(PW_i)$ and stores K_1, K_2, R, and $H(\cdot)$ into the smart card SC_i, where b is a random number unique to the user U_i. Finally, S releases SC_i to U_i and the registration phase is completed.

2.2 Authentication Phase

(A.1) $SC_i \longrightarrow S : ID_i, T_{U_i}, C_1, C_2$
The user U_i enters ID_i and PW_i and the smart card SC_i computes $C_1 = R \oplus H(PW_i)$ and checks if C_1 is equal to the stored K_1. If it does not hold, SC_i terminates U_i's login request; otherwise, it computes $C_1' = K_2 \oplus H(PW_i \oplus H(PW_i))$ and $C_2 = H(C_1' \oplus T_{U_i})$, where T_{U_i} is the current timestamp generated by U_i. Then, SC_i submits $\{ID_i, T_{U_i}, C_1, C_2\}$ to the server.

(A.2) $S \longrightarrow SC_i : T_S, C_3$
Upon receiving the login request, S verifies the validity of T_{U_i}. If it is invalid, S rejects U_i's login request; otherwise, S checks if the hashed value $H(H(ID_i \oplus X \oplus M') \oplus T_{U_i})$ is equal to received C_2, where $M' = C_1 \oplus H(ID_i \oplus X)$. If it does not hold, SC_i terminates communication; otherwise, S succeeds to authenticate U_i and submits T_S and $C_3 = H(H(ID_i \oplus X \oplus M') \oplus C_2 \oplus T_S)$ to SC_i, where T_S is the current timestamp generated by S. Upon receiving the message from S, SC_i verifies the validity of T_S. If it is invalid, U_i terminates communication; otherwise, U_i checks if the hashed value $H(C_1' \oplus C_2 \oplus T_S)$ is equal to received C_3. If it holds, U_i succeeds to authenticate the remote server S.

2.3 Password Update Phase

In this phase, U_i inserts SC_i into the card reader and enters ID_i and PW_i. Then, SC_i computes $K_1' = R \oplus H(PW_i)$ and checks if the value K_1' is equal to stored K_1. If it does not hold, SC_i rejects U_i's password update request; otherwise, U_i enters a new password PW_i' and SC_i computes $R' = K_1' \oplus H(PW_i')$ and $K_2' = K_2 \oplus H(PW_i \oplus H(PW_i)) \oplus H(PW_i' \oplus H(PW_i'))$ and replaces (R, K_2) with (R', K_2').

3 The Various Kinds of Attacks with Smart Card Security Breach

In this section, we show some attacks with smart card security breach in Kim et al.'s authentication scheme. Let us consider the following scenarios. If a user's smart card is lost and it is picked up by an attacker U_A or an attacker steals user's smart card. The secrets stored in the smart card can be extracted by monitoring its power consumption [2,8], then the attacker can off-line guess user's password and masquerade as a legitimate user.

3.1 Off-Line Password Guessing Attack on Kim et al.'s Scheme

In Kim et al.'s scheme [1], the attacker U_A can breach the secrets $K_1 = H(ID_i \oplus X) \oplus b$, $R = K_1 \oplus H(PW_i)$ and $H(\cdot)$, which are stored in the smart card. Then, U_A can use the breached secrets K_1, R and $H(\cdot)$ to perform the following steps:

Step 1. Select a guessed password PW_i^*.
Step 2. Compute $K_1' = R \oplus H(PW_i^*)$.
Step 3. Compare K_1 to K_1'.

A match in Step 3 above indicates the correct guess of user's password. Therefore, the attacker succeeds to guess the low-entropy password PW_i and Kim et al.'s scheme is vulnerable to off-line password guessing attack.

3.2 Masquerading Attack on Kim et al.'s Scheme

Once the attacker U_A has correctly derived the user's password PW_i, he/she can also use the stored information on the stolen or lost smart card to forge a valid login request to masquerade as a legal user.

During the authentication phase of Kim et al.'s scheme, the attacker U_A can use the information on the lost or stolen smart card to make a valid login request with ease. For example, U_A is able to compute $C_1^* = R \oplus H(PW_i^*)$ and $C_2^* = K_2 \oplus H(PW_i^* \oplus H(PW_i^*) \oplus T_{U_A})$ by using the current timestamp T_{U_A} and the derived password PW_i^* on the lost or stolen smart card. Finally, U_A can successful make a valid login request message to impersonate U_i by sending $\{ID_i, T_{U_A}, C_1^*, C_2^*\}$ to the server S.

4 The Proposed Scheme

In this section, we describe a robust remote user authentication scheme which resolves all the above security flaws of smart card security breach. There are four phases in our scheme - registration, login, verification and password update.

4.1 Registration Phase

(R.1) $U_i \Longrightarrow S : ID_i, H(H(PW_i \oplus RN_1))$
To register, the user U_i chooses his/her identity ID_i and password PW_i and generates a random number RN_1. Then, U_i computes $H(H(PW_i \oplus RN_1))$ and sends ID_i and $H(H(PW_i \oplus RN_1))$ over a secure communication channel to S.

(R.2) $S \Longrightarrow SC_i : ID_i, C_1, H(\cdot)$
Upon receiving ID_i and $H(H(PW_i \oplus RN_1))$, S maintains a account table (AT) for a registration service and the format of AT is shown as follows:

User identity	Registration times	Verification parameter
ID_i	$N = 0$	$H(H(PW_i \oplus RN_1))$

where the 1st field of AT records the user's identity, the 2nd field of AT records $N = 0$ if it is U_i's initial registration, otherwise, S sets $N = N + 1$ in the existing field for U_i, and the 3rd field records U_i's verification parameter $H(H(PW_i \oplus RN_1))$ for a later login request.

Finally, S computes $C_1 = H(ID_i||X||N) \oplus H(H(PW_i \oplus RN_1))$ and stores $\{ID_i, C_1, H(\cdot)\}$ into the smart card SC_i and releases it to U_i.

(R.3) $U_i \Longrightarrow SC_i : ID_i, C_1, H(\cdot), RN_1$

Upon receiving SC_i, U_i stores RN_1 into SC_i and U_i finishes the registration procedure. Note that U_i's SC_i contains $\{ID_i, C_1, H(\cdot), RN_1\}$ and U_i does not need to remember RN_1 after finishing this phase. Note that the bit length of random numbers RN_i and S's master secret key X are assumed to be 256. That is, RN_i and X are two high entropy random numbers.

4.2 Login Phase

When U_i wants to login S, the following operations will perform:

(L.1) $U_i \Longrightarrow SC_i : ID_i, PW_i, RN_2$

U_i inserts his/her SC_i into the smart card reader and enters ID_i, PW_i and a new random number RN_2, where RN_2 is used for next login request. Then, SC_i generates a random number RC and computes $C_2 = H(PW_i \oplus RN_1)$, $C_3 = C_1 \oplus H(C_2)$, $C_4 = C_3 \oplus C_2$, and $C_6 = E_{K_{U_i}}(C_5, RC)$, where $C_5 = H(H(PW_i \oplus RN_2))$ and $K_{U_i} = H(C_2||C_3)$.

(L.2) $SC_i \longrightarrow S : ID_i, C_4, C_6$

SC_i sends $\{ID_i, C_4, C_6\}$ over a public communication channel to the remote server S.

4.3 Verification Phase

Upon receiving the login request from U_i, the remote server S and the smart card SC_i performs the following operations:

(V.1) $S \longrightarrow SC_i : E_{K_S}(RC, RS, C_5)$

If ID_i is invalid, S rejects U_i's login request. Otherwise, S computes $C_7 = H(ID_i||X||N)$, $C_8 = C_4 \oplus C_7$, and $C_9 = H(C_8)$ and compares the third entry $H(H(PW_i \oplus RN_1))$ to the computed C_9. If equal, S successfully authenticates U_i and computes symmetric key $K'_{U_i} = H(C_8||C_7)$, which equals to $K_{U_i} = H(C_2||C_3)$, to obtain (C_5, RC) by decrypting $D'_{K_{U_i}}(C_6)$. Then, S replaces the third entry $H(H(PW_i \oplus RN_1))$ with $C_5 = H(H(PW_i \oplus RN_2))$ and sends $E_{K_S}(RC, RS, C_5)$ over a public communication channel to the smart card SC_i, where RS is a random number generated by S and $K_S = H(C_7||C_8)$. Finally, the format of AT is shown as follows:

User identity	Registration times	Verification parameter
ID_i	$N = 0$	$H(H(PW_i \oplus RN_2))$

(V.2) $SC_i \longrightarrow S : H(RS)$
Upon receiving the message from S, SC_i computes symmetric key $K'_S = H(C_3||C_2)$, which equals to $K_S = H(C_7||C_8)$, to obtain (RC, RS, C_5) by decrypting $D'_{K_S}(E_{K_S}(RC, RS, C_5))$. Then, SC_i verifies if generated (RC, C_5) equals received (RC, C_5). If not equivalent, SC_i terminates communication; otherwise, SC_i now successfully authenticates S and replaces original RN_1 and C_1 with new RN_2 and $C_3 \oplus C_5$, respectively. Finally, SC_i sends a response $H(RS)$ to S and S can make sure that it is communicating with a legitimate U_i. Note that both U_i and S can compute the agreed session key $SK = H(RC \oplus RS)$ for securing future communications.

4.4 Password Update Phase

This phase is extremely similar to the login and verification phases of the proposed scheme and U_i is strongly recommended not to use any previous parameters for his/her update request, e.g. random number RN_2. When a user U_i wants to update his/her password PW_i with a new password PW'_i, U_i inserts his/her SC_i into the smart card and enters his/her ID_i, the original password PW_i, the new password PW'_i, and a new random number RN_3. Then, SC_i computes $C_2 = H(PW_i \oplus RN_2)$, $C_3 = C_1 \oplus H(C_2)$, $C_4 = C_3 \oplus C_2$, and $C_6 = E_{K_{U_i}}(C'_5, RC)$, where $C'_5 = H(H(PW'_i \oplus RN_3))$ and $K_{U_i} = H(C_2||C_3)$. Finally, SC_i sends $\{ID_i, C_4, C_6\}$ over a public communication channel to the remote server S. Upon receiving the message, S performs Step (V.1) and finally the format of AT is shown as follows:

User identity	Registration times	Verification parameter
ID_i	$N = 0$	$C'_5 = H(H(PW'_i \oplus RN_3))$

Note that the new password PW'_i and the new random number RN_3 stored in S's AT are simultaneous updated. Moreover, SC_i replaces original RN_2 and C_1 with new RN_3 and $C_3 \oplus C'_5$, respectively. Now, the new password PW'_i and the new random number RN_3 are successfully updated and this phase is terminated.

5 Security Analysis of the Proposed Scheme

The proposed authentication scheme benefits from the protection of smart cards to prevent the secret information for an attacker to steal and guess the real secrets stored in the stolen smart card or in the exchange of authentication messages. In the following propositions, we give an in-depth analysis of the proposed scheme in terms of security properties.

Proposition 1. *The present scheme is secure against off-line password guessing attack with smart card security breach.*

Proof. With the assumption that the attacker can collect the transmitted messages $\{ID_i, C_4 = H(ID_i||X||N) \oplus H(PW_i||RN_i), C_6 = E_{K_{U_i}}(H(H(PW_i \oplus RN_{i+1}))), E_{K_S}(RC, RS, H(H(PW_i \oplus RN_{i+1}))), H(RS)\}$ and extract the secrets

$\{ID_i, C_1 = H(ID_i||X||N) \oplus H(H(PW_i \oplus RN_{i+1})), H(\cdot), RN_{i+1}\}$ stored in the lost or stolen smart card, where $i = 1, 2, 3, \ldots$, $K_{U_i} = H(H(PW_i \oplus RN_i)||H(ID_i||X||N))$ and $K_S = H(H(ID_i||X|| N)||H(PW_i||RN_i))$.

Throughout the proposed scheme, U_i's password PW_i makes four appearances as $C_4 = H(ID_i||X||N) \oplus H(PW_i||RN_i)$, $C_6 = E_{K_{U_i}}(H(H(PW_i \oplus RN_{i+1})))$, $E_{K_S}(RC, RS, H(H(PW_i \oplus RN_{i+1})))$ and $C_1 = H(ID_i||X||N) \oplus H(H(PW_i \oplus RN_{i+1}))$. However, for each new login request, the previous random number RN_i stored in the smart card have to be replaced with new random number RN_{i+1}. Therefore, an attacker cannot launch off-line password guessing attack without knowing the previous secret RN_i and our proposed authentication scheme can resist off-line password guessing attack with smart card security breach.

Proposition 2. *The proposed scheme can withstand masquerade attack with smart card security breach.*

Proof. Let us assume an attacker U_A has extracted smart card's secrets and has got the transmitted messages between U_i and S. U_A inserts U_i's SC_i into the card reader and then enters the guessing password PW_i^* and a random number RN_i^*. As described above, throughout the proposed scheme, if any trial value of the password is used during an on-line session, U_A has only one chance to guess the original password to pass server's validation. Once U_A's guessing password is wrong, the server can immediately detect the validity of fake login request and terminate U_A's login session. In this case, U_A cannot masquerade as a legal user to send a valid login request message and the masquerade attack cannot work in the proposed scheme.

Proposition 3. *The proposed scheme is able to provide mutual authentication and a agreed session key between U_i and S in every login session.*

Proof. By the proposed scheme, let us assume that A and B be the two communication parties, namely the login user and the remote server. Let $A \overset{SK}{\longleftrightarrow} B$ denotes the agreed session key SK shared between A and B. Hence, the mutual authentication is achieved between A and B if there exists a session key SK, then A would believe $A \overset{SK}{\longleftrightarrow} B$, and B would believe $A \overset{SK}{\longleftrightarrow} B$. As a result, we have stated that a strong mutual authentication should satisfy the following equations:

$$A \;\; believes \;\; B \;\; believes \;\; A \overset{SK}{\longleftrightarrow} B. \tag{1}$$

$$B \;\; believes \;\; A \;\; believes \;\; A \overset{SK}{\longleftrightarrow} B. \tag{2}$$

In Step (L.2) of the login phase, after B receives the login request $\{A, C_4 = H(A||X||N) \oplus H(PW_A \oplus RN_i), C_6 = E_{K_A}(H(H(PW_A \oplus RN_{i+1})), RC)\}$, B will verify $H(PW_A \oplus RN_i)$ by computing $C_4 \oplus H(A||X||N)$ and check whether the hashed value $H(C_4 \oplus H(A||X||N))$ is equal to $H(H(PW_A \oplus RN_i))$. If it holds, B decrypts C_6 and gets RC in Step (V.1) of the verification phase. Moreover, B generates RS and submits $E_{K_S}(RC, RS, C_5 = H(H(PW_A \oplus RN_{i+1}))$ to A. After A receives the response message, A will verify $H(H(PW_A \oplus RN_{i+1}))$ and RC by computing $D_{H(H(A||X||N))||H(PW_A \oplus RN_i))}(E_{K_S}(RC, RS, C_5 = H(H(PW_A \oplus RN_{i+1})))$.

If these values are valid, A computes the session key $SK = H(RC \oplus RS)$ and believes $A \overset{SK}{\longleftrightarrow} B$. Since RC is chosen by A, A believes B believes $A \overset{SK}{\longleftrightarrow} B$. Also, in Step (V.2) of the verification phase, a response $H(RS)$ will be sent to B. After B received the response message from A, B uses RS to compute $H(RS)$ and checks whether the hashed value contains a response RS. If it holds, B believes $A \overset{SK}{\longleftrightarrow} B$. Since RS is chosen by B, B believes A believes $A \overset{SK}{\longleftrightarrow} B$. Finally, after Equations (1) and (2) are satisfied, and together they accomplish the mutual authentication and dynamic session key agreement in the proposed scheme.

6 Conclusions

This paper proposed a robust user authentication scheme using smart cards. We have showed that the proposed scheme avoids smart card security breach attacks and maintains the merits of related works such as provision of mutual authentication, prevention of password guessing attack, detection of masquerade attack, session key agreement, and so on. In our future works, a formal security proof and a experimental simulation would have been a better picture to demonstrate the feasibility of the proposed scheme. and the proposed scheme can be further extended with the countermeasure against the Denial-of-Service (DoS) attacks.

References

1. Kim, S.K., Chung, M.G.: More secure remote user authentication scheme. Computer Communications 32(6), 1018–1021 (2009)
2. Kocher, P., Jaffe, J., Jun, B.: Differential power analysis. In: Proceedings of Advances in Cryptology, pp. 388–397 (1999)
3. Lamport, L.: Password authentication with insecure communication. Communications of the ACM 24(11), 770–772 (1981)
4. Li, C.T., Hwang, M.S.: An efficient biometrics-based remote user authentication scheme using smart cards. Journal of Network and Computer Applications 33(1), 1–5 (2010)
5. Li, C.T., Hwang, M.S.: An online biometrics-based secret sharing scheme for multiparty cryptosystem using smart cards. International Journal of Innovative Computing, Information and Control 6(5), 2181–2188 (2010)
6. Li, C.T., Lee, C.C.: A novel user authentication and privacy preserving scheme with smart cards for wireless communications. Mathematical and Computer Modelling, article (in press, 2011)
7. Liao, I.E., Lee, C.C., Hwang, M.S.: A password authentication scheme over insecure networks. Journal of Computer and System Sciences 72(4), 727–740 (2006)
8. Messerges, T.S., Dabbish, E.A., Sloan, R.H.: Examining smart-card security under the threat of power analysis attacks. IEEE Transactions on Computers 51(5), 541–552 (2002)

N-Gram Based Secure Similar Document Detection

Wei Jiang and Bharath K. Samanthula

Department of Computer Science, Missouri S & T, Rolla, MO 65401
{wjiang,bspq8}@mst.edu

Abstract. Secure similar document detection (SSDD) plays an important role in many applications, such as justifying the need-to-know basis and facilitating communication between government agencies. The SSDD problem considers situations where Alice with a query document wants to find similar information from Bob's document collection. During this process, the content of the query document is not disclosed to Bob, and Bob's document collection is not disclosed to Alice. Existing SSDD protocols are developed under the vector space model, which has the advantage of identifying global similar information. To effectively and securely detect similar documents with overlapping text fragments, this paper proposes a novel n-gram based SSDD protocol.

Keywords: privacy, security, n-gram.

1 Introduction

Textual information is ubiquitous and plays major roles in information dissemination. There are many practical situations where detecting documents that are similar to a given query document in a privacy-preserving way is beneficial. Consider an FBI agent looking for the data related to potential terrorist suspect. He or she may wish to check whether there are reports that are related to the suspect from local police databases. However, neither the FBI agent nor the local police wants to exchange their data unless there is a need to share. One way to identify such a need is to detect similarities or correlations between the the FBI's query (in form of textual document) and the local police's database of reports on criminal activities. Once the need for sharing information is verified, the FBI and the local police can exchange only the needed information. During the process of identifying similar or correlated information, it is the best interest for both parties not to disclose the query document and the database. Such a process is referred as secure similar document detection (SSDD).

The SSDD problem was first introduced in [6], where vector space model and Cosine Similarity are adopted to detect similar documents. Under the vector space model, each document is represented as a vector of terms or words, and each entry of the vector indicates certain frequency information of the corresponding term. When the vectors contain normalized term frequency values, secure dot product protocols (e.g., [2]) can be used as the building block for an

Y. Li (Ed.): Data and Applications Security and Privacy XXV, LNCS 6818, pp. 239–246, 2011.

SSDD protocol that identifies similar documents through Cosine Similarity. The same work was later extended in [8] to improve computation efficiency.

The vector space model is not the only way to compute document similarity, and n-gram based document representation [7] can also be adopted to detect similar documents. The vector space model has the advantage of detecting global similarity, e.g., a bag of similar terms. On the other hand, the n-gram model has the advantage of finding local similarity, e.g., overlapping of pieces of texts. Also, n-gram model is language independent and has simple representation. Plus, n-gram based document modeling is less sensitive to document modification. Thus, the goal of this paper is to propose a n-gram based SSDD protocol under the semi-honest model [3].

1.1 Related Work

The SSDD problem was first introduced in [6]. The key in their work is how to securely compute the similarity between two documents. Initially, both participating parties, Alice and Bob, compute local (their own) vector spaces for their document collections. Then each of their documents can be represented as a vector of terms or words. Cosine similarity is adopted to measure similarity between any two documents. The same work was later extended in [8] to improve computation efficiency by combining text clustering techniques.

2 The Proposed Method

We follow the same setting as in [6,8]. Let Alice and Bob represent two entities, each of whom has a collection of documents. Given a query document u from Alice, the goal of an SSDD protocol is to detect whether or not Bob's collection (denoted by $\mathcal{D} = \{v_1, \ldots, v_n\}$) contains a document similar to u without disclosing Bob's database to Alice and vice versa. SSDD is defined as follows [6]:

$$\text{SSDD}(u, \mathcal{D}) \rightarrow \sigma_1, \ldots, \sigma_n \qquad (1)$$

Instead of returning the actual similar documents, SSDD returns n[1] similarity scores $\sigma_1, \ldots, \sigma_n$ to Alice. If one or more are particularly close, arrangements can be made (e.g., via agreed access control policies) to investigate further.

The SSDD protocol proposed in this paper is based on the n-gram model. In general, an n-gram is a subsequence (substring) of size n from a given sequence (string). An n-gram of size 1, 2 or 3 is referred as an uni-gram, bi-gram or tri-gram receptively. An n-gram of size 4 or more is simply called n-gram. If a text document is treated as a one big string, under the n-gram model, each document can be represented by a set of successive n-gram. Table 1 shows four pieces of texts and their corresponding unique tri-gram representations.

[1] Note that in this paper, n is used to indicate either Bob's document collection size or the length of the n-gram depends on the context.

Table 1. Sample Texts

	Text	n-gram representation
u	aabbc abbde	{aab, abb, bbc, bca, cab, bbd, bde}
v_1	ca aabbc ddf	{caa, aaa, aab, abb, bbc, bcd, cdd, ddf}
v_2	xaab xyyyz	{xaa, aab, abx, bxy, xyy, yyy, yyz}
v_3	xxx yyy xyyz	{xxx, xxy, xyy, yyy, yyx, yxy, yyz}

Under the n-gram model, the similarity between any two documents can be calculated using set similarity. A commonly accepted way to measure set similarity is to use *Jaccard Coefficient* (JC). Suppose u and v are two documents under the n-gram model, then JC between u and v is given by:

$$\mathrm{JC}(u,v) = \frac{|u \cap v|}{|u \cup v|} = \frac{|u \cap v|}{|u| + |v| - |u \cap v|} \tag{2}$$

Referring to Table 1, assume u is a query document and $\{v_1, v_2, v_3\}$ is Bob's document collection. The similarity between u and v_1 can be calculated by $\mathrm{JC}(u, v_1) = \frac{3}{7+8-3} = 0.25$. JC will be adopted as the similarity measure in our proposed SSDD protocol.

2.1 Secure Similarity Computation

In order to return only the JC scores, our SSDD protocol consists of two stages. Each stage is summarized as follows:

- **Stage 1** - Computing Random Shares of $|u \cap v_i|$:
  At the end of this stage, Alice receives a random number a_{1i} and Bob receives a random number a_{2i}, such that $a_{1i} + a_{2i} \mod N = |u \cap v_i|$, where N is a security parameter or an encryption key.
- **Stage 2** - Computing JC Score:
  Alice sets $b_{1i} = |u| - a_{1i} \mod N$ and Bob sets $b_{2i} = |v_i| - a_{2i} \mod N$. Alice and Bob securely compute $\frac{a_{1i}+a_{2i} \mod N}{b_{1i}+b_{2i} \mod N}$, without disclosing a_{1i}, b_{1i} to Bob and a_{2i}, b_{2i} to Alice.

To implement the first stage, Bob first generates a global space of n-gram based on his document collection, denoted by S. Then S is mapped to an integer domain from 1 to $|S|$. Let M denote such a mapping function and S_j denote the jth element in S, then $M(S_j) = j$. Under the domain of $M(S)$, each document v_i can be represented by a binary vector $\boldsymbol{v}_i$ (i.e., a vector with 0/1 entries). The following properties hold for each $\boldsymbol{v}_i$:

- $|\boldsymbol{v}_i| = |S|$
- $\boldsymbol{v}_i[j] = 1 \Rightarrow S_j \in v_i$ and $\boldsymbol{v}_i[j] = 0 \Rightarrow S_j \notin v_i$, where $\boldsymbol{v}_i[j]$ denotes the jth entry or dimension of $\boldsymbol{v}_i$.

Example 1. Following the documents in Table 1, Table 2 shows a global n-gram space based on Bob's document collection and the vector representation of each

Table 2. Global n-gram space

Global n-gram space and its mapping to integer domain																		
S	*aaa*	*aab*	*abb*	*abx*	*bbc*	*bcd*	*bxy*	*caa*	*cdd*	*ddf*	*xaa*	*xxx*	*xxy*	*xyy*	*yxy*	*yyx*	*yyy*	*yyz*
$M(S)$	1	2	3	4	5	6	7	8	9	10	11	12	13	14	15	16	17	18
Binary vector representation of each document in the global n-gram space																		
$\boldsymbol{u}$	0	1	1	0	1	0	0	0	0	0	0	0	0	0	0	0	0	0
$\boldsymbol{v}_1$	1	1	1	0	1	1	0	1	1	1	0	0	0	0	0	0	0	0
$\boldsymbol{v}_2$	0	1	0	1	0	0	1	0	0	0	1	0	0	1	0	0	1	1
$\boldsymbol{v}_3$	0	0	0	0	0	0	0	0	0	0	0	1	1	1	1	1	1	1

document on the global space. Note that not all n-gram in u appear in S because S is only derived from Bob's document collection. However, this does not affect the set intersection computation. To compute the intersection between u and v_i, we merely calculate the dot product of $\boldsymbol{u}$ and $\boldsymbol{v}_i$, i.e., $|u \cap v_i| = \boldsymbol{u} \bullet \boldsymbol{v}_i$. □

The above example shows that to securely compute $|u \cap v_i|$, we can use a secure dot product protocol that computes $\boldsymbol{u} \bullet \boldsymbol{v}_i$. We will adopt the homomorphic encryption based secure dot product protocol given in [2].

2.2 Stage 1 - Securely Computing a_{1i} and a_{2i}

Let E_{pk} and D_{pr} be the encryption and decryption functions in Paillier's public-key homomorphic encryption system [9]. The encryption function has the following additive homomorphic property: $E_{pk}(x_1) * E_{pk}(x_2) = E_{pk}(x_1 + x_2)$.

Given two documents $\boldsymbol{u}$ and $\boldsymbol{v}_i$, represented under the global n-gram model, the main steps computing a_{1i} and a_{2i} is given in Algorithm 1. The algorithm takes $\boldsymbol{u}$ from Alice and $\boldsymbol{v}_i$ from Bob's document collection, and returns a_{1i} to Alice and a_{2i} to Bob, such that $a_{1i} + a_{2i} \mod N = \boldsymbol{u} \bullet \boldsymbol{v}_i$. During this process, Alice does not know anything that is computationally feasible about Bob's input vector, and vice versa. At the beginning, Alice encrypts her private input vector component-wise and sends the encrypted vector to Bob denoted as $\boldsymbol{z}$. Upon receiving $\boldsymbol{z}$, At step 2(b), Bob computes $E_{pk}(\boldsymbol{u} \bullet \boldsymbol{v}_i)$, the encryption of the dot product of $\boldsymbol{u}$ and $\boldsymbol{v}_i$, denoted by s. At step 2(c), Bob computes $E_{pk}(\boldsymbol{u} \bullet \boldsymbol{v}_i + r)$. At step 2(d), Bob computes his share a_{2i} and sends $E_{pk}(\boldsymbol{u} \bullet \boldsymbol{v}_i + r)$ to Alice. Alice can get her share a_{1i} by decrypting the value received from Bob. Note that Alice's private vector $\boldsymbol{u}$ is not disclosed to Bob because only the encrypted vector is sent to Bob. No one (except Alice) can decrypt the vector to get the actual values regarding $\boldsymbol{u}$. In addition, because $a_{1i} = \boldsymbol{u} \bullet \boldsymbol{v}_i + r$ and $a_{2i} = N - r$, it is certain that $a_{1i} + a_{2i} \mod N = \boldsymbol{u} \bullet \boldsymbol{v}_i$.

The protocol in Algorithm 1 is secure in the semi-honest model. The main reason is that the messages communicated during the execution of the protocol are random shares, which can be simulated based on the input and the output.

Algorithm 1. Computing_Random_Shares($\boldsymbol{u}, \boldsymbol{v}_i$) $\rightarrow (a_{1i}, a_{2i})$

Require: Alice's input: Query Document $\boldsymbol{u}$ and (g, N); Bob's input: $\boldsymbol{v}_i$ and (g, N); $|\boldsymbol{u}| = |\boldsymbol{v}_i| = |S|$ (Note: the private key pr is only known to Alice)

1: Alice:

(a). Encrypt $\boldsymbol{u}$ component-wise: $\boldsymbol{z}[j] \leftarrow E_{pk}(\boldsymbol{u}[j])$ for $j = 1, \ldots, |S|$
(b). Send $\boldsymbol{z}$ to Bob

2: Bob:

(a). Receive $\boldsymbol{z}$ from Alice
(b). $s \leftarrow \prod_{j=1 \wedge \boldsymbol{v}_i[j]=1}^{|S|} \boldsymbol{z}[j]$
(c). $s \leftarrow s * E_{pk}(r)$, where r is randomly chosen from $\mathbb{Z}_N^*$
(d). $a_{2i} \leftarrow N - r$
(e). Send s to Alice

3: Alice:

(a). Receive s from Bob
(b). $a_{1i} \leftarrow D_{pr}(s)$

Complexity Analysis. The complexity of Computing_Random_Shares consists of local computation cost and communication cost between the two parties. Since the protocol is asymmetric, the local computation cost is different for each party. The main computation cost for Alice is encrypting her input vector, and we calculate her computation complexity based on the number of encryptions she performs. According to Algorithm 1, Alice's computation cost is determined by step 1(a) where the number of encryptions performed is linearly bounded by the size of her input vector. Therefore, the computation complexity for Alice is bounded by $O(|S|)$ number of encryptions.

Step 2(b) of Algorithm 1 determines Bob's computation cost, and it requires at most $|S|$ multiplications of ciphertexts received from Alice. In general, one encryption operation (or exponentiation) under the Paillier's system is much more expensive than one multiplication (depends on the size of encryption key). Here, we assume that the time it takes to perform one encryption at step 2(c) is less than $|S|$ multiplications performed at step 2(b). Then, the computation complexity for Bob is bounded by $O(|S|)$ number of multiplications.

Let k denote the size of encryption key in number of bits. (In practice, the encryption key N should be at lest 1,024-bit long.) The communication complexity of the protocol is bounded by step 1(b). Because the size of each ciphertext is bounded by k, the communication complexity is given by $O(k \cdot |S|)$ in bits.

2.3 Stage 2 - Securely Computing JC Scores

Once Alice and Bob obtain a_{1i} and a_{2i} respectively, Alice sets $b_{1i} = |u| - a_{1i} \mod N$ and Bob sets $b_{2i} = |v_i| - a_{2i} \mod N$. Alice and Bob can securely compute $\frac{a_{1i}+a_{2i} \mod N}{b_{1i}+b_{2i} \mod N}$, without disclosing a_{1i}, b_{1i} to Bob and a_{2i}, b_{2i} to Alice. Suppose

Algorithm 2. Computing_JC_Scores$(\alpha_1, \alpha_2) \rightarrow \sigma_1, \ldots, \sigma_n$

Require: Alice's input: $\alpha_1 = \langle a_{11}, \ldots, a_{1n} \rangle$; Bob's input: $\alpha_2 = \langle a_{21}, \ldots, a_{2n} \rangle$, and $|\alpha_1| = |\alpha_2| = n$
1: Alice: Compute $\beta_1 = \langle b_{11}, \ldots, b_{1n} \rangle$, where $b_{1i} = |u| - a_{1i} \mod N$ for $1 \leq i \leq n$
2: Bob: Compute $\beta_2 = \langle b_{21}, \ldots, b_{2n} \rangle$, where $b_{2i} = |v_i| - a_{2i} \mod N$ for $1 \leq i \leq n$
3: Alice (with input α_1, β_1) and Bob (with input α_2, β_2): For $1 \leq i \leq n$, compute $\sigma_i \leftarrow$ Secure_Division$((a_{1i}, b_{1i}), (a_{2i}, b_{2i}))$

Bob's collection contains n documents, at the end, Alice and Bob needs to compute n JC scores, one for each pair of u and v_i. Algorithm 2 lists the main steps to achieve this. The inputs to the algorithm are α_1 and α_2, from Alice and Bob respectively. α_1, privately owned by Alice, contains n random shares generated from stage 1. Similarly, α_2, privately owned by Bob, contains n random shares generated from stage 1. Initially, Alice and Bob independently compute β_1 and β_2, so for $1 \leq i \leq n$, JC score of u and v_i is given by $\sigma_i = \frac{a_{1i}+a_{2i} \mod N}{b_{1i}+b_{2i} \mod N} = \frac{|u \cap v_i|}{|u \cup v_i|}$. To securely compute σ_i (without disclosing α_1 to Bob and α_2 to Alice), step 3 of Algorithm 2 adopts the appropriate Secure_Division protocol proposed in [1]. The protocol takes private input (a_{1i}, b_{1i}) from Alice and private input (a_{2i}, b_{2i}) from Bob. It returns $\sigma_i = \frac{a_{1i}+a_{2i} \mod N}{b_{1i}+b_{2i} \mod N}$ to either or both parties.

Complexity Analysis. The secure dot product protocol can be easily implemented using Paillier's crypto system as suggested in [2]. Without giving further details, the computation cost of Secure_Division for both party is bounded by O(1) number of encryptions. The communication cost of Secure_Division is bounded by O(k) bits, where k is the size of an encryption key in bits. Computing_JC_Scores requires n executions of Secure_Division, so its computation complexity is bounded by O(n) encryptions for each party, and the communication complexity is bounded by O($k \cdot n$) bits.

2.4 N-Gram Based SSDD

Once we know how to securely implement Stage 1 and Stage 2, we can combine the two stages together to derive a n-gram based SSDD protocol. The main steps of the protocol are highlighted in Algorithm 3. Initially, Bob generates the global n-gram space S from his document collection $\mathcal{D}$. Then a one-to-one mapping $M(S)$ is created to map S to $\{1, \ldots, |S|\}$. At step 1(c) of Algorithm 3, Bob, according to S and $M(S)$, computes the vector representation of each document in his document collection $\mathcal{D}$ under the n-gram model. Once Alice receives S and $M(S)$, Alice generates $\boldsymbol{u}$, the vector representation of her query document u under the n-gram model. After that Alice and Bob can proceed to Stage 1 and Stage 2. At the end of stage 2, Alice receives a set of similarity scores, or these scores can be shared by both parties. The security of the protocol is determined by the Secure_Division protocol adopted at stage 2.

Algorithm 3. NGram_SSDD$(u, \mathcal{D}) \rightarrow \sigma_1, \ldots, \sigma_n$

Require: Alice's input: u; Bob's input: $\mathcal{D}$

1: Bob:

(a). Compute S and $M(S)$ from $\mathcal{D}$
(b). Compute $\boldsymbol{v}_i$ from $\mathcal{D}, S, M(S)$, for $1 \leq i \leq |\mathcal{D}|$
(c). Send $S, M(S)$ to Alice

2: Alice: Compute $\boldsymbol{u}$ from $u, S, M(S)$
3: Alice and Bob:

(a). **Stage 1** - Computing_Random_Shares$(\boldsymbol{u}, \boldsymbol{v}_i)$, for $1 \leq i \leq |\mathcal{D}|$ (At the end, Alice obtains $\alpha_1 = \langle a_{11}, \ldots, a_{1n} \rangle$, and Bob obtains $\alpha_2 = \langle a_{21}, \ldots, a_{2n} \rangle$)
(b). **Stage 2** - Computing_JC_Scores(α_1, α_2)

Complexity Analysis. The main cost of the protocol occurs at step 3 of Algorithm 3. Stage 1 initiates n executions of Computing_Random_Shares protocol. From Alice's point of view, based on the computation complexity analysis of Computing_Random_Shares, Alice needs to encrypt her query document $\boldsymbol{u}$ n times. However, during the actual implementation, Alice only needs to encrypt $\boldsymbol{u}$ once, and uses the same encrypted $\boldsymbol{u}$ for each of the n instantiations of the Computing_Random_Shares protocol. As a result, the computation cost for Alice at stage 1 is $O(|S|)$ number of encryptions. Since each instantiation of Computing_Random_Shares requires Bob to perform $O(|S|)$ multiplications, the computation cost for Bob at stage 1 is $O(n \cdot |S|)$ multiplications. Alice needs to send the encrypted $\boldsymbol{u}$ once, so the communication complexity for stage 1 is $O(k \cdot |S|)$ bits where k is the encryption key size in Paillier's system.

Stage 2 only calls the Computing_JC_Scores once; thus, its complexity analysis is the same as that of Computing_JC_Scores. Combining the two stages together, the computation complexity of NGram_SSDD for Alice is bounded by $O(|S| + n)$ number of encryptions. The computation complexity of NGram_SSDD for Bob is bounded by $O(n \cdot |S|)$ number of multiplications plus $O(n)$ number of encryptions. The total communication complexity of NGram_SSDD is bounded by $O(k \cdot |S| + k \cdot n)$ bits.

3 Future Work

We will empirically study the performance of the proposed protocol. To further improve the efficiency and instead of fixing the global n-gram space based on Bob's entire document collection, we could apply winnowing techniques [10] on each Bob's document and select representative n-gram (or fingerprints) for each document. Since winnowing selects few fingerprints by adjusting window size and noise threshold, it is possible to reduce the global space to a larger extent thereby reducing the computational cost.

Acknowledgment

This material is based upon work supported by the Office of Naval Research under Award No. N000141110256.

References

1. Atallah, M., Bykova, M., Li, J., Frikken, K., Topkara, M.: Private collaborative forecasting and benchmarking. In: Proceedings of the 2004 ACM Workshop on Privacy in the Electronic Society, WPES 2004, pp. 103–114 (October 2004)
2. Goethals, B., Laur, S., Lipmaa, H., Mielikainen, T.: On secure scalar product computation for privacy-preserving data mining. In: Park, C.-s., Chee, S. (eds.) ICISC 2004. LNCS, vol. 3506, pp. 104–120. Springer, Heidelberg (2005)
3. Goldreich, O.: General Cryptographic Protocols. In: The Foundations of Cryptography, vol. 2. Cambridge University Press, Cambridge (2004)
4. Goldreich, O.: Encryption Schemes. In: The Foundations of Cryptography, vol. 2. Cambridge University Press, Cambridge (2004)
5. Goldwasser, S., Micali, S., Rackoff, C.: The knowledge complexity of interactive proof systems. In: Proceedings of the 17th Annual ACM Symposium on Theory of Computing, Providence, Rhode Island, U.S.A., May 6-8, pp. 291–304 (1985)
6. Jiang, W., Murugesan, M., Clifton, C., Si, L.: Similar document detection with limited information disclosure. In: Proceedings of the 24th International Conference on Data Engineering (ICDE 2008), Cancun, Mexico, April 7-12 (2008)
7. Manber, U.: Finding similar files in a large file system. Technical Report TR 93-33, Department of Computer Science, The University of Arizona, Tucson, Arizona (October 1993)
8. Murugesan, M., Jiang, W., Clifton, C., Si, L., Vaidya, J.: Efficient privacy-preserving similar document detection. The VLDB Journal, January 16 (2010)
9. Paillier, P.: Public key cryptosystems based on composite degree residuosity classes. In: Stern, J. (ed.) EUROCRYPT 1999. LNCS, vol. 1592, pp. 223–238. Springer, Heidelberg (1999)
10. Schleimer, S., Wilkerson, D.S., Aiken, A.: Winnowing: Local algorithms for document fingerprinting. In: Proceedings of the ACM SIGMOD Conference on Management of Data, San Diego, California, United States, June 9-12, pp. 76–85. ACM, New York (2003)

An Index Structure for Private Data Outsourcing

Aaron Steele and Keith B. Frikken

Department of Computer Science and Software Engineering,
Miami University, Oxford, OH 45056
{steelea,frikkekb}@muohio.edu

Abstract. Data outsourcing provides companies a cost effective method for their data to be stored, managed, and maintained by a third-party. Data outsourcing offers many economical benefits, but also introduces several privacy concerns. Many solutions have been proposed for maintaining privacy while outsourcing data in the data as plain-text model. We propose a method that can maintain a similar level of privacy while improving upon the query performance of previous solutions. The motivating principle behind our solution is that if the data owner possesses a small amount of secure local storage, it can be used as a pseudo-index table to improve query performance for selection queries involving conjunctions. We offer a heuristic approach for calculating the required storage resources and provide experimental analysis of the scheme.

Keywords: Data Outsourcing, Privacy, Indexing.

1 Introduction

For small organizations the burden of maintaining large volumes of information can be overwhelming. In an attempt to lessen the burden, organizations turn to third-parties to maintain the data for them. On one hand the economic savings from outsourcing the data is tremendous, but on the other hand concerns arise about the confidentiality of sensitive information being outsourced.

As an example, a credit card company maintains a large collection of financial information, shopping patterns, and personal information about their customers. To minimize costs, the company wants to use a third-party to host the data. The credit card company then accesses the data for billing and advertising. The drawback with such outsourcing is that the data cannot be revealed to the hosting party, for fear of compromising their customers' privacy. The scheme proposed in this paper attempts to minimize the risks of data outsourcing while improving the efficiency of data access.

Several solutions have been proposed to address this problem (Section 2.1). Several of these solutions allow the data owner to efficiently query the data using equality selections for single attributes. However, most prior solutions do not allow the data owner to efficiently query the data using conjunction. This would be most problematic if the same pair of attributes were queried frequently together in such a selection. In this paper, we introduce an indexing technique that can be applied on top of previous solutions, that facilitates answering such queries efficiently.

The remainder of the paper is structured as follows. First, we describe some recent solutions that have been introduced to solve the data outsourcing problem (Section 2).

Y. Li (Ed.): Data and Applications Security and Privacy XXV, LNCS 6818, pp. 247–254, 2011.

Next, we introduce our scheme that extends previous solutions by incorporating a small amount of secure local storage and a method for calculating the required amount of local storage (Section 3). We provide experimental results (Section 4) that support the flexibility and robustness of the scheme. Finally, we present some related work (Section 5) and summarize our results (Section 6).

2 Background

The scenario we consider is the same one addressed by [1,3,4,5,6], primarily that the data to be outsourced is represented as a relational schema $R(a_1, a_2, \ldots, a_n)$ where R is a set of tuples over the set of all attributes $\{a_1, a_2, \ldots, a_n\}$ where the domain of attribute a_i is denoted by D_i. Formally, we let A be the set of all attributes and D be the set of all domains in R. We use the privacy model of confidentiality constraints that was originally introduced in [12], and subsequently has been used in [1,3,4,5,6,7,11]. Confidentiality constraints are sets of attributes within R that cannot be revealed together. The set of confidentiality constraints are written as $C = \{c_0, c_1, \ldots, c_m\}$ where $c_i \subseteq R$ for $i \in (0, m]$. Confidentiality constraints can be singletons, implying that privacy will be compromised if that specific attribute is visible. In the case of non-singleton constraints privacy is compromised through the association of the attributes, not any single attribute.

A sample relational dataset and corresponding confidentiality constraints are shown in Fig. 1. For instance, c_0, a singleton confidentiality constraint, indicates that to maintain data privacy the **SSN** must be obscured. Similarly, c_3, indicates that privacy will be violated if **Zip, Dob,** and **CardNumber** all appear in plaintext together. To satisfy this constraint, the relationship needs to be obscured, not every attribute in the tuple.

CardNumber	Name	DoB	Zip	SSN	Code
1234 5678 9012 3456	J. Johnson	03/01/85	98765	012-34-5678	135
2345 6789 0123 4567	B. Roberts	04/02/86	87654	123-45-6789	246
3456 7890 1234 5678	S. Smith	05/03/87	76543	234-56-7890	357
4567 8901 2345 6789	M. Michaels	06/04/88	65432	345-67-8901	468
5678 9012 3456 7890	A. Alexander	07/05/89	54321	456-78-9012	579

$c_0 = \{\text{SSN}\}$, $c_1 = \{\text{Name, Zip, DoB}\}$, $c_2 = \{\text{Name, CardNumber}\}$
$c_3 = \{\text{Zip, DoB, CardNumber}\}$, $c_4 = \{\text{CardNumber, Code}\}$

Fig. 1. Credit Card Relational Dataset and corresponding Confidentiality Constraints

2.1 Previous Solutions

Several solutions have presented methods to outsource a portion of the database as plaintext, which allows the client to query parts of the database efficiently. The first method proposed for outsourcing data as plaintext was introduced in [1]. This method divides the outsourced data into two fragments that are to be stored on separate, non-communicating servers. These fragments are constructed in such a way as to satisfy the maximum number of confidentiality constraints. Any remaining unsatisfied confidentiality constraints are then satisfied either through encoding or encrypting specific

salt	enc	Name	Zip	Code
s_1	α	J.Johnson	98765	135
s_2	β	B. Roberts	87654	246
s_3	γ	S. Smith	76543	357
s_4	δ	M. Michaels	65432	468
s_5	ϵ	A. Alexander	54321	579

salt	enc	CardNumber	DoB
s_6	ζ	1234 5678 9012 3456	03/01/85
s_7	η	2345 6789 0123 4567	04/02/86
s_8	θ	3456 7890 1234 5678	05/03/87
s_9	ι	4567 8901 2345 6789	06/04/88
s_{10}	κ	5678 9012 3456 7890	07/05/89

Fig. 2. Correct fragmentation of dataset in Fig 1

attributes. The second method proposed for outsourcing data as plaintext was introduced in [4] and refined in [3]. This method is similar to the method in [1] except it doesn't require the strong assumption of non-communicating servers. This method divides the data into fragments to be stored on one or more servers. Encryption is applied at the attribute level to satisfy confidentiality constraints and prevent the linking of data between fragments. Similarly, salt is applied to each encryption to prevent frequency attacks. An example of correct fragmentation using this method can be seen in Fig. 2. The final method proposed for outsourcing data as plaintext was introduced in [6,5]. This method, similar to the method in [1] divides the data into two fragments. The first fragment, which is maintained by the data owner, contains all sensitive attributes, or attributes in a relationship that could be used as a quasi-identifier. The second fragment contains the remaining attributes and is outsourced. A summary of methods for outsourcing data with plaintext can be found in [7,11].

2.2 Problem Definition

The solution in [6,5] describes a scheme that relies on that the data owner to maintain a significant portion of the data. The amount of storage needed to store a single fragment only differs from storing the entire database by a constant factor. Similarly, [1] requires the assumption that the servers hosting the data lack the ability to communicate with one another. This is a strong assumption that is impossible to mandate in a real-world implementation.

A drawback of the solutions described in [3,4], occurs when there exists a set of attributes where each attribute isn't highly selective by itself, but the conjunction of the attributes is highly selective. More formally, suppose attributes $R.A$ and $R.B$ are in different fragments and many queries of the from $\sigma_{A=p_1 \wedge B=p_2}(R)$ are issued. To answer using the method in [4,3] one needs to obtain $\sigma_{A=p_1}(R)$ or $\sigma_{B=p_2}(R)$. The main contribution of this paper is an index-strategy that allows the system to answer the query $\sigma_{A=p_1 \wedge B=p_2}(R)$ efficiently. This technique could be used for multiple pairs of attributes. Having such an index adds a cost to the system, but the benefits and disadvantages can be considered by the data owner, much like a DBA considers the pros and cons of adding an index to a traditional DBMS to improve performance.

3 Proposed Scheme

Our scheme is presented in the context of maintaining privacy in a relational dataset where there are two attributes; scenarios involving more than two attributes are not formally addressed and are left as potential extensions to the scheme. For our scheme we also assume that the data owner has access to a unspecified amount of secure local storage(T). Our scheme is most effective when used in conjunction with the scheme in [4,3]. That is these schemes will be used to handle most queries, and our index technique will only be used to handle conjunctive selection queries over R. Before describing our scheme we introduce the Attribute Matrix as a method for representing the relationships between two attributes in a dataset.

Definition 1. *(Attribute Matrix)*
An attribute matrix M for two attributes A_1 and A_2, is an mxn matrix, where $m = |D_1|, n = |D_2|$ and D_1 is the domain of A_1 and D_2 is the domain of A_2. Each entry in M_{ij} corresponds to the number of records in the data set where $a_1 = v_i$ and $a_2 = v_j$ ($v_i \in D_1$ and $v_j \in D_2$). Every attribute matrix has a set of row and column totals V and W s.t. $V_i = \sum M_{i*}$ and $W_j = \sum M_{*j}$.

Given an attribute matrix M for two attributes a_1 and a_2 that are stored on different fragments. We would like the server to be able to answer queries of the form $\sigma_{a_1=c_1 \wedge a_2=c_2}(R)$ for constants $c_1 \in D_1$ and $c_2 \in D_2$. In this example, suppose that the confidentiality constraints state that information about the relationship between a_1 and a_2 must be hidden. Ideally, a solution would return only $M_{c_1c_2}$ records, but this may reveal information about the relationship between a_1 and a_2. As an example, suppose that the first attribute has a domain $\{A, B\}$, and the second attribute also has a domain $\{\epsilon, \delta\}$, and that the server knows that there are 9 A's, 6B's, 11 δ's, and 4 ϵ's (which it knows since it has a_1 in plaintext form in one table and a_2 in plaintext from in the other table). Suppose that the adversary discovered that the conjunction of $A\delta = 7$ then the adversary also discovers the remaining cells in the attribute matrix (that is there must be 2 $A\epsilon$, 4 $B\delta$, and 1 $B\epsilon$. Hence, in order for a solution to be secure against such leakage, it must not reveal anything that is not deducible from the V and W values. It is acceptable to reveal such information, because the adversary has the V and W values.

The main idea of our approach is to designate a query response size b, where if $M_{ij} < b$ then additional records will be added to pad to b. Similarly, for every $M_{ij} > b$, then b records will be outsourced and $M_{ij} - b$ records will be stored locally by the data owner. To answer a query $\sigma_{A=p_1 \wedge B=p_2}(R)$, the querier simply obtains the b cells corresponding to this entry and retrieves any values in its local storage. In the situation the data owner can select a larger b to reduce the number of records to be stored locally or select a smaller b and store more records locally. Therefore, our scheme creates an inverse relationship between query performance and required storage, thus making it a potential solution for all datasets regardless of the amount of available local storage.

3.1 Calculating Storage

The amount of local storage (T) required depends on the number of records in the dataset, the attribute distribution within these records, and the query response size (b). We assume that the server hosting the data doesn't know the attribute matrix M, but that it does know the row totals V, the column totals W, the query size requirement b, and the amount of secure local storage being used T. The goal is to determine if it is possible to outsource the data using these parameters. With this capability, the outsourcer could choose either b or T and then calculate the minimum T or b values.

A naive approach is to calculate the required storage directly by using the attribute matrix. For elements in the attribute matrix that exceed the b, store the excess locally. That is, $T = \sum_{i=1}^{m} \sum_{j=1}^{n} max\{M_{ij} - b, 0\}$. If the storage is calculated this way, then the hosting server will be able to use V, W, b, and the amount of local storage, T, to infer a large portion, if not all, of the original attribute matrix. For example, if we return to the example in the previous section and the server sees that $b = 5$ and $T = 2$, then the server is able to infer that the number of values with $A\delta$ is 7 (as this is the only such combination that requires $T = 2$ when $b = 5$.

Therefore, in order to guarantee that additional information isn't leaked to the server, we need to calculate our storage needs based on information already known to the server, primarily V, W, and b. By restricting our technique to information already known to the server we don't reveal any additional information to the server. Thus the goal is to determine if every attribute matrix M that satisfies $V$and W can be stored using T local storage and b query time. The following problem can be used to determine if such a (b, T) pair is sufficient for V and W.

Problem 1. (Optimal Storage) Given an attribute matrix row total V, attribute matrix column total W, the query response size b, and a target amount of local storage T, does there exist an attribute matrix M, such that $\sum_{i=1}^{m} \sum_{j=1}^{n} max\{M_{ij} - b, 0\} \leq T$.

Theorem 1. *The Optimal Storage Problem is NP-Hard*

Proof. (Sketch) The proof is a reduction from Subset Sum. Recall that Subset sum is: Given natural numbers $s_1, \ldots s_n$, and a target number t, is there $S' \subseteq S$ whose sum is precisely t?

The reduction can be constructed in the following way. First, we assume the existence of a black box function $H(\cdot, \cdot, \cdot, \cdot)$ that can solve the Optimal Storage problem in a polynomial amount of time. If we construct the input as follows, $V = S$, set $|W| = 2$ where $w_1 = t$ and $w_2 = \sum_{s \in S}(s - t)$, let $b = 1$ and finally set $T = \sum\limits_{s \in S}(s) - (b \cdot m)$. If H returns 1, then this implies there is a solution to subset sum, otherwise there is not. Therefore, Optimal Storage must be NP-HARD. □

3.2 Approximating Storage

Since determining the necessary storage, based upon V and W is NP-Hard, we propose an approximation($APRX$) that determines the storage requirement for a dataset. The approximation is based upon a few basic observations. The first observations is, $\forall_i$ where $V_i \leq b$ no local storage will be required for this row of the attribute matrix. The rationale behind this is that if a single row total is less than or equal to b, then it is impossible for any entry in the row to be greater than b. Therefore, when approximating the storage, we discard all rows whose total is not greater than b. Thus, without loss of generality, we assume that each V_i and W_j are larger than b.

The second observation is when $V_i > b$, then the most that an individual row can contribute to the local storage is $V_i - b$, because the worst case would be that all values are placed in a single cell. It is straightforward to see this observations holds true when considering columns as well as rows. Using these two observations we then formulate our approximation algorithm as follows: $APRX(V, W, b) = (\sum_{i=0}^{m} V_i) - max\{m, n\}b$.

We offer an additional method of approximating the required local storage. This method is similar to the first, but requires that we reveal a value u to the local server, with the claim that there does not exist a value in the attribute matrix that exceeds u. This reveals some additional information to the adversary, but this leakage may be acceptable in some circumstances. Since the adversary knows that there does not exist an entry in the matrix that exceeds u, he can discover a minimum of how many non-zero entries exist in a particular row or column of the attribute matrix. This information is the crux of our new approximation algorithm. $APRX'(V, W, b, u) = \sum_{i=0}^{m} V_i - max\{1, \lfloor V_i/u \rfloor\}b$

By divulging more information to the adversary we can help minimize the amount of wasted storage space. It is apparent that $u \in [max\{A_{ij}\}, max\{V \cup W\}]$. If we let $u < max\{A_{ij}\}$ then the amount of storage will be insufficient because there exists an entry in the attribute matrix that exceeds u. Thus, by using $APRX'$ the data owner can achieve an adequate balance between privacy and required storage.

Theorem 2. *The storage required for $APRX \geq OPT$, where OPT is the maximum storage required for any attribute matrix that can produce the row and column totals V, W.*

Proof. (Sketch)

First, we are given the row and column totals V, W for an attribute matrix and a query response size b. It is known that all row and column totals must be greater than b otherwise that row or column will not contribute to the required storage. It is also obvious that each row and column must have at least one non-zero entry in it. Therefore, it can be inferred that at least b elements from each row or column can be outsourced, thus leaving the remaining data to be stored locally. Since this requirement holds for both rows and columns, we can determine the minimum amount to be outsourced based upon whether there are more rows or columns. Thus, the data to be stored must be less than the the entire dataset minus b times the maximum of m and n. The proof that $APRX' \geq OPT$ follows a similar construction. □

4 Experiments and Results

The approximation algorithms presented in Section 3.2 have been implemented to obtain experimental data to assess the quality of the algorithms in terms of the accuracy of the calculated storage and query response size. For both $APRX$ and $APRX'$ we generated 100,000 random attribute matrices. For every possible b value we calculated the percentage of the dataset that would have to be stored locally based on our approximation as well as the average query response size as a percentage of the average query response size for the same matrix using the methods in [4,3]. Figure 3 shows the matrix that produced the best and worst results for each approximation.

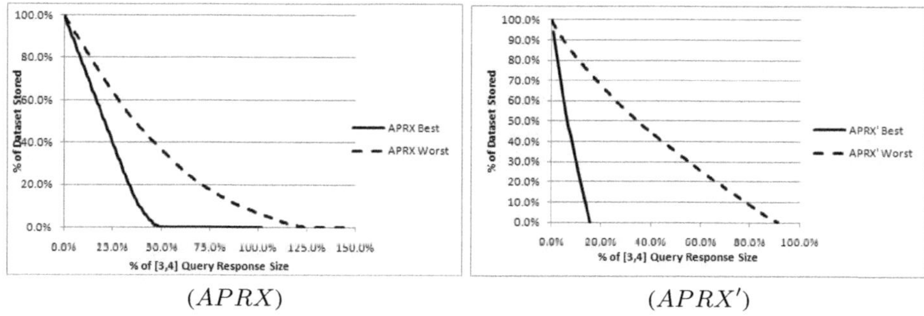

$(APRX)$ $(APRX')$

Fig. 3. Experimental Storage and Query Response Size

5 Related Work

The data outsourcing paradigm has been the focus of a significant amount of research. The work in [2,8,9,13] propose encrypting the data entirely and propose novel methods for efficient query evaluation. The encrypted data usually is accompanied by an index of the data to aid in query evaluation. Similar to all these methods is the solution in [14], where the authors propose a method for allowing people to query statistical information from the data, while protecting the data itself. Work done by the authors in [10] claim that it is infeasible to traditionally query encrypted data efficiently while maintaining security. The authors propose a system that meets a revised definition of security and an efficient query processing method.

6 Conclusions

This paper presented an approach to improve query performance when outsourcing data in the data as plaintext model. Specifically we were interested in improving the performance of queries where the attributes in the query are not highly selective independently, but the conjunction of the attributes is highly selective. The solution presented achieves the desired query performance by leveraging the data owner's secure local storage. The amount of storage required is independent of the dataset and is determined by the data owner based upon desired query performance and availability of storage. In this paper we offer two approximation algorithms for calculating the required storage for a given dataset. We also provide experimental results showing that the approximations we offer are a relatively good estimate for the actual amount of storage.

Acknowledgments

The authors would like to thank the anonymous reviewers for their comments and useful suggestions. Portions of this work were supported by Grant CNS-0915843 from the National Science Foundation.

References

1. Aggarwal, G., Bawa, M., Ganesan, P., Garcia-molina, H., Kenthapadi, K., Motwani, R., Srivastava, U., Thomas, D., Xu, Y.: Two can keep a secret: A distributed architecture for secure database services. In: Proc. CIDR (2005)
2. Cesell, A., Damiani, E., De Capitani Di Vimercati, S., Jajodia, S., Paraboschi, S., Samarati, P.: Modeling and assessing inference exposure in encrypted databases. ACM Trans. Inf. Syst. Secur. 8, 119–152 (2005)
3. Ciriani, V., De Capitani di Vimercati, S., Foresti, S., Jajodia, S., Paraboschi, S., Samarati, P.: Fragmentation design for efficient query execution over sensitive distributed databases. In: 29th IEEE International Conference on Distributed Computing Systems, ICDCS 2009, pp. 32–39 (22-26, 2009)
4. Ciriani, V., De Capitani di Vimercati, S., Foresti, S., Jajodia, S., Paraboschi, S., Samarati, P.: Combining fragmentation and encryption to protect privacy in data storage. In: ACM TISSEC (2010)
5. Ciriani, V., De Capitani di Vimercati, S., Foresti, S., Jajodia, S., Paraboschi, S., Samarati, P.: Keep a few: Outsourcing data while maintaining confidentiality. In: Backes, M., Ning, P. (eds.) ESORICS 2009. LNCS, vol. 5789, pp. 440–455. Springer, Heidelberg (2009)
6. Ciriani, V., De Capitani di Vimercati, S., Foresti, S., Jajodia, S., Paraboschi, S., Samarati, P.: Enforcing confidentiality constraints on sensitive databases with lightweight trusted clients. In: Gudes, E., Vaidya, J. (eds.) Data and Applications Security XXIII. LNCS, vol. 5645, pp. 225–239. Springer, Heidelberg (2009)
7. De Capitani di Vimercati, S., Foresti, S.: Privacy of outsourced data. In: Bezzi, M., Duquenoy, P., Fischer-Hübner, S., Hansen, M., Zhang, G. (eds.) IFIP AICT, vol. 320, pp. 174–187. Springer, Heidelberg (2010)
8. Iyer, B., Hacigümüş, H., Mehrotra, S.: Providing database as a service. In: Proc. of ICDE (2002)
9. Hacigümüş, H., Iyer, B., Li, C., Mehrotra, S.: Executing sql over encrypted data in the database-service-provider model. In: SIGMOD 2002: Proceedings of the 2002 ACM SIGMOD International Conference on Management of Data, pp. 216–227. ACM, New York (2002)
10. Kantarcioglu, M., Clifton, C.: Security issues in querying encrypted data. Technical Report TR-04-013, Purdue University (2004)
11. Samarati, P., De Capitani di Vimercati, S.: Data protection in outsourcing scenarios: Issues and directions. In: ASIACCS 2010: Proceedings of the 5th ACM Symposium on Information, Computer and Communications Security, pp. 1–14. ACM, New York (2010)
12. Agrawaland, R., Srikant, R.: Privacy-preserving data mining. SIGMOD Rec. 29, 439–450 (2000)
13. Wang, H., Lakshmanan, L.: Efficient secure query evaluation over encrypted xml databases. In: Proceedings of the 32nd International Conference on Very Large Data Bases, VLDB 2006, pp. 127–138. VLDB Endowment (2006)
14. Xiong, L., Chitti, S., Liu, L.: Preserving data privacy in outsourcing data aggregation services. ACM Trans. Internet Technol. 7(3), 17 (2007)

Selective Disclosure on Encrypted Documents

Hao Lei* and Dengguo Feng

State Key Laboratory of Information Security(SKLOIS), China
leiyokster@gmail.com

Abstract. With tackling the dilemma between the privacy concern and information utilization in mind, an efficient pairing-based instantiation of a new primitive, which we call Selective Disclosure scheme, is proposed in this paper. Selective Disclosure scheme allows the document issuer to distribute and publish the outsourced document in a secure way such that it achieves fine-grained authorized reading by selective parts in a document to different visitors and only one copy is needed. It is proved secure against fully adaptive adversaries in the random oracle model. The Selective Disclosure technique will be of use by embedding or integrating it into various word processors, e-mail,.etc.

Keywords: Selective Disclosure, Privacy-Preserved Information Utilization, Plaintext Awareness Secure.

1 Introduction

With respect to all content in an outsourced document, it is reasonable that the content is selective disclosure to different visitors for the sake of document owner's privacy. That is, every visitor only has access to the information specified by the document owner, who totally controls and puts on different restrictions for different visitors. So, for the same document, the content read by different visitors is different. For example, in the case of a Blog document, a document visitor may be Blog owner's soul-mate, real friend, good friend, or just a simple friend. In this case, although they are all permissible visitors, it is reasonable that what a simple friend can read is different from what a soul-mate can.

In general, assume there are n kinds of permissible visitors related to a document, that is, n is the number of selective disclosure views stemming from this document. Once attempting to achieve above selective disclosure goals, a common approach appears below using known techniques (1) According to the dedicated content to be presented, the document owner creates n different copies from the original document. (2) For every copy, document owner selects n different keys, generates n different encrypted copies, and outsources them to the storage server. (3)The document owner distributes the corresponding decryption key to every matched permissible visitor. (4) Every permissible visitor can decrypt the encrypted dedicated copy and obtain the selective disclosure view.

* This is the extended abstract, June 3, 2011.

Y. Li (Ed.): Data and Applications Security and Privacy XXV, LNCS 6818, pp. 255–262, 2011.

This way has two significant drawbacks in terms of efficiency, functionality and security analysis: (1) It is very troublesome for the document owner to generate n different dedicated copies and n different encrypted copies. (2) These n encrypted dedicated copies would require more storage space because of the redundant content among them.

Besides the above two applications, we find the selective disclosure also plays an important role in the scenario of outsourced storage [9], peer-to-peer storage systems [6,10], long-term archives[11], and web-service object stores [16], all of which share both information utilization and privacy concerns. In general, for the sake of data security and privacy, the outsourced document must be encrypted by the document owner before outsourcing to a third party storage provider.

1.1 Requirements, and Related Technologies

From above observations, the main security requirements of Selective Disclosure (SD for short) on outsourced documents can be phased as (1) It is the document owner that controls the content disclosed to different visitors, which means that the restrictions to every parts of the outsourced document are to be set by the document owner on his/her own, instead of a so-called trusted administrator, and SD guarantees the restrictions can be enforced correctly and strictly. This is termed as *document owner centric control property.* (2) Visitors with different permission can review different content, but they cannot read more content even if all of them collude against the document owner.

In the view of practical concerns such as functionality and performance, the following three requirements must also be taken into accounts (1) It admits any selective part (Paragraphs, Sections, Pages, etc.) contained in a document, and any subset of possible visitors, both of which are chosen ad hoc by the document owner. (2) It allows that every visitor can perform decryption independently without cooperation or any help from others. (3) Last but not the least, regardless of multiple views stemming from the original document, only one real copy of this document remains in storage and it incurs no additional storage costs.

Besides the above 5 requirements, a practical Selective Disclosure scheme must be provably secure without doubt.

The technologies that are closely related to Selective Disclosure are in three different areas, namely (1) *Traditional Access Control Approach*, (2)*Revocation and Broadcast Encryption[3,15,14,12,5,4,7,13]*, and *Attribute-Based Encryption[1,8]*. The detailed introduction about related work as well as the difference between SD and them is listed in full version.

1.2 Key Idea, Challenges, and Our Contribution

The key idea to achieve the five requirements of SD at the same time is to aggregate all impermissible visitors for each part as a whole and use it to construct cipher text.

Our approach presents us with two challenges. First, we need to make sure that an impermissible visitor cannot do anything useful with his/her private key,

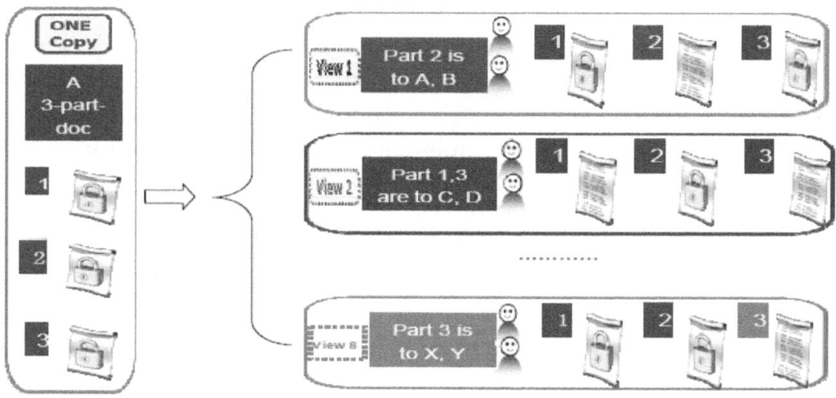

Fig. 1. SD enables eight views stemming from a three-part-document

even they collude against the document owner. Second, simply combining the ABE and revocation technologies is not sufficient, and we must ensure that not only the public and private keys, but also the ciphertext are of size independent of the number of permissible visitors.

With tackling the dilemma between the privacy concern and information utilization in mind, we propose an efficient pairing-based instantiation of a new primitive, which we call Selective Disclosure scheme. It allows the document issuer to distribute and publish the outsourced document in a secured way such that it achieves fine-grained authorized reading by selective parts in a document to different visitors and only one copy is needed. We then proved it is secure against fully adaptive adversaries in the random oracle model. To the best of our knowledge, there is no previous solution to enable selective disclosure on a document while incurs no additional storage consumption. The following Figure 1 presents a document with 3 parts which are selective disclosure to 8 different subsets of permissible visitors.

2 Syntax for SD Scheme

Before presenting our SD scheme we briefly review the definition as well as its security formulation for an SD scheme. If S is a set then $s \in_R S$ denotes the operation of picking an element s of S uniformly at random. We write $A(x, y, \ldots)$ to indicate that A is an algorithm with inputs $x, y, \ldots$ and by $z \stackrel{R}{\leftarrow} A(x, y, \ldots)$ we denote the operation of running probabilistic algorithm A with inputs $x, y, \ldots$ and letting z be the output. $z \leftarrow A(x, y, \ldots)$ indicates that A is a deterministic algorithm.

2.1 Syntax for SD Scheme

Regarding to a part m contained in document, let Q denote all visitors who are represented by his/her public key pk_i, and $\overline{Q}_R \subset Q$ be a subset of impermissible visitors to m. A SD scheme consists of the following four algorithms:

$(Msk, Params) \stackrel{R}{\leftarrow} Setup(1^k)$. The setup algorithm, on input security parameter 1^k, outputs a master secret key Msk and public parameters $Params$.

$(PK_i, SK_i) \stackrel{R}{\leftarrow} KeyGen(Msk, Params, ID_i)$. The key generation algorithm takes as input master secret key Msk , public parameters $Params$ and user's identifier ID_i, outputs the corresponding public key PK_i and private key SK_i.

$C \stackrel{R}{\leftarrow} Enc(\overline{Q}_R, Params, m, SK_s)$. The encryption algorithm takes as input a document's portion $m \in \{0,1\}^{k_0}$ together with public parameters $Params$, the owner's private key SK_s , and $\overline{Q}_R \subset Q$ which are impermissible visitors to m, outputs C which is the encryption of m for permissible visitors $Q/\overline{Q}_R$. The encryption algorithm is run by the document owner.

$m/\perp \leftarrow Dec(C, \overline{Q}_R, Params, SK_i, PK_i)$. The decryption algorithm takes as input the cipher text C together with public parameters $Params$, the permissible visitor private key SK_i and all the public keys of impermissible visitors $\overline{Q}_R$ to m , outputs correct plaintext $m \in \{0,1\}^{k_0}$. Otherwise, it returns $\perp$. This algorithm is run by anyone of the permissible visitors independently.

2.2 The IND-SD-CPA Security Game and Plaintext Awareness

The security for a SD scheme $\Pi = (Setup, KeyGen, Enc, Dec)$ is formulated by the following IND-SD-CPA experiment between an attacker A and a challenger B. Furthermore, we strengthen the standard definition of IND-CPA game by allowing the attacker A to issue chosen private key extraction queries.

Experiment $Exp_{A,\Pi}^{IND-\mathrm{SD-CPA-b}}(k)$

$(Msk, Params) \stackrel{R}{\leftarrow} \mathrm{Setup}(g_1, g_2, \mathrm{e}(\cdot,\cdot))$.

$\forall ID_i \in \{0,1\}^*, (pk_i, sk_i) \stackrel{R}{\leftarrow} \mathrm{KeyGen}(Msk, Params, ID_i)$.

$Q = \{pk_1, ..., pk_n\}$.

$(m_0, m_1, ID_c) \leftarrow \mathrm{A}^{\mathrm{O}_H, \mathrm{O}_{sk}}(Params, Q)$.

$pk_c \leftarrow \mathrm{KeyGen}(Msk, Params, ID_c)$.

$\mathrm{b} \in_R \{0,1\}; \bar{Q}_R = Q/\{(x_c, pk_c)\}; C^* \leftarrow \mathrm{Enc}_{\bar{Q}_R}(m_\mathrm{b})$.

$\mathrm{b}' \leftarrow \mathrm{A}^{\mathrm{O}_H, \mathrm{O}_{sk}}(C^*, Params, Q)$.

return b′

Definition 1(IND-SD-CPA Secure)[2]. A SD scheme Π is secure against IND-CPA if for $k \in N$ and $b \in_R \{0,1\}$, $Adv_{A,\Pi}^{IND-\mathrm{SD-CPA}}(k) = |Pr[Exp_{A,\Pi}^{IND-\mathrm{SD-CPA-1}}(k) = 1] - \Pr[Exp_{A,\Pi}^{IND-\mathrm{SD-CPA-0}}(k) = 1]|$ is negligible. The probability is over the random bits consumed by both the challenger B and adversary$A$.

Plaintext Awareness(PA) was defined in [2] and it formalizes an adversary's inability to create ciphertext without knowing its corresponding plaintext m. PA can be achieved through constructing a $\lambda(k)$-Knowledge Extractor K on the basis of proved secure in the sense of IND-CPA, and PA implies SD is security against IND-CCA2 [2]. The following is a formal definition for PA and $\lambda(k)$-Knowledge Extractor.

Let Π = (Setup, KeyGen, Enc, Dec) be an encryption scheme, let B be an adversary, and let K be a knowledge extractor. For every $k \in N$ define:

$$Succ^{PA}_{\Pi,B,K}(k) \stackrel{def}{=} \Pr[H \leftarrow Hash; (pk, sk) \leftarrow K(k);$$
$$(hH, C, y) \leftarrow \mathrm{runB}^{O_H, Enc^H_{pk}}(pk) : \mathrm{K}(hH, C, y, pk) = \mathrm{D}^H_{sk}(y)] \geq \lambda(k)$$

Definition 2 ($\lambda(k)$-Knowledge Extractor [2]). We say that K is a $\lambda(k)$-extractor if K has running time polynomial in the length of its inputs and for every B, $Succ^{PA}_{\Pi,B,K} \geq \lambda(k)$ where $1 - \lambda(k)$ is negligible and $y \notin C$, where C is the queried cipher text set.

Definition 3 (Plaintext Awareness Secure [2]). We say that Π is secure in the sense of PA if Π is secure in the sense of IND-CPA and there exists a $\lambda(k)$-extractor K.

3 A CCA2 Secure SD Scheme and Its Application

SD scheme is a pairing-based cryptology methodology based on the following general decisional q-BDHI assumption. Let G_1, G_2 and G_T be cyclic groups with the same prime order $p(|p| = k)$,where $k = k_0 + k_1$ is the security parameter. The parameter k_0 determines the size of plaintext to be encrypted, i.e.,$m \in \{0,1\}^{k_0}$. There exists an efficient computationally bilinear map $e : G_1 \times G_2 \rightarrow G_T$ with bilinearity and non-degeneracy properties, and a computable isomorphism ψ : $G_2 \rightarrow G_1$.

General Decisional q-BDHI Assumption is defined as follows.

Definition 4(General Decisional q-BDHI Assumption). Taking a $(q+4)$-tuple $(x_c, g_1, g_2, g_2^{\gamma}, g_2^{\gamma^2}, \cdots, g_2^{\gamma^q}, T) \in Z_p^* \times G_1 \times G_2^{q+1} \times G_T$ as input where $\gamma \in_R Z_P^*$, no P.P.T. adversary$A$ has non-negligible advantage $\varepsilon(k)$ in distinguishing whether T is $e(g_1, g_2)^{1/(\gamma+x_c)}$ or a random in group G_T. That is, with respect to $|\Pr[A(x_c, g_1, g_2, g_2^{\gamma}, g_2^{\gamma^2}, \cdots, g_2^{\gamma^q}, e(g_1, g_2)^{1/(\gamma+x_c)}) = 1] - \Pr[A(x_c, g_1, g_2, g_2^{\gamma}, g_2^{\gamma^2}, \cdots, g_2^{\gamma^q}, T) = 1]|$, the advantage $\varepsilon(k)$ for any P.P.T. adversary A is negligible.

Let g_1 and g_2 be a generator of G_1 and G_2 respectively. Let $Q = \{pk_1, ..., pk_{q-1}\}$ denotes all of the visitors (including document owner) in a SD scheme where $pk_i = (ID_i, x_i, B_i)$ and the ID_i is the identifier of visitor i. The IND-SD-CCA2 scheme is proposed in the following Table 1.

It is easy to see that the decryption algorithm is consistent. Indeed, if C is a valid cipher text, then we have

$$\begin{aligned} D_2 &= e(C_1, F^{\bar{Q}_R \cup \{x_i\}}) \cdot e(A_i, C_2) \cdot D_1 \\ &= e(u^t, F^{\bar{Q}_R \cup \{x_i\}}) \cdot e(A_i, w^t \cdot (F^{\bar{Q}_R})^t) \cdot e(u^t, B_i)^{-x_i} \\ &= e(h^{\gamma t}, (F^{\bar{Q}_R})^{\frac{1}{\gamma+x_i}}) \cdot e(h^{\frac{x_i}{\gamma+x_i}}, (F^{\bar{Q}_R})^t) \cdot e(h^{\frac{x_i}{\gamma+x_i}}, g_2^{\gamma t}) \cdot e(h^{\gamma t}, g_2^{\frac{1}{\gamma+x_i}})^{-x_i} \\ &= e(h, F^{\bar{Q}_R})^t \in G_T. \end{aligned}$$

Then $\frac{C_3}{D_2} = \frac{e(A_s,v)^t \cdot e(h,F^{\bar{Q}_R})^t}{e(h,F^{\bar{Q}_R})^t} = e(A_s, v)^t$, hence $\hat{M} = C_4 \oplus \mathrm{H}_2(\frac{C_3}{D_2}) = C_4 \oplus \mathrm{H}_2(V) = \hat{m}||\hat{s}$.

The algorithm for computing $F^{\bar{Q}_R} = g_2^{\frac{1}{(\gamma+x_1)\cdot(\gamma+x_2)\cdots(\gamma+x_d)}} \in G_2$ can be found in [14], i.e., to aggregate all impermissible visitors $\bar{Q}_R$ on m. In addition, for efficiency consideration as well as avoiding the direct application of private key

Table 1. The IND-SD-CCA2 scheme

Setup(1^k)
$g_1, h \in_R G_1, g_2, v \in_R G_2, \gamma \in_R Z_p^*, u = h^\gamma \in G_1, w = g_2^\gamma \in G_2$, $\mathrm{H}: \{0,1\}^* \rightarrow \mathrm{Z}_p^*$, H_1: $\{0,1\}^k \rightarrow \mathrm{Z}_p^*$, H_2: $\mathrm{G}_T \rightarrow \{0,1\}^k$, $Msk \leftarrow \gamma$, $Params \leftarrow (g_1, h, u = h^\gamma, g_2, w = g_2^\gamma, v, e(\cdot,\cdot), \mathrm{H}, \mathrm{H}_1, \mathrm{H}_2)$. Output$(Msk, Params)$
KeyGen$(Msk, Params, ID_i)$
$\mathrm{H}(ID_i) = x_i, SK_i = A_i = h^{\frac{x_i}{\gamma + x_i}} \in G_1, B_i = g_2^{\frac{1}{\gamma + x_i}} \in G_2, PK_i = (ID_i, x_i, B_i)$. Output$(SK_i, PK_i)$
Enc$(m, Params, SK_s, \bar{Q}_R)$
$s \in_R \{0,1\}^{k_1}, t = \mathrm{H}_1(m\|\|s) \in Z_p^*, V = e(A_s, v)^t \in_R G_T$, $F^{\bar{Q}_R} = g_2^{\frac{1}{(\gamma+x_1)\cdot(\gamma+x_2)\cdot\cdots\cdot(\gamma+x_d)}} \in G_2$, $C \leftarrow \{u^t, w^t \cdot (F^{\bar{Q}_R})^t, e(A_s, v)^t \cdot e(h, F^{\bar{Q}_R})^t, (m\|\|s) \oplus \mathrm{H}_2(e(A_s, v)^t)\}$. Output(C,$\bar{Q}_R$)
Dec$(C, \bar{Q}_R, Params, SK_i, PK_i)$
Parse C $as\{\mathrm{C}_1, \mathrm{C}_2, \mathrm{C}_3, \mathrm{C}_4\}$. $If\ PK_i \notin \bar{Q}_R: \quad F^{\bar{Q}_R \cup \{x_i\}} = g_2^{\frac{1}{(\gamma+x_1)\cdot(\gamma+x_2)\cdot\cdots\cdot(\gamma+x_v)} \cdot \frac{1}{(\gamma+x_i)}} = (F^{\bar{Q}_R})^{\frac{1}{\gamma+x_i}}$. $D_1 = e(C_1, B_i)^{-x_i} = e(A_i, g_2^{\gamma t})^{-1} \in G_T$, $D_2 = e(C_1, F^{\bar{Q}_R \cup \{x_i\}}) \cdot e(A_i, C_2) \cdot D_1 = e(h, F^{\bar{Q}_R})^t \in G_T$, $\hat{M} = C_4 \oplus \mathrm{H}_2(\frac{C_3}{D_2}) = C_4 \oplus \mathrm{H}_2(e(A_s, v)^t), \quad \hat{t} = \mathrm{H}_1(\hat{M}) \in Z_p^*$. $If\ C_1 \neq u^{\hat{t}}, C_2 \neq w^{\hat{t}} \cdot (F^{\bar{Q}_R})^{\hat{t}}$, output $\perp$. Output $m = [M]_{k_0}$.

A_s in practical use, the component $e(A_s, v)$ of C_3 can be pre-computed and one time pairing can be saved.

To testify the potential practical use of SD scheme, we show that SD scheme enables us to add selective disclosure property to the Microsoft Word in a secure manner.Firstly,the document owner highlights the dedicated part that desires to put restrictions on, then s/he selects the impermissible visitors from a list of all the potential visitors, which is analogous to the one of selecting recipients from the mail list. Secondly,the dedicated part will be encrypted according to SD scheme. Thus, every visitor only has access to the information specified by the document owner, who totally restricts the information content and puts on different restriction for different visitors.

4 Security Proof for IND-SD-CCA2

Informally, the security of SD scheme is equivalent to the nonexistence of an adversary that is capable, within the confines of a certain game, of decrypting the cipher text on the condition that she/he is impermissible visitor.

By the definition 4.1 in [2], the security in the sense of IND-CPA and the existence of a knowledge extractor imply the security in the sense of Plaintext Awareness, which implies security against the adaptive chosen-ciphertext attack

(IND-CCA2) in virtue of the Theorem 4.2 in [2]. The detailed proof related to Theorem 1, Lemma 1 and Theorem 2 have been omitted because of space limit, and they are provided in the full version.

Firstly, the above SD scheme is IND-CPA secure according to Theorem 1.

Theorem 1. Let A be an adversary that has non-negligible advantage $\varepsilon(k)$ against the SD scheme in the sense of IND-SD-CPA. If the hash functions $\mathrm{H}(\cdot)$, $\mathrm{H}_1(\cdot)$ and $\mathrm{H}_2(\cdot)$ are modeled as random oracles, and we let $q > 0$, $q_1 > 0$, $q_2 > 0$ and $q_{sk} > 0$ be the number of queries that A makes to $\mathrm{H}(\cdot)$, $\mathrm{H}_1(\cdot)$, $\mathrm{H}_2(\cdot)$ and key generation oracle respectively. Then there is an algorithm B to solve the general decision q-BDHI problem in groups of order p with non-negligible advantage $\varepsilon(k)/2$.

Before conducting a knowledge extractor K, the following Lemma 1 elaborates $f_{u,v,w,h,\bar{Q}_R}(A_s, t)$ is injective. The partially trapdoor one-way function implied in the encryption function Encryption$(m, Params, SK_s, \bar{Q}_R)$is defined as $f_{u,v,w,h,\bar{Q}_R}(A_s, t) \mapsto \{u^t, w^t \cdot (F^{\bar{Q}_R})^t, e(A_s, v)^t \cdot e(h, F^{\bar{Q}_R})^t\}$.

Lemma 1. The function $f_{u,v,w,h,\bar{Q}_R}(A_s, t)$ is injective.

Now we turn to construct a knowledge extractor K in Theorem 2.

Theorem 2. Let B be an adversary for PA. Then there is a knowledge $\lambda(k)$-extractor K and hence the SD scheme is secure in the sense of PA, thus it is IND-CCA2.

5 Conclusion

In this paper, we proposed a secure Selective Disclosure Scheme that enables not only its content is selective disclosure to different document visitors, but also the dedicated information to every visitor is strict under the control of the document owner, while just requiring one real copy in storage and no additional storage consumption incurred.

Our work motivates two interesting open problems.The first is to find an efficient Selective Disclosure scheme in the case of a large number of impressible visitors. The second is to explore a Dynamic Selective Disclosure scheme, which comprises of the two requirements: (1) It allows new visitor added into existing permissible visitor set. Recall the proposed SD scheme only admits static visitor set, i.e., the impermissible visitor set must be determined prior to encryption. Otherwise, the new added member is able to read all the parts because he is not in *any* impressible visitor set. (2) It suits well to revoke permissible visitor, and/or make an impermissible visitor to be a permissible one, without constructing the cipher text from scratch.

Acknowledgments

Part of the work was done while the author was at High Privacy and Security group, NEC Labs., China. We are grateful to Ph.D Ke Zeng, and Ph.D Wenbin Chen for helpful discussions, and the anonymous reviewers for their comments.

References

1. Attrapadung, N., Imai, H.: Conjunctive Broadcast and Attribute-Based Encryption. In: Shacham, H., Waters, B. (eds.) Pairing 2009. LNCS, vol. 5671, pp. 248–265. Springer, Heidelberg (2009)
2. Bellare, M., Desai, A., Pointcheval, D., Rogaway, P.: Relations among Notions of Security for Public-key Encryption Schemes. In: Krawczyk, H. (ed.) CRYPTO 1998. LNCS, vol. 1462, pp. 26–45. Springer, Heidelberg (1998)
3. Fiat, A., Naor, M.: Broadcast Encryption. In: Stinson, D.R. (ed.) CRYPTO 1993. LNCS, vol. 773, pp. 480–491. Springer, Heidelberg (1994)
4. Goodrich, M.T., Sun, J.Z., Tamassia, R.: Efficient tree-based revocation in groups of low-state devices. In: Franklin, M. (ed.) CRYPTO 2004. LNCS, vol. 3152, pp. 511–527. Springer, Heidelberg (2004)
5. Halevy, D., Shamir, A.: The LSD Broadcast Encryption Scheme. In: Yung, M. (ed.) CRYPTO 2002. LNCS, vol. 2442, pp. 47–62. Springer, Heidelberg (2002)
6. Kubiatowicz, J., Bindel, D., Chen, Y., et al.: Oceanstore: An architecture for global-scale persistent
7. Kurosawa, K., Desmedt, Y.: Optimum traitor tracing and asymmetric schemes. In: Nyberg, K. (ed.) EUROCRYPT 1998. LNCS, vol. 1403, pp. 145–157. Springer, Heidelberg (1998)
8. Li, J., Ren, K., Kim, K.: A^2BE: Accountable Attribute-based Encryption for Abuse Free Access Control. Cryptology ePrint Archive, Report 2009/118 (2009)
9. Millstein, J.S., King, M., Morrison, Foerster, L.L.P.: Cloud Computing and Outsourcing: Is Data Lost in the Fog? (2009), `http://www.tawpi.org/uploadDocs/CloudComputingandOutsourcing.pdf`
10. Muthitacharoen, A.A., Morris, R., Gil, T.M., Chen, B.: Ivy: A read/write peer-to-peer file system. In: Proceedings of OSDI 2002, pp. 31–44 (2002)
11. Maniatis, P., Roussopoulos, M., Giuli, T., Rosenthal, D., Baker, M., Muliadi, Y.: The LOCKSS peer-to-peer digital preservation system. ACM Trans. on Computing Systems 23(1), 2–50 (2005)
12. Naor, D., Naor, M., Lotspiech, J.: Revocation and Tracing Schemes for Stateless Receivers. In: Kilian, J. (ed.) CRYPTO 2001. LNCS, vol. 2139, pp. 41–62. Springer, Heidelberg (2001)
13. Naor, M., Pinkas, B.: Efficient trace and revoke schemes. In: Frankel, Y. (ed.) FC 2000. LNCS, vol. 1962, pp. 1–20. Springer, Heidelberg (2001)
14. Delerablée, C., Paillier, P., Pointcheval, D.: Fully Collusion Secure Dynamic Broadcast Encryption with Constant-Size Ciphertexts or Decryption Keys. In: Takagi, T., Okamoto, T., Okamoto, E., Okamoto, T. (eds.) Pairing 2007. LNCS, vol. 4575, pp. 39–59. Springer, Heidelberg (2007)
15. Sahai, A., Waters, B.: Revocation Systems with Very Small Private Keys. Cryptology ePrint Archive, Report 2008/309 (2008)
16. Yumerefendi, A.Y., Chase, J.: Strong accountability for network storage. In: Proc. of FAST 2007, Trans. Storage, vol. 3(3) (2007)

A New Leakage-Resilient IBE Scheme in the Relative Leakage Model

Yu Chen*, Song Luo, and Zhong Chen

Information Security Lab, School of EECS, Peking University, Beijing, China
Key Laboratory of High Confidence Software Technologies, Ministry of Education
{chenyu,luosong,chen}@infosec.pku.edu.cn

Abstract. We propose the first leakage-resilient Identity-Based Encryption (IBE) scheme with full domain hash structure. Our scheme is leakage-resilient in the relative leakage model and the random oracle model under the decisional bilinear Diffie-Hellman (DBDH) assumption.

Keywords: identity based encryption, leakage-resilient, relative leakage, bilinear Diffie-Hellman assumption.

1 Introduction

Cryptographic schemes are used to be analyzed in an attack model in which the internal secret states are completely hidden from the adversary/attacker. However several works [13, 12] indicated that the attack model fails to capture many attacks in the real world, since the attacker may obtain some partial information about the secret states via various *key leakage attacks*. Therefore it is urgent to design leakage-resilient cryptographic schemes which remain provably secure in the strengthened attack model which takes *key leakage attacks* into account.

Recently, the research community pay a lot of attention to construct IBE schemes with leakage-resilience. Alwen et al. [1] presented three leakage-resilient IBE schemes from the Gentry IBE [10], the Boneh-Gentry-Hamburg IBE [4], and Gentry-Peikert-Vaikuntanathan IBE [11], respectively. Among them, the first scheme is secure in the standard model, while the other two schemes are secure in the random oracle model. Chow et al. [6] gave three new leakage-resilient IBE schemes from the Boneh-Boyen IBE [2], the Waters IBE [16], and the Lewko-Waters IBE [14], respectively. All of them are secure in the standard model.

Our Contributions. According to [5], IBE schemes from pairings can be classified into three broad families, the full-domain hash family (e.g. Boneh-Franklin IBE [3]), the exponent inversion family (e.g. Gentry-IBE [10]), and the commutative blinding family (e.g. Boneh-Boyen IBE [2]). The existing work [1, 6] have shown that IBE schemes from the exponent inversion family and commutative

* Supported by National Natural Science Foundation of China (No.61073156).

Y. Li (Ed.): Data and Applications Security and Privacy XXV, LNCS 6818, pp. 263–270, 2011.

blinding family can be tailored to be leakage-resilient ones. It is natural to ask if we can strengthen the IBE schemes from the full domain hash family to be leakage-resilient.

We give an affirmative answer to the above question by presenting an IBE scheme with the full domain hash structure based on a variant of Boneh-Franklin IBE [7]. Its leakage-resilient chosen plaintext security can be tightly reduced to the DBDH assumption in the relative leakage model and the random oracle model.

2 Preliminaries

Notations. $x \xleftarrow{R} S$ denotes that x is picked uniformly at random from the set S. We write PPT for probabilistic polynomial time. By $\mathsf{negl}(n)$ we denote a negligible function of n. We denote the bit-wise XOR operation by $\oplus$. We denote by $\mathcal{I}$ the identity space and by $\mathcal{SK}$ the private key space.

2.1 Bilinear Diffie-Hellman Assumption

The decisional BDH (DBDH) assumption [3, 2] is defined via the following game: the challenger runs the bilinear group generator $\mathsf{GroupGen}(1^\kappa)$ to generate $(p, \mathbb{G}, \mathbb{G}_T, e)$, picks four random exponents x, y, z, w from $\mathbb{Z}_p$, then computes g^x, g^y, g^z, $T_0 = e(g,g)^{xyz}$ and $T_1 = e(g,g)^{xyw}$. We denote by D the tuple $(p, \mathbb{G}, \mathbb{G}_T, e, g, g^x, g^y, g^z)$. The challenger picks a random bit c and gives to the adversary $\mathcal{B}$ the challenge instance (D, T_c). We say $\mathcal{B}$ succeeds in solving the DBDH problem if it outputs the right guess c' for c at the end of the game, whose advantage is defined as:

$$|\Pr[c = c'] - 1/2| = |\Pr[\mathcal{B}(D, e(g,g)^{xyz}) = 0] - \Pr[\mathcal{B}(D, e(g,g)^{xyw}) = 0]|$$

Definition 2.1. *The (t, ϵ)-DBDH assumption holds if no t-time adversary has at least ϵ in solving the DBDH problem in $\mathbb{G}$.*

2.2 Randomness Extractors

The following notions and primitives will be used in our construction. We refer the readers to [15, 1] for a complement knowledge.

For a random variable X, we define $\mathbf{H}_\infty(X) = -\log(\max_x \Pr[X = x])$ as its min-entropy. We use the notion of *average min-entropy* [8] which captures the remaining unpredictability of a random variable X conditioned on another random variable Y, formally defined as

$$\tilde{\mathbf{H}}_\infty(X|Y) = -\log\left(E_{y \leftarrow Y}\left[\max_x \Pr[X = x|Y = y]\right]\right)$$

where $E_{y \leftarrow Y}$ denotes the expected value over all values of Y.

The average min-entropy measures exactly the optimal probability of guessing X given knowledge of Y. The following lemma was proved in [9] regarding average min-entropy:

Lemma 1. *For any random variables X, Y, Z, if Y has 2^ℓ possible values, then* $\tilde{\mathbf{H}}_\infty(X|(Y,Z)) \geq \tilde{\mathbf{H}}_\infty(X|Z) - \ell$.

The statistical distance between two random variables X, Y over a finite domain Ω is defined as

$$\mathbf{SD}(X,Y) = \frac{1}{2}\sum_{\omega\in\Omega} |\Pr[X=\omega] - \Pr[Y=\omega]|$$

Same as [15, 1, 6], a main tool used in our construction is the strong randomness extractor, which is formally defined as follows to the setting of the average min-entropy.

Definition 2.2. *A polynomial-time function* $\mathsf{ext} : \mathbb{G} \times \{0,1\}^\mu \to \{0,1\}^m$ *is an average case* (k,ϵ)*-strong extractor if for all pairs of random variables* (X,Y) *such that* $X \in \mathbb{G}$ *and* $\tilde{\mathbf{H}}_\infty(X|Y) \geq k$, *we have that*

$$\mathbf{SD}((\mathsf{ext}(X,U_\mu),U_\mu,Y)),(U_m,U_\mu,Y)) \leq \epsilon$$

where $\mathbb{G}$ is a non-empty set, and U_μ, U_m are two uniformly distributed random variables over $\{0,1\}^\mu$, $\{0,1\}^m$ respectively.

Dodis et al. [8] proved that any strong extractor is in fact an average-case strong extractor, for a proper setting of the parameters:

Lemma 2. *For any* $\delta > 0$, *if* ext *is a worst case* $(m - \log(1/\delta), \epsilon)$*-strong extractor, then* ext *is also an average-case* $(m, \epsilon + \delta)$*-strong extractor.*

As a specific example, they proved the following lemma which essentially gives an explicit construction of an average-case strong extractor:

Lemma 3. *Let* X, Y *be two random variables such that* $X \in \mathbb{G}$ *and* $\tilde{\mathbf{H}}_\infty(X|Y) \geq k$. *Let* $\mathcal{H} = \{H : \mathbb{G} \to \{0,1\}^m\}$ *be a family of universal hash functions. If* $m \leq k - 2\log(1/\epsilon)$ *then we have*

$$\mathbf{SD}((H(X),U_s,Y)),(U_m,U_s,Y)) \leq \epsilon$$

2.3 Leakage Model for IBE Setting

In this paper we use the relative leakage model suitable for the IBE setting. The leakage-resilient chosen plaintext security is defined by the following $\mathsf{LeakCPA}$ game, which is refined from the $\mathsf{CpaLeak}$ game introduced in [6].

Setup. The challenger generates the public parameters mpk and the master secret key msk. It gives mpk to the adversary and keeps msk to itself.

Phase 1. The adversary can make one of the following two types of queries to the challenger:

1. $\mathsf{Leak}(I, h_i)$ query, where $h_i : \mathcal{SK} \to \{0,1\}^{\ell_i}$. The challenger checks if the overall amount leakage will exceed ℓ. If not, it responds with $h_i(sk)$. Otherwise it responds with a reject symbol $\perp$.

2. $\mathsf{Reveal}(I)$ query, where I is the identity. The challenger responds with the associated private key sk.

Challenge. The adversary submits two messages M_0, M_1 of equal size and a challenge identity I^*, with the restriction that I^* has not been revealed. The challenger picks a random bit β and encrypts M_β under I^*. It sends the resulting ciphertext C^* to the adversary.

Phase 2. The same as Phase 1 with the restriction that no leakage queries or reveal queries related to I^* are allowed.

Guess. The adversary outputs a bit β'. We say it succeeds if $\beta = \beta'$.

The advantage of an adversary $\mathcal{A}$ on breaking an IBE scheme $\mathcal{E}$ with security parameter κ and leakage bound ℓ is defined as $\mathrm{Adv}_{\mathcal{A},\mathcal{E}}^{\mathsf{CPALeak}}(\kappa, \ell) = |\Pr[\beta = \beta'] - \frac{1}{2}|$.

Definition 2.3. *An IBE scheme $\mathcal{E}$ is ℓ-leakage fully secure if for all PPT adversaries $\mathcal{A}$ it holds that* $\mathrm{Adv}_{\mathcal{A},\mathcal{E}}^{\mathsf{CPALeak}}(\kappa, \ell) \leq \mathsf{negl}(\kappa)$.

3 Our Scheme

Our scheme consists of the following four algorithms:

Setup. Run $\mathsf{GroupGen}(1^\kappa) \rightarrow (p, \mathbb{G}, \mathbb{G}_T, e)$, pick $x \xleftarrow{R} \mathbb{Z}_p$, $g_2 \xleftarrow{R} \mathbb{G}^*$, and a cryptographic hash function $H : \{0,1\}^* \rightarrow \mathbb{G}$. Let $g_1 = g^x$, $\ell = \ell(\kappa)$ be an upper bound on the amount of leakage. Then set an average-case $(\log|\mathbb{G}_T| - \ell, \epsilon_{\mathsf{ext}})$-strong extractor function $\mathsf{ext} : \mathbb{G}_T \times \{0,1\}^\mu \rightarrow \{0,1\}^n$. The message space is $\mathcal{M} \in \{0,1\}^n$, while $mpk = (g, g_1, g_2)$ and $msk = x$.

KeyGen. For a given identity I, pick $t \xleftarrow{R} \mathbb{Z}_p$, compute $u = H(I)$, and then generate the private key for I as $sk = (d_1, d_2) = (t, (ug_2^{-t})^x)$.

Encrypt. To encrypt a message M under identity I, pick an exponent $r \xleftarrow{R} \mathbb{Z}_p$ and a seed $s \xleftarrow{R} \{0,1\}^\mu$ for the extractor function, generate the ciphertext as $C = (c_1, c_2, c_3, c_4) = (g^r, s, e(g_1, g_2)^r, M \oplus \mathsf{ext}(e(u, g_1)^r, s))$.

Decrypt. To decrypt a ciphertext $C = (c_1, c_2, c_3, c_4)$ encrypted under I using the associated private key $sk = (d_1, d_2)$ to compute $M = c_4 \oplus \mathsf{ext}(e(c_1, d_2)c_3^{d_1}, c_2)$. It is easy to verify that if the private key matches, we get the right decryption.

3.1 Security Analysis

Theorem 3.1. *If the DBDH assumption holds and the extractor's second parameter ϵ_{ext} is negligible in κ, then the proposed scheme is ℓ-leakage secure, where $\ell = \log|\mathbb{G}_T| - k$ and k is the extractor's first parameter.*

To prove the theorem, we organize the proof as a sequence of games, which are defined as follows:

Game$_{\mathbf{Real}}$. The real $\mathsf{CPALeak}$ game.

Game$_{\mathbf{Final}}$: The real CPALeak game except in the challenge phase the challenger generates the ciphertext as follows:

$$\begin{array}{ll} z, w \xleftarrow{R} \mathbb{Z}_p, \beta \xleftarrow{R} \{0,1\} & W = e(u^*, g_1)^z e(g_1, g_2)^{t^*(w-z)} \\ c_1^* = g^z & c_2^* \xleftarrow{R} \{0,1\}^\mu \\ c_3^* = e(g_1, g_2)^w & c_4^* = M_\beta \oplus \mathsf{ext}(W, c_2^*) \end{array}$$

where t^* is the tag of private key sk^* of the challenge identity I^*, z and w are randomly picked from $\mathbb{Z}_p$. The challenge ciphertext is $C^* = (c_1^*, c_2^*, c_3^*, c_4^*)$. Note that if $w \neq z$, then C^* is not a valid ciphertext since it is only decrypted correctly when using the private key with tag t^*.

Lemma 3.2. *If there exists a PPT algorithm $\mathcal{A}$ such that $\mathrm{Adv}_{\mathcal{A},\mathcal{E}}^{\mathbf{Game_{Real}}} - \mathrm{Adv}_{\mathcal{A},\mathcal{E}}^{\mathbf{Game_{Final}}} = \epsilon$, then we can build a PPT algorithm $\mathcal{B}$ with advantage ϵ in breaking the DBDH problem.*

Proof. Suppose $\mathcal{B}$ is given a DBDH challenge $(p, \mathbb{G}, \mathbb{G}_T, e, g, g^x, g^y, g^z, T)$. We now describe how it interacts with $\mathcal{A}$ in the following game:

Setup. $\mathcal{B}$ sets $g_1 = g^x$ (implicitly sets $msk = x$), $g_2 = g^y$, picks a suitable extractor function ext, then gives $\mathcal{A}$ the public parameters $mpk = (p, \mathbb{G}, \mathbb{G}_T, e, g, g_1, g_2, \mathsf{ext})$.

Hash queries. For a fresh hash query on I, $\mathcal{B}$ picks $a, t \xleftarrow{R} \mathbb{Z}_p$ and responds with $u = g^a g_2^t$.

KeyGen queries. For an arbitrary identity I, $\mathcal{B}$ computes a private key for it as follows: (1) compute $u = H(I)$; (2) set $d_1 = t$, $d_2 = g_1^a = (u g_2^{-t})^x = (g^a g_2^t g_2^{-t})^x$; (3) return $sk = (d_1, d_2)$.

We note that the keygen queries are always implicitly called by $\mathcal{B}$ when it answers the associated leak queries and reveal queries.

Phase 1. To answer the leak queries and reveal queries issued by $\mathcal{A}$, $\mathcal{B}$ creates two lists L and K, which are initially empty. L is a list of triples of identities, private keys, and a leakage counter, while K is a list of tuples of identities, private keys.

– $\mathsf{Leak}(I, h_i)$ query: $\mathcal{B}$ checks if there is a tuple $\langle I, sk \rangle$ in the existing K list. If it is not $\mathcal{B}$ runs $sk \leftarrow \mathsf{KeyGen}(msk, I)$, inserts the tuple (I, sk) to the K list and the triple $\langle I, sk, 0 \rangle$ to the L list. After this step there must exists a triple $\langle I, sk, num \rangle$ in the L list, $\mathcal{B}$ checks if $num + \ell_i \leq \ell$. If this is true, it responds with $h_i(sk)$ and sets $num \leftarrow num + \ell_i$ in $\langle I, sk, num \rangle$. Otherwise $\mathcal{B}$ responds with a reject symbol $\perp$.

– $\mathsf{Reveal}(I)$ query: $\mathcal{B}$ checks if there is a tuple $\langle I, sk \rangle$ in the K list. If it is $\mathcal{B}$ responds with sk. If it is not $\mathcal{B}$ runs $sk \leftarrow \mathsf{KeyGen}(msk, I)$, inserts the tuple $\langle I, sk \rangle$ to the K list and the triple $\langle I, sk, 0 \rangle$ to the L list, and responds the leak query with sk.

Notice that $\mathcal{B}$ can calculate a valid private key for any identity. Therefore, $\mathcal{B}$ is able to answer all the leakage queries $\mathsf{Leak}(I, h_i)$ and reveal queries $\mathsf{Reveal}(I)$, with the corresponding private key $sk = (d_1, d_2)$.

Challenge. $\mathcal{A}$ submits two messages M_0, M_1 and an identity I^* on which it want to be challenged to $\mathcal{B}$. $\mathcal{B}$ computes $sk^* = (d_1^*, d_2^*) = (t^*, g_1^{a^*})$, then generates the challenge ciphertext as follows:

$$\begin{array}{ll} \beta \xleftarrow{R} \{0,1\} & c_1^* = g^z \\ c_2^* \xleftarrow{R} \{0,1\}^\mu & c_3^* = T \\ W = e(c_1^*, d_2^*)(c_3^*)^{d_1^*} = e(g^z, g_1^{a^*})T^{t^*} & c_4^* = M_\beta \oplus \mathsf{ext}(W, c_2^*) \end{array}$$

Phase 2. The same as Phase 1.

Guess. $\mathcal{A}$ outputs a guess β'. $\mathcal{B}$ returns 0 if $\beta = \beta'$ or 1 if $\beta \neq \beta'$.

We will prove that the advantage of $\mathcal{B}$ in breaking the DBDH problem is ϵ. To see this, notice that if $T = e(g,g)^{xyz}$ the challenge ciphertext is a correct ciphertext according to the original encryption algorithm and thus $\mathcal{A}$ plays the $\mathbf{Game}_{\mathbf{Real}}$. This is because $W = e(g^z, g_1^{a^*})T^{t^*} = e(g^{a^*}, g_1^z)e(g_2^{t^*}, g_1^z) = e(g^{a^*} g_2^{t^*}, g_1^z) = e(u^*, g_1)^z$ as one can easily verify. Thus the probability that $\mathcal{A}$ succeeds in the game is exactly $\frac{1}{2} + \mathrm{Adv}_{\mathcal{A},\mathcal{E}}^{\mathbf{Game}_{\mathbf{Real}}}$. Since $\mathcal{B}$ outputs 0 when $\mathcal{A}$ succeeds we get that

$$\Pr[\mathcal{B}(D, e(g,g)^{xyz}) = 0] = \frac{1}{2} + \mathrm{Adv}_{\mathcal{A},\mathcal{E}}^{\mathbf{Game}_{\mathbf{Real}}}$$

On the other hand if $T = e(g,g)^{xyw} = c_3^*$ then $\mathcal{A}$ essentially plays the $\mathbf{Game}_{\mathbf{Final}}$, because $W = e(g^z, g_1^{a^*})T^{t^*} = e(g^{a^*}, g_1^z)e(g_2^{t^*}, g_1^{(w-z)+z}) = e(u^*, g_1)^z e(g_1, g_2)^{t^*(w-z)}$ as one can easily verify. Therefore we have that

$$\Pr[\mathcal{B}(D, e(g,g)^{xyw}) = 0] = \frac{1}{2} + \mathrm{Adv}_{\mathcal{A},\mathcal{E}}^{\mathbf{Game}_{\mathbf{Final}}}$$

Combining the above equations we get that the advantage of $\mathcal{B}$ in DBDH is $\left|\Pr[\mathcal{B}(D, e(g,g)^{xyz}) = 0] - \Pr[\mathcal{B}(D, e(g,g)^{xyw}) = 0]\right| = \mathrm{Adv}_{\mathcal{A},\mathcal{E}}^{\mathbf{Game}_{\mathbf{Real}}} - \mathrm{Adv}_{\mathcal{A},\mathcal{E}}^{\mathbf{Game}_{\mathbf{Final}}} = \epsilon$. Therefore we prove the lemma. □

Lemma 3.3. *For any PPT adversary $\mathcal{A}$ we have* $\mathrm{Adv}_{\mathcal{A},\mathcal{E}}^{\mathbf{Game}_{\mathbf{Final}}} \leq 2\epsilon_{\mathsf{ext}}$.

Proof. In the $\mathbf{Game}_{\mathbf{Final}}$, it is true that $W = e(u^*, g_1)^z e(g_1, g_2)^{t^*(w-z)}$. where t^* is the tag of the private key for I^*. If we assume that the exact private key with tag t^* is perfect hidden from the adversary, then W distributes uniformly at random in $\mathbb{G}_T$, and therefore the challenge ciphertext C^* is totally independent of M_β in an PPT adversary $\mathcal{A}$'s view. This is because $w = z \bmod p$ with negligible probability in κ and t^* is chosen randomly for I^*.

Suppose we denote by R the set of all terms (public parameters, private keys, challenge ciphertext) given to the adversary $\mathcal{A}$ except the leakage, the random seed c_2^*, and the part of the challenge ciphertext c_4^*, then according to the above argument $\tilde{\mathbf{H}}_\infty(C|R) = \log|\mathbb{G}_T|$. But the attacker has access to at most ℓ bits of leakage from the private key, i.e. to a random variable Y with 2^ℓ values, thus by lemma 1 we know that

$$\tilde{\mathbf{H}}_\infty(C|(Y,R)) \geq \tilde{\mathbf{H}}_\infty(C|R) - \ell = \log|\mathbb{G}_T| - \ell$$

According to the definition of $(\log|\mathbb{G}_T| - \ell, \epsilon_{\mathsf{ext}})$-strong extractor we have that $\mathbf{SD}((\mathsf{ext}(W,S), S, Y, R), (U_m, S, Y, R)) \leq \epsilon_{\mathsf{ext}}$, where S is the random variable for the seed $c_2^* \in \{0,1\}^\mu$ distributed uniformly at random, Y, R are the values of all the random variables known to the adversary: leakage and the rest, respectively. Thus the statistical distance of $c_4^* = M_\beta \oplus \mathsf{ext}(W, c_2^*)$ from the uniform distribution is at most ϵ_{ext} for each β. The statistical distance between the two possible ciphertexts is at most $2\epsilon_{\mathsf{ext}}$ and no adversary (even an unbounded one) can distinguish them with advantage more than this. □

Suppose ϵ_{DBDH} is the maximum advantage of all PPT adversaries in the DBDH game. Then according to the above lemma, for any PPT adversary $\mathcal{A}$ we have $\mathrm{Adv}_{\mathcal{A},\mathcal{E}}^{\mathbf{Game_{Real}}} - \mathrm{Adv}_{\mathcal{A},\mathcal{E}}^{\mathbf{Game_{Final}}} \leq \epsilon_{DBDH}$. Therefore

$$\mathrm{Adv}_{\mathcal{A},\mathcal{E}}^{\mathbf{Game_{Real}}} \leq \mathrm{Adv}_{\mathcal{A},\mathcal{E}}^{\mathbf{Game_{Final}}} + \epsilon_{DBDH}(\kappa) \leq 2\epsilon_{\mathsf{ext}}(\kappa) + \epsilon_{DBDH}(\kappa)$$

The proposed scheme is leakage-resilient CPA secure if both $\epsilon_{DBDH}(\kappa)$ and $\epsilon_{\mathsf{ext}}(\kappa)$ are negligible functions of κ. This proves the theorem. □

References

1. Alwen, J., Dodis, Y., Naor, M., Segev, G., Walfish, S., Wichs, D.: Public-key encryption in the bounded-retrieval model. In: Gilbert, H. (ed.) EUROCRYPT 2010. LNCS, vol. 6110, pp. 113–134. Springer, Heidelberg (2010)
2. Boneh, D., Boyen, X.: Efficient Selective-ID Secure Identity Based Encryption without Random Oracles. In: Cachin, C., Camenisch, J.L. (eds.) EUROCRYPT 2004. LNCS, vol. 3027, pp. 223–238. Springer, Heidelberg (2004)
3. Boneh, D., Franklin, M.K.: Identity-Based Encryption from the Weil Pairing. SIAM Journal on Computation 32, 586–615 (2003)
4. Boneh, D., Gentry, C., Hamburg, M.: Space-efficient identity based encryption without pairings. In: 48th Annual IEEE Symposium on Foundations of Computer Science (FOCS 2007), pp. 647–657. IEEE Computer Society, Los Alamitos (2007)
5. Boyen, X.: General ad hoc encryption from exponent inversion ibe. In: Naor, M. (ed.) EUROCRYPT 2007. LNCS, vol. 4515, pp. 394–411. Springer, Heidelberg (2007)
6. Chow, S.S.M., Dodis, Y., Rouselakis, Y., Waters, B.: Practical leakage-resilient identity-based encryption from simple assumptions. In: Proceedings of the 17th ACM Conference on Computer and Communications Security, CCS 2010, pp. 152–161. ACM, New York (2010)
7. Coron, J.S.: A variant of Boneh-Franklin IBE with a tight reduction in the random oracle model. Des. Codes Cryptography 50(1), 115–133 (2009)
8. Dodis, Y., Ostrovsky, R., Reyzin, L., Smith, A.: Fuzzy extractors: How to generate strong keys from biometrics and other noisy data. SIAM J. Comput. 38(1), 97–139 (2008)

9. Dziembowski, S.: Intrusion-resilience via the bounded-storage model. In: Halevi, S., Rabin, T. (eds.) TCC 2006. LNCS, vol. 3876, pp. 207–224. Springer, Heidelberg (2006)
10. Gentry, C.: Practical Identity-Based Encryption Without Random Oracles. In: Vaudenay, S. (ed.) EUROCRYPT 2006. LNCS, vol. 4004, pp. 445–464. Springer, Heidelberg (2006)
11. Gentry, C., Peikert, C., Vaikuntanathan, V.: Trapdoors for hard lattices and new cryptographic constructions. In: Proceedings of the 40th Annual ACM Symposium on Theory of Computing, STOC, pp. 197–206. ACM, New York (2008)
12. Halderman, J.A., Schoen, S.D., Heninger, N., Clarkson, W., Paul, W., Calandrino, J.A., Feldman, A.J., Appelbaum, J., Felten, E.W.: Lest we remember: Cold boot attacks on encryption keys. In: Proceedings of the 17th USENIX Security Symposium, pp. 45–60 (2008)
13. Kocher, P.C., Jaffe, J., Jun, B.: Differential power analysis. In: Wiener, M. (ed.) CRYPTO 1999. LNCS, vol. 1666, pp. 388–397. Springer, Heidelberg (1999)
14. Lewko, A.B., Waters, B.: New techniques for dual system encryption and fully secure hibe with short ciphertexts. In: Micciancio, D. (ed.) TCC 2010. LNCS, vol. 5978, pp. 455–479. Springer, Heidelberg (2010)
15. Naor, M., Segev, G.: Public-key cryptosystems resilient to key leakage. In: Halevi, S. (ed.) CRYPTO 2009. LNCS, vol. 5677, pp. 18–35. Springer, Heidelberg (2009)
16. Waters, B.: Efficient Identity-Based Encryption Without Random Oracles. In: Cramer, R. (ed.) EUROCRYPT 2005. LNCS, vol. 3494, pp. 114–127. Springer, Heidelberg (2005)

Accurate Accident Reconstruction in VANET

Yuliya Kopylova, Csilla Farkas, and Wenyuan Xu

Dept. of CSE, University of South Carolina
{kopylova,farkas,wyxu}@cse.sc.edu

Abstract. We propose a forensic VANET application to aid an accurate accident reconstruction. Our application provides a new source of objective real-time data impossible to collect using existing methods. By leveraging inter-vehicle communications, we compile digital evidence describing events before, during, and after an accident in its entirety. In addition to sensors data and major components status, we provide relative positions of all vehicles involved in an accident. This data is corroborated by observations provided by witness vehicles to rectify inconsistencies. Our application utilizes the mandatory form of VANET communication (beacons), making it non-obtrusive in terms of resource and bandwidth consumption.

Keywords: Accident reconstruction, EDR, in-vehicle applications, VANET.

1 Introduction

One of the most active research areas of mobile ad-hoc networks is the Vehicular Ad-hoc NETworks (VANET). The dramatic increase in the number of vehicles equipped with computing and wireless technologies enabled new applications previously infeasible. These applications fall into safety and comfort categories. Safety VANET applications include imminent collision warning, obstacle detection/avoidance, emergency message dissemination, intersection decision support, cooperative driving etc. Comfort VANET applications include traffic congestion advisories, route updates, automated toll and parking services, etc. [5,2]. While safety applications have been in the focus of academic and industrial research, the topic of forensic applications using VANET data has been under-explored. In this paper we propose a forensic application that harvests inter-vehicle communication for the purpose of post accident analysis. Our objective is to collect data sufficient for establishing the chain of events associated with the accident.

The contributions of this work include the following: (1) we identify desirable properties of data collection process for accurate accident reconstruction,(2) we propose a viable solution that achieves these properties based on vehicular communications, (3) we provide some details on application logic, architecture, and integration of the proposed application, (4) we discuss mechanisms to protect confidentiality of the data collected by our application

The rest of the paper is organized as follows. Section 2 overviews data collection practices for accident reconstruction. Section 3 presents the proposed

Y. Li (Ed.): Data and Applications Security and Privacy XXV, LNCS 6818, pp. 271–279, 2011.

solution. Section 4 provides a limited discussion on security and privacy issues associated with our solution. Section 5 concludes the paper.

2 Accident Reconstruction Overview

Conducted by law enforcement agencies, accident reconstruction is defined as a process of determining the cause and the circumstances of a collision from available evidence [9]. The data of interest involves movement, relative positions, and interaction of the involved vehicles. Accident reconstruction is usually conducted in two steps: (1) data collection and (2) data fitting. Data collection involves measurements of parameters relevant to trajectory and impact reconstruction, such as speed, position, acceleration, point of impact, etc. Data fitting is accomplished through trajectory modeling based on the data collected in the first step. Supplying accurate data to the modeling software is the key to the successful reconstruction especially in complicated incidents [7].

The data gathered through conventional means (close-ups of skid marks, tire prints, evidence of the area of impact, collision debris distribution, etc.) is often incomplete and occasionally misleading [9]. More reliable crash data is collected by Event Data Recorders (EDR). The main purpose of EDR is to verify proper functioning of the safety systems in place. Even though EDR data was not originally intended for accident reconstruction, its use in post-accident analysis is becoming a more accepted practice [11,1]. However, information collected from a single EDR is often insufficient for obtaining accurate reconstruction of an accident. This is especially true in multi-vehicle collisions, hit-and-run scenarios, and accidents that span multiple events [6,7,12].

Shortcomings of the existing data collection practices are summarized below:

1. Insufficiency of data in scope and duration:
   - Triggered exclusively via airbag deployment. A near rollover event, skidding off the road, etc. do not trigger EDR recording [6,7];
   - Insufficient history of recording especially pre-crash. In more than half of the cases investigated with the help of EDR, insufficient recording history renders EDR data inadequate for accident reconstruction [7].
2. Insufficiency of relevant data:
   - Geared towards assessing functionality of safety systems (airbags, seatbelts and mechanical parts), not trajectory reconstruction;
   - Limited to a single event; subsequent events, even if caused most of the injury or fatality are not recorded [6];
   - No existing means of recording data related to other vehicles trajectories.
3. Inaccuracy of data:
   - Inaccuracy of values due to indirect measurements;
   - Inaccuracy of values due to error propagation through accident phases;
   - No existing means to counter sensor malfunction/miscalibration [7,12].

Redesigning EDR to expand data collection can only partially these limitations. However, this task is not straightforward from architectural standpoint due to intra-vehicle communication constraints [10]. We propose a solution that addresses all limitations without the need of redesigning EDR.

3 Proposed Solution

Our solution addresses the above limitations in the following manner:

1. We improve the log recording triggering mechanisms by integrating our application into existing in-vehicle applications (access to rollover sensor, diagnostic module, etc.) in section 3.1;
2. We expand the scope of the data through recording positions and dynamics of all nearby vehicles (VANET communication data) in section 3.2;
3. We provide a mechanism to rectify GPS sensor malfunction/mal-calibration through submitting corroborating witness data in section 3.3;
4. We provide sufficiency of data duration by the means of rotating log centered around the accident event in section 3.4.

3.1 Architecture Philosophy

The application we propose derives data from two sources: sensory data obtained locally on the vehicle and external communication data arrived from vehicles nearby. On the one hand, our application needs to fit and benefit from sensor data collection mechanisms in place for in-vehicle applications; on the other hand, our application needs to be able to process significant volumes of data and share this data across multiple VANET applications that base their decisions on a similar subset of data to ensure consistency of decisions made across safety applications. We approach this challenge from the architectural standpoint.

Many VANET applications are proposed as standalone applications: they assume (1) direct access to sensor data and (2) autonomy from other VANET applications. Designing a standalone application might lead to either impractical (sensor data belongs to different functional domains) or inefficient application (redundancy in data processing, competing for resources). To avoid this pitfall, we discuss in a follow up paper how to fit our application into the framework of both existing in-vehicle applications (Figure 1) and future VANET applications (Figure 2). Fitting our application into the framework of existing in-vehicle applications allows for expanding log recording triggering mechanisms to include

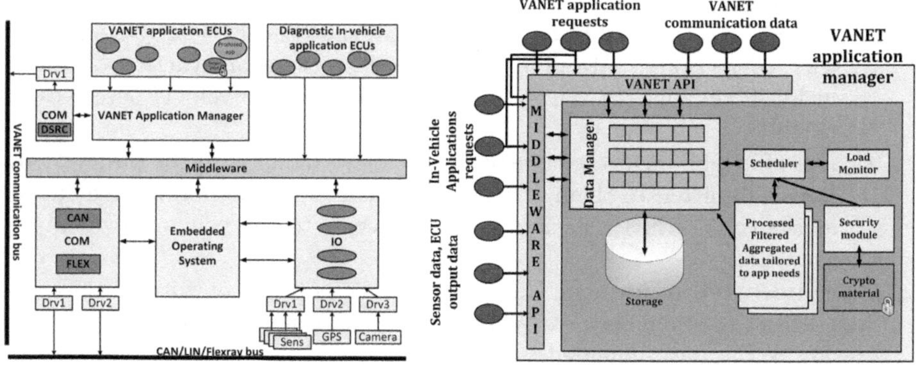

Fig. 1. Proposed architecture

Fig. 2. VANET Application Manager

rollover sensor data and output from Diagnostic Module. Fitting our application into the framework of VANET applications promotes applications cooperation.

3.2 VANET Communication Data

To obtain data related to other vehicles, we propose to use beacons already being exchanged by the VANET vehicles. A fundamental aspect of VANET communication is periodic beaconing; that is transmission of position, heading, status, along with additional parameters. Beacons contain the most relevant pieces of information necessary for accident reconstruction such as GPS position, heading, current speed, lateral and longitudinal acceleration, engine rpm, break status, etc. They are required for normal operation irrespectively of number and types of applications. According to [4,13], for operation of a typical traffic safety application in VANET beacons are assumed to have the following characteristics:

Generation Rate	Dissemination Latency	Communication Type	Communication Range	Size
10 beacons/sec	up to 100 ms	one hop broadcast	up to 300 m	80 bytes

3.3 Accident Reconstruction Application Data

To provide a complete suite of data necessary for accurate accident reconstruction including mechanisms to counter sensor malfunctions, we propose to create a two-piece digital evidence:

1. **Primary evidence:** the first piece contains data necessary for trajectory reconstruction of *all vehicles* in the proximity of an accident. This data is stored on the vehicle directly involved in the accident and can be retrieved through explicit permission of the owner or court decision. Primary evidence consist of three parts:
   (a) History of vehicle's own **sensor data.** This allows trajectory reconstruction of the vehicle collecting the data (directly involved in the accident). This data represents how the vehicle perceives itself.
   (b) History of overheard **beacon data** from the vehicles nearby augmented with correctional data. This allows trajectory reconstruction of all vehicles in the vicinity. This data represents how the vehicle perceives its neighbors.
   (c) List of neighbors at the time of the accidents along with the **encryption keys** submitted to them. This allows retrieval of corroborative evidence at the time of investigation, i.e. after access to the primary evidence is granted.
2. **Corroborative evidence:** The second piece consists of witness data obtained from the vehicles nearby. It contains information necessary for verification of the data included in the primary evidence file. This data corresponds to how witness vehicles perceive each other. The goal of this piece is to counter falsified/mal-calibrated GPS data submitted by other witnesses;

offset missing data due to path obstruction and out-of-range scenarios; protect against dishonest vehicles directly involved in the accident (owners of the primary evidence). Corroborative evidence submitted by a witness vehicle v_i is beacon log augmented with correctional data (vehicle v_i would store this log as a part of its own primary evidence should v_i itself get into an accident). Corroborative evidence is submitted to a road side unit (RSU), a trusted and impartial party. This data is encrypted with a key stored in the primary evidence file to prevent power abuse by investigating authorities.

Correctional data in the beacon log is used for cross referencing evidence. The same data can be utilized by routing protocols for position verification in VANET. There are many ways to accomplish this task. The most common approach is to rely on additional functionality of wireless antennas such as capability of assessing Time Difference of Arrival (TDoA), Time of Arrival (ToA), or Angle of Arrival (AoA). A method proposed in [15] is suitable for our application. It is resilient to node collaboration and does not rely on RSU for verification. Thus, the beacon log in both the primary and corroborative evidence files is augmented with three measures of TDoA, ToA and AoA per every entry.

Table 1 summarizing proposed digital evidence uses the following notation: Δt is sampling interval,$(b_i)_{t_j}$ stands for beacons received from vehicle i within time $t_j + \Delta t$, $(\delta_{v_i v_k})_{t_j}$ stands for correctional data on vehicle v_i regarding vehicle v_k with respect to GPS data in beacon received within time $t_j + \Delta t$.

The data in the primary evidence file allows detailed reconstruction of relative trajectories of all vehicles before, during and after the accident; the data submitted by witness vehicles allows to corroborate the story and counter falsified/malcalibrated GPS data submitted by other witnesses.

Table 1. Digital Evidence Summary

Primary evidence on V_0		
Sensor Data	$((s_1, s_2, \ldots, s_n)_{t_0}, (s_1, s_2, \ldots, s_n)_{t_1}, \ldots, (s_1, s_2, \ldots, s_n)_{t_k}$	self perception
Beacon Log	$((b_{v_1}, \delta_{v_0 v_1})_{t_0}, (b_{v_1}, \delta_{v_0 v_1})_{t_1}, \ldots, (b_{v_1}, \delta_{v_0 v_1})_{t_k}),$ $(b_{v_2}, \delta_{v_0 v_2})_{t_0}, (b_{v_2}, \delta_{v_0 v_2})_{t_1}, \ldots, (b_{v_2}, \delta_{v_0 v_2})_{t_k}),$ $\ldots$ $(b_{v_n}, \delta_{v_0 v_n})_{t_0}, (b_{v_n}, \delta_{v_0 v_n})_{t_1}, \ldots, (b_{v_n}, \delta_{v_0 v_n})_{t_k}))$	v_0 perceives v_1 v_0 perceives v_2 v_0 perceives v_n
Set of Keys	$(E_{v_0 v_1}, E_{v_0 v_2}, \ldots, E_{v_0 v_n})$	encryption keys
Corroborative Evidence on RSU		
Witness Data	$[((b_{v_0}, \delta_{v_1 v_0})_{t_0}, (b_{v_0}, \delta_{v_1 v_0})_{t_1}, \ldots, (b_{v_0}, \delta_{v_1 v_0})_{t_k}),$ $((b_{v_2}, \delta_{v_1 v_2})_{t_0}, (b_{v_2}, \delta_{v_1 v_2})_{t_1}, \ldots, (b_{v_2}, \delta_{v_1 v_2})_{t_k}),$ $\ldots$ $((b_{v_n}, \delta_{v_1 v_n})_{t_0}, (b_{v_n}, \delta_{v_1 v_n})_{t_1}, \ldots, (b_{v_n}, \delta_{v_1 v_n})_{t_k})]_{E_{v_0 v_1}}$ $\ldots$ $[((b_{v_0}, \delta_{v_i v_0})_{t_0}, (b_{v_0}, \delta_{v_i v_0})_{t_1}, \ldots, (b_{v_0}, \delta_{v_i v_0})_{t_k}),$ $((b_{v_1}, \delta_{v_i v_1})_{t_0}, (b_{v_1}, \delta_{v_i v_1})_{t_1}, \ldots, (b_{v_1}, \delta_{v_i v_1})_{t_k}),$ $\ldots$ $((b_{v_n}, \delta_{v_i v_n})_{t_0}, (b_{v_n}, \delta_{v_i v_n})_{t_1}, \ldots, (b_{v_n}, \delta_{v_i v_n})_{t_k})]_{E_{v_0 v_i}}$	v_1 perceives $(v_0, v_2, \ldots, v_n)$ v_i perceives $(v_0, v_2, \ldots, v_n)$

3.4 Application Operation

A threaded approach as shown in Fig. 3 can be adopted if memory space is not a concern. In the absence of abnormal sensor readings, the accident reconstruction application monitors sensor data and updates rotating data log via Monitoring thread and Logging thread. Abnormal events of crash and witness type are processed by launching Accident thread and Witness thread respectively. Logging thread is responsible for data recording within $t_{accident} \pm \tau$ interval. Threaded approach allows a vehicle to be a witness to multiple accidents while being itself involved in a crash. Abnormal events are triggered by two kinds of input: internal (e.g., sensor readings, output of in-vehicle applications) and external (e.g., witness request from other vehicles, receipt from RSU when witness data is received). A crash type event is generated based on internal input. In addition to airbag sensor reading (current EDR), we allow for readings from rollover sensor, lateral acceleration sensor, crash impact sensor, and output from the DM. Monitoring thread maintains a list of neighbors (witnesses) within communication range and analyzes data for suspicious events:

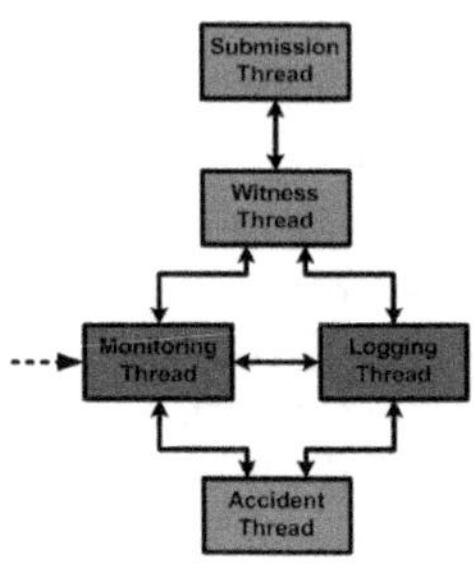

Fig. 3. App. threads

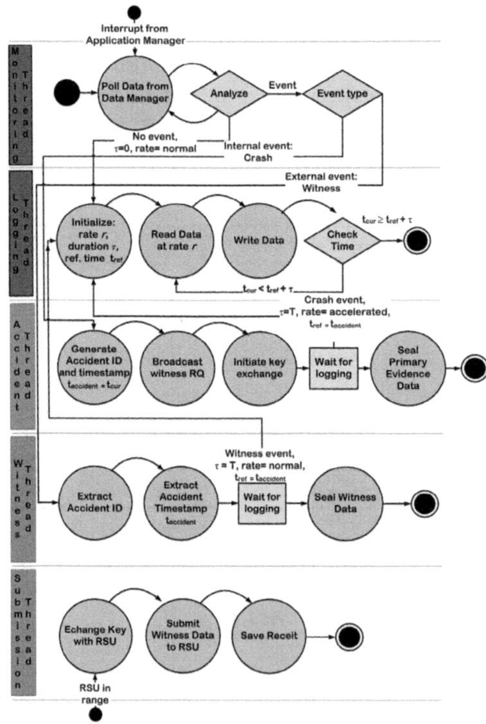

Fig. 4. Application State Diagram

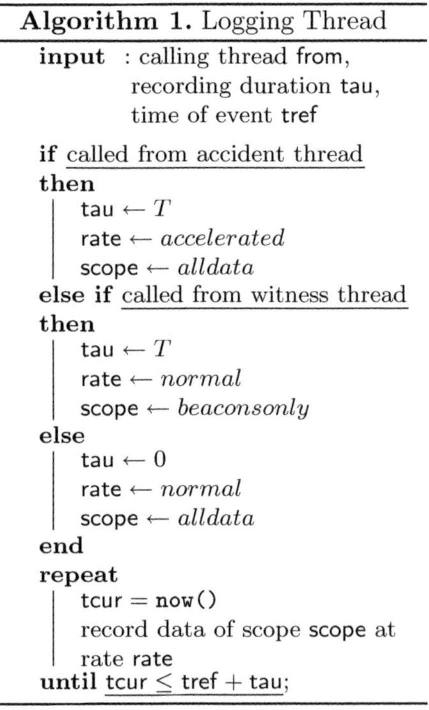

Algorithm 1. Logging Thread

input : calling thread from, recording duration tau, time of event tref

if called from accident thread **then**
  tau ← T
  rate ← *accelerated*
  scope ← *alldata*
else if called from witness thread **then**
  tau ← T
  rate ← *normal*
  scope ← *beaconsonly*
else
  tau ← 0
  rate ← *normal*
  scope ← *alldata*
end
repeat
  tcur = now()
  record data of scope scope at rate rate
until tcur ≤ tref + tau;

Fig. 5. Logging Thread Algorithm

Sensor data is obtained through the AM by polling; events, generated by the DM or cooperative driving applications, are delivered by the AM via asynchronous notification. A crash type event is processed when digital evidence is compiled and sealed. A witness type event is triggered by the reception of a request to submit corroborating evidence originated on another vehicle. A witness type event is processed when evidence data is successfully delivered to the nearest RSU. Fig. 3 illustrates thread interaction; Fig. 4 details individual threads; Fig. 5 presents Logging thread pseudocode.

4 Security and Privacy

In this section we present a brief summary of the security and privacy concerns of our application.

Authenticity, Integrity, Non-repudiation: Since our application only harvests VANET communication data, authenticity, integrity, and non-repudiation of individual entries in the evidence file are predicated on correct and secure implementation of the communication protocol. These mechanisms are provided in 1609.2 standard.

Confidentiality: We consider four distinct situations with different confidentiality requirements:

1. *Beacon exchange: no confidentiality.* Beacon messages do not contain confidential information: they are transmitted in the clear but digitally signed for integrity protection and proper attribute authentication [8].
2. *Primary Evidence: confidentiality against all but authorized parties.* Digital evidence on the vehicle directly involved in the accident is encrypted and stored in a tamper proof location. To prevent involvement of non-governmental institutions (issuers of secure VANET communication keys as per 1609.2) in law-enforcement mechanisms, a separate set of keys for digital evidence is issued by the law-enforcement authorities (preloads and replenish scheme [14]). Thus, the evidence can be decrypted only by the law enforcement authorities. Other interested parties (insurance companies) would have to legally obtain the decryption key from the police.
3. *Corroborative evidence request-response sequence: confidentiality against all except direct communication partners.* These are safety messages encrypted as required by 1609.2. During this step, another key is generated: the encryption key for corroborative evidence (simple Diffie-Hellman key exchange after mutual authentication will suffice).
4. *Witness data: confidentiality against authorities with too much power.* The secret key obtained in the previous step insures witness protection. Corroborative evidence submitted by witness vehicles to a RSU is encrypted with the key stored in the digital evidence file on the vehicle directly involved

in an accident. Corrupt, overzealous or curious authorities can access witness statements (submitted to RSU), but unable to decrypt them without obtaining a subpoena of the vehicle under investigation.

Non-frameability: Intention of corroborative evidence is twofold: (1) to protect against misbehaving nodes by submitting correctional data to the vehicle involved in an accident (perceived position history from other witness vehicles) and (2) to protects against dishonest nodes directly involved in an accident by submitting witness package to the nearest RSU.

Privacy: The privacy goal of our application is to ensure that access to the digital evidence"does not enable one to learn anything about individual that could not be learned without access to some other external data"[3]. External data includes physical evidence from the scene, EDR data, eye witness statements, cameras along public roads, etc. The advantage we provide is completeness and relevance of the data compared to traditional means. If proper investigation procedures are followed, no impact on privacy of individuals is expected.

5 Conclusions and Discussion

We propose a forensic application for accurate accident reconstruction. It leverages VANET communication to create a two-piece digital evidence. The data in the primary evidence (stored on a vehicle) allows detailed reconstruction of relative trajectories of all vehicles before, during and after the accident; witness data (stored on RSU) corroborates the story. Our ongoing work includes evaluation/simulation studies and technical details for individual components.

References

1. Croft, A.: Sensing Diagnostic Module: The modern motor vehicle's "black box"
2. Dotzer, F., et al.: Secure Communication for Intersection Assistance. In: 2nd International Workshop on Intelligent Transportation (2005)
3. Dwork, C.: Differential privacy. In: Bugliesi, M., Preneel, B., Sassone, V., Wegener, I. (eds.) ICALP 2006. LNCS, vol. 4052, pp. 1–12. Springer, Heidelberg (2006)
4. van Eenennaam, E., et al.: Exploring the Solution Space of Beaconing in VANETs. In: 1st IEEE Vehicular Networking Conference (2009)
5. Elbatt, T., et al.: Cooperative Collision Warning Using Dedicated Short Range Wireless Communications. In: 3rd IW on VANET, pp. 1–9. ACM Press, New York (2006)
6. Gabler, H., Hampton, C.: Estimating Crash Severity: Can event data recorders replace crash reconstruction? Accident Analysis & Prevention 40, 548–558 (2008)
7. Haight, W.: Automobile Event Data Recorder (EDR) Technology - Evolution, Data, and Reliability. Tech. rep., Collision Safety Institute (2001)
8. Hartenstein, H., Laberteaux, K.: VANET Vehicular Applications and Inter-Networking Technologies. John Wiley & Sons, Chichester (2010)
9. Lofgren, M.: Handbook for the Accident Reconstructionist. IPTM (1983)
10. Navet, N., et al.: Trends in Automotive Communication Systems. IEEE 93, 1024–1223 (2005)

11. NHTSA: Final Rule: Event Data Recorders (2006)
12. Niehoff, P., et al.: Evaluation of Event Data Recorderss in Full Systems Crash Tests. Tech. rep., NHTSA (2006)
13. project, C..D.: C&D WP-1 Requirements Document. Tech. rep. (2009)
14. Raya, M., Hubaux, J.P.: Security Aspects of Inter-Vehicle Communications. In: 5th Swiss Transport Research Conference (2005)
15. Shmatikov, V., Wang, M.-H.: Secure Verification of Location Claims with Simultaneous Distance Modification. In: Cervesato, I. (ed.) ASIAN 2007. LNCS, vol. 4846, pp. 181–195. Springer, Heidelberg (2007)

Cyber Situation Awareness: Modeling the Security Analyst in a Cyber-Attack Scenario through Instance-Based Learning

Varun Dutt*, Young-Suk Ahn, and Cleotilde Gonzalez

Dynamic Decision Making Laboratory, 4609 Winthrop Street, Pittsburgh, PA, 15213, USA
Tel.: +1-412-628-1379; Fax: +1-412-268-6938
varundutt@cmu.edu, ysahn@altenia.com, coty@cmu.edu

Abstract. In a corporate network, the situation awareness (SA) of a security analyst is of particular interest. A security analyst is in charge of observing the online operations of a corporate network (e.g., an online retail company with an external webserver and an internal fileserver) from threats of random or organized cyber-attacks. The current work describes a cognitive Instance-based Learning (IBL) model of the recognition and comprehension processes of a security analyst in a simple cyber-attack scenario. The IBL model first recognizes cyber-events (e.g., execution of a file on a server) in the network based upon events' situation attributes and the similarity of events' attributes to past experiences (instances) stored in analyst's memory. Then, the model reasons about a sequence of observed events being a cyber-attack or not, based upon instances retrieved from memory and the risk-tolerance of a simulated analyst. The execution of the IBL model generates predictions of the recognition and comprehension processes of security analyst in a cyber-attack. An analyst's decisions are evaluated in the model based upon two cyber SA metrics of accuracy and timeliness of analyst's decision actions. Future work in this area will focus on collecting human data to validate the predictions made by the model.

Keywords: cyber-situation awareness; cyber-attack; dynamic decision-making; instance-based learning theory; intrusion-detection system; security analyst; threat event.

1 Introduction

Recently, President Barack Obama declared that the "cyber threat is one of the most serious economic and national security challenges we face as a nation" [1]. According to his office, the nation's cyber-security strategy is twofold: (1) improve our resilience to cyber incidents; and, (2) reduce the cyber threat [1]. Similarly, in the United Kingdom, organizers of the London 2012 Olympic Games believe that there is an increased danger of cyber-attacks that could fatally undermine the technical network

* Corresponding author.

Y. Li (Ed.): Data and Applications Security and Privacy XXV, LNCS 6818, pp. 280–292, 2011.

that supports everything from recording world records to relaying results to commentators at the Games [2]. At the lowest level, meeting both the objectives of the Whitehouse and those of the organizers of the Olympic Games in a corporate network requires cyber situation-awareness (SA), a three stage process which includes: recognition (or the awareness of the current situation in the network); comprehension (or the awareness of malicious behavior in the current situation in the network); and, projection (assessment of possible future courses of action resulting from the current situation in the network) [3, 4].

In cyber SA, the ability of a security system to protect itself from a cyber-attack without any interventions from a human decision-maker is still a distant dream [5]. Thus, the role of human decision-makers in security systems is one that is crucial and indispensible [6, 7]. A key role in the cyber-security process is that of a security analyst: a decision-maker who is in charge of observing the online operations of a corporate network (e.g., an online retail company with an external webserver and an internal fileserver) from threats of random or organized cyber-attacks. The purpose of this paper will be to describe a cognitive model of the recognition and comprehension processes of a security analyst, where the model is based on the Instance-Based Learning Theory (IBLT, hereafter, IBL model) [8]. Furthermore, we evaluate the IBL model of the security analyst using two cyber SA measures: accuracy and timeliness [5]. The IBLT is well suited to modeling the decisions of a security analyst as the theory provides a generic decision-making process that starts by recognizing and generating experiences through interaction with a changing decision environment, and closes with the reinforcement of experiences that led to good decision outcomes through feedback from the decision environment.

2 A Simple Scenario of a Cyber Attack

The cyber-infrastructure in a corporate network typically consists of a webserver and a fileserver [9, 10]. The webserver handles customer interactions on a company's webpage. However, the fileserver handles the working of many workstations that are internal to the company and that allow company employees to do their daily operations. A bidirectional firewall (firewall 1 in Figure 1) protects the path between the webserver and the company's website on the Internet. Thus, firewall 1 allows both the incoming "request" traffic and the outgoing "response" traffic between the company's website and the webserver. Another firewall (firewall 2 in Figure 1) protects the path between the webserver and the fileserver. Firewall 2 is a much stronger firewall than the firewall 1 as it only allows a very limited Network File System (NFS) access of the fileserver from the webserver, but an easy access of the webserver from the fileserver (this latter access allows company employees to make changes on the webserver that would later show-up on the company's website). For this cyber-infrastructure, attackers follow a sequence of an "island-hopping" attack[5, pg. 30], where the webserver is compromised first, and then the webserver is used to originate attacks on the fileserver and other company workstations (the workstations are directly connected to the fileserver).

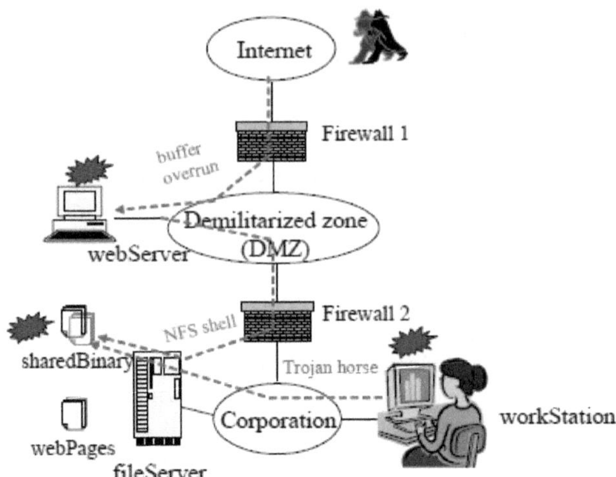

Fig. 1. A simple scenario of a cyber-attack. The attacker (shown as a black person) tries to gain access of a company's fileserver indirectly through the company's webserver. Source: [10].

Ou et al. [9] and Xie et al. [10] defined a simple scenario of an island-hopping cyber-attack within the cyber-infrastructure discussed above (see Figure 1). In the simple scenario, a security analyst is expose to a sequence of 25 network events (consisting of both threat and non-threat events) whose nature (threat or non-threat) is not precisely known to a security analyst. Out of the total of 25 events, there are 8 predefined threat events in the sequence that are initiated by an attacker. The attacker, through some of these 8 events, first compromises the webserver by remotely exploiting vulnerability on the webserver and getting a local access to the webserver. If the cyber-attack remains undetected by the security analyst by the 8th event out of a total of 25 events, then the attacker gains full access of the webserver. Since typically in a corporate network and in the simple scenario, a webserver is allowed to access the fileserver through only a NFS event, the attacker then modifies data on the fileserver through the vulnerability in the NFS event. If the cyber-attack remains undetected by the security analyst by the 11th event out of a total of 25, then the attacker gains full access of the file server. Once the attacker gets an access to modify files on the fileserver, he then installs a Trojan-horse program (i.e., a virus) in the executable binaries on fileserver that is used by different workstations (event 19th out of 25). The attacker can now wait for an innocent user on a workstation to execute the virus program and obtain control of user's workstation (event 21st out of 25).

During the course of the simple scenario, a security analyst is able to observe all the 25 events corresponding to file executions and packets of information transmitted on and between the webserver, fileserver, and different workstations. He is also able to observe alerts that correspond to some network events using an intrusion-detection system (IDS) [5]. The IDS raises an alert for a suspicious file execution or a packet transmission event that is generated on the corporate network. However, among the alerts generated by the IDS in the simple scenario, there is both a false-positive and a false-negative alert and one alert that correspond to the 8th event, but which is received by the analyst after the 13th event in the sequence (i.e., a time delayed alert).

Most importantly, due to the absence of a precise alert corresponding to a potential threat event, the analyst does not have precise information on whether a network event and its corresponding alert (from the IDS) are initiated by an attacker or by an innocent company employee. Even through the analyst lacks this precise information, he needs to decide, at the earliest possible and most accurately, whether the sequence of events in the simple scenario constitutes a cyber-attack. The earliest possible or proportion of timeliness is determined by subtracting the percentage of events seen by the analyst before he makes a decision about cyber-attack in the simple scenario to the total number of events (25) in the scenario from 100%. The accuracy of the analyst is determined by whether the analyst's decision was to ignore the sequence of events or declare a cyber-attack based upon the sequence of observed network events.

3 Motivation

Prior literature has shown that the SA of a security analyst is a function of the a priori experiences and knowledge level of the analyst about a cyber-attack scenario [5], and the willingness of the analyst to take risks, i.e., analyst's risk-tolerance [11, 12]. Prior research in judgment and decision making (JDM) has also discussed how our prior experiences of events in the environment shape our decision choices [13, 14]. Typically, having a greater number of bad experiences in memory about an activity makes a decision-maker avoid the activity; whereas, good experiences with an activity boost the likelihood of a decision-maker to undertake the same activity [13, 14]. Although there is abundant literature that discusses the role of prior experiences in general and the relevance of risk-tolerance in network security, there exists lack of a study that empirically investigates the role of both these factors together on the SA of a security analyst.

We believe that an analyst's correct and timely classification of a sequence of network events in the simple scenario as a cyber-attack or not, is based upon the following two factors:

1. The knowledge level of the analyst in terms of the mix of experiences stored in analyst's memory, and,
2. The analyst's risk-tolerance level, i.e., the willingness of an analyst to classify a sequence of events as a cyber-attack.

The above two factors as well as many other cognitive factors that may limit on enhance the cyber-SA of an analyst can be studied through computational cognitive modeling. In this paper, we use IBLT to develop a model of the security analyst and we assess the effects on the two factors on the accuracy and timeliness of the analyst to detect a cyber-attack in the simple scenario.

4 Instance-Based Learning Theory (IBLT) and IBL Model of Security Analyst

IBLT is a theory of how people make decisions from experience in a dynamic task [8]. In the past, computational models based on IBLT have proven to be accurate in generating predictions of human behavior in many dynamic-decision making situations like those faced by the security analyst [15, 16].

IBLT proposes that people represent every decision making situation as *instances* that are stored in memory. For each decision-making situation, an instance is retrieved from memory and reused depending on the similarity of the current situation's attributes to the attributes stored in instances in memory. An instance in IBLT is composed of three parts: situation (S) (the knowledge of situation attributes in a situation event), decision (D) (the course of action to take for a situation event), and utility (U) (i.e., a measure of the goodness of a decision made or the course of action taken for a situation event).

In the case of the decision situations faced by the security analyst, these attributes are those that characterize potential threat events in a corporate network and that needs to be investigated continuously by the analyst. The situation attributes that characterize potential threat events in the simple scenario are the *IP* address of the location (webserver, fileserver, or workstation) where the event took place, the *directory* location in which the event took place, whether the IDS raised an *alert* corresponding to the event, and whether the *operation* carried out as part of the event (e.g., a file execution) by a user of the network succeeded or failed.

In the IBL model of the security analyst, an instance's S slots refers to the situation attributes defined above; the D slot refers to the decision, i.e., whether to classify a sequence of events as constituting a cyber-attack or not; and, the U slot refers to the accuracy of the classification of an situation as a threat. IBLT proposes five mental phases in a closed-loop decision making process: recognition, judgment, choice, execution, and feedback (see Figure 2). The five decision phases of IBLT represent a complete learning cycle where the theory explains how knowledge is acquired, reused, and learnt by human decision-makers. Because the focus of this study is on the recognition and comprehension process in the SA of a security analyst, we will only focus on and discuss the recognition, judgment, choice, and execution phases in the IBLT (for details on the feedback phase, refer to [8, 15]). In addition to the IBLT's decision-making process, IBLT borrowed some of the proposed statistical-learning mechanisms from a popular cognitive architecture called ACT-R [17, 18]. Thus, most of the previous cognitive models that have used IBLT were developed within the ACT-R architecture.

The IBLT's process starts in the recognition phase in search for alternatives and classification of the current situation as *typical* or *atypical*. The current situation is typical if there are memories of similar situations (i.e., instances of previous trials that are similar enough to the current situation). If the situation is typical, then in the judgment phase, the most similar instance is retrieved from memory and is used in determining the value of the expected utility of the situation being evaluated. In the IBL model of the security analyst, the decision alternatives refer to whether a sequence of events constitutes a cyber-attack or not. For the model, the determination of the utility in the judgment phase means whether to comprehend a potential network event as a threat to the network or not. The actual determination of the utility is based upon the value in the utility slot of an instance retrieved from memory. The decision to retrieve an instance from memory for a situation event is determined based upon a comparison of the instance's memory strength, called *activation*. Thus, an instance is retrieved from memory if the instance has the highest activation among all instances in memory.

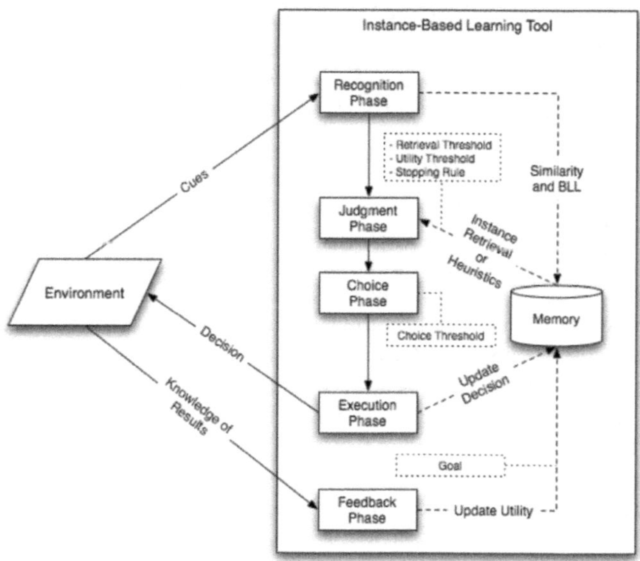

Fig. 2. The five phases of IBL theory (right) and an environment, i.e., a decision task with which a model developed according to the IBLT interacts (left).

However, if the situation event in the network is atypical (i.e., no instance similar to the situation event is found in memory), then a judgment heuristic rule is applied to determine the value of the utility of a new instance corresponding to a decision alternative. In the IBL model of the security analyst, we prepopulate the memory of a simulated analyst with certain instances to start with. These are assumed to be pre-stored experiences of past situations in the analyst's memory, and thus all situation events are treated by the model as typical.

Next, in the choice phase, a decision alternative is selected based upon the utility determined in the judgment phase (above). Thus, the choice phase in the IBL model of the security analyst consists of whether to classify a set of network events seen up to the current event in the scenario as constituting a cyber-attack, or whether to accumulate more evidence by further observing incoming situation events before such a classification could be made. According to IBLT, this decision is determined in the "necessity level" which represents a satisficing mechanism to stop search of the environment and be "satisfied" with the current evidence (e.g., the *satisficing strategy*) [19]. In the IBL model of the security analyst, we will call this parameter the "risk-tolerance level" (a free parameter) to represent the number of events the model has to classify as threats in the simple scenario before it classifies the scenario to constitute a cyber-attack. For the risk-tolerance level, each time the model classifies a situation event in the network as a threat (based upon retrieval of an instance from memory), a counter increments and signifies an accumulation of evidence in favor of a cyber-attack. If the value of the accumulated evidence (represented by the counter) becomes equal to the analyst's risk-tolerance level, the analyst will classify the scenario as a cyber-attack based upon the sequence of already observed network events; otherwise, the model will decide to continue obtaining more information from the environment, and observe the next situation event in the network. We manipulate the risk-tolerance parameter in this study at different number of events 2, 4, or 6 (more details ahead). Regardless, the main outcome of the choice phase in the model is whether to classify a set of network events as a cyber-attack or not.

The choice phase in the model is also based upon a property of analyst to exhibit "inertia," i.e., simply not to decide to classify a sequence of observed network events as a cyber-attack due to lack of attention and continue to wait for the next situation event. The inertia in the model is governed by a free parameter called *probability of inertia* (Pinertia) [15, 20]. If the value of a random number derived from a uniform distribution between 0 and 1 is less than Pinertia, the model will choose to observe another event in the scenario and will not classify the sequence of already observed events as a cyber-attack; otherwise, the model will make a decision to classify the sequence of already observed events based upon the set risk-tolerance level. We assumed a default value of Pinertia at 0.3 (or 30%).

The choice phase is followed by the execution of the best decision alternative. The execution phase for the IBL model of the security analyst means either to classify a sequence of observed events as a cyber-attack and stop online operations in the company, or *not* to classify the sequence of events as a cyber-attack and to let the online operations of the company continue undisrupted.

In IBLT, the activation of an instance i in memory is defined using the ACT-R architecture's activation equation:

$$A_i = B_i + \sum_{l=1}^{k} P_l \times M_{li} + \varepsilon_i \,. \tag{1}$$

where, B_i is the base-level learning parameter and reflects the recency and frequency of the use of the ith instance since the time it was created, which is given by:

$$B_i = ln\left(\sum_{t_i \in \{1,\dots,t-1\}} (t - t_i)^{-d} \right) \tag{2}$$

.

The frequency effect is provided by $t - 1$, the number of retrieval of the ith instance from memory in the past. The recency effect is provided by $t - t_i$, i.e., the event since the tth past retrieval of the ith instance (in equation 2, t denotes the current event number in the scenario). The d is the decay parameter and has a default value of 0.5 in the ACT-R architecture and it is the value we assume for the IBL model of the security analyst.

The $\sum_{l=1}^{k} P_l \times M_{li}$ summation is the similarity component and represents the mismatch between a situation event's attributes and the situation (S) slots of an instance i in memory. The k is the total number of attributes of a situation event that are used to retrieve the instance i from memory. In the IBL model of the security analyst, the value of k = 4, as in the simple scenario, there are 4 attributes that characterize a situation event in the network and that are also used to retrieve instances from memory. As mentioned above, these attributes are *IP*, *directory*, *alert*, and *operation* in an event. The match scale (P_l) reflects the amount of weighting given to the similarity between an instance *i*'s situation slot *l* and the corresponding situation event's attribute. P_l is generally a negative integer with a common value of -1.0 for all situation slots *k* of an instance *i*. We assume a value of -1.0 for the P_l in the IBL model of the security analyst. The M_{li} or match similarities represents the similarity between the value *l* of a situation event's attribute that is used to retrieve instances from memory and the value in the corresponding situation slots of an instance *i* in memory. Typically, M_{li} is defined using a squared distance between the situation event's attributes and corresponding situation slots in instances in memory [21]. Thus, in the IBL model of the security analyst, M_{li} is equal to sum of squared differences between a situation event's attributes and the corresponding situation slots of an instance. In order to find the sum of these squared differences, the situation events' attributes and the values in the corresponding slots of instances in memory were coded using numeric codes. Table 1 shows the codes assigned to the SDU slots of instances in memory and the situation events' attributes in the simple scenario.

Table 1. The coded values in the slots of an instance in memory and attributes of a situation event

Attributes	Values	Codes
IP (S)	Webserver	1
	Fileserver	2
	Workstation	3
Directory (S)	Missing value	-100
	File X	1
Alert (S)	Present	1
	Absent	0
Operation (S)	Successful	1
	Unsuccessful	0
Decision (D)	Cyber-attack	1
	No Cyber-attack	0
Threat (U)	Yes	1
	No	0

Due to the $\sum_{l=1}^{k} P_l \times M_{li}$ specification, instances that encode a similar situation to the current situation event's attributes, receive a less negative activation (in equation 1). In contrast, instances that encode a dissimilar situation to the current situation event's attributes receive a more negative activation.

Furthermore, ε_i is the noise value that is computed and added to an instance *i*'s activation at the time of its retrieval attempt from memory. The noise value is characterized by a parameter *s*. The noise is defined as,

$$\varepsilon_i = s \times ln\left(\frac{1-\eta_i}{\eta_i}\right). \tag{3}$$

where, η_i is a random draw from a uniform distribution bounded in [0, 1] for an instance *i* in memory. We set the parameter *s* in an IBL model to make it a part of the activation equation (equation 1). The *s* parameter has a default value of 0.25 in the

ACT-R architecture and we assume the default value of s in the IBL model of the security analyst.

5 Implementation and Execution of the IBL Model

The IBL model of the security analyst was created using Matlab software (the Matlab representation has already been evaluated to work similarly to the ACT-R representation, see [22]). The IBL model of the security analyst goes over a sequence of 25 network events in the simple scenario (Figure 1). We pre-populated the memory of a simulated analyst in the model with instances encoding all possible sequences of network events based upon values of events' attributes. Some of these instances in memory contained a threat value as the utility and some which do not (more information below). Unbeknownst to the model (but known to the modeler), out of the 25 events in the scenario (mentioned above), there are 8 pre-defined threat events that are executed by an attacker outside the company [9-10]. For each event in the scenario, the IBL model uses equation 1 – 3, to retrieve an instance that is most similar to the encountered event. Based upon the value of the utility slot of a retrieved instance, the situation event is classified as a threat or not a threat. Depending upon the inertia mechanism and the risk-tolerance level of a simulated analyst in the model, a decision is made to classify a sequence of observed events as a cyber-attack and stop company's online operations, or to let the company continue its online operations (no cyber-attack).

The IBL model was executed for a set of 500 repeated simulated trials of the same scenario where each simulated trial made the model to process 25 situation events in the network. For each set of 500 simulated trials, we manipulated the mix of threat and non-threat instances in memory of a simulated analyst, i.e., experience of the analyst, and the risk-tolerance level of the analyst.

The mix of threat and non-threat instances in the IBL model's memory could be one of the following three kinds: ambivalent analyst (Ambi): 50% of threat instances and 50% non-threat instances for each situation event in the scenario; an extra-careful analyst (Extra): 75% of threat instances and 25% of non-threat instances for each situation event in the scenario; and, a less-careful analyst (Less): 25% of threat instances and 75% of non-threat instances for each situation event in the scenario. The risk-tolerance level of analyst was manipulated as the following three levels: low (2 events out of a possible 25 event need to be classified as threats before the analyst classifies a sequence of observed events as cyber-attack); medium (4 events out of a possible 25 event to be classified as threats before the analyst classifies a sequence of observed events as cyber-attack); and, High (6 events out of a possible 25 event to be classified as threats before the analyst classifies a sequence of observed events as cyber-attack).

We wanted to derive predictions of the effect of the above manipulations in the IBL model upon the performance of the analyst. The performance of a simulated analyst was measured using the accuracy and timeliness of the analyst. The accuracy was evaluated using two different cyber-SA metrics, recall and precision, and the timeliness was evaluated in the model using a single timeliness cyber-SA metric [5]. Recall is the percent of events correctly detected as threats out of the total number of known threat events observed by the model before the model stopped (Recall is the same as hit rate in Signal Detection Theory). Precision is percentage of events correctly detected as threats out of the total number of threat events detected by the model before the model stopped. Timeliness is 100%-percentage of events, out of a total 25, after which the model stops and classifies the scenario to be a cyber-attack (the timeliness could be defined as the number of events out of 25, but defining it as a percentage allows us to compare it to other two SA measures). We expected best performance for the IBL model representing an extra-careful analyst with a low risk-tolerance, and the worst performance for the IBL model representing a less-careful analyst with a high risk-tolerance. This is because an extra-careful analyst with a low risk-tolerance will be classifying network events more cautiously as constituting a cyber-attack compared to a less-careful analyst with a high risk-tolerance.

6 Results

Figure 3 shows the predictions from the IBL model of the effects of manipulating the memory and the risk-tolerance upon the performance of the security analyst. Generally, as per our expectation, an extra-careful analyst with a low risk-tolerance did better on all three performance measures compared to a less-careful analyst with a high risk-tolerance. Furthermore, risk-tolerance and memory seem to impact all three performance measures; however, the Precision is always smaller than the Recall and Timeliness measures and this observation is to do with the fact that a model that is able to retrieve more threat instances from memory not necessarily retrieves them correctly, i.e., retrieve a threat instance from memory that *always* corresponds to a network threat event. Also, the effect of memory appears to be more impacting that the risk-tolerance of the analyst.

7 Discussion

In this paper, we have proposed that computational models based on the IBLT can be used to make predictions of the SA of a security analyst. Particularly, the model can make concrete predictions of the level of recall, precision, and timeliness of the security analyst given some level of experience (in memory) and risk-tolerance.

We created an IBL model of the analyst for a simple scenario of a typical island-hopping cyber-attack. Then, using the scenario, we evaluated the performance of a simulated analyst on three commonly used measures of cyber-SA. These measures are based upon accuracy of analyst (Precision and Recall) and the timeliness of the analyst (Timeliness). Our results reveal that both the risk-tolerance level of an analyst and the mix of threat and non-threat instances in analyst's memory affect the analyst's cyber SA with the effect of the analyst's experiences (in memory) slightly more impacting compared to analyst's risk-tolerance. The less impact of the risk-tolerance factor compared to memory could be due to the nature of IBL models that are strongly dependent upon retrieval of instances from memory to make choice decisions.

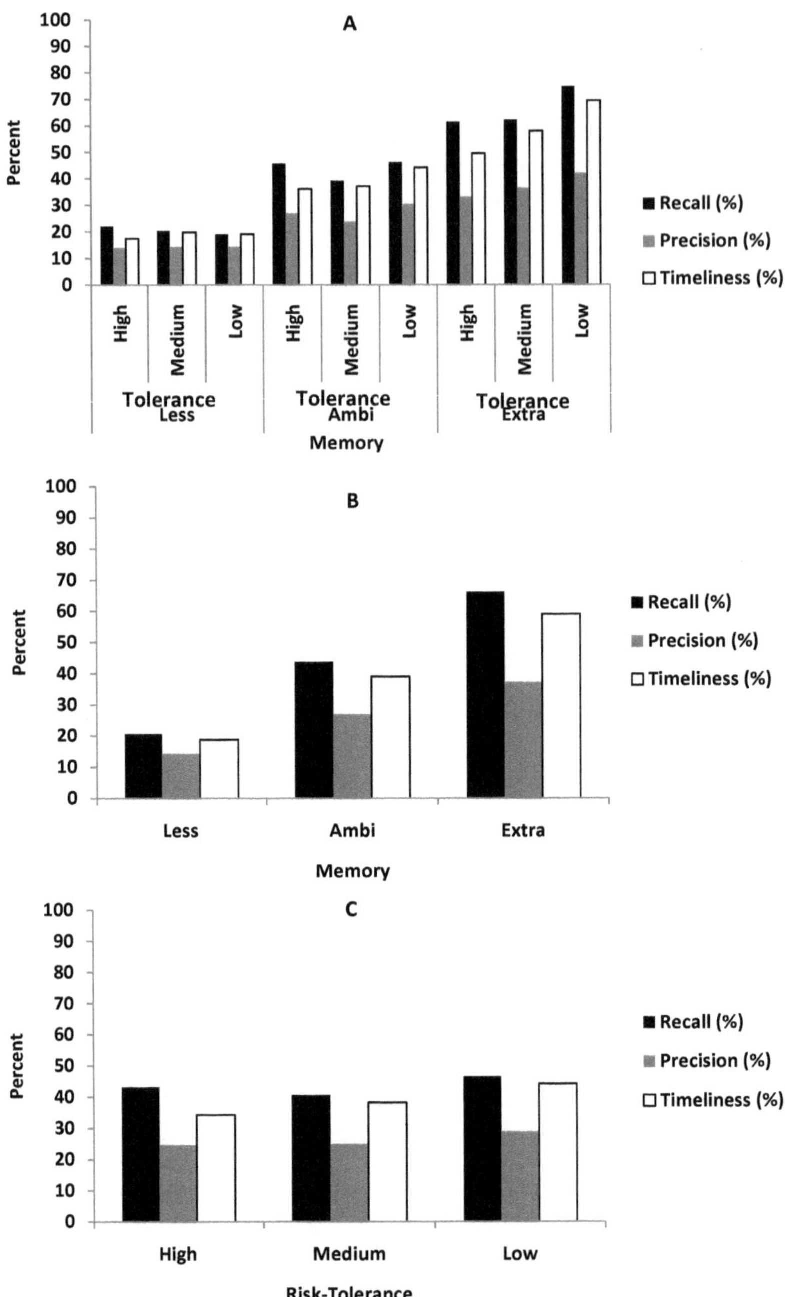

Fig. 3. (A) The interaction effect of memory and risk-tolerance on cyber SA of an analyst. (B) The effect of memory alone on cyber SA of an analyst. (C) The effect of risk-tolerance alone on cyber SA of an analyst. A greater percentage on all three cyber SA measures is more desirable as it makes the simulated analyst more efficient.

When the simulated analyst is less-careful, then for any situation event the model has only a 25% chance of retrieving threat instances and 75% chance of it retrieving non-threat instances. As a consequence, the model has a lesser chance to classify actual threats in the simple scenario as threats and it takes more time for the model to accumulate evidence that is more than the risk-tolerance level (decreasing the Timeliness). However, when the simulated analyst is more-careful, then for any situation event there is a 75% chance of the model retrieving threat instances and 25% chance of it retrieving non-threat instances. As a consequence, the model has a greater chance to classify actual threats in the simple scenario as threats and it takes less time for the model to accumulate evidence that is equal to the risk-tolerance level (increasing the Timeliness).

The important aspect of the model is the fact that although the Recall and Timeliness increase as a direct function of the ability of the model to retrieve threat instances from the memory and its risk-tolerance, there is not a substantial increase in model's Precision when either of the two factors is favorable (Figure 3 A, B, and C). The slow increase in Precision is expected because a model that is able to retrieve more threat instances from memory and is less risk-tolerant, might not necessarily be more precise in its actions. However, there is still an increase in Precision with a manipulation of both factors and this suggests that making a security analyst less risk-tolerant as well as extra-careful might help increase the job-efficiency of the analyst. These are only some of the many predictions that the IBL model is able to make regarding the Cyber-SA of human analysts.

Although the current model is able to make precise predictions, these need to be validated with human data, i.e., observed behavior from a human security analyst operating in the simple scenario. We plan to run laboratory studies in the near future to assess human behavior in this simple scenario. An experimental approach will allow us to validate our model predictions and improve the relevance of the model and assumptions made in it on its free parameters. In these experimental studies, we believe that some of the interesting factors to manipulate would include the experiences of the human analyst (stored in memory). One method we have thought currently is to make the analyst read examples of more and less threat scenarios before the analyst participates in the act of detecting cyber-attacks in the simple scenario. Also, we plan to record the risk-taking and risk-averse behavior of the analyst in the study to control for the risk-tolerance factor. Thus, our next goal will be to validate the predictions from the IBL model.

If our model is able to represent the Cyber-SA of human analysts accurately, this model would have significant potential to contribute towards the design of training and decision support tools for security analysts.

Acknowledgements

This research was a part of a Multidisciplinary University Research Initiative Award (MURI; # W911NF-09-1-0525) from Army Research Office for a research project on Cyber Situation Awareness. We would like to thank Hau-yu Wong, Dynamic Decision Making Laboratory, for help with editorial work in the paper.

References

1. Cybersecurity, http://www.whitehouse.gov/the_press_office/Remarks-by-the-President-on-Securing-Our-Nations-Cyber-Infrastructure/
2. London 2012 Olympics faces increased cyber attack threat, http://www.guardian.co.uk/uk/2011/jan/19/london-2012-olympics-cyber-attack
3. Endsley, M.: Toward a Theory of Situation Awareness in Dynamic Systems. Hum. Fact. 37, 32–64 (1995)
4. Tadda, G., Salerno, J.J., Boulware, D., Hinman, M., Gorton, S.: Realizing Situation Awareness Within a Cyber Environment. In: Proceedings of SPIE, vol. 6242, p. 624204. SPIE, Kissimmee (2006)
5. Jajodia, S., Liu, P., Swarup, V., Wang, C. (eds.): Cyber Situational Awareness. Springer, New York (2001)
6. Gardner, H.: The Mind's New Science: A History of the Cognitive Revolution. Basic Books, New York (1987)
7. Johnson-Laird, P.: How We Reason. Oxford University Press, London (2006)
8. Gonzalez, C., Lerch, J.F., Lebiere, C.: Instance-Based Learning in Dynamic Decision Making. Cog. Sci. 27(4), 591–635 (2003)
9. Ou, X., Boyer, W.F., McQueen, M.A.: A Scalable Approach to Attack Graph Generation. In: Proceedings of the 13th ACM Conference on Computer and Communications Security, pp. 336–345. ACM, Alexandria (2006)
10. Xie, P., Li, J.H., Ou, X., Liu, P., Levy, R.: Using Bayesian Networks for Cyber Security Analysis. In: Proceedings of the 2010 IEEE/IFIP International Conference on Dependable Systems and Networks (DSN), pp. 211–220. IEEE Press, Hong Kong (2010)
11. McCumber, J.: Assessing and Managing Security Risk in IT Systems: A Structured Methodology. Auerbach Publications, Boca Raton (2004)
12. Salter, C., Saydjari, O., Schneier, B., Wallner, J.: Toward a Secure System Engineering Methodology. In: Proceedings of New Security Paradigms Workshop, pp. 2–10. ACM, Charlottesville (1998)
13. Lejarraga, T., Dutt, V., Gonzalez, C.: Instance-Based Learning: A General Model of Decisions from Experience in Repeated Binary Choice. J. Behav. Dec. Mak. (in press)
14. Hertwig, R., Barron, G., Weber, E.U., Erev, I.: Decisions from Experience and the Effect of Rare Events in Risky Choice. Psych. Sci. 15, 534–539 (2004)
15. Gonzalez, C., Dutt, V.: Instance-Based Learning: Integrating Sampling and Repeated Decisions from Experience. Psych. Rev. (in press)
16. Dutt, V., Cassenti, D.N., Gonzalez, C.: Modeling a Robotics Operator Manager in a Tactical Battlefield. In: Proceedings of the IEEE First International Multi-Disciplinary Conference on Cognitive Methods in Situation Awareness and Decision Support (CogSIMA), pp. 82–87. IEEE Press, Miami Beach (2011)
17. Anderson, J.R., Lebiere, C.: The Atomic Components of Thought. Lawrence Erlbaum Associates, Hillsdale (1998)
18. Anderson, J.R., Lebiere, C.: The Newell Test for a Theory of Mind. Behav. Brain Sci. 26, 587–639 (2003)
19. Simon, H.A., March, J.G.: Organizations. Wiley, New York (1958)
20. Gonzalez, C., Dutt, V., Lejarraja, T.: A Loser Can Be a Winner: Comparison of Two Instance-based Learning Models in a Market Entry Competition. Games 2(1), 136–162 (2011)
21. Shepard, R.N.: The Analysis of Proximities: Multidimensional Scaling with an Unknown Distance Function. Psychometrika 2, 125–140 (1962)
22. Gonzalez, C., Dutt, V., Lebiere, C.: Building a New Instance-Based Learning Modeling Tool (unpublished manuscript in preparation, 2011)

Leveraging UML for Security Engineering and Enforcement in a Collaboration on Duty and Adaptive Workflow Model That Extends NIST RBAC

Solomon Berhe[1], Steven Demurjian[1], Swapna Gokhale[1], Jaime Pavlich-Mariscal[2,3], and Rishi Saripalle[1]

[1] Department of Computer Science & Engineering, University of Connecticut, U-2155, 371 Fairfield Road, Storrs, CT, USA
{solomon.berhe,steve,ssg,rishikanth}@engr.uconn.edu
[2] Pontificia Universidad Javeriana, Cra 7 N 40-62, Bogota, Colombia
[3] Universidad Catolica del Norte, Angamos 0610, Antofagasta, Chile
jpavlich@ucn.cl, jpavlich@javeriana.edu.co

Abstract. To facilitate collaboration in the patient-centered medical home (PCMH), our prior work extended the NIST role-based access control (RBAC) model to yield a formal collaboration on duty and adaptive workflow (COD/AWF) model. The next logical step is to place this work into the context of an integrated software process for security engineering from design through enforcement. Towards this goal, we promote a secure software engineering process that leverages an extended unified modeling language (UML) to visualize COD/AWF policies to achieve a solution that separates concerns while still providing the means to securely engineer dynamic collaborations for applications such as the PCMH. Once defined, these collaboration UML diagrams can be utilized to generate the corresponding aspect oriented policy code upon which the enforcement mechanism can be applied to at runtime.

1 Introduction and Motivation

Over the last five years there has been a dramatic shift towards collaborative computing in multiple domains. One such application domain is the patient-centered medical home (PCMH) where a primary physician coordinates care for a patient across a range of providers, who all must interact with one another across distance and time [1]. Our prior work in this regard has been a formal model for obligated collaboration on duty and adaptive workflow (COD/AWF) [3] that extends the National Institute of Standards and Technology (NIST) Role-Based Access Control (RBAC) model [11]. This COD/AWF model adds capabilities to NIST RBAC that include: secure collaboration to control access to data; obligated collaboration which denotes individuals that must participate and how they interact; team-based collaboration, which defines the collaboration with multiple individuals; and coordinated collaboration, which characterizes

Y. Li (Ed.): Data and Applications Security and Privacy XXV, LNCS 6818, pp. 293–300, 2011.

the way that individuals are allowed to interact with one another. These four components are grouped together into the following definition:

Def. 1 *COD = [$\mathcal{COD}_{ID}$, $\mathcal{COD}_{NAME}$, $\mathcal{TEAM}$, $\mathcal{CODC}$, $\mathcal{P}$, $\mathcal{CW}$] is a uniquely $\mathcal{COD}_{ID}$ named collaboration $\mathcal{COD}_{NAME}$ with a team of role types $\mathcal{TEAM}$, a set of collaboration constraints $\mathcal{CODC}$, a set of permissions $\mathcal{P}$, and a collaboration workflow $\mathcal{CW}$ composed out of collaboration steps.*

The next logical step is to explore its integration into a software process that includes security engineering from design through enforcement. Towards this goal, we promote security engineering that leverages an extended unified modeling language (UML) to visualize COD/AWF policies to separate concerns while still providing the means to securely engineer collaborations for applications such as the PCMH. Defining collaborative security for PCMH will require role teams, obligations, collaboration steps, and workflows, resulting in requirements that are tangled with one another. The contribution of this work is two-fold, first we propose a set of new UML slice diagrams for COD/AWF that extends prior work on UML with roles, delegation, and user authorization diagrams [10]. Second, these COD/AWF diagrams will be utilized to generate the corresponding policy code upon which the enforcement mechanism can be applied to. There has been a myriad of related work with regard to UML and access control and workflows [4,7,8,10,12,14,15], however none of it considers an integrated Collaboration on Duty (COD) approach which integrates the four components (Obligation, Access Control, Workflow and Teams) into a single formal model. Moreover, to the best of our knowledge no MDA-based approach has been done which extends UML with the four components facilitating separation of concerns and generating COD policy code. The remainder of this paper contains three sections. Section 2 introduces an approach for security engineering of COD/AWF with UML and proposed extensions. Section 3 presents the code templates that are collected together followed by concluding remarks in section 4.

2 Security Engineering of COD/AWF with UML

This section proposes four new UML diagrams that are utilized to constrain and define permissions associated with collaboration, namely: the positive and negative role slice diagrams and the team slice diagram in Section 2.1; the obligation slice diagram and the collaboration workflow slice diagram in Section 2.2. By differentiating between these four diagrams, we essentially separate the concerns to allow the different aspects of permissions to be characterized in different diagrams as illustrated in Figure 1.

2.1 UML Role and Team Slice Diagram

The role slice diagram in Fig. 1a defines permissions [6] for the Emergency Room Collaboration (ERC) has CS Triage (others not shown). Triage negates permission getBillingHistory and getAppointmentHistory. During the collaboration, all activated permissions must be a subset of $\mathcal{P}$ (Def. 1), which is modeled using

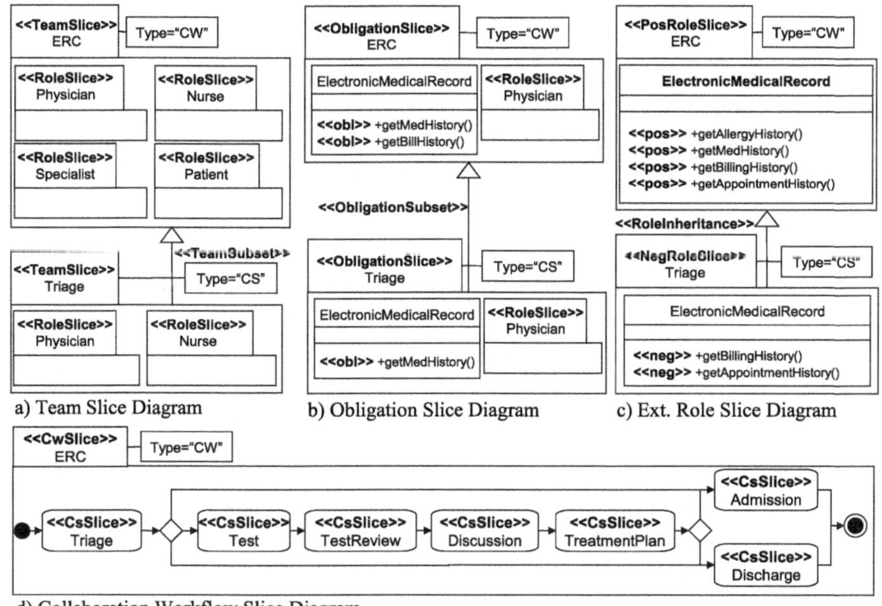

Fig. 1. COD UML Slice Diagrams

$<< \mathit{RoleInheritance} >>$ stereotype, such that the assigned $\mathcal{P}$ to the collaboration workflow (CW) is represented as the root role slice (Fig. 1c). This CW type is tracked through the use of UML tagged values (Type="CW" and Type="CS"). It's used to match role slices with the corresponding CW, CSs, and roles in the remaining slices (Figs. 1a, 1b, and 1d). All collaboration steps that are activities in the CW are only allowed to activate a subset of $\mathcal{P}$. The current inheritance semantics allows adding additional positive permissions to any role slice [10]. Our objective is to capture COD role slice inheritance semantics in which CSs are only permitted to activate the set of permissions which is not specified as negative and is present in the parent role slice [5]. To enforce this semantic, we extend this notion of role slice with two new annotations: $<< \mathit{PosRoleSlice} >>$ which only allows the specification of positive permissions and is used in the root role slice to set the scope of allowed privileges throughout the collaboration; and, $<< \mathit{NegRoleSlice} >>$ which only allows the specification of negative permissions which is utilized to further restrict privileges in a particular collaboration step (CS).

The team slice diagram in Fig. 1a depicts a separate concern to capture permissions for the entire team. In the ERC example, each team contains the specific role slices that are needed; the latter is inclusive of all roles (entire team of four roles), the former limited to roles within a step. Using the subset $<< \mathit{TeamSubset} >>$ relationship for the team slice diagram, the root slice represents $\mathcal{TEAM}$ (Def. 1) and all CSs subset team members from this root team slice. A team slice is depicted as a UML package with the stereotype

<< *TeamSlice* >>. This package contains a set of role slices. Permissions are not specified - they are given in the role slice diagram in Fig. 1c - and the focus for team slices is to specify the participants of each step. For permission activation, team membership allows a role to be authorized to permissions.

2.2 UML New Obligation and Workflow Slice Diagram

The obligation slice diagram in Fig. 1b defines the set of permissions that are required to be activated and roles that must participate. These complement RBAC constraints and model the obligation requirement (who is allowed to perform which method at which time) [9]. In Fig. 1b, for the ERC team, a physician is a role that is obligated to participate. For example, during "Triage" CS, the physician must participate. In COD/AWF, obligated participation implies that a role must activate at least one of its permissions. With regard to obligated permission activation, getMedHistory *must* be activated before the collaboration terminates. The obligated activation of a permission requires its activation of any authorized role in the collaboration before it can terminate. Permissions from Fig. 1c are used to constrain the role slice elements within the obligation slice. Permission activation requirements are modeled as classes along with their obligated permissions that are elements of the obligation slice marked using the << *obl* >> stereotype. Similar to the team slices, the root obligation slice represents the set of obligations that must be activated during the entire collaboration, while each collaboration step only must fulfill a subset of it. This is depicted using the << *ObligationSubset* >> stereotype.

The collaboration workflow diagram leverages and extends the UML activity diagram and allows the security engineer to focus only on the design of the healthcare coordination requirements. In Fig. 1d, the ERC package is composed of 7 collaboration steps into a workflow. The annotation << *CwSlice* >> is in charge of matching the collaboration steps in the other COD slices with the corresponding collaboration workflow $\mathcal{CW}$ (Def. 1). Access control, obligation and team requirements are unified in this diagram by essentially linking across the four diagrams (1a-1d); while the concerns are separate, they are tied with one another though naming convention and are linked through the unique identifier where matching CS identifiers are located in the previous three slices.

3 Mapping to Enforcement Policies for COD/AWF

Section 2 visually specified COD/AWF via extended UML, and using that as a basis, this section explores the generation of enforcement code that exactly meets the COD/AWF requirements as defined in the UML slices (see Fig. 1a to 1d). Specifically, this section presents the mapping of the four new/extended COD/AWF UML diagrams to a policy code-based model, which are interfaces/ templates from which actual collaboration domain application can then be enforced at runtime. Accompanying these policy code templates is an authorization enforcement algorithm which checks if a user in a particular collaboration is permitted to activate a permission in a workflow at a particular step (not shown).

Our intent in this section is to demonstrate the generated policy code model (templates) for the example as given in Section 2. Note that the COD/AWL UML new/extended diagrams and the code model are extensions to the formal UML Class meta model (not shown)[13]. Finally, this work uses Java-like code templates to illustrate the code mapping of the COD/AWL diagrams.

The remainder of this section is organized as follows. Section 3.1 presents the code template for the role slice and the team slice diagram. Section 3.2 details the code template for the obligation slice and the collaboration workflow slice diagram.

3.1 Policy Code Template for the Role and Team Slice Diagram

The negative and positive role slices allow us to define the set of allowable permissions during the Emergency Room Collaboration (ERC) at the root slice node. In this context, we utilize role slices to define the specific privileges that are associated with the ERC and each of its collaboration steps (e.g. Triage, Admission, etc.). The permissions assigned to the collaboration step/workflow are specified as interfaces which can be implemented by specific classes (e.g. Triage interface can be implemented for an ERTriage or RegularTriage class); this is shown by the code template a) for the slice of Fig. 1c. This allows this COD/AWF framework to be generic enough to adapt to the particular sub-domain (e.g., CDC, Hospital, Clinic, Family Practice, etc.). We utilize the ElectronicMedicalRecord (EMR) class to specify all of the privileges that can be performed against this patients' clinical data. The annotations @PosRoleSlice and @NegRoleSlice are applied to interfaces and enforce sub-interfaces to only specify positive (@pos) or negative (@neg) permissions. This requirement can be verified at runtime using meta programming. In this example, every class that implements the Triage collaboration step interface in the context of ERC is not allowed to activate both permissions getBillingHistory but only getMedHistory (see Code Template b).

```
Policy Code Template a)
@PosRoleSlice
public interface ERC{
  public interface EMR {
    @pos getMedHistory();
    @pos getBillingHistory();
  }
}
```

```
Policy Code Template b)
@NegRoleSlice
public interface Triage ext ERC{
  public interface EMR {
    @neg getBillingHistory();
  }
}
```

In the code template for the collaboration team slice diagram, the root team slice specifies the entire team (from Triage to Admission/Discharge); this is shown by the code template c) for the slice of Fig. 1a. Each team is marked using the @TmSlice annotation. A particular collaboration step further restricts the participation of roles depending on the context using the subset relationship. In the policy code, this relationship is expressed through the @TmSubset annotation. Both annotations can only be applied to interface, which allows the specification of generic teams which can be customized in a particular domain through specific implementation. In this example, the ERC team is composed out of all roles depicted in Fig. 1a. During the Triage collaboration step, only users with the Physician is allowed to participate (policy code template d); all other roles are prohibited to participate in this collaboration step. Fig. 1a only contains a partial representation of who can participate in which steps; for a full collaboration, the diagram would have additional TeamSlice definitions for all collaboration steps.

```
Policy Code Template c)
@TmSlice
public interface ERC{
  public interface Roles {
    public interface Nurse();
    public interface Physician();
  }
}
```

```
Policy Code Template d)
@TmSlice
  @TmSubset(name=TmSlice, val=ERC)
  public interface Triage {
    public interface Roles {
      public interface Physician();
    }
  }
```

3.2 Policy Code Template for the Obligation and Workflow Slice Diagram

The obligation slice policy defines the permissions that must be activated and roles that must participate during a particular collaboration step. The root node defines the obligations that can be specified throughout the ERC collaboration workflow; this is shown by the code template e) for the slice of Fig. 1b. This is denoted using the @CodcSlice annotation. The @CodcSubest annotation further subsets the obligation requirements for a child collaboration step. All of the required roles and permissions are marked using @obl annotation. For example, during the Triage step (policy code template f), it is required to review the patients' medication history but not to read the billing. In terms of participation, Triage requires the Physician to participate. Again, the policy code templates e) and f) only presents a partial definition of the obligation slices. The final part

```
Policy Code Template e)
@CodcSlice
public interface ERC{
  public interface Roles {
    public interface Nurse();
    public interface Physician();
  }
  public interface EMR {
    @pos getMedHistory();
    @pos getBillingHistory();
  }
}
```

```
Policy Code Template f)
@CodcSlice
@CodcSubest(name=CodcSlice, val=EMC)
  public interface Triage ext ERC{
    public interface Roles {
      public interface Physician();
    }
    public interface EMR {
      @pos getMedHistory();
    }
  }
```

of the COD/AWF policies specifies all of the collaboration steps and the order in which they must be activated. The << *CollabSlice* >> marks an interface as a collaboration step and the << *NextCollabSlice* >> states the subsequent collaboration steps; this is shown by the code template g) for the slice of Fig. 1d. The ERC interface name along with its collaboration step names are utilized to link them to the code as given in Figs. 1a-1c. The collaboration workflow is annotated using @CollabWorkflowSlice, and each of its collaboration steps with @CollabSlice. Moreover, each collaboration step contains the information about the subsequent collaboration steps using @NextCollabSlice. Again, the code template g) only shows the first two steps of the collaboration in Fig. 1d; the full code template would have all of the steps and represent the entire needed workflow for each collaboration.

```
Policy Code Template g)
@CollabWorkflowSlice
public interface ERC{
  @CollabSlice
  @NextCS(name=CollabSlice value="Test, Admission, Discharge")
  public interface Triage();

  @CollabSlice
  @NextCS(name=CollabSlice value="TestReview, Admission, Discharge")
  public interface Test();
}
```

4 Conclusion

Collaboration applications such as the patient-centered medical home (PCMH) require individuals to interact with one another towards a common goal (treat a patient) across time and under certain limitations; such applications must provide a means to facilitate access and interaction across a sophisticated workflow that is adaptable. The work reported herein extends our prior work on adding collaboration on duty and adaptive workflow (COD/AWF) to NIST RBAC by considering security engineering for collaborative applications that can leverage existing, extended, and new UML diagrams, thereby elevating security to a first class citizen in an integrated software process. Towards this objective, the paper: proposed four new collaboration diagrams that extend and augment UML to separate concerns for the COD/AWF model in Section 2; presented policy code templates a-g for the four new UML diagrams (Fig. 1a-d) of Section 2. Overall, we believe this work is a crucial step forward for both collaborative security and security engineering, particularly in applications like PCMH.

References

1. American Academy of Family Physicians (AACP), http://www.aafp.org/pcmh
2. Ahn, G., Sandhu, R.: Role-based authorization constraints specification. ACM Transaction on Information and System Security 3, 207–226 (2010)
3. Berhe, S., Demurjian, S., Agresta, T.: Emerging Trends in Health Care Delivery: Towards Collaborative Security for NIST RBAC. In: Gudes, E., Vaidya, J. (eds.) Data and Applications Security XXIII. LNCS, vol. 5645, pp. 283–290. Springer, Heidelberg (2009)
4. Bertino, E., Ferrari, E., Atluri, V.: The Specification and Enforcement of Authorization Constraints in Workflow Management Systems. ACM Trans. Inf. Syst. Secur. 2(1), 65–104 (1999)
5. Budd, T.: An Introduction to Object-Oriented Programming. Addison-Wesley, Reading (1997)
6. Centonze, P., Naumovich, G., Fink, J.S., Pistoia, M.: Role-Based access control consistency validation. In: Proceedings of the International Symposium on Software Testing and Analysis (2006)
7. D'Amour, D., Goulet, L., Jean-Francois, L., Martin-Rodriguez, S.L., Raynald, P.: A model and typology of collaboration between professionals in healthcare organizations. BMC Health Services Research (2008)
8. Juerjens, J.: Secure Systems Development with UML. Springer, Heidelberg (2003)
9. Li, N., Tripunitara, M., Bizri, Z.: On mutually exclusive roles and separation-of-duty. ACM Transaction of Information System Security (2007)
10. Pavlich-Mariscal, J., Demurjian, S., Laurent, D.M.: A framework of composable access control features: Preserving separation of access control concerns from models to code. Science Direct, Special Issue on Software Engineering for Secure Systems 29, 350–379 (2010)
11. Sandhu, R., Ferraiolo, D.F., Kuhn, R.: The NIST Model for Role Based Access Control: Toward a Unified Standard. In: Proceedings of the 5th ACM Workshop on Role Based Access Control, Berlin, pp. 47–63 (2000)
12. Sun, Y., Shijun, X., Peng, P.L.: Flexible Workflow Incorporated with RBAC. In: Shen, W.-m., Chao, K.-M., Lin, Z., Barthès, J.-P.A., James, A. (eds.) CSCWD 2005. LNCS, vol. 3865, pp. 525–534. Springer, Heidelberg (2006)
13. Teilans, A., Kleins, A., Sukovskis, U., Merkuryev, Y., Meirans, I.: A Meta-Model Based Approach to UML Modelling. In: Proceedings of the 10th International Conference on Computer Modeling and Simulation, pp. 667–672 (2008)
14. Thomas, K.R.: Team-based access control (TMAC): a primitive for applying role-based access controls in collaborative environments. In: Proceedings of the 2nd ACM Workshop on Role-based Access Control (1997)
15. Zarnett, J., Tripunitara, M., Lam, P.: Role-based access control (RBAC) in Java via proxy objects using annotations. In: Proceedings of the 15th ACM Symposium on Access Control Models and Technologies (2010)

Preserving Privacy in Structural Neuroimages

Nakeisha Schimke, Mary Kuehler, and John Hale

Institute of Bioinformatics and Computational Biology,
The University of Tulsa,
800 South Tucker Drive,
Tulsa, Oklahoma 74104

Abstract. Evolving technology has enabled large-scale collaboration for neuroimaging data. For high resolution structural neuroimages, these data are inherently identifiable and must be given the same privacy considerations as facial photographs. To preserve privacy, identifiable metadata should be removed or replaced, and the voxel data de-identified to remove facial features by applying skull stripping or a defacing algorithm. The Quickshear Defacing method uses a convex hull to identify a plane that divides the volume into two parts, one containing facial features and another the brain volume, and removes the voxels on the facial features side. This method is an effective alternative to existing solutions and can provide reductions in running time.

Keywords: Medical image privacy, neuroimaging, de-identification, HIPAA.

1 Introduction

The digitization of health records and medical images has transformed healthcare and medical research. New technologies provide instant access to patient and subject data by automatically disseminating the information to healthcare providers and research collaborators. Expanded storage and transfer capabilities have made feasible the addition of medical images to these electronic records, but as the demand for capturing and storing images increases, so does the need for privacy measures. For shared data sets, the need for removing protected health information (PHI) is agreed upon, but the extent to which medical images constitute PHI is still debated.

The Health Insurance Portability and Accountability Act (HIPAA) Privacy Rule [12] defines “full face photographic images and any comparable images” as PHI. With respect to identifiability, high resolution structural magnetic resonance imaging (MRI) datasets are comparable to full face photographs, and volume rendering software is freely available. Fig. 1 is a volume rendering of a structural MRI using 3D Slicer [1], an open source software package for medical image analysis. The result is clearly identifiable as a human face.

The challenges of removing identifiable metadata are well documented, and there are numerous tools for automating the process. There are also formal

Y. Li (Ed.): Data and Applications Security and Privacy XXV, LNCS 6818, pp. 301–308, 2011.

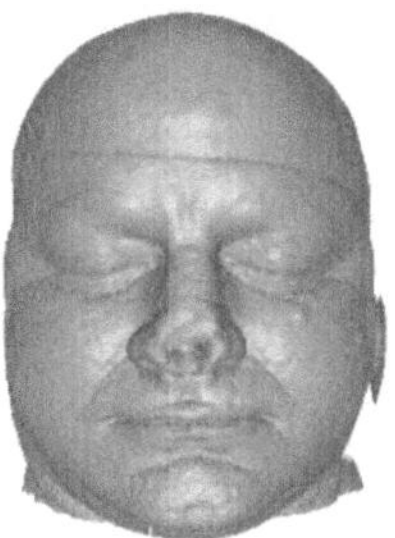

Fig. 1. Volume rendering using 3D Slicer. Sample MRI data is from 3D Slicer.

models for privacy, such as *k-anonymity* [23]. However, the inherent privacy risks of the neuroimages themselves is less well defined. The relative anonymity of subjects in structural MRI may be compromised by the image itself. This paper explores the potential privacy hazards associated with neuroimage datasets. It also proposes a new algorithm for image-based de-identification of neuroimages and evaluates its effectiveness and performance.

2 Background

Large scale collaborative research efforts have the potential to transform neuroscience. The Alzheimer's Disease Neuroimaging Initiative (ADNI) [2] is a multisite collaborative research project that has collected images from over 40 sites and distributed data to more than 1,300 investigators to date [13, 15]. Its success has inspired similar initiatives for other diseases.

There are, however, obstacles to neuroimage data sharing that hamper collaboration. Solutions to technical challenges, including data storage, transmission, management, and dissemination, continue to evolve. The task of maintaining subject privacy while disseminating data has made significant progress. Metadata removal is routinely integrated into the scientific workflow. However, the determination of when and how to apply de-identification to the neuroimage itself has yet to be made. The benefits of sharing neuroimaging data are clear, but pressing concerns over subject privacy must first be addressed.

The terms *anonymization* and *de-identification* are often used interchangeably, but their subtle differences are significant to subject privacy. The core idea mechanism for patient privacy relies on obscuring the subject's identity by hiding medical and personal data, often applied to meet the de-identification requirements of HIPAA. A dataset de-identified under the HIPAA Privacy Rule can be distributed and used. HIPAA designates eighteen identifiers as PHI, including "full face photographic images and any comparable images" [12].

Anonymization is not as clearly defined. True anonymity would prevent a dataset from ever being re-identified but is difficult to achieve while retaining useful data [18]. Neuroimaging studies often require metadata such as gender and age for analysis, and removing these could negatively impact results. Practical anonymity inhabits a grey area between true anonymity and an acceptable yet undefined limit to the possibility of re-identification.

The need for re-evaluation of PHI is evident when a few pieces of seemingly innocuous data can be re-linked to identify a subject. Medical images belong to a class of health data that is inherently self identifying and laden with contextual information about the subject, their condition, treatment, and medical and personal history. The privacy issues associated with the storage and use of medical images warrant special consideration, and the current approaches of simply removing metadata may be insufficient.

3 Privacy Issues in Medical Images

While textual data can be redacted by simply removing or replacing the offending field, the image, which can constitute self identifying data, is not so easily sanitized. Removing identifying features in medical images may destroy the very information a researcher needs.

Table 1. Threats to subject privacy from medical images

Type	Description	Example
Direct	Reveals a condition	X-ray reveals fractured wrist
Re-linkage	Metadata reveals identity	Metadata includes gender, age, and zip code and tied back to patient
Existential Inference	Image known to exist	Subject in imaging study assumed to be a case rather than control
Identification	Inherently identifiable	Facial features identify subject

The primary threats to subject privacy from medical images are listed in Table 1. A direct threat occurs when the image reveals a condition or other private information, but a more likely scenario is re-linkage, where the image is used to identify the subject along with metadata. The existence of a medical image or participation in a study may also suggest the presence of a condition, perhaps incorrectly. Neuroimages are particularly challenging because they are inherently identifiable. High resolution neuroimages contain detailed facial features that can be used to re-identify the subject. The neuroimage could be used to discover an identity from a large database of faces or to confirm a subject's identity.

3.1 Neuroimage Re-identification

There are many potential avenues for re-identifying a subject using their neuroimage. Re-identification occurs in two phases, reconstruction and recognition. The reconstruction phase produces a likeness of the subject to be used in the recognition phase for discovering the subject's identity.

In forensic science, facial reconstruction requires a blend of artistic and scientific skills to reproduce a likeness of the subject. Reconstruction is more straightforward using structural MRI because of the high spatial resolution. Several packages for analyzing neuroimage data provide built-in volume rendering capabilities, including AFNI [3], 3D Slicer [1], and MRIcron [20]. Typical volume rendering software offers the ability to change lighting conditions and viewing angles. These features can be used to match rendered volumes against photographic facial images.

Facial recognition can be applied using a variety of techniques to achieve novel identification, attempting to discover an identity, or identity confirmation. Metadata can be used to guide a facial recognition search, narrowing down the potential subjects using basic non-PHI fields such as gender and age. The current limitations and relatively poor performance of facial recognition techniques make it tempting to dismiss the potential for re-identification based on flawed assumptions: (1) facial recognition will never improve, and (2) only correct identifications are problematic. The latter fails to consider the damage caused by incorrect identification. Challenging a false re-identification may require the individual to reveal their records.

The problems plaguing facial recognition techniques are not easily confronted, but researchers in the field are making progress. Facial recognition techniques are detailed with links to recent advances at the Face Recognition Homepage [10]. A NIST report on face recognition illustrates significant improvements in the field[11].

Hardware advances can also improve the results of facial recognition. Increased storage capacity and computing power allow higher quality images to be stored and compared more quickly. Facial recognition software struggles when viewing angles and lighting vary [24], but volume rendering software can generate multiple images with a wide range of light sources and angles to match source photographs. Therefore, if neuroimage-based recognition can perform with comparable results, they must be offered the same protection.

3.2 Neuroimage De-identification

There are two common approaches to de-identifying neuroimages, skull stripping and defacing. Skull stripping is the identification and removal of non-brain tissue as part of the typical analysis workflow. It has many benefits, including improved registration between images, removal of acquisition artifacts [22], and de-identification by removing facial features.

There are several methods for skull stripping, and many are integrated with widely used neuroimage analysis software [3, 5, 9, 22, 8, 21]. Several skull stripping methods are compared and analyzed in detail in [7]. Skull stripping methods are highly sensitive to parameters, which may often result into loss of desirable brain tissue. The results may also vary between methods and can require manual correction. Differences in data sets may impact further analysis, such as segmentation. Skull stripping may also favor a particular region based on the particular study [6]. This complicates meta-analysis, data re-use, and collaboration by discarding potentially relevant voxels.

Unlike skull stripping, defacing techniques [6] preserve non-brain tissue. The MRI Defacer approach removes only voxels with zero probability of containing brain tissue and non-zero probability of containing facial features using a manually labeled face atlas. The result appears as though the facial features were eroded, leaving the brain volume intact.

It is tempting to de-identify with skull stripping since it is part of analysis, but defacing techniques allow for more flexibility. Simply skull stripping an image may discard useful data. Defacing is an effective method for removing facial features, and it does not interfere with subsequent analysis. MRI Defacer relies on a face atlas to identify features, which may not apply well to all datasets.

4 Quickshear Defacing

Quickshear Defacing is a new technique for removing facial features from structural MRI. The primary objective is to provide an efficient and effective defacing mechanism that does not rely on external atlases. It uses a binary mask to identify the brain area to protect, as illustrated in Fig. 2. It identifies a plane that divides the volume into two parts: one containing the brain volume and another containing facial features. The voxels that fall into the latter volume **F** are removed, leaving the brain volume **B** untouched. Removing all facial features is not necessary to de-identify the image, and the subject's identity can sufficiently be obscured by removing the primary features (eyes, nose, mouth).

The brain mask is created using a skull stripping technique, with the flexibility to use an existing skull stripped volume. Non-brain tissues such as cerebrospinal fluid and the optic nerve, among others, are often problematic for skull stripping techniques, which aim to include only brain tissue. Quickshear, however, does not need to fully distinguish between brain and non-brain tissue. To reduce complexity and simplify the process, a flattened, two-dimensional sagittal view of the brain is considered. The edge mask is used to find the convex hull. By definition, the convex hull of the brain will form a polygon so that all brain voxels are either on the boundary or inside.

Andrew's monotone chain algorithm is used to find the convex hull [4], The algorithm sorts the points lexicographically and finds the lower and upper halves

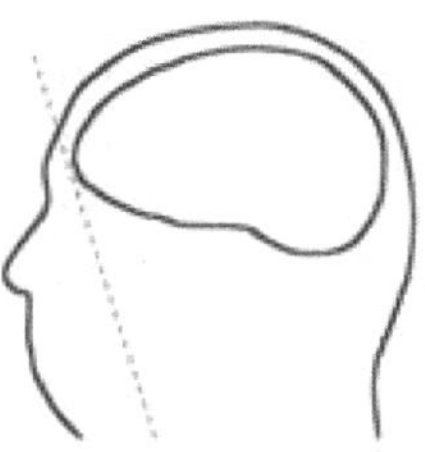
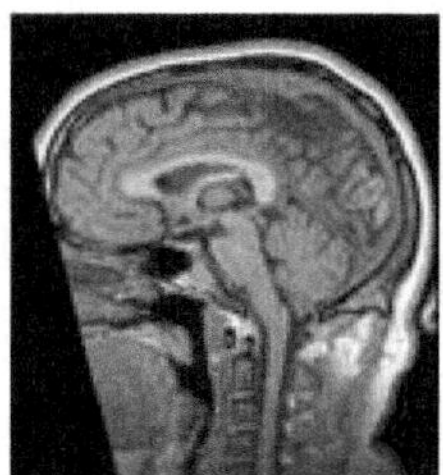
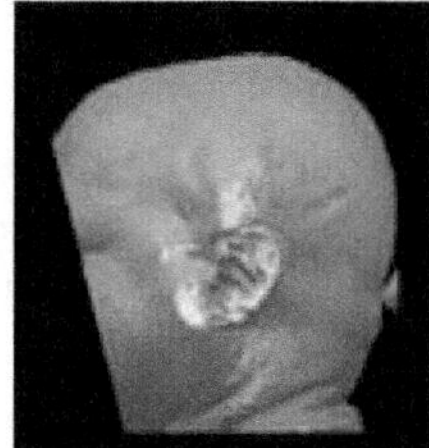

Fig. 2. Quickshear Defacing illustrated (left). Sample slice (middle) and volume rendering (right) after defacing.

of the hull. Selecting the leftmost point (x_0, y_0)[1] and the adjacent point (x_1, y_1) on the hull ensures that all of the brain voxels are contained in the remaining portion of the hull.

The three-dimensional defacing mask is created by discarding all voxels that lie below the line formed by the points defined by

$$w_j = \left(\frac{y_1 - y_0}{x_1 - x_0}\right)(j - x_0) + y_0 - b \ . \tag{1}$$

The value of b specifies a buffer to ensure preservation of the brain volume by shifting the line by $-b$ values in the j direction.

The methods were tested with the Multimodal Reproducibility Study data set from Landman, et al., using MPRAGE scans with a 1.0x1.0x1.2 mm^3 resolution. Acquisition is detailed in [14]. The data set contains 42 images from 21 health subjects. Defacing was performed on Ubuntu 10.10 running in VirtualBox on an Intel i7-2600k with 2GB RAM. Running time is shown in Table 2 as an average per image, averaged over five runs.

Table 2. Performance for defacing per image of sample data set, averaged over five runs

Method	Skull Stripping Time (s)	Defacing Time (s)
MRI Defacer	-	260.17
Quickshear	205.71	4.30

Table 3. Average number of brain voxels discarded for each defacing mechanism (Number of images with voxels discarded)

	Brain Mask		
Defacing Method	AFNI	BET	HWA
MRI Defacer	408.74 (12)	75271.93 (42)	422.0 (7)
Quickshear	0.0 (0)	5560.76 (13)	0.0 (0)

By design, Quickshear Defacing should not remove any voxels identified as brain by the binary mask it is given. This is a basic sanity check, where the defaced volume is compared voxelwise with the brain mask identified by each of three skull stripping techniques (AFNI 3dSkullStrip, FSL BET, and FreeSurfer HWA). On average, Quickshear Defacing discarded fewer brain voxels from fewer images than MRI Defacer.

Volume rendering was applied using MRIcron [20] to the resulting defaced images and passed through the OpenCV Haar classifier [19] to detect faces. For

[1] The leftmost point is chosen as the starting point based on a space where $+x$-axis is the inferior to superior (front to back).

Quickshear, 12 of 42 images were classified as containing a face, and for MRI Defacer, 9 of 12 contained faces. Quickshear tended to leave behind features such as the eye sockets and nasal cavity that may be triggering a false positive. Upon visual inspection, defacing appeared adequate using both methods. MRI Defacer left behind extreme features like the nose in some cases.

5 Conclusions

While the practical and effective discussion concerning privacy in structural neuroimages continues, there are effective measures that can be taken immediately to improve subject privacy. Adopting such measures to protect both metadata and pixel data can increase the flow of data both internal and external to research organizations and encourage collaboration.

Metadata can be removed using existing anonymizing tools, such as the LONI De-identification Debabelet [16] and DICOMBrowser [17]. To remove pixel data, skull stripping or one of the defacing algorithms is recommended. Skull stripping is an effective method for removing facial features, but it may discard desirable tissue. If reproducibility and peer review are the motivations for data sharing, skull stripping may be sufficient and can save time if it is part of the workflow. For data reuse, a defacing approach such as the one presented in this paper may be preferred.

Quickshear Defacing uses a two-dimensional view of the data to create a convex hull, which identifies a plane that divides the volume into two parts, one containing the entire brain and the other facial features. By removing all voxels on the face side, the image data is de-identified.

Quickshear Defacing preserves more brain voxels in more images than MRI Defacer. After MRI Defacer, fewer volumes were identified as containing faces by the Haar classifier. Visual inspection of both techniques showed that the remaining volumes were unlikely to be identified.

Further tests on the data should be applied to determine the effects of the new defacing technique proposed in this paper on further skull stripping. Additionally, implementing other techniques in addition to the Haar classifier to verify the removal of facial features may illuminate the performance of both defacing methods.

Acknowledgments

We gratefully acknowledge support from the William K. Warren Foundation.

References

[1] 3D Slicer, `http://www.slicer.org` (accessed 2010)
[2] ADNI: Alzheimer's Disease Neuroimaging Initiative, `http://www.loni.ucla.edu/ADNI/` (accessed 2011)

[3] AFNI, http://afni.nimh.nih.gov (accessed 2011)
[4] Andrew, A.M.: Another efficient algorithm for conex hulls in two dimensions. Inform. Process Lett., 216–219 (1979)
[5] BET - Brain Extraction Tool, http://www.fmrib.ox.ac.uk/fsl/bet2/index.html (accessed 2010)
[6] Bischoff-Grethe, A., et al.: A technique for the deidentification of structural brain MR images. Hum. Brain Mapp. 28, 892–903 (2007)
[7] Fennema-Notestine, C., et al.: Quantitative evaluation of automated skull-stripping methods applied to contemporary and legacy images: Effects of diagnosis, bias correction, and slice location. Hum. Brain Mapp. 27, 99–113 (2006)
[8] FreeSurfer, http://surfer.nmr.mgh.harvard.edu (accessed 2011)
[9] FMRIB Software Library, http://www.fmrib.ox.ac.uk/fsl/ (accessed 2010)
[10] Grgic, M., Delac, K.: Face recognition homepage, http://face-rec.org (accessed 2011)
[11] Grother, P.J., Quinn, G.W., Phillips, P.J.: Report on the evaluation of 2D still-image face recognition algorithms. Tech. rep., National Institute of Standards and Technology (2010)
[12] HIPAA Administrative Simplification: Regulation Text (2009)
[13] Kolata, G.: Rare Sharing of Data Leads to Progress on Alzheimers. New York Times (August 12, 2010)
[14] Landman, B.A., et al.: Multi-parametric neuroimaging reproducibility: A 3T resource study. NeuroImage (2010)
[15] Mueller, S.G., et al.: Ways toward an early diagnosis in Alzheimer's disease: The Alzheimer's Disease Neuroimaging Initiative (ADNI). Neuroimag. Clin. N Am. (2005)
[16] Neu, S.C., Valentino, D.J., Toga, A.W.: The LONI Debabeler: a mediator for neuroimaging software. NeuroImage 24, 1170–1179 (2005)
[17] Neuroinformatics Research Group: DICOM Browser, http://nrg.wustl.edu/software/dicom-browser/ (accessed 2011), Washington University School of Medicine
[18] Ohm, P.: Broken promises of privacy: Responding to the surprising failure of anonymization. UCLA Law Rev. 57(6) (2010)
[19] OpenCV, http://opencv.willowgarage.com (accessed 2011)
[20] Rorden, C.: MRIcron, http://www.cabiatl.com/mricro/mricron/index.html (accessed 2010)
[21] Ségonne, F., et al.: A hybrid approach to the skull stripping problem in MRI. NeuroImage 22, 1060–1075 (2004)
[22] Smith, S.M.: Fast robust automated brain extraction. Hum. Brain Mapp. 17, 143–155 (2002)
[23] Sweeney, L.: k-anonymity: a model for protecting privacy. Int. J. on Uncertain Fuzz 10(5), 557–570 (2002)
[24] Zhao, W., Chellappa, R., Phillips, P.J., Rosenfeld, A.: Face recognition: A literature survey. ACM Comput. Surv. 35, 399–458 (2003)

Author Index

GPSR Compliance

The European Union's (EU) General Product Safety Regulation (GPSR) is a set of rules that requires consumer products to be safe and our obligations to ensure this.

If you have any concerns about our products, you can contact us on ProductSafety@springernature.com

In case Publisher is established outside the EU, the EU authorized representative is:

Springer Nature Customer Service Center GmbH
Europaplatz 3
69115 Heidelberg, Germany

Batch number: 09474011

Printed by Printforce, the Netherlands